D.N. DUNLOP

D.N. Dunlop

A Man of Our Time

T.H. Meyer

TEMPLE LODGE
London

First English edition 1992

Authorised Translation from the German by Ian Bass

Originally published in German under the title *D.N. Dunlop - Ein Zeit-und Lebensbild* by Philosophisch-Anthroposophischer Verlag am Goetheanum, Dornach in 1987

The publishers wish to thank The Anthroposophical Society in Great Britain, The Michael Wilson Fund, ASEE Exhibitions Ltd, and all others who kindly offered practical support for this book.

A catalogue record for this book is available from the British Library

ISBN 0 904693 38 4

Typeset by DP Photosetting, Aylesbury, Bucks
Printed and bound in Great Britain by Cromwell Press Ltd.

Universal History, the history of what man has accomplished in this world, is at the bottom the History of the Great Men who have worked here . . . We cannot look, however imperfectly, upon a great man, without gaining something by him. He is the living light-fountain, which is good and pleasant to be near.

Thomas Carlyle, *Heroes and Hero-Worship*

What is the most important task of all human thinking? It is this: to grasp the human being as a free individuality—one founded within itself.

Rudolf Steiner, *Truth and Science*

CONTENTS

3
PRACTICAL OCCULTISM 65

4
THE MEETING WITH RUDOLF STEINER 129

5
THE IMPUSE OF THE WORLD POWER CONFERENCE 199

6
'ANTHROPOSOPHY FORMED A NEW ORGAN IN ME' 247

7
PERSPECTIVES 331

APPENDIX 373

FOREWORD

Many people have contributed, in a variety of ways, to bringing this book into existence. The author would like to ask all those whom he may have forgotten or overlooked to bear with him and consider themselves mentioned here between the lines.

Miss Constance Winney of London has greatly supported the research into D.N. Dunlop's position within the Anthroposophical Society in Great Britain. Mrs Skip Gordon kindly arranged for the author to spend several nights at the Steiner Press 'Hotel' in the immediate vicinity of the British Museum. Through the good offices of Nick Thomas the author was able to trace D.N. Dunlop's daughter Edith Young, who died in 1989. Her biography *Inside Out* contains some valuable insights, especially with regard to Dunlop's 'Dublin Period'. Thanks are also due to David Clement, John Wood and the late Alistair Macdonald for indicating other matters of importance. John Fletcher from London provided some important material concerning Mrs Merry.

Most aspects of the World Power Conference would have remained in the dark had it not been for the very willing assistance afforded to us by C.H. Gray, the late Secretary of this organization, and his successor Eric Ruttley who were kind enough to provide a variety of detailed accounts and important documents.

Emanuel Zeylmans from Reutlingen, Germany, has constantly and tirelessly helped with references of various kinds, putting valuable material at the author's disposal with regard to Dunlop's contribution to the medical work in England and particularly to the events occurring during the last days of his life.

Wandering along the blind-alleys of bibliographical references the author could always count on a short cut with the help of Madlen Hauser in the Goetheanum Library.

After the publication of this biography in German five years ago, many new details about D.N. Dunlop have come to light. It was particularly through Crispian Villeneuve, Devon, for whose untiring help in reviewing and commenting on the final script the author is deeply indebted, that substantial further material on Dunlop was provided. This has led to a thorough revision of the whole book with occasional modifications and enlargements in some of its parts.

*

'The eternal is discovered most fully in what appears to hide it most effectually,' D.N. Dunlop once wrote to his friend Eleanor C. Merry. This may also apply to the basic question with regard to every biography: does the material collected for it contribute more to hiding or to discovering its subject? If the 'almost quixotic wealth' of details of which Owen Barfield speaks in his Afterword might sometimes seem to hide the subject of this biography, the reader may be well advised to keep an eye on its formal structure which occasionally breaks strict chronological order of external events in order to follow up the inner continuity of some core motif in Dunlop's life. For it is rather through the form or *the how* and not through the richness of *the what* alone that something of the ever present individuality of D.N. Dunlop might be found within or rather between the pages of this book.

It is with great pleasure that the author witnesses the embarkation of his 'favourite child' on its journey into the English speaking world.

T.H. Meyer
Basel, 3 February 1992

Author's note:
Quotations from material orginally published in German have occasionally been translated from the source, and may differ from the published English translation.

Some of the most frequently quoted sources have been indicated in brackets in the text by the following abbreviations:

StN = Letter from W.J. Stein to the engineer Zur Nedden. See page 5.
St = W.J. Stein, 'An appreciation of D.N. Dunlop', in *The Present Age*, Vol. I, No. 1, December 1935.
StS = An unpublished biographical sketch of D.N. Dunlop written by W.J. Stein.
DS = D.N. Dunlop: 'Rudolf Steiner and the Fulfilment of a Quest'. See page 3.
MD = Unpublished manuscript by E.C. Merry on D.N. Dunlop.

INTRODUCTION

Remember that you have looked upon cataclysms many times and have always risen triumphant. D.N.D.

As a result of the Chernobyl disaster in 1986, all the problems connected with modern energy technology have moved into the forefront of world-wide consciousness. A new dimension of urgency has been added to the already existing preoccupations with alternative sources of energy, and there is mounting opposition to a steadily growing atomic industry largely dominated by economic and monopoly interests. In the second decade of this century (in association with one of the characters in his *Mystery Plays*, Dr Strader), Rudolf Steiner drew attention to the necessity of discovering a new kind of energy—one of the future which would be based upon the principle of rhythmic vibration.[1] At the same time he pointed out the dangers that this discovery would automatically bring if this form of energy were ever to be discovered and used for technological purposes before the idea of a threefold social order had taken root on at least a small part of the planet. Consequently, the energy problem—and with it the whole problem of the economy as such—will have to be considered in the future more and more as indissolubly linked with the social question, and its solution should only be sought for in the light of this latter question. As a separate individual, however, man is not only a social being; he is also an antisocial entity. Indeed, at first, it is only on the basis of this antisocial aspect of his nature that the individual actually learns to unfold his conscious, self-determined being as a free spirit. This aspect must therefore also be fully taken into account in any attempt to restructure our society in the future—that is, if the spiritual and cultural life is to be founded upon the free spiritual activity of the individual.

The various preoccupations, fears and anxieties predominant today with regard to the energy problem are often only based on material considerations which just 'touch the surface' of what is really at stake; they clearly indicate the deficit of awareness which still exists in regard to the social and spiritual dimensions of this problem. However, if the present civilization, founded above all on materialistic ideas and impulses, is not to 'roll on into the abyss', as Rudolf Steiner once put it,[2] then the future *practice* of this civilization will have to join hands with a true, spiritual *vision* of the universe.

This is where the remarkable yet comparatively unknown figure of D.N. Dunlop fits into the picture, for this figure is significantly and intimately interwoven into this same threefold complex of problems stretching over the whole of our century.

Inspired by a truly profound spiritual impulse, D.N. Dunlop founded the *World Power Conference*, which still exists and operates today under the name of the *World Energy Council*. The purpose of this private international organization is to bring about world-wide co-ordination and co-operation in all fields related to the various sources of energy and their corresponding forms of technology. By conceiving and setting up this world-wide organization, Dunlop endeavoured to reap the harvest of certain ideas sown by Rudolf Steiner, which are ripening with the millennium. It was a first step towards providing a material basis for a future restructuring of society—a society more suitable and worthy of the human race, a first step towards providing a social framework which might be used as a healthy basis for the development of a free cultural and spiritual life.

*

Daniel Nicol Dunlop did not leave any 'memoirs' behind. Very few personal letters have been found, and he hardly seems to have 'showered' even those who were closest to him during his life-time with oral communications or other indications of an autobiographical kind. This fact is revealing in itself. It corresponds to two striking traits of Dunlop's nature: a fundamental mode of expression transcending all personal considerations, and an ability to wait silently for the moment in which *to act*. He would wait for the right moment to practise what he was most fond of calling 'skill in action'. Dunlop was a man of action, but he acted without any trace of hastiness. He put his personality at the service of goals he had spiritually perceived as being those of humanity. His biography can be roughly divided into two parts: during the first half of his life, on the basis of certain far-reaching spiritual experiences of his youth and intensive studies of occult and mystical literature, he develops his personality and perfects it as an instrument; in the second half we bear witness to how he uses this instrument to accomplish acts of world-wide significance—all forces of the personality are ever more strongly put at the service of the 'world' as such. However, if Dunlop was rarely given to making comments of a purely personal kind it was not that he had any intention of hiding or holding anything back. It must have been as natural to him as breathing, and it seems to have been the method he used to establish and maintain the function of the personality as an 'instrument'. Fortunately, however, during his theosophical phase he did include a few autobiographical remarks in various essays and lectures he was then producing. They serve to illustrate some point he was making at the time and often do so in the most refreshing, heart-warming and humorous manner.

The only coherent autobiographical source we have consists of a contribution Dunlop made to a book which was unfortunately never completed. It was planned by English anthroposophists to be a collection of reminiscences of meetings with Rudolf Steiner. He and certain other (predominantly English and Dutch) anthroposophists were invited to describe three fundamental stages in their lives:

1 'where one stood before the meeting';
2 'the meeting itself';
3 'what came of the meeting'.

Dunlop's contribution, which was entitled 'Rudolf Steiner and the Fulfilment of a Quest', was published for the first time[3] in the magazine *Anthroposophical Movement* two months after his death in the summer of 1935. As this sketch is the only account of Dunlop's life which stems from his own hand, it represents an important biographical source and is also included in the Appendix of this book. Moreover, this is not the only reason it is of great significance for us: as far as this biography is concerned, it provides us with a method and approach which is particularly relevant to the years of Dunlop's youth and childhood. At the very beginning of this autobiographical sketch, Dunlop himself singles out two reminiscences as being truly *symptomatic* of the whole course his spiritual life was subsequently to take.

We owe the most detailed descriptions of Dunlop's life as a whole to Walter Johannes Stein. During the Summer School at Westonbirt in 1934, one year before Dunlop's death, Stein had an intuition which proved to be extremely fortunate. He asked Dunlop, on one of the rare occasions he had a free moment—presumably during the midday interval—to give him a simple and straightforward account of his life. As we can surmise from the still extant notes, Stein must have taken down on the spot what he considered to be the most important points and used his notes to write an appreciation of his great friend and companion. He subsequently published it in the first issue of *The Present Age*.[4] It had been Dunlop's idea to bring out this magazine to begin with and so it was only natural that Stein should want to erect a monument to the memory of his departed friend in the opening pages.

However, even Walter Johannes Stein's account is inevitably fragmentary and incomplete when it comes to tracing a real external continuity of events. For this reason we must attach all the more importance to the autobiographical 'interview'. In it Dunlop describes a number of other striking scenes from his life. They speak a powerful language and betray something of the symptomatic and significant role they played in the whole course of his destiny.

Another important source consists of all the essays, printed lectures and books, as well as a number of letters. To this must be added the numerous obituaries which appeared in a great variety of newspapers and journals, some remarks by the only son, R.O. Dunlop, and one of D.N. Dunlop's two daughters, Edith Young, as well as a number of statements made by friends still alive today. In a report entitled *D.N. Dunlop and the World Power Conference now renamed the World Energy Conference*, C.H. Gray, the former Secretary of the World Power Conference, throws some important light on the role Dunlop played within the whole of this international organization. Lastly, we should mention certain notes compiled by E.C. Merry, who was very actively and closely linked to Dunlop during the years of his anthroposophical activity, and several statements made by Rudolf Steiner and Ita Wegman. These statements and, in particular, Rudolf Steiner's allusion to the karmic background of this individuality were of decisive importance in helping the author to discover the most essential points of view for the writing of this biography.

*

In May 1935, D.N. Dunlop was taken to a private hospital in London with acute appendicitis. A series of complications, which the doctors were not able to diagnose with any degree of certainty, led to his death on 30 May. It was Ascension Day. The following day there was an earthquake in Pakistan and the city of Quetta was almost entirely destroyed. Dr Ita Wegman, who was called from Stuttgart in order to lend medical assistance, was convinced that the death was also, and above all, due to a certain exercising of spiritual 'economy'.

One week after Dunlop's death, W.J. Stein wrote a letter to a certified Engineer, Zur Nedden,[5] who was also active within the framework of the World Power Conference. It included the following lines:

> Mr Dunlop expressed no last wishes and I had the impression that for him the best guarantee of continuity was to be found in human beings rather than in anything that could be written down in fixed terms. He

> believed in humanity and for him the living human being was the *real* continuous factor . . . He was silent; he liked to weigh his plans in stillness, to wait a long time and in the right moment—objectively and psychologically speaking—transform into deeds as much as seemed possible to him. I had the good fortune to be 'educated' by him so to speak. And he instructed more by his exemplary attitude to things than by the words he spoke; more by goodness than by forceful energy, more by a simple ability to wait than by any haste in action. He was full of plans, and every now and then he would give those near to him a glimmering of what it was he was planning . . . If one did anything with Mr Dunlop one felt freer than when one did it quite alone. For there was something about his interest and his love that encouraged you to unfold your real self. At the crematorium there were so many flowers that it was impossible to bring them all into the chapel. More than half of them lay outside in front of the door and people passing by paused to ask who had died and what manner of man he was.

The sheer number of obituaries[6] published in various newspapers and journals is in itself impressive. *The Times* laid particular emphasis on the personal and permanent significance of D.N. Dunlop as the father of the World Power Conference—his 'favourite' child. Willem Zeylmans van Emmichoven depicted the deceased as a '"spectator" on the world-stage, one who recognizes the true needs of the times and then, with unshakable will and determination, *acts*'. George Adams opened his memorial address for friends in London with the simple words, 'D.N. Dunlop was our friend'; and C.H. Gray, whom Dunlop had appointed Secretary of the WPC in 1928 and who was to retain this office until 1966, still spoke 50 years after Dunlop's death of the 'enormous charm' and 'combination of vision and ability' of this 'remarkable man'.[7]

*

Even though we may be approaching these scenes from quite a distance and travelling across a certain period of time, let us none the less pause a moment in front of all those flowers and attempt to mingle with those passers-by in order to ask 'who had died and what manner of man he was'.

1

YOUTH ON A SCOTTISH ISLAND

Thou Who hast made me an immortal soul,
give me the courage of one who is immortal. D.N.D.

Origins

Daniel Nicol Dunlop was born on 28 December 1868, the only child of Alexander and Catherine Dunlop, at Kilmarnock, in Scotland. It was during the 13 Holy Nights, when the sun was in the sign of Capricorn.

Kilmarnock today numbers about 50 thousand inhabitants and lies about 30 miles south of Glasgow. Apart from the façade of one house bearing Masonic symbols and a somewhat dilapidated old theatre, the town seems to possess little of interest on the architectural and cultural level. On entering Kilmarnock, the visitor is greeted by a sign reminding him that the town is the birthplace of 'Johnny Walker, Scotch Whisky'. In rather dismal contrast to this tribute to the joys of drinking are these words from Psalm 118 set beside a church portal: 'It is better to find refuge in the Lord, than to trust in man.'

The mother, Catherine (née Nicol), died at the age of 26, when Daniel was 5 years old. The boy was brought to live with his maternal grandfather on the Isle of Arran, and thereby he set foot on ground which, for the next seven or eight years, would form the principal stage upon which the most decisive experiences of his youth and childhood were to be enacted. Arran is one of the special places of this earth. The island is almost egg-shaped and can be driven around by car in about two hours. It was already inhabited in the Neolithic Age, as is witnessed by the numerous cairns, stone circles and standing stones which one encounters particularly on the southern half of the island. Geologists have called Arran 'a Scotland in miniature' and 'a complete synopsis of Scottish geology'[8] because the most characteristic land-formations, varieties of stone and climatic conditions of the whole of the rest of Scotland are all assembled here in this one, narrow space. The climate is mild on account of the Gulf Stream. In the valleys near the coast subtropical plants are to be found, although the island is not without rain. In the north several mountains rise to a height of up to two thousand feet above sea-level.

The grandfather,[9] in whose house Dunlop's mother had also grown up, was a Gaelic-speaking fisherman living at Kildonan, one of the small villages on the south-east side of the island, in the neighbourhood of Lamlash, and not far from the Holy Island. The name of this village is derived from St Donan who, in the sixth century, came with St Columba to Arran to evangelize the heathen inhabitants.

'Mother evoked this vision of the sea in me'

Daniel's relationship to his mother seems to have been a very tender one. On the Isle of Arran he was shown a rock-cave by the sea-shore, sheltered from the wind.[10] She had, so he was told, often sought out this place where, deeply immersed in thought, she would gaze out to sea. So Daniel, who greatly missed his mother, many a time sought out this place himself. He would sit down on the rocky ground and look out at the wide-open, surging sea, thinking of his mother and seeking her presence there. 'I imagined,' he later recalled (StN) 'my mother evoked this vision of the sea in me.' One day, as he was sitting in the sheltered rock-cave, her voice seemed to come to him from out of the very wind and waves, whispering, 'See Daniel, I have not left you. I live on in the wind and the waves, in everything that surrounds you. Behold the blue mantle which I cast around you by day and the gold-gleaming garment which envelopes you by night. I have become one now with the Great Mother, Mother Nature. In *her* your mother will always be with you.' On the hills around Kildonan, again and again Daniel's gaze fell upon those stones—enigmatic, though somehow long familiar and akin to him—rising up all alone towards the sky, or else joined together in groups or circles. Not far out to sea, on the eastern side of Arran, lay the 'Holy Island'. People spoke frequently of the Irish monks who had visited it and lived there, of the chalice-shaped circular engravings in the rock, and of the runic symbols in the caves. In the child's perceptive, awakening soul another level of experience was now emerging. Just as nothing less than the mysteries of space had begun to dawn on him from beyond the wide expanses of the sea and the starry heavens at night, from behind the veils of the Great Mother, so now these age-old stones and stone circles which had remained silent for so long seemed to want to reveal to him secrets from the very depths of Time.

The Father

Alexander Dunlop was a powerfully built man who cut a very stern and patriarchal figure. He worked as an architect on the mainland. A strong adherent of the Quaker movement, he was widely active in the surrounding area as an energetic lay-preacher. Both these activities, in metamorphosed form, were destined to play an important role in the life of his son who was later to create, thanks to a profound spiritual impulse and an extraordinary gift of eloquence, a world-wide technical and economic organization upon which the whole of humanity could build. On the sparsely populated island Daniel kept house for his grandfather and himself. He learned how to fish and how to make and repair nets. One day, soon after the death of Daniel's mother, Alexander Dunlop told his son, concisely and in no uncertain terms, to read the Bible 'beginning with the creation of the world and finishing up with the Apocalypse, chapter by chapter, day by day'.(St) After overcoming his initial resistance, Daniel began more and more to enjoy his daily Bible-readings; they became a habit which he was to retain for the whole of his life. 'And I am doing it still,' he told Stein in 1934, 'up to five chapters a day. I have actually read the whole of it several times.' (St)

The Bible-reading activity thus demanded of Daniel—and which was to be of such consequence for his future—was in striking contrast to the principles Alexander Dunlop, as a Quaker preacher, was generally wont to uphold. He would certainly relate parts of the Bible to his various congregations, but he would 'spare' his listeners any obligation to take up the 'Book of Books' in order to read it for themselves. For some reason he deemed it necessary, in his son's case, to make an exception to this rule. And his word carried considerable weight. Only a few years ago, shortly before her death, Dunlop's eldest daughter, Edith Young, vividly recalled the awesome austerity of that towering figure in the background of her early youth. The Bible-readings required of his son were evidently the only reading Alexander Dunlop would tolerate in his house. Thus, one day when his granddaughter was staying with him on holiday, he took away all the books which she had brought with her, and placed them under lock and key—for good and all!

Almost inevitably we are reminded by this scene of that misanthropic dictum set beside the church-portal in Kilmarnock. Could the setting of it perhaps have been inspired by a certain Alexander Dunlop?

The 'Crystallized' Word

Apparently, Daniel was soon able to forget that the original impetus for his Bible-reading activity had been a decree of a very severe and patriarchal nature; for remarkably soon these readings bore fruit—and at a point in time and under circumstances which are, themselves, no less remarkable.

At the age of 9, Daniel had 12 friends who came regularly on Sundays, from all directions and covering considerable distances on the island, in order to seek him out. 'I would preach to them out in the middle of nature, standing on a rock.' (StS) In his short autobiographical summary Dunlop wrote: 'I read to them the Gospel of St John, dimly aware that here was something magical, infinitely more real than all the lessons at the village school.' (DS) On account of his great enthusiasm he would usually lose all notion of what he had just been talking about. But whenever he got himself into such a state, his voice began to take on the quality and tone of song.

In connection with the Gospel of St John, he tried one Sunday to explain to his friends what it actually meant that 'the Word' had once 'become flesh', and what it was which necessarily made Christ different from all other men. And he said: 'Christ cannot be compared with other human beings, because we cannot say of any others that they are the Crystallized Word. So Christ must have been different from all others in this respect.' (St) In the autobiographical sketch, he spoke of this enthusiastic reading and preaching to his Sunday circle of friends as belonging to 'the two memories' which 'have remained with me and may be recounted here as symptomatic of the course which my spiritual life was afterwards to take.' (DS)

It is possible to see a link between this recollection (the second one will be dealt with at a later point), the lecture on St John's Gospel Dunlop was to give many years later, and the 'Morning Meditation' (see page 267) he occasionally passed on to certain friends of his. Thus, this early 'enthusiasm' of the young boy was going to play an important role throughout his life. Finally, let us in passing draw the reader's attention to another remarkable circumstance in connection with this youthful recollection—a circumstance which, likewise, is to be considered in the light of a later event in this biography. It is the fact that Dunlop's extraordinary group of friends numbered 12.

Once again we see this youthful soul—in his *entourage*—touched by the enigma of space, only this time it is as though on a higher level. For wherever the number 12 is the constituting factor, spiritual principles or their heavenly and earthly images in the world of space are always involved. Space is constituted according to the number 12: seen from a cosmic point of view, by the spiritual forces represented in the 12 signs of the zodiac. And a human community based on the number 12 is the social expression of this principle of cosmic order (as in the 12 apostles, the 12 Arthurian knights, etc.). The central principle is represented by a thirteenth, a sun-hero. A human community constituted according to cosmic principles and spiritual impulses: this seems to be the biographical impulse flashing up in this scene. And one could hardly think of a number of eager listeners more wonderfully suited to this young enthusiast.

'From then on I was an I'

The next significant event which occurred in Dunlop's youth could also be regarded in certain respects as the most central one, although it is not alluded to in his autobiographical sketch as 'symptomatic' recollection. In fact Dunlop does not refer to it at all and only spoke of it to Stein and others in a small circle of friends.

It was the summer of 1882. 'One day,' Stein recalls, 'it was raining and very stormy and Daniel's clothes were very wet. As evening drew on the storm increased. He and his grandfather were in the little house with no other human being at hand. As he lay in his little bed a feeling of eeriness crept over him, and so he asked his grandfather to allow him to come into his bed. There, in the arms of his grandfather, he fell asleep. But that night the old man died, and when the boy awakened he found himself lying in a pool of blood.' One of his grandfather's frontal veins had burst during the night. 'He was shocked but not frightened. He stood up and stirred the fire, dried his wet clothes in front of it and sat on a little bench in the window looking out to sea. He had fried a herring and began to eat it. After this light meal he began to think. "I was fully conscious that my grandfather was dead and that I was alone, but I had no feeling of urgency. So I started thinking and my thoughts turned to dreams, and from dreams to visions."'(St)

Out of that experience of death, free as it had been from any feeling of fear, arose a star that could illuminate certain fields of human experience which otherwise must remain hidden from ordinary waking consciousness bound to the senses and the intellect. It is as though the boy's devoted attachment to his grandfather—of a similar nature no doubt to the love he bore his mother—had opened an inner eye. For the *curtain*, upon which the forms of the sense-world are usually traced (and even appear so 'close to us' and 'real' that we hardly ever suspect or recognize the presence of a veil) opened up at the moment his grandfather disappeared behind it. And thus the one who had passed beyond began, in metamorphosed form, to appear before the mind's eye of the one seeking him in retrospect—he appeared in a series of images which wove their beholder ever more closely into their fabric.

'"I could see myself riding upon a camel and others joined us, and I saw my grandfather, but with another face, on horseback. He was wearing rich white clothes."

'I asked Mr Dunlop if they had been Arabian clothes and he replied, "No, much richer ones, maybe Egyptian." Then pictures came, constantly changing as in a kaleidoscope. He described another one to me. He saw himself as a young officer looking up to a much older and very fine-looking man, riding beside him through the desert. Then he saw himself as a Greek youth, wearing white garments and a golden girdle; he stood leaning against the pillar of a temple, watching a procession as it entered the temple. It was in one of the sacred groves dedicated to the cult of the Orphic Mysteries and he felt great sorrow because the woman he loved was being taken away from him for initiation in the temple. He felt completely desolate.'(St)

This last picture, and the experience described in it, is strangely evocative of something else: it is as though it were a kind of reversal of one of the scenes in Rudolf Steiner's Fourth Mystery Drama—the scene of the 'Egyptian woman' leaning against the pillar of a temple, gazing with inner longing after the beloved 'Neophyte' who is being 'torn away' from her by the temple . . . 'I did not know about reincarnation then. I just had the experience of my previous lives, but I had no theory about such things.'(St) This is how Dunlop later characterized these inner experiences.

After these visions had gradually faded away, Daniel set out for the one and only post office on the island which was equipped with a telegraph system. It was in a shop in Brodick, about three hours away on foot. When Daniel asked the shopkeeper to send a telegram to his father on the mainland and inform him of his grandfather's death, the man could not at first bring himself to believe him—perhaps on account of the perfectly normal and tranquil manner in which the boy formulated his request. 'But after all, I said to him, it was my affair; he was obliged to send the telegram even if the whole thing was untrue. So then he sent it off.' (StS)

The father came over to the island. And with pony and cart he and his son transported the grandfather to the burial place, a simple plot of ground far away from the cemeteries. There was no minister and there were no mourners, no undertakers, no public.[11]

Dunlop ends the description of these scenes and experiences which had so deeply marked him with the observation: 'At that moment I awoke. I had a kind of vision of the future, and all my ideas go back to it.' (StN)

*

In context that can mean one thing only: that from then on a sure feeling for the reality of the 'ego'—as an entity enduring beyond all changes governed by birth and death—was present in him. From then onwards the star of his 'Entelechy' began to shine ever more constantly and powerfully over the horizon of his consciousness. It was the birth of that spiritual process whereby the ego grasps itself as it stands on its own foundation, and therewith the moment in which the true seed of all external independence was born. The initiating consciousness, or 'Telest', had awakened in the boy.[12]

The specific period into which fall the two last mentioned events of Dunlop's youth (i.e. the 'sermon' and the inner experience and vision following his grandfather's death) is especially worth noting—and not only in the context of this biography but also with respect to the 'biography of mankind'. They are situated at approximately equal intervals before and after the autumn of the year 1879, a date which introduces a new epoch, with a different Spirit of the Age—a happening we know about from Rudolf Steiner's spiritual-scientific research. Michael, who gives the impulses for cosmopolitan activity and the spiritualization of the intellect, relieves Gabriel, who has acted up to this point as effective Spirit of the Times. With this occurrence, from the occult background of history, new forces are available to the reach of human beings; they make it possible to grasp spiritual experiences by means of a spiritual science, experiences which, from this time onwards, begin to enter with great force into the consciousness of numerous individuals.[13]

The History of the World

The boy's father decided to bring him onto the mainland. Thus the time had come to take leave of the island which had become so dear to him, the faithful circle of friends, and of those enigmatic stones, witnesses of a long-distant past.

Little is documented concerning the next seven years. However, we do know that Daniel went for a while to school in Ardrossan Academy, then newly opened on the South Beach in Ardrossan,[14] a port situated opposite Arran and today about an hour's journey away by boat. Soon afterwards, the father put his son—who in the meantime would have reached about his fourteenth year of age—to work in an office. And at this point an event occurred which was further to strengthen his independence. It is the second experience during his youth which was later to be described by Dunlop as 'symptomatic'.

Daniel was in charge of the small cash-box which as a rule had only a few shillings in it. One day a representative of a publishing company or book-club, a kind of commercial traveller for popular education, passed by. He had a prospectus advertising a set of works entitled the History of the World in several small volumes. Daniel immediately felt as though magically attracted to this work. The History of the World? How marvellous! How wonderful it must be to know the history of the whole world! To have a complete view of everything that ever happened! It must be something like the feeling—only a thousand times more glorious—I often had out there on the island where my grandfather lived, when I used to seek out mother's cave by the shore and look out into the wide-open sea! Or maybe it is similar to the feeling I had the morning after grandfather's death when I sat for ages sunk in thought, looking out to sea, until space seemed to vanish all around me and from a distant past images unrolled before my inner eye and I could feel my way into the mysteries of time . . . How promising now the possibility of tracing not only my own history and that of my grandfather, but the history of the whole world and everybody in it ! Such were, perhaps, his thoughts and feelings on viewing the prospectus.

And suddenly one thing was clear to him: he had to have it. But he had no money. So he told the agent that he was very, very sorry that he could not buy it. At the time Daniel was earning exactly the same amount as the book cost. He could pay the weekly instalments if he went without his supper. But the man wanted two and sixpence and he did not have them. The agent pointed to the cash-box. 'Here,' he said, 'you have a little cash, take it. You can pay it back later.' (St) So Daniel let himself be persuaded and thus obtained the first volume. He placed an IOU in the cash box each week. But when, after some time, he was at a loss to know how to pay back the money he owed his employer, he informed him. The latter, beside himself with rage, dismissed him on the spot. And his father refused to advance him the money and wanted never again to set eyes on him.

On his own Feet

So, suddenly, Daniel was out on the street with no money, no roof over his head, no work, and with a heavy debt on his hands. Immersed in thought, he slowly turned his steps towards the harbour. There he saw a ship loading its cargo, and he decided to offer his services. 'And in 24 hours he had earnt all the money he needed by carrying sacks.'(StS) He sent the money he owed to his former employer and informed his father that he had put the matter in order. In the meantime, however, the latter had had second thoughts and had already paid off the debt. So Daniel wanted to pay back the money to his father who was unable to bring himself to believe that his son had earned it by honest means.

Finally, however, he let himself be persuaded and even allowed Daniel to obtain the whole of *The History of the World.*

The next day Daniel again went down to the harbour, earned a pound, and decided from now on to be the sole master of his own fortune. He put 14 advertisements in 14 newspapers and received 14 replies giving him a possible 14 different occupations to choose from. He turned in prayer to his heavenly Father for wise and gracious guidance and eventually decided to seek out each and every one of the people who had answered his advertisements—and to do this in alphabetical order of their names. This path brought him to Glasgow, where he got to know life in the suburbs and was confronted for the first time with the noise and bustling activity especially characteristic of the poorer parts of the city.

Under the letter 'H' he found a job but gave it up after a few days and took on employment with a Frenchman who bore the handsome name of 'Fontaine'. Fontaine owned a bicycle business in East Glasgow. The work began at six o'clock in the morning and brought in 12 shillings a week, three shillings of which went to paying the rent. To earn extra money he did a paper round before going to work. The house in which he lived was very shabby. At the weekends there was a lot of heavy drinking with accompanying scenes. But his room in the attic was clean and cheap, and that was what mattered to him. It belonged to the landlady's son who was a seafaring man and was away most of the time, but occasionally returned. And then, whilst the seaman was on leave, the room had to be shared with him.

Daniel lived modestly spending very little money. His lunch was provided for him at work by his employer and the money he thus saved was immediately invested in a penny or two-penny booklet. And so with time he came to own a certain number of penny booklets and other volumes he had found in second-hand bookstalls—for the greater part, books concerning history or the occult. By the light of two carefully preserved candles he would read them at night in the small attic room. According to his daughter Edith Young, the small library also included Greek and Roman classics: Sophocles, Euripides, Aristotle, Cicero, Marcus Aurelius, etc. And maybe it also included some strange writings, then being published in Glasgow, by an American author of the name of Thomas Lake Harris.

*

Certainly—Daniel may well have mused on contemplating the small blue circle tattooed at the base of his thumb—he felt closer to these great minds than to his colleagues both at the harbour and later in the bicycle-shop. Nonetheless, it was in that workshop that he first became acquainted with the world of machinery and technology—acquainted with something of his own future in fact. For by means of the prospectuses available, and from careful observation, he obtained his first knowledge of a technical and practical nature. In this field as well he was determined to supplement, through his own drive and initiative, the fragmentary, dull and deficient education he had received at school.

2

IRISH RENAISSANCE

Strong friendship is but the visible link
in the long chain of events through many lives,
and the renewed feeling is but the taking up
of the friendship of the past. Friends will be drawn
together as naturally as a magnet attracts iron . . .
it is just as if they had parted an hour before. D.N.D.

Spiritual Renaissance in Dublin

Ireland, in the eighties and nineties of the last century, was in the process of giving birth to a literary movement whose most famous protagonist was later to be recognized as W.B. Yeats, born in 1865. In 1878, as part of a series of works on the history of Ireland, Standish O'Grady published the volume entitled *Heroic Period*. Ireland thus came to discover the heroes of her Celtic past. This gave rise to the 'Literary Revival', the cultural and literary renaissance which found a natural centre of gravity in Dublin. Throughout his life W.B. Yeats showed a deep interest in occult phenomena. The literary renaissance had started out from a revival of certain aspects of Celtic-Irish culture, permeating them with a strong kind of enthusiasm orientated towards the future. It fell upon Yeats to contribute decisively to the creation and introduction into all this of a subsidiary movement based on concrete spiritual experience: the movement of Theosophy.

One day in the year 1883 or 1884, in the house of a friend of his who was a professor, Yeats witnessed a lively discussion concerning a work which had just been published, A.P. Sinnett's *Esoteric Buddhism*. After he had read the book he recommended it to Charles Johnston, an old school-friend of his, in whom these ideas kindled a deep and passionate interest. Johnston influenced a whole circle of friends who became enthusiastic about Sinnett's ideas and in 1885, ten years after the founding of the Theosophical Society by H.P. Blavatsky, H.S. Olcott and W.Q. Judge in New York, he called a Hermetic Society into being. He then travelled to London in order to make the personal acquaintance of Sinnett and was introduced by him into theosophical circles there. He became a member of the Theosophical Society and returned to Ireland intent upon founding a Lodge in Dublin; as early as 1886, permission was granted for it. Thus the Hermetic Society which had been founded one year earlier now became superfluous. The Dublin Lodge itself survived in its original form until 1897 when it was dissolved as a result of various diverging tendencies.

This theosophical impulse, appearing within a period of only a few years, 'provided a literary, artistic and intellectual centre from which radiated influences whose effect was felt even by those who did not belong to it,' wrote E.A. Boyd in 1916 in his book *Ireland's Literary Renaissance.*[15] Yeats was able to win yet another friend over to theosophical ideas: the painter-poet George William Russell, who has become known under the pen-name 'A.E'. Yeats and Russell (who was two years younger) already knew each other from the Metropolitan School of Art which they had attended together. According to the essayist John Eglinton, who was another friend in this gradually emerging circle, Yeats and Russell were the undisputed leaders of the 'Literary Revival'.[16]

The Making of a Lifelong Friendship

Although Yeats constantly encouraged Russell to write, and even dedicated the first volume of his poems to him, the latter became so enflamed with enthusiasm for theosophical ideas that for a long time everything else seemed to him to be of secondary importance. For these ideas answered a deep-seated feeling of reality concerning the spiritual world, a feeling which had lived in him since his early childhood and which had one day surfaced in his consciousness in a very unusual way. In his autobiographical reflections, *The Candle of Vision*, he describes this event which determined the whole of the further course of his life as follows:

> I was aged about sixteen or seventeen years, when I, the slackest and least ideal of boys, with my life already made dark by those desires of body and heart with which we so soon learn to taint our youth, became aware of a mysterious life quickening within my life. Looking back I know not of anything in friendship, anything I had read, to call this forth. It was, I thought, self-begotten. I began to be

> astonished with myself, for, walking along country roads, intense and passionate imaginations of another world, of an interior nature began to overpower me. They were like strangers who suddenly enter a house, who brush aside the doorkeeper, and who will not be denied. Soon I knew they were the rightful owners and heirs of the house of the body, and the doorkeeper was only one who was for a time in charge, who had neglected his duty, and who had pretended to ownership. The boy who existed before was an alien. He hid himself when the pilgrim of eternity took up his abode in the dwelling. Yet, whenever the true owner was absent, the sly creature reappeared and boasted himself as master once more . . . The visible world became like a tapestry blown and stirred by the winds behind it. If it would but raise for an instant I knew I would be in Paradise. Every form on that tapestry appeared to be the work of the gods. Every flower was a word, a thought. The grass was speech; the trees were speech; the waters were speech; the winds were speech.[17]

The young Russell soon came to make a fine distinction between human wisdom achieved by personal endeavour and spiritual visions of this kind: 'We may indeed have a personal wisdom, but spiritual vision is not to speak of as ours any more than we can say at the rising of the sun: "This glory is mine." '[17] And ever more rare were the occasions when he would start to say, with respect to his visions: 'I imagined this,' rather than 'The curtain was lifted that I might see.' But Russell did not wait passively until this 'curtain' was lifted again. He seems very quickly to have discovered the secret of active waiting just as it is described in a single sentence in Rudolf Steiner's *Knowledge of the Higher Worlds*. It runs as follows: 'I must do everything I can to further the development of my soul and spirit, but I will wait calmly until higher powers have found me worthy of enlightenment.'[18] This sentence sets one the task of harmoniously co-ordinating the greatest possible activity with the greatest possible passivity and is a key to understanding two fundamental and, if left unconnected, potentially one-sided attitudes which can easily predominate in human striving.

Russell was soon undertaking exercises in concentration and meditation; he even engaged in the exercise of a special kind of retrospection, contemplating the sequence of daily events in reversed order. In this way he was able to strengthen his powers of recollection and even recall certain experiences of his youth long since buried and lost to memory, including

> . . . the greatest of all wonders in my boyhood, when I lay on the hill of Kilmasheogue and Earth revealed itself to me as a living being, and rock and clay were made transparent so that I saw lovelier and lordlier beings than I had known before, and was made partner in memory of mighty things, happenings in ages long sunken behind time. Though the walls about the psyche have thickened with age and there are many heavinesses piled about it, I still know that the golden age is all about us and that we can, if we will, dispel that opacity and have vision once more of the ancient Beauty.[19]

By cultivating such inner experiences and working them over in his mind in thought and meditation, a kind of magnetic core was formed in Russell's soul, magically attracting as it were experiences and events in the outside world which corresponded to his own stage of development:

> I became aware of a swift echo or response to my own moods in circumstance which had seemed hitherto immutable in its indifference. I found every intense imagination, every new adventure of the intellect endowed with magnetic power to attract to it its own kin. Will and desire were as the enchanter's wand of fable, and they drew to themselves their own affinities. Around a pure atom of crystal all the atoms of the element in solution gather, and in like manner one person after another emerged out of the mass, betraying their close affinity to my moods as they were engendered. I met these people seemingly by accident along country roads, or I entered into conversation with strangers and found they were intimates of the spirit. I could prophesy from the uprising of new moods in myself that I, without search, would soon meet people of a certain character, and so I met them. Even inanimate things were under the sway of these affinities. They yielded up to me what they had specially for my eyes. I have glanced in passing at a book left open by someone in a library, and the words first seen thrilled me, for they confirmed a knowledge lately attained in vision. At another time a book taken down idly from a shelf opened at a sentence quoted from an Upanishad,

> scriptures then to me unknown, and this sent my heart flying eastwards because it was the answer to a spiritual problem I had been brooding over an hour before. It was hardly a week after my first awakening that I began to meet those who were to be my lifelong comrades on the quest.[20]

One of those 'life-long comrades' whom Russell—inwardly prepared in this way—was soon to meet was D.N. Dunlop. The first meeting between them must have taken place about 1887, at a time when the Dublin Lodge already existed and Russell was assimilating theosophical ideas with fiery enthusiasm, while Yeats was just moving to London where he was to stay for the next four years. Whether the encounter with Dunlop was one of those which occurred seemingly by accident out on a country road or whether he was one of those 'strangers' with whom Russell entered into conversation cannot be said with certainty. Perhaps the first meeting took place in the context of a theosophical gathering in Dublin; what is certain beyond the shadow of a doubt is that Dunlop soon belonged amongst those whom Russell considered to be 'intimates of the spirit'. The alchemical process of mutual attraction seems to have worked quickly and spontaneously. Perhaps all that had been necessary was for Russell to have made some passing remark about the reincarnation of the human spirit to open up in 'Dan' (as he was soon to call him) certain heart-chambers which had, for a long time, been carefully kept closed. After all, in the years which lay between the first meeting with Russell and the death of his grandfather on the island of Arran he had spoken to no one at all of the inner experiences which, in the form of somewhat dreamlike imaginations, had visited his soul at that time. Enshrouded by silence, like the standing stones and stone circles on Arran, these experiences had lain at rest. Nothing of their potential energy had been 'wasted'. This whole force had flown towards the 'I', an 'I' awakened by vision, and had strengthened it. Dunlop's ego, which 'had awakened at that moment' in Arran, had for several years been both reinforced and shaped by the changes endured: the hard struggle to earn his daily bread and the nocturnal studies in occult literature. Yet he must have felt the growing need at long last to talk about these most intimate of matters to a fellow spirit—from heart to heart. In the first conversations nothing less than floodgates of the heart must have opened up between the two of them. This is simply borne out by the development of their friendship in the following years.

'Windows Facing Quite Another World' (A Methodical Aside)

Dunlop's first encounter with G.W. Russell falls into the period of his first 'moon node'. This phenomenon, the moon or lunar nodes, is based on a particular rhythm in the life of every human being, comprising approximately 18 years and 7 months reckoned from the moment of birth; it is a recurring astronomical configuration between the orbits of the earth and the moon in the context of the zodiac. Research by spiritual science discovers this astronomical fact to have an important correlation within the human soul. Such moments are, according to Rudolf Steiner, of special importance in the course of every human life; in the biography of particularly outstanding individuals they often appear in the unmistakable shape of powerfully intervening experiences and events. On 16 April 1920, Rudolf Steiner introduces this subject with the words: 'These are things in which the spiritual and material (as we call it) touch each other, or let us say the psychical and material,' and he goes on to establish the importance of this rhythm of approximately 18 years within the whole context of human biography:

> He who can faithfully observe what is contained within his own self will find the following . . . These things must gradually be brought to the attention of humanity. There are, I believe, many among you, who have already passed the point of 18 years and about 7 months in age. That was an important point. Others will have passed twice that number of years—37 years and 2 months—again an important point of time. After that we have a third very significant point, 18 years and 7 months later, at the age of 55 years and 9 months. Few can notice as yet, not having been trained to do so, the effects and important changes taking place within the individual soul at these times. The

> nights passed during these points of time are the most important nights in the life of the individual. It is here that the Macrocosm completes its 18 respirations, completes one minute—and man as it were, opens a window facing quite another world. But as I said, man cannot yet watch for these points in his life. Everyone, however, could try to let his mental eye look back over the years he has passed, and if he is over 55 years old to recognize three such important stages; others two, and most of you at any rate one! In these stages events take place, which rush up into this world of ours out of quite a different one. Our world opens at these moments onto another world.[21]

Now though this 'window' is opened for us every night, apart from these decisive moments, it is really only 'a fraction' wide as it were.

From the further context of what Rudolf Steiner explains concerning this matter we can infer the following: at such moments it is first and foremost prenatal experiences and 'decisions' which penetrate with special intensity—albeit totally unconsciously as a rule—into the human soul incarnated in the body, a body which, even at night, is never completely detached from the soul. And as a result of this interpenetration—precisely at such moments of biographical importance when the 'windows are open'—special meetings, occurrences, and changes can be brought about, or a way be opened up for them.

This aside is made at this point in order to draw the reader's attention to an important aspect of biographical study which will prove particularly productive when considering the life of D.N. Dunlop.

Thomas Lake Harris—an 'Intermezzo' of Far-reaching Significance

There can be little doubt that Russell, in his theosophical enthusiasm, tried to fill 'Dan' as well with enthusiasm for theosophical literature and especially for the works of H.P. Blavatsky or Mabel Collins. And he walked straight into a house with open doors. Dunlop may even have already got to know Blavatsky's first great work, *Isis Unveiled*, in Glasgow, the book having been published in 1877, two years after the founding of the Theosophical Society. At any rate, her next great work, *The Secret Doctrine*, which came out in 1888, was soon to become a common subject of study for the young Dublin theosophists.

It is probable that Russell also tried to persuade Dunlop to move to Dublin immediately. However, this only materialized about 1889, that is to say, some two years after their first meeting. Again, what took place in between remains somewhat obscure as far as biographical details are concerned. After the preliminary period in Dublin, Dunlop probably returned to Glasgow but in any case set out soon afterwards on the first of several journeys to America. This journey was motivated by his acquaintance with Thomas Lake Harris whom he may have got to know whilst he was still in Ireland.

Harris, who lived from 1823 to 1906, established a 'Brotherhood of the New Life' in the state of New York which moved over to California in 1875. It was a kind of agricultural and later viticultural commune founded on a religious basis. Harris was a convinced Swedenborgian and the author of numerous books concerning mysticism and the occult.[22] The adherents of his teachings 'were to learn to deny themselves completely in order to deliver themselves over to the divine power in man.'[23]

Although Harris evidently possessed certain occult and prophetic powers it has to be said that he largely misused these in dominating and manipulating those people with whom he came into contact. To his followers he prescribed rigid celibacy and occasionally exercised his spiritual authority both in breaking up existing marriages and prohibiting others. The complex web of karmic entanglements which association with Harris came to entail was maybe nowhere better illustrated than in the life of the great adventurer and occultist-writer Laurence Oliphant who lived for a long period in the American commune, but eventually succeeded in breaking himself free from Harris's influence.[24] He died in 1888, about the very time when Dunlop came into contact with Harris.

Whether it was Harris's teachings or rather his personality that attracted the young Scotsman we do not know, just as little as we know whether other motives, for instance the search for new work, might have given rise to this first journey to America. In any case he must have made strong personal links to Harris, for when, some time in 1889 or 1890, he returned to Dublin, he was in possession of all of Harris's written works along with some of the latter's unpublished manuscripts as well. At the same time he had been constantly engaged in studying Blavatsky's writings (as already stated, *The Secret Doctrine* had come out in the meantime), and thereby a strange kind of dissension was gradually arising in him. For giving way to a deep inner feeling he wrote to Blavatsky telling her that he was in possession of Harris's works and some of his unpublished manuscripts: should he read them? If not, what should he do with them? Blavatsky's reply was that he should send the whole lot back, unread, to America—a piece of advice which, with certain other components as we shall see in one of the next chapters, was to give rise to a very remarkable conflict.

No. 3 Upper Ely Place

In April 1891, in the same building which accommodated the Theosophical Lodge, the engineer Frederick J. Dick and his wife created a permanent place of residence for a few young theosophists. D.N. Dunlop along with George Russell and H.M. Magee, the brother of the above-mentioned John Eglinton, were among the first tenants. They formed a kind of nucleus in a house where numerous guests were constantly coming and going.

W.B. Yeats, who returned to Ireland in July of that year and became an occasional visitor, gives the following account of Ely Place and its inhabitants, looking back over a period of about two decades:

> The one house where nobody thought or talked politics was a house in Ely Place, where a number of young men lived together, and, for want of a better name, were called Theosophists. Besides the resident

> members, other members dropped in and out during the day, and the reading-room was a place of much discussion about philosophy and about the arts. The house had been taken in the name of the engineer to the Board of Works, a black-bearded young man, with a passion for Manichaean philosophy, and all accepted him as host; and sometimes the conversation, especially when I was there, became too ghostly for the nerves of his young and delicate wife, and he would be made angry. I remember young men struggling, with inexact terminology and insufficient learning, for some new religious conception, on which they could base their lives; and some few strange or able men.[25]

Even if we cannot determine whom Yeats rated as the 'strange' or 'able' men or who it may have been who spoke with 'inexact terminology' and 'insufficient learning', nevertheless, we can in the following description of the two occupants on the upper floor certainly identify one of them:

> At the top of the house lived a medical student who read Plato and took hashish, and a young Scotsman who owned a vegetarian restaurant, and had just returned from America, where he had gone as the disciple of the Prophet Harris, and where he would soon return in the train of some new prophet.[25]

No doubt about it: the Scotsman whom Yeats does not actually mention by name is Dunlop! And when Yeats enquired of this Scotsman—presumably in a tone of friendly irony—what it was that had set him on his wanderings, 'he told', doubtless with a corresponding tinge of gentle irony, 'of a young Highlander, his friend in boyhood, whose cap was always plucked off at a certain twist in the road, till the fathers of the village fastened it upon his head by recommending drink and women.'[25]

Indeed, for several months Dunlop actually ran a vegetarian restaurant in Dublin created by members of the Harris community; in this undertaking he was supported by the enegetic participation of one Eleanor Fitzpatrick, whom he had met at a lecture on Dante. In this restaurant a special non-alcoholic wine was offered to those theosophists who had gone so far as to renounce the pleasure of savouring wine upon the palate but could, however, not yet free themselves entirely from the delights of beholding it.

Apart from the fact that he was somewhat older and had already made a name for himself as a poet, Yeats's rather peripheral rapport with the occupants at Ely Place may also have been determined by the circumstance that he, who had indirectly been responsible for the founding of the Dublin Lodge in the first place, had already been received into the Hermetic Order of the Golden Dawn in March 1890.[26] This order, founded in 1888, with its turbulent and sometimes dubious history, used Rosicrucian instruction on the one hand along with Cabbalistic sources on the other; it also had a predilection for all kinds of ceremonial and ritualistic magic. Thus, it may well have seemed to Yeats (who in the meantime had become wise to a thing or two) that the young theosophists at Ely Place were amiable but somewhat naive greenhorns.

Nonetheless, over a period of time, a friendly understanding was established between them, and one day 'Dan' was even invited by 'Willy', as he was soon to call him, to witness a remarkable ceremony of ritualistic magic with Yeats at the heart of it. Edith Young, who as a young girl frequently succeeded in coaxing her father to give live descriptions of his time in Dublin, relates the following:

> In a fine old Georgian house a staircase took him to a bare backroom in which he was to join the privileged few chosen by Yeats to witness the rite. An opulent marble mantelpiece stood in the stead of an altarpiece. Wine bottles acted as sconces for the candles by whose light Yeats was to chalk a pentagram on the floorboards. The stage thus set, the audience squatted cross-legged against the wall. Into their midst strode Yeats, garbed in black, like the priest of some forgotten cult, a raven lock sweeping his brow, to chant a mantra designed to call into being apparitions from the nether world. Into his hand a participant placed a slaughtered cock; and in accordance with the instructions of those versed in the black arts, Yeats, holding the sacrificial bird at arm's length, whilst droning an incantation, sprinkled blood from its matted feathers into the middle of the mystical five pointed star.

> 'What happened? Did you see anything?' I eagerly enquired. 'All I saw,' father confessed, 'was Willy turning away in disgust from the dead bird at his feet.'[27]

It may well have been the experiencing of just this kind of scene which led Dunlop in later years to develop a very different attitude towards 'practical magic', as we shall see. But although experiments of this sort would have tended to alienate him, in other respects he nonetheless held Yeats in great esteem, as is evidenced by the following words of Edith Young:

> To hear him expound the mysteries of the Cabbala or recite one of his early lyrics over a bottle of wine afterwards was an experience I'm not likely to forget. Tone deaf though he was reported to be, I have yet to meet the man who had as fine an ear for the music of words as had Willy. He was too intellectual ever to have become a medium.[27]

But let us return to the house at Ely Place. H.M. Magee later recalled that 'life at Ely Place was quite monastic. The urge of sex, natural to youngsters in their twenties, was hardly spoken of (except under the disguise of "Kama") and was sternly suppressed.'[28]

Most of the young 'chelas' had every intention of remaining single for the whole of their lives because in theosophical circles it was not rarely believed to be impossible for a man properly to divide his attention between the earnest pursuit of occultism and a wife. Therefore the news that Charles Johnston, the founder of the Dublin Lodge, had married (a niece of Blavatsky, at that!) was quite shocking to some of the residents.

And yet in her then recently-published book *The Key to Theosophy* (1889) Blavatsky gives a more differentiated picture of the question. In a section entitled 'Theosophy and Marriage', she answers the question 'Must a man marry or remain celibate?' in the following way:

> It depends on the kind of man you mean. If you refer to one who intends to live in the world, one who, even though a good, earnest Theosophist, and an ardent worker for our cause, still has ties and

> wishes which bind him to the world, who, in short, does not feel that he has done for ever with what men call life, and that he desires one thing and one thing only—then for such a one I say there is no reason why he should not marry, if he likes to take the risks of that lottery where there are so many more blanks than prizes. Surely you cannot believe us so absurd and fanatical as to preach against marriage altogether? On the contrary, save in a few exceptional cases of practical Occultism, marriage is the only remedy against immorality.

Dunlop might have had good reason to ponder just these remarks. For ever since his meeting with Eleanor Fitzpatrick he had other things on his mind beside Theosophy.

'I think of my mother in her youth as a firebird,' Edith Young, Eleanor Fitzpatrick's daughter, writes in her autobiography, 'moulting in the confines of her home . . . set free by the attractive Scotsman.'

Looking at the picture (see Plate 5) of this 'attractive Scotsman', with the 'delicate and beautiful hands', we can almost imagine that it is a sensitive pianist or poet that we see before us here. 'My grandmother,' writes Edith Young, 'had not at first approved of the ideas father had absorbed at the weekly meetings he attended at the Theosophical Headquarters at Ely Place. But since he always had a soft word for her and an engaging twinkle in his eye he succeeded in gaining her permission to allow my mother to accompany him . . .'

When Eleanor found that she was with child, her friend might have felt at a loss what to do. At any rate he decided to write to both Harris and Blavatsky in London asking whether he should now get married. Harris's answer was 'no', Blavatsky's 'yes'. These answers can hardly have reached D.N. Dunlop more than a few days before the news came through that Helena Petrovna Blavatsky had died on 8 May 1891. For Dunlop in particular, but also for the whole community, still in its opening phase, this news came as a powerful shock. It resulted in an even more intensive study and discussion of her books in the evenings—as though to create a new element of community to compensate for her passing on.[29]

The 'Masters'—who were referred to from time to time with

awe and great respect—what would they, indeed what had they decided for the future? Which individuality would they select as their new instrument?

Such questions would have been seriously discussed in 'The Household', as the community was called. But at the same time the earnestness of its members was healthily counterbalanced by other activities. Often in the evenings Frederick Dick would sit down at the piano in the reading-room and play Chopin or Beethoven while Russell, who did not have a great affinity for music, would sketch charcoal caricatures of those listening—unless at that particular moment he happened to be immersed in *The Secret Doctrine.*

'A Mingling of Natures'

Let us take a closer look at the person and nature of George William Russell. To make such an attempt at this point seems to be unavoidable given the fact that certain fundamental qualities of this remarkable man play a strange role in the inner conflict, yet to be described, of his friend 'Dan'.

Russell, born on 10 April 1867, entered a well-known school of art in Dublin at the age of 13. Two years later, besides regularly attending secondary school he again resumed evening classes at the Metropolitan School of Art where, in 1884, he became closely acquainted with Yeats. In the following year he also met Charles Johnston and from 1888 onwards he attended meetings at the Theosophical Lodge, subsequently becoming a member. In December 1890, with the usual probationary period, he was received into the 'Esoteric Section of the Theosophical Society'. The certificate of admission bore Blavatsky's own signature.

During the time Russell was living at Ely Place he was also working as an accountant at Pim's, a well-known drapery store in Dublin. This was after he had no longer been able to reconcile his conscience with the idea of earning his living in a brewery.

'Russell's great delight and consolation when he returned from Pim's,' says Eglinton, 'was to study *The Secret Doctrine*, though I'm bound to say I don't remember seeing him "study" for long without breaking off for argument or discussions.' And in Dan he would often have found a committed partner just as ready as he was himself to participate in these discussions: 'I remember, however, the heartfelt way in which he told me how he was supported through the day's routine by the prospect of immersing himself in its pages—to him a contact with a high Reality.'[30]

Russell took theosophical ideas very seriously. This is clear from the following example found in a letter to a girlfriend of his youth: 'I do not think I will ever try to get either literary or artistic fame; art and literature do not interest me now, only one thing interests me and that is life or truth. I want to become rather than to know.'[30]

Approximately 20 years later Dunlop was to write something comparable to this himself. In a book entitled *The Path of Attainment*, compiled from three lectures he had given to theosophists, he describes how the 'true esotericist' strives 'not so much to know as to become, and herein lies the tremendous import of the Delphic inscription "Know thyself", which is the key-note of all true esoteric development, for the true esoteric student understands that self-knowledge can be attained only through self-development in the highest possible sense of the term.'[31] Such authentic will to *become*, to attain selfhood beyond ambition or vanity, was a deeply founded element of common striving in the bond of friendship arising between Russell and Dunlop.

Even so, however much Russell took theosophical ideas and ideals to heart, he never for a moment lost another quality inborn in him—a loving interest and sympathy for the world around him and his fellow men. In a most extraordinary fashion he was able to feel his way into the soul-experiences of friends or sometimes even people quite unknown to him; indeed this occurred in such a manner as would seem to prefigure, in a germinal form, certain future capacities of mankind in the social sphere. Russell writes in *The Candle of Vision*:

Once in an idle interval in my work, I sat with my face pressed in my

> hands, and in that dimness pictures began flickering in my brain. I saw a little dark shop, the counter before me, and behind it an old man fumbling with some papers, a man so old that his motions had lost swiftness and precision. Deeper in the store was a girl, red-haired with grey watchful eyes fixed on the old man. I saw that to enter the shop one must take two steps downwards from a cobbled pavement without. I questioned a young man, my office companion, who then was writing a letter, and I found that what I had seen was his father's shop. All my imaginations—the old man, his yellow-white beard, his fumbling movements, the watchful girl, her colour, the steps, the cobbled pavement—were not imaginations of mine in any true sense, for while I was in a vacant mood my companion had been thinking of his home, and his brain was populous with quickened memories, and they invaded my own mind, and when I made question I found their origin. But how many thousand times are we invaded by such images and there is no speculation over them?[32]

To what extent this kind of visionary participation was linked to a motive of compassion (in the sense of totally experiencing something *with* someone), indeed, to what extent it had its deepest roots in this very motive, can be seen from another passage in which Russell relates certain experiences of his youth:

> I was living in the country and was told of a woman who was dying, how, a quarter of an hour or so before she went, she wept that she was unable to rise and nurse a sick neighbour; and there came on me a transfiguring anguish because of this self-forgetfulness of hers, and though the mood was too high for me to sustain and I passed from it to many egoisms, yet this was the starting-point of whatever selflessness was in my life.[33]

According to the literary critic Ernest Boyd, 'the basic element in AE's work . . . is its absolute sincerity'[34] and indeed, the more one finds passages of the kind quoted in this chapter, the more the truth of these words seems to be borne out.

Crisis and Decision

In the years following his return from America a strange inner conflict had been developing deep within Dunlop's soul. However, it remained unnoticed by outsiders, indeed by most of his friends as well, except for Russell. Initially it was no doubt linked to the inner dilemma—Harris or Blavatsky? This was a problem that was becoming more and more acute. On the other hand, factors of a more external nature may also have contributed to creating the conflict. There was not only Dunlop's relationship with Eleanor, but also the uncertainty of material prospects for the future—the vegetarian restaurant had to be closed down after a few months because the cook gave in his notice. At all events, as time went on the conflict assumed the character of an extensive crisis with regard to the whole of his spiritual orientation.

It was as though an invisible sword had cut through his soul, for many of the inner qualities and natural tendencies which had hitherto functioned together as a unity in his thought and striving were now, before his soul's eye, being mercilessly divided into their separate components—which were becoming ever more recognizable as such. Russell, who underwent an intimate experience of his friend's crisis at the moment of its dramatic climax, gives the following account of it in a short narrative published in May 1893 under the title *The Secret of Power*.[35]

> The incident here related is burned into my mind and life, not because of its dramatic intensity or personal character, but because it was a revelation of the *secret of power*, a secret which the wise in good and the wise in evil alike have knowledge of.
>
> My friend Felix[36] was strangely disturbed; not only were his material affairs unsettled, but he was also passing through a crisis in his spiritual life. Two paths were open before him. On one side lay the dazzling mystery of passion; on the other 'the small old path' held out its secret and spiritual allurements. I had hope that he would choose the latter, and as I was keenly interested in his decision, I invested the struggle going on in his mind with something of universal significance, seeing in it a symbol of the strife between 'light and darkness which are the world's eternal ways'. He came in late one

evening. I saw at once by the dim light that there was something strange in his manner. I spoke to him in enquiry; he answered me in a harsh dry voice quite foreign to his usual manner. 'Oh, I am not going to trouble myself any more, I will let things take their course.' This seemed the one idea in his mind, the one thing he understood clearly was that things were to take their own course; he failed to grasp the significance of any other idea or its relative importance. He answered 'Aye, indeed,' with every appearance of interest and eagerness to some trivial remark about the weather and was quite unconcerned about another and most important matter which should have interested him deeply. I soon saw what had happened: his mind, in which forces so evenly balanced had fought so strenuously, had become utterly wearied out and could work no longer. A flash of old intuition illumined it at last—it was not wise to strive with such bitterness over life—therefore he said to me in memory of this intuition, 'I am going to let things take their course.' A larger tribunal would decide; he had appealed unto Cæsar. I sent him up to his room and tried to quiet his fever by magnetization with some success. He fell asleep and as I was rather weary myself I retired soon after.

Thus far Russell describes and interprets the state of his friend as he outwardly appeared at the beginning. What now follows is a description of experiences which took place beyond the threshold of the world accessible to the senses and the intellect, and this is a world in which a far deeper 'mingling of natures' is possible, to use an expression from *The Candle of Vision.* Russell used it, in fact, as a title for the chapter in which the above-mentioned experience with his office colleague is described.

This was the vision of the night. It was surely in the room I was lying in and on my bed, and yet space opened on every side with pale, clear light. A slight wavering figure caught my eye, a figure that swayed to and fro; I was struck with its utter feebleness, yet I understood it was its own will or some quality of its nature which determined that palpitating movement towards the poles between which it swung. What were they? I became silent as night and thought no more. Two figures awful in their power opposed each other; the frail being wavering between them could by putting out its arms have touched them both. It alone wavered, for they were silent, resolute and knit in the conflict of will; they stirred not a hand nor a foot; there was only a still quivering now and then as of intense effort, but they made no other movement. Their heads were bent forward slightly, their arms folded, their bodies straight, rigid, and inclined slightly backwards from each other like two spokes of a gigantic wheel. What were they, these figures? I knew not, and yet gazing upon them, thought which took no words to clothe itself mutely read their meaning. Here were the culminations of the human, towering images of the good and evil man may aspire to. I looked at the face of the evil adept. His bright red-brown eyes burned with a strange radiance of power; I felt an answering emotion of pride, of personal intoxication, of psychic richness rise up within me gazing upon him. His face was archetypal; the abstract passion which eluded me in the features of many people I knew, was here declared, exultant, defiant, giantesque; it seemed to leap like fire, to be free. In this face I was close to the legendary past, to the hopeless worlds where men were martyred by stony kings, where prayer was hopeless, where pity was none. I traced a resemblance to many of the great Destroyers in history whose features have been preserved, Napoleon, Rameses, and a hundred others, named and nameless, the long line of those who were crowned and sceptered in cruelty. His strength was in human weakness. I saw this, for space and the hearts of men were bare before me. Out of space there flowed to him a stream half invisible of red; it nourished that rich radiant energy of passion; it flowed from men as they walked and brooded in loneliness, or as they tossed in sleep. I withdrew my gaze from this face which awoke in me a lurid sense accompaniment, and turned it on the other. An aura of pale soft blue was around this figure through which gleamed an underlight as of universal gold. The vision was already dim and departing, but I caught a glimpse of a face godlike in its calm, terrible in the beauty of a life we know only in dreams, with strength which is the end of the hero's toil, which belongs to the many times martyred soul; yet not far away nor in the past was its power, it was the might of life which exists eternally. I understood how easy it would have been for this one to have ended the conflict, to have gained a material victory by its power, but this would not have touched on or furthered its spiritual ends. Only its real being had force to attract that real being which was shrouded in the wavering figure. This truth the adept of darkness knew also and therefore he intensified within the sense of pride and passionate personality. Therefore they stirred not a hand nor a foot, while under the stimulus of their presence culminated the

> good and evil in the life which had appealed to a higher tribunal to decide. Then this figure wavering between the two moved forward and touched with its hand the Son of Light. All at once the scene and actors vanished, and the eye that saw them was closed. I was alone with darkness and a hurricane of thoughts . . . I knew that although the gods and cosmic powers may war over us for ever, it is we alone declare them victors or vanquished. For the rest the vision of that night was prophetic, and the feet of my friend are now set on that way which was the innermost impulse of his soul.

The impression given at a first reading of this scene might well be, despite Russell's words of introduction, that it is first and foremost a narration of his own soul-experiences. However, one need only recall his own description (quoted above)—of how he was aware of other people's experiences, of contents of consciousness foreign to himself—to find the idea plausible that we are indeed dealing with the same phenomenon here.

From the account Dunlop gave Stein, it is quite clear that the former was *himself* the focal-point of the imaginative 'drama' experienced by Russell; this whole scene had indeed 'dawned upon' the latter in rather the same way as on the other occasion the mental pictures of his office colleague had emerged in his own consciousness. Russell's inner participation was in fact so strong in this case that he included this visionary scene in one of the murals with which he had begun to decorate the walls of 'The Household' at Upper Ely Place.

*

'In an important decision in which he had to choose between Harris and Blavatsky,' Stein writes in his reminiscences, Dunlop 'decided in a way that was illustrated by a vision. Mr. Dunlop told me the content of this vision . . . and told me that this vision appeared not only to him but also to his friend George Russell, who was present in the same house at the same moment.' Stein inserts Russell's description at this point and continues: 'Mr. Dunlop described this vision to me and even many years afterwards, speaking about it, I could see how intensely alive both these figures had been. He described two beings, the red one in red clothing and red light: and the blue one in blue clothes and blue light, both very beautiful and impressive.'(St) It is particularly worth noting that whilst Russell felt a distinct aversion for the red figure, both figures appeared 'very beautiful and impressive' to Dunlop—a fact that must have intensified the difficulty as well as the scope involved in making this inner choice.

However, two complementary elements later provided by Dunlop, and which are totally lacking in Russell's version of the experience, are even more significant: 'And a voice sounded and asked him to choose between them, and he said, "I decided for the blue, and I felt that it was a great decision that I was making."'

This adds an *inspirational* element to Russell's version. The very fact that it is lacking in his account attests to its objectivity. Since Russell himself was in no way the one who had to make the decision, the voice could only be heard by his friend, Dunlop, who appeared in the vision as the frail figure, and possibly only to Russell in this particular way.

The other illuminating element provided by Dunlop follows on immediately in Stein's report: 'First the red figure disappeared, then the blue one, and finally a wise old man appeared and began to teach me.' (St)

This last 'picture' can also be seen as a crowning conclusion to the whole series of images experienced by Dunlop, for it points significantly to an important stage reached on the path of esoteric development. Indeed, we should never for a moment forget that we are here dealing with someone who already had far-reaching spiritual experiences 'behind him', and in whose life, as he was to relate it about a month before his death, 'a feeling of the reality of the spiritual world had always been present'. It was a life in which 'a deliberate seeking after spiritual knowledge began . . . with the very first stirrings of independent thought. In short, we are dealing with someone whose ego had 'awakened early'.

If one takes Dunlop's words seriously and quite concretely, and on the basis of the preceding biographical considerations there is no reason to do otherwise, then the old man might appear to an impartial judgement as embodying the purely spiritual intervention of a certain individuality whose spiritual guidance now begins in the individual human being (in such a way as to be consciously perceived by him). Thus, in the crowning conclusion of these scenes experienced by Dunlop, we can also decipher the presence of a third, *intuitive* element in so far as the closing scene points to a meeting of two beings on a purely spiritual level. Again, the fact that this final image did not figure in Russell's experience attests to the objectivity of *his* description.

The conflict arising from the alternative—Harris or Blavatsky?—as well as the various external difficulties besetting him at the time, merely provided an internal and an external setting for a drama of far deeper dimensions: the drama of human knowledge and consciousness which every human being must sooner or later experience on the path of esoteric development.

The real choice, and the two paths which are ultimately at stake here, are described in a deeper sense by Rudolf Steiner in the last two chapters of his book *Knowledge of the Higher Worlds.* A description is given in these chapters of how the 'lesser' and the 'greater' Guardian of the Threshold come to meet the pupil at a certain moment on the inner path of knowledge. In the 'lesser' Guardian 'the extent to which the individual is entangled in the physical world of the senses is made concretely perceptible' (this entanglement initially being expressed by the presence of instincts, impulses, desires, egoistical wishes, all forms of selfishness and so forth); however, 'when the pupil has recognized the things from which he must free himself, an exalted Being of Light stands before him on his path. The beauty of this Being is difficult to describe in human language.' Rudolf Steiner then relates, in imaginative form, how this 'greater' Guardian advises the pupil of the necessity of making a decision between the 'black path' and the 'white path', and of consequences inevitably linked to such a decision: 'I therefore forbid you admission,' so speaks the 'greater' Guardian, 'into the highest regions of the supersensible world as long as you have not applied all the powers you have acquired to the redemption of the world to which you belong.'[37]

The path of esoteric training had brought the two friends, each in his own way, to a crossroads where a decision of this kind had become a real necessity. And each one had, again in his own way, already developed the faculties which make it possible to 'sojourn in the lower regions of the supersensible world'. It was now time, within these very regions, to establish whether henceforth they intended to tread the 'black' or the 'white' path.

The same individuality who, in the Imagination of his youth, stood leaning against the pillar of a temple watching his Beloved enter in, passed into that temple himself in this incarnation—accomplishing this act in a totally conscious way. For in his soul he had found 'the means whereby the lips of the Initiates will be unsealed.'[38]

New Impulses and New Horizons

These profound spiritual experiences not only had the effect, in different ways, of advancing Russell and Dunlop in their moral development, they also gave birth to intense new impulses in the bond of friendship which united them. 'To work, with a new will and enthusiasm!' No doubt this would have been the call resounding in their hearts after that 'night of visions', experienced in extraordinary communion and yet in such an individual and personal way. Both of them had recognized the danger of coming to a kind of 'dead end' on the inner path. Now the way was cleared for completely fresh and energetic activity with goals that stood under a special star, embracing as they did much more than the everyday aims that the isolated individual can set himself. A new morning was beginning to dawn in the life of the two young friends, with fresh horizons and wide perspectives. They decided to create a magazine in order to participate actively in the spreading of spiritual ideas. Of course during the long evenings at Ely Place they still continued to study Blavatsky's 'Stanzas of Dzyan' which 'seemed to be a voice of thunder from a bygone age, carrying their one conviction of spiritual reality, but remote and imperfectly understood'. (DS) However, from now on the fruits of such studies, enriched by their own experiences and decisions, were to be made into a source of joy and spiritual nourishment for people quite unknown to them. The new magazine was simply named *The Irish Theosophist*. 'We wanted to awaken people to the wonders surrounding them.' (StS) Thus Dunlop later characterized one of the common motives they shared in this work. 'We printed it and even learned to do the illustrations ourselves. The printing-press was in one of the bedrooms, and we greatly increased our sales by using coloured illustrations.' (St) The first number of the magazine, which was published until 1897, came out in October 1892.

Fortunately the whole magazine has recently been republished and so can be studied at length by anybody interested, but here we must content ourselves with a few cursory references to its content. While Dunlop concentrated on his editorial responsibilities (writing those enthusiastic articles with an occasionally humorous touch which gave the magazine its bold and generous external contours), Russell began, for the first time in his life, actually to write down poetry and publish it. For although many of his poems had reached the stage of 'oral perfection', it was only in 1894 (the same year in which Rudolf Steiner's *Philosophy of Spiritual Activity* appeared) that these poems were published, in a handsome little volume entitled *Homeward—Songs by the Way*, thanks to the efforts and persuasive powers of yet another friend belonging to that circle, the amiable Charles Weekes, who was later to work together with Dunlop in the electrical industry in London. The collection was positively received and much attention was paid to it at the time.

Russell often signed his poems 'AE'. This was also the pseudonym under which he was to publish his later works. The way in which he came by this pseudonym is in many respects so enlightening that it would be a pity not to mention it here. In *The Candle of Vision* Russell describes how he tried once in meditation to imagine 'the apparition in the Divine Mind of the idea of the Heavenly Man'. He subsequently attempted to distil the resulting imaginative experience into a picture, feeling that 'something ancient and eternal seemed to breathe through my fancies'. He lay awake long into the night wondering what he should call the picture now that it was finished. 'And I felt like one who is in a dark room and hears the breathing of another creature, and himself waits breathless for its utterance, and I struggled to understand what wished to be said, and at last, while I was prenaturally dilated and intent, something whispered to me, "Call it the Birth of Aeon." The word "Aeon" thrilled me, for it seemed to evoke by association of ideas, moods and memories most ancient, out of some ancestral life where they lay hidden.'[39]

A few days after this experience Russell was in a library when his eyes fell quite by chance on a dictionary of religions lying open in front of him. They came to rest on an expression which he had never seen or heard before: 'Aeon'. This expression, so the explanation went, was that used by the Gnostics to designate the first created worlds or beings. When Russell subsequently signed an article for the theosophical journal *Lucifer* with the word 'AEON', the proof-reader, who could not decipher it, put a question-mark after the E and thereafter Russell simply signed himself 'AE'. *The Irish Theosophist* provided its readers with both stimulating and independent-minded commentaries on the whole of the 'theosophical scene' of that period. Everything was reviewed in a pertinent and totally undogmatic manner (a valuable achievement given the fact that after Blavatsky's death things by no means always proceeded harmoniously and without a certain 'fracas').

Judge or Besant? That was the question concerning the future leadership of the 'Esoteric School' of the Theosophical Society which preoccupied so many minds at the time. Colonel Olcott, president of the society until his death in 1907, after having acted as mediator and negotiator, decided to divide the 'Esoteric School' into two parts, conferring the direction of the East (Eurasia) on Annie Besant and that of the West on William Quin Judge. (A Dubliner by birth, Judge worked as a lawyer in New York. He had been one of the founder members of the Theosophical Society in 1875 but subsequently he and his American followers had begun to turn away from the Anglo-Indian leadership.)

Judge and Besant had given theosophical lectures in Dublin so that they were personally known to both the 'Irish theosophists'. Dunlop had, however, never actually met 'Madame Blavatsky' whom he so greatly revered, while Russell had only met her briefly. Thus one day Dunlop asked his friend Yeats (who had got to know 'Madame' in London shortly before her death) for an interview in which he was to describe quite freely and openly his personal impressions of this unusual and controversial lady. It appeared in the November 1893 issue of *The Irish Theosophist* (and is printed in full in the Appendix of this book). At the end of the interview 'Dan' asked 'Willie' about his work in progress and characterized him as someone who 'combines the man of thought with the man of action'.

*

After that remarkable nocturnal experience and decision, Dunlop's life underwent radical changes on other 'fronts' as well. With regard to his relationship with Eleanor Fitzpatrick, he soon acted according to Blavatsky's advice. He and Eleanor were married on 12 August 1891. He then left the theosophical residence at Ely Place which had become so familiar and dear to him and joined his wife in her parents' house. The young couple lived in the top storey of a house in Drumcondra Road, which served as editorial address of *The Irish Theosophist*. There, in January 1892, a daughter, the above-mentioned Edith, was born.[40] Two years later she was followed by the only son, Ronald.[41] According to Edith Young, her father was, at that time, earning the income necessary for the upkeep of the family as an employee in an insurance company.

*

Meanwhile, *The Irish Theosophist* continued to report on the numerous events and activities going on inside the Theosophical Society. Of particularly striking importance seems to have been the year 1896. After the death of Judge, the president of the American Society, in March of that same year, an international theosophical convention was called in New York on 26/27 April. The new situation had to be clarified and a solution found. Dunlop attended the convention as a representative of the Dublin Lodge. Short as it was, the following address which he delivered there gives us a good picture of his attitude towards the Theosophical Society and theosophical matters at that time:

> Comrades. You know of course that I come from a very small part of the world, a part which compared with this vast continent is almost infinitesimal, but although it is small geographically, yet as you know it has not played an altogether unimportant part in the history of this movement.
>
> The one thing which unites us, apart from any feelings of nationality or race distinction is the endeavour to realize brotherhood all over the world, and to engage in unselfish work for others. So that Theosophical Conventions are not gatherings for mutual admiration but that we may with united devotion and harmony take the opportunity to bring about better organization for our work, and to strengthen the links that bind us together all over the world, and thus extend the Theosophical movement in every direction.
>
> Now, as our worthy Chairman has said, it seems perhaps rather conceited on our part to talk of having some particular solution of the problems of life that other people have not. Patent medicines are produced almost every day for the physically ill, likewise for the morally sick you find quack remedies brought forward almost every other week. But there is one thing perhaps that you will find in looking into Theosophical philosophy and that is that it not only affords a great deal of intellectual food, but at the same time it justifies itself on intellectual and logical grounds. And still further you will find that from a devotional point of view it is satisfactory in the very highest degree. You will find in Theosophy a philosophy which is as old as time and which has come forward at different periods in the history of the world and been scattered broadcast, through the agency of those 'elder brothers' of ours, in order that mankind may gradually be led back to that knowledge which it has lost.[42]

If one is attentive to the finer undertones of this simple and unassuming address, one discovers that it touches on certain points of fundamental importance for anyone attempting to cultivate and further a truly spiritual impulse. If one were to remove the somewhat charming and amiable 'padding' around these thoughts one could perhaps 'translate' this address into the following fundamental terms. Selfless activity for others on the basis of a true spiritual impulse is incompatible with the human (all-too-human) craving to revere and want to be revered. Without the genuine will to work on the basis of world-wide co-ordination and co-operation, a movement such as the theosophical one can achieve nothing. No theosophist should deem himself as 'having' the truth in his possession and therefore able to look down upon his fellow men. On the contrary he should show his reverence towards Theosophy by not merely avidly consuming it, but by making an effort to *understand* its substance by means of precise logic and sound common sense. And if in the midst of his endeavours he can also remind himself that the *substance* of Theosophy has been passed on to us by spiritual beings far advanced on the path, then his soul may well be stirred by the warm breath of genuine devotion.

Whether or not this is reading too much into Dunlop's intentions and we would do better to consider these as rather beautiful and conventional words with no further significance will become clear in the course of our considerations. Obviously, from the mere words as such we shall not be able to deduce with any certainty what spiritual substance may be latent in them. Let us therefore continue our investigations into who it is who is saying this type of thing.

*

W.Q. Judge had designated in his will that a certain person named 'Promise' should succeed him as leader of the American Section of the Theosophical Society. This section had become *officially* separated from the original society in 1895, whereas the latter had in the meantime taken up its quarters in Adyar, India, after coming under the exclusive leadership of Colonel Olcott. This 'Promise' arrived at the forefront of the American Society in the following way: 'In a spiritualistic séance, in which Catherine Tingley participated as an active medium, the spirit of H.P. Blavatsky was said to have appeared and declared Mrs Tingley to be this "Promise".'[43]

Tingley, whom Dunlop had met at the April convention in New York, regarded herself as 'leader of the entire Theosophical Movement throughout the world' and accordingly prepared for a world-crusade to spread this news and gather active followers. In the beginning of August Tingley arrived at Dublin and visited the group at Ely Place. Presently the 'leader' and her crusaders travelled down to Killarney in search of a stone to go with others from various countries to form the corner for the School for the Revival of the Lost Mysteries of Antiquity. A camp was erected for several days, and amongst those attending the various ceremonies we also find AE and D.N. Dunlop. Probably it was on this occasion that Catherine Tingley asked Dunlop to become her secretary in America and help her to form what was going to become the 'International Brotherhood League'—Tingley's alternative to the Adyar society. The editor of *The Irish Theosophist*, who had also personally known Judge, accepted this offer from his successor with great enthusiasm. It was, however, going to take him more than a year actually to move to America.

At first sight it might be difficult to understand why Dunlop immediately accepted this offer. But, as it was obviously of importance to him to know exactly what was going on in the movement, he would have wanted to be directly acquainted with its leading figures in order to judge and assess the whole of its future orientation and development. For this reason it may have seemed important to him to enter into a closer kind of relationship with this new 'Promise'. But as it turned out 'many disillusionments were still in store through the years of activity in more than one branch of the Theosophical Society which followed the reading of H.P. Blavatsky's works. (DS)

However, it may well have been also for other reasons that Dunlop moved with the whole of his family to America. At any rate one of Tingley's followers present on this occasion at Killarney, a certain F.R. Price, who owned an engineering firm in New York, arranged for Dunlop to be given a post in the firm's sales department. But no doubt 'the lure of American engineering' alone could certainly not have drawn him to America as some obituaries suggested.

Personality and Individuality on the Occult Path

In view of the difficult and often turbulent developments prevailing within the Theosophical Society in the middle of the nineties, in which disputes about individuals and struggles involving them were constantly the focal-points of attention, Dunlop considered it incumbent on *The Irish Theosophist* to present its readers every now and then with a completely lucid and unsentimental view of theosophical matters and theosophical aspirations. This also meant occasionally exposing certain exaggerated attitudes in the striving of aspiring, over-zealous theosophists. Thus, in December 1896, Dunlop on one occasion speaks of those theosophists who believe that their one and only duty towards humanity consists in so cultivating 'their nerves into a state of "abnormal sensitiveness" . . . that they shriek almost when they enter a room with ugly wallpaper'.

An article which Dunlop published in March 1897 sheds light on other areas even more deeply buried within human experience. It bears the title 'By-paths in Occult Progress',[44] and much of its richness is the direct product of that unique night now some years behind him. It gives us a real insight into what Dunlop considered to be the true nature and purpose of occult development; it also expresses a view of these things which, on the whole, he would continue to hold throughout the following decades as well. For this reason the most essential passages of this essay may here be given:

> One of the objects which we, as members of the Theosophical Society, set before ourselves, is to strive after a realization of man's higher destiny in our own selves. We believe in the existence of higher powers, and a sublimer state of consciousness than that which we experience now. We believe that the attainment of this exalted condition depends upon the abandonment of personal interests, which are a snare and a delusion, and the aspiring towards a universal consciousness which we shall share with all creation, and in which we shall feel by sympathy the throb of every human heart, and have no secret joys or sorrows unshared by others. Sick of the narrow limits of our personality; weary of private ambitions, loves, and specula-

tions; distracted by the never-ceasing panorama of our own moods, now of gratulation, now of remorse; now of cold cynicism, now of morbid sentimentality, we long to escape from that importunate demon of self-consciousness which is ever at our side instilling into our cup of joy the poison of pleasure, and marring our healthy spontaneity of feeling with its whisperings of vanity and egotism. 'Let me feel myself in these people, let me share their joys and sorrows that so I may help them!' is the cry of the soul; but the personality—exacting spouse created by our self in the past—steps between and snatches our love for itself.

To paralyse this personality, to make it an obedient slave, and to learn to take away our attention from it and listen to the voice of the Oversoul—this is . . . true practical occultism. Shall we then cultivate occult powers? Is it right to try to develop them? Or should we leave them alone, and confine our attention to the ethics and the philosophy? Such questions are often asked, but have we not here a touchstone by which they are easily solved? Would such and such a power increase or diminish the strength of our personality? Would its attainment hinder or help us in our chosen aim?

There are many occult powers and faculties which are mere adornments of the personality, and it is quite possible to imagine a being superbly gifted with clairvoyance, magnetic power, intellectuality, control over his inner bodies, and what not—and yet an intensely personal individual. He might fill the world with his charities and attract crowds by his personal gifts, but still be the victim of self-consciousness, egotism and vanity. Well, some may deem this a desirable goal to attain, and even imagine that such a being would be happy; but for those who do not care to merely swell their personality, the cultivation of such powers will be of no use whatever. There are some of us who, so far from having powers to gain, have positively powers to lose, ere we can make any progress on the true path. Having in a past life strayed on the path of personal aggrandisement, we unexpectedly arouse a latent tendency to do the same in this life. A fatal facility to study along the lines of various occult arts tempts us to leave the straight path of spiritual development and to wander on the by-path of useless knowledge. Some have bodies over-sensitive to psychic impressions, whereby the evil forces of a great city are able to invade them and lead them astray. Others find they can leave their physical body and travel in an inner body, and thus they encounter new fields of temptation and subtler attacks which they cannot resist. Such powers are obviously hindrances, not helps, unless indeed our motives are other than we care to confess.

The fact is that the brain-mind is not fit to judge what powers we ought to develop. The powers are supposed to be for the use of the higher self in its work, but the brain-mind only caters for the lower self. It is never safe, therefore, to make the acquisition of powers an object; we should aspire after selflessness, and leave the powers to grow naturally as an outcome of our success in realizing that aspiration.

As it is our personality is so strong that it invariably twists and distorts every bit of knowledge and power that comes within its reach. All our good motives get tinctured with vanity and greed, because we cannot yet altogether eliminate the personal element from them. Our responsibilities for the right use of our ordinary faculties are great indeed; which one of us dare take the far greater responsibility of rightly using wider powers? An occult force is not a mere quiescent machine ready to be used and capable of being turned off at will. It is a good deal more, and must be controlled to prevent it from controlling its master. Let us beware how we waken it.

Is it possible to stumble into the wrong path by accident and through heedlessness? Yes, I believe it is, and that some of us are inclined to fall in danger of doing so occasionally. The danger usually arises from a mistaken notion as to the object of certain ceremonies or practical aids that may be recommended. Suppose, for instance, we are told to visualize some symbol or what not, as an aid to concentration on the Higher Self. This hint is intended—not as an object in itself—but as an aid towards a higher object. If we find it does aid us, well and good; but if we forget the main object and allow our mind to be taken up altogether with the practice, we miss the point. It is of no use to visualize a double triangle until it grows objective and follows you about everywhere like a dog. This is simply the unintelligent cultivation of an occult art, and will lead you astray . . . Use the symbol to start a good current if you like, but then forget it. Again, we may be over-anxious to protect ourselves from the antagonistic forces that surround us, and may indulge in some such practice as the building of an imaginary wall or shell round us. The mainspring of this conduct is fear, we are afraid, we feel weak, and we want to shut ourselves up in a comfortable house where we can be safe. But courage is the best protection; courage builds a far

> stronger wall round its possessor than could be built in the other way. It can even stop bullets in a battle. The wall built by courage is a real wall, and it is built in the right way—by dwelling on the *idea* and letting the material effect follow of itself. The psychic wall which some people try to build round themselves is built in the wrong way; they dwell on the material side of the question . . .
>
> Black magic always begins at the wrong end. It begins at the bottom. It attempts to achieve spiritual results by the adjustment of material conditions. Thus it resembles the Tower of Babel, which was built upon the ground and reared towards heaven. But the creative power evolves from spirit downwards to matter. One of the symbols of the Tarot is the lightning-struck tower, which typifies a material system smitten by the wrath of heaven. Pranayama, or the restraint of breath, is a good instance of this. The idea is to tranquilize the mind by regulating the vital currents. But the right way is to regulate the mind, and then the vital currents will regulate themselves. There is a little vital god in your body who understands how to govern it much better than you do. Leave the regulation of breath to him, and attend to your mind . . .

Are we not dealing here with the consequences of that decisive, nocturnal experience, the vision having now been transformed into conceptual language? It is not very difficult to sense the presence of the two adepts in the background of these depictions. The red one, who appeals to the lust for power within the human being and to vanity and ambition, is able to give tremendous strength to these same desires; he leads the personality, as it strives to develop occult powers, onto the 'black path'. The blue figure is not concerned with the personality; it can, however, accompany and inspire the true individuality upon the 'white path', provided the latter has awoken to self-consciousness. Thus there is a clear inner congruity between this essay and the spiritual experience earlier described.

Dunlop did not sign the article with his own name nor did he use a pseudonym; instead he signed it with his 'cosmic' name: Capricorn. This was well-suited to a point of view which aimed at transcending the personal in its description of the essential nature and dangers on the occult path.

How can the 'individuality', the true, cosmic being of the ego, be awakened within the personality? How can the true being of the 'I' be cultivated? This is the basic question we might well ponder as we follow the striking thoughts of this man of now 28 years. For D.N. Dunlop there are basically three ways of achieving this aim: firstly, by practising true and selfless brotherhood as recommended at the end of this essay; then by discovering within the sheaths of the personality the immortal self which is active in human thinking; and lastly by cultivating certain forms of sacrifice within the life of will.

'Personality', 'individuality'—here we touch on one of the real 'leitmotifs' of all of Dunlop's future activity. We shall encounter it on numerous occasions, for the question as to whether it is possible to 'cultivate' a higher self within the sheaths of the personality is indeed of cardinal importance. In fact, as Dunlop observes at the end of this essay, both in daily life as upon the occult path itself 'all the rest depends thereon'.

Glancing Back and Looking Forwards

The time has come for us to take leave of Dublin. Of course this period could have been looked at and illuminated from other and very different points of view. The nineties were also years of great political ferment and the power and influence of the Irish Movement of Independence was steadily growing—a fact which the English motherland had increasingly to confront and accept. However, in the context of this particular biography it was, above all, the spiritual significance and development of this city with its inhabitants and visitors which had to be highlighted. And whilst the history books record as a most prominent event of the year 1891 the death of the freedom-fighter Parnell, the Dublin theosophists were far more preoccupied by the death of 'Madame' Blavatsky which occurred in the course of that same year.

What was it, we may ask, that brought together all these unique individuals and seekers after truth, enabling them to discover in Theosophy the most vital substance and nourishment they needed for their lives? It was undoubtedly a kind of 'homelessness' in the very depths of their souls. Indeed it was as 'homeless souls'[45] too that Rudolf Steiner described them three septenniads after he had begun working in the Theosophical Society; they were homeless souls who could not bring themselves to become part of the establishment. And there were many such souls at the time in Berlin and Vienna. Today, of course, they are to be found all over the world. At the turn of the century the 'Blavatsky phenomenon'[46] was able to make a deep impression on such homeless souls that found their way into the Theosophical Movement.

Considered from an external point of view this extraordinary personality certainly had one or two weaknesses and dubious traits; indeed one of the most remarkable things about her was the way in which highly advanced spiritual faculties were combined in her being with a naivety which at times was nothing short of abysmal. Nonetheless, deep down in her was an individuality to whom great credit must be given—for being, as it were, the first pioneering spirit to break completely with the practice of keeping occult knowledge secret and, in the process, defying the interests of certain very one-sided, power-seeking occultists. And though Rudolf Steiner later found it necessary to rectify many things in her works and above all to make a radical break with the mediumistic methods which had often been employed in the research of certain theosophical truths, nonetheless an extremely interesting assessment of the significance of the so-called Stanzas of Dzyan in *The Secret Doctrine* is to be found in a lecture he gave exactly one lunar-node period after Blavatsky's death. These are the very stanzas that Dunlop described as seeming to be 'a voice of thunder from a bygone age', albeit 'remote and imperfectly understood'. Rudolf Steiner observes that 'those stanzas of Dzyan in *The Secret Doctrine* . . . contain much of what, coming from the teaching of the holy Rishis, has flowed down through the sanctuaries of the East . . . Much that is to be found in the Stanzas of Dzyan will only be gradually understood in all its depth.'[47]

*

'I did not know about reincarnation then,' Dunlop explained to Stein in 1934 during a conversation in which he described all that he had undergone after his grandfather's death, 'I just had the experience of my previous lives, but I had no theory about such things.'(St) And in 1935, in his brief memoirs, he wrote:

> For years I was engrossed, in company with the Irish poet 'A.E.' and others whose names have since become well-known, in the study of H.P. Blavatsky's works, and *an overwhelming wish was born in me: to meet an initiate in the physical body, to be able to recognize, here on Earth, a knower of spiritual truth*, and then to take my share in spreading this truth for the well-being of humanity.

This desire of Dunlop's to meet an incarnated initiate, together with his habit of waiting long periods of time before interpreting his spiritual experiences, seem to have constituted the very forces which led him towards a meeting with that 'knower of spiritual truth'—a meeting which was to take place on the physical level in the year 1922. And it was Rudolf Steiner himself who, in his autobiography, *The Course of my Life*, had this to say about his own experiences when he was approximately 28 years of age:

> It was at the very time of my life I am now describing that I succeeded in attaining to definite perceptions of repeated earth lives of man. Before this time I was not far from them but they had not yet come out of indeterminate lines into sharply defined impressions. Theories, however, in regard to such things as repeated earth lives I did not form in my own thoughts; I took them into my understanding, of course, out of literature or other sources of information as something intelligible, but I did not myself theorize about them.[48]

Given our attempt to portray the 'Irish phase' of Dunlop's life against the background and birth of the Irish Theosophical Movement, the words which follow on directly from these lines offer us a rather strange parallel. Rudolf Steiner writes:

> During the time when concrete perceptions were more and more forming within me in regard to repeated earth-lives, I became

> acquainted with the Theosophical Movement, which had been initiated by H.P. Blavatsky. Sinnett's *Esoteric Buddhism* came into my hands through a friend to whom I had spoken about these things. This book, the first from the Theosophical Movement with which I became familiar, made upon me no impression whatever. And I was glad that I had not read the book *before* having experienced perceptions out of the life of my own soul. For the content of this book was repellent to me, and my antipathy against this way of representing the supersensible might well have prevented me from advancing further at once upon the road that had been pointed out to me.

What a strange paradox! The book which introduced the Theosophical Movement into Ireland (a movement that was to fructify and so strongly influence certain domains of life and culture) was the very same book which had enabled Rudolf Steiner to 'make the acquaintance of the Theosophical Movement' and, what is more, in a manner which already seems to foreshadow the whole of his future position and attitude within this movement right up to his final decision to detach himself from it altogether.

*

During his Irish years there was always a warm welcome for 'Brother Dunlop' at the theosophical gatherings where he often appeared. On one occasion he afforded everyone a very amusing surprise when, in spite of all the odds, he actually made it to the Tingley convention that was being held in New York in April 1897. The following account of this appeared in the first May issue of *The Theosophical News*:

> A burst of enthusiastic excitement was caused in the middle of the evening by the utterly unexpected appearance of Brother Dunlop, just off the steamer, and still showing the effect of the salt breezes. His attendance at the Convention was another proof of the prescience of the Leader (Mrs Tingley) who had told him that he would be present here. The vigorous propaganda carried on in Dublin, the work on The Irish Theosophist and the present low

financial condition of Theosophists there, made it seem utterly impossible for them to have a delegate here. But, just in time to catch the steamer which landed him in New York Saturday evening, brother Dunlop was unceremoniously hustled off to America by the business house where he is engaged, to attend to a sudden business emergency, so that that became a fact which when foretold seemed an impossibility.

A few days later we encounter Dunlop at a theosophical meeting in Philadelphia, and in the middle of August he was attending the European Convention at Stockholm. Thus his horizon started to widen far beyond Ireland.

*

Of course there were also other cultural trends of an entirely different nature in the Dublin of that period whose protagonists completely rejected Theosophy, if indeed they went to the trouble at all to acquaint themselves with it. James Joyce, born in 1882, later to become world-famous by his works *Ulysses* and *Finnegan's Wake*, can be considered as a representative of such an 'anti-theosophical' tendency. In his *Ulysses* there are several ironically styled passages caricaturing the Dublin theosophists and other theosophical literary figures.

'My literary efforts have had the good fortune to meet with the approval of the eminent poet A.E. (Mr. Geo Russell),'[49] he observes ironically, and in another passage he asks: 'What do you think really of that hermetic crowd, the opal hush poets: A.E. the master mystic? That Blavatsky woman started it. She was a nice old bag of tricks . . .'[50]

And in the hero Leopold Bloom's consciousness, which runs rich with all kinds of associations, James Joyce will have AE, John Eglinton and their spiritual associates appear as 'those literary ethereal people . . . dreamy, cloudy, symbolistic . . .'[51]

A few pages further on, as he pursues the associations of this witch-hunt, we come across: 'Dunlop, Judge, the noblest . . . of them all, A.E . . . K.H.; their master, whose identity is no secret to adepts. Brothers of the great white lodge always watching where they can help.'[52]

In 1903 D.N. Dunlop was personally introduced to James Joyce in London—by his friend Yeats. Years afterwards he was able to give a poignant description of Joyce to his daughter:[53] 'A shy, proud man—was Joyce. He used his native wit as a weapon to defend himself against the literary set in Dublin who regarded him as an outsider. His attitude to religion was that of an apostate priest.' Outwardly he appeared 'a nondescript, shabby-genteel young fellow, thin-lipped and taciturn, who would as well bark at you as give you a civil answer to a question you were bold enough to put to him.'

And Edith Young describes how her father 'had many a time seen him sitting by himself at a table in a far corner of a vegetarian restaurant they had mutually frequented. Picking at a nut cutlet, he kept his head buried in a newspaper lest anyone should have the temerity to address him. Should father venture to hail him, he'd be met with a curt nod. When in the . . . thirties I drew my father's attention to Joyce's reference to him in *Ulysses*, he looked surprised. "Well," he said suavely, "I'm in good company anyway."'

3

PRACTICAL OCCULTISM

Yes, you can do the impossible—
what else is worth doing? D.N.D.

Horizons New

On a warm day in October 1897 D.N. Dunlop, accompanied by his wife and children, docked at New York Harbour. He already knew the city and some of its surrounding areas from the repeated visits and short stays he had made in this country before. This time, however, he was manifestly planning to settle down for a longer period. The autumn of that same year saw the last number of *The Irish Theosophist* come out in print and the official existence of the original Dublin Lodge also came to an end.

In the last edition of this lively and enterprising magazine, so rich in substance and thought, we find the following original and somewhat illuminating lines written by a certain Robert Coates, Honorary Secretary of the Dublin Lodge; in a humorous vein Coates gives a kind of warm 'appreciation' of Dunlop's work within the Lodge. And from his words it soon becomes clear just how much the latter was already being missed, and how great and unfillable the gap was which his departure had created:

> Our autumn session opens with a strain of sadness, for we will miss at our meetings the best President, the most kindly brother, and the hardest worker for the cause, our comrade Dunlop, who will be in America ere this appears. He has laughed and joked with us through nights of innumerable cigarettes and pipes and discussions and many intellectual battles; and yet we have never lost through familiarity the sense of the bright spirit behind, whose face shone at our public meetings, and with whose words seemed often to bubble up the sweet waters of immortality. They all go like that, one after another. O America, what a populous lodge this would be if you only restored us our own again![54]

Indeed, one is almost tempted to apply that same truth which

Dunlop had once formulated in a leading article of *The Irish Theosophist* to Dublin itself: 'When the great man is absent, the age produces nothing.'[55]

*

Dunlop's work in the sales department of the Pierce and Miller engineering firm began immediately upon his arrival. But soon he found himself at least equally involved in working for the theosophical crusades of Catherine Tingley.

'The Purple Mother', as Tingley was known to her followers, was busily developing numerous activities in the New York centre. Dunlop took over the organizational aspect of these initiatives, giving lectures himself within the American society and contributing to the cause of Tingley's 'Universal Brotherhood' by writing articles and reports for such periodicals as *The New Century* and *The Crusader*.

*

Not that his enthusiastic work in these new surroundings relieved him and his family from financial hardship. They dwelt in a densely populated area often living on a diet of maize, porridge and milk. And, to crown it all, Christmas was drawing on apace and there was no money left, either for a Christmas lunch or for presents for the children. However, when the time came and the family was about to sit down at the festively decorated table to celebrate Christmas, a stranger appeared at the door. He was carrying an enormous Christmas hamper. And everything was in it: presents for the children, the traditional turkey, fruit, bread and wine. Dunlop said to the stranger at the door: 'There must be some mistake. We have no friends here, and nobody knows us.' But the stranger insisted: 'You are Daniel Nicol Dunlop, are you not? Well then, this is your Christmas hamper.' And nothing else could be got out of the man. He just disappeared. (St)

'It always gave me new strength, even after many years, whenever I thought of this event,' Dunlop remarked to Stein.

'From then onwards I knew that there were souls and spirits who take care of human beings which seemed a truly wonderful thing!'

*

On one occasion he was required to hold a lecture in a huge hall in front of several thousand people. 'I was just a tiny speck down there looking up to the gallery,' he told Stein with what, one imagines, would have been a gentle smile around the corners of his mouth. 'I had never given a lecture on that scale before and I had not the faintest idea what to say.' (StS) But he calmly assimilated the impression that the weary-eyed faces made on him and suddenly he found the inspiration for his subject. He grasped the immediate mood of many of those present and spoke of the state of depression into which one can often be cast by everyday life; this was, however, no good reason not to turn one's gaze upwards, again and again. 'And then I spoke of the heavens and eternity; and of the great mother whom we all have and who embraces us with such might and power. And they applauded and I had won the interest of a large number of people!' (StS) The 'Great Mother'? Does this not remind us of the young boy by the rock-cave in Arran, 'dreaming' of his mother—feeling, sensing, gradually finding his way into the bosom of a far greater and all-embracing Mother?

*

Dunlop's activities for Tingley seem to have reached their climax in the summer of 1899 when the American theosophists at last made their way across the continent to the chosen site of the 'School for the Revival of the Lost Mysteries' on the Californian coast. He later described his first impressions on arriving there as follows:

> I remember well my excitement on reaching Point Loma in California to see the beginnings of what I then fondly hoped might be a realization of Utopia. Mrs. Tingley had inspired my enthusiasm

> with her glowing descriptions of the place, and the possibility of founding institutions, under her direction, which would usher in the golden age, when once again the gods would walk among men. When I arrived the place was, of course, in a very primitive state, with only one building, which had been erected at the expense of one of the members of the Society. The climate was ideal and the natural surroundings fulfilled expectations. A convention of the Society had been called and there was a representative gathering of delegates from many parts of the United States and a few from other countries.

However, from the very first moment he also had a foreshadowing of all the difficulties to come:

> Even in this initial gathering the seed of future disruption could be seen in the field of observation, and I left Point Loma with a somewhat heavy heart. My anticipations were fully justified as a number of my comrades reported to me afterwards.[56]

In fact he was now coming to find himself at impossible odds with the 'Purple Mother' who sometimes had recourse to militant tactics in her direct opposition to Annie Besant and the Adyar society. Dunlop, by contrast, was throughout his life always concerned with arriving at, and subsequently maintaining, a standpoint that could transcend all oppositional tendencies and polarities. Thus it will no doubt have been on account of certain 'ideological differences' that—about three years after she had discovered him in Dublin—Mrs Tingley relieved of his office as Secretary that same person whom she had previously engaged with such enthusiasm. In all probability it was because he had fallen out with Mrs Tingley that Dunlop's work for Pierce and Miller also came to an end.

*

During the period of his unemployment, Dunlop took up the study of electricity. His immediate preoccupation with this phenomenon was occasioned by the forthcoming World Exhibition in Paris in 1900. Several newspapers were already publishing information about it and some shorter or longer essays on the subject had also appeared. By means of a letter of recommendation Dunlop gained access to one of these papers, and, in connection with the Paris Exhibition, was commissioned to write 16 articles on the various uses that can be made of electricity in different fields. In one of the articles he describes how electricity is used in agriculture.

The writing as such presented no problem to Dunlop; as editor of *The Irish Theosophist* he had already accumulated a wealth of experience and developed a clear and unimposing style. But as far as the subject matter was concerned, for him it was entirely new territory. The brief period of his apprenticeship at the Howe Machine Company in Ardrossan and later in the bicycle-shop in Glasgow as well as his recent employment with the Pierce and Miller Engineering Company in New York had certainly given him the opportunity of familiarising himself with the fundamental principles of mechanics, but hardly introduced him to the phenomenon of electricity itself. So now it was up to him in a very short space of time to gain a bold and yet clear survey of the subject to be treated! To achieve this a great deal of courage and presence of mind was necessary, two qualities which he did not lack and had already put to the test more than once.

The series of articles was published, translated into French—and had consequences. For George Westinghouse, the founder of the American Westinghouse Electric Company, sought an interview with the author; Dunlop was offered a position in the New York Branch of the Pittsburgh firm, and for the next two years he was to be concerned with the manufacturing of electrical apparatus and with research into statistics as well.

He returned home in high spirits from this interview which had changed the course of his destiny and proclaimed the news to his hardly tasked family. Edith Young recalls his first words as he solemnly quoted Walt Whitman: 'Henceforth I ask not good fortune. I, myself, am good fortune.'[57]

It must have been during this period that Dunlop was able personally to inspect the 'Keely Motor', which he already knew about from Blavatsky's *Secret Doctrine* (as he later revealed to Stein). This motor could be set in motion by its inventor (of that name) purely by means of psychic energies and must be considered as the first, clearly forerunning achievement of a new spiritual technology, of a sort which Rudolf Steiner predicted would appear in the not too distant future.

In the late autumn of 1899, Dunlop was appointed assistant manager of Westinghouse's European publicity department and moved with his family to London.

*

Not that all connections with the American continent were immediately severed. In 1900, he was still a contributor and even a co-editor of the Canadian theosophical magazine *The Lamp*, which published several articles of his. And for some years he even continued to speak with a slight American drawl!

By 1902, Dunlop had already become sole head of the publicity department and, before much time had passed, of the 'supply' sales department as well. This was at a time when the whole sector of electrical industry was crossed by strong segregational tendencies. Enormous struggles between competitive groups, uncontrollable prices produced by massive undercutting—all this had created chaos in the industry's economy. The several attempts that had been made to realize some kind of project based on associative co-operation had not met with much success. Just how Dunlop himself managed to introduce an extensive impulse based upon co-operation into this field will be described in a later chapter.

Apart from a short period near Manchester, London was to remain Dunlop's domicile for the whole of the second part of his life. For his two-year sojourn in America clearly separates his life into two halves. Up to the beginning of the century, it is his spiritual experiences, interests and studies which stand at the fore, combined at times with a hard, existential struggle on the material level. Then, from the beginning of the century onwards, these experiences, having thus matured and firmly grounded themselves, begin to flow in a single stream, slowly but constantly, into external life—into professional and social practice. If one considers his life and activities up to this point, in relatively elementary terms, as unfolding on an a more occult level as it were, then it could be said that from the turn of the century onwards this occultism becomes ever more practical and adapted to external life—on the very widest of fronts.

But let us at first attempt to obtain a somewhat clearer vision of the occult foundation itself—of that which formed the basis of his ever increasing activity on the external plane during the decades to come.

The Occult Path and the Zodiac

Returning from his sojourn in the West, Dunlop not only brought with him the achievement of having gained a secure position and situation in life, he also brought important impulses to deepen and extend the spiritual foundations of his external activity; and foundations such as those D.N. Dunlop had been looking for could only be found within the constellations of the heavens. It has already been shown that the cosmic number 12 had featured significantly in the Sunday 'sermons' Dunlop held upon the Isle of Arran, where a 12-strong host of friends had gathered around him as a 9-year-old boy. Later on, so as to acquaint himself thoroughly with the signs of the zodiac—the cosmic representatives of the principle 12—he would often have practised himself what he later recommended to his American audience on the occasion of a lecture when he had invited them to 'turn their eyes upward'.

Then again, in *The Irish Theosophist*, he had assumed a clearly cosmic standpoint when writing about the purpose and dangers of occult development, signing himself 'Capricorn'. And now, during the American period and the years immediately following it, he had progressed considerably in the art of deciphering the script of the heavens itself.

It was above all the influence of H.W. Percival, occultist, Freemason and theosophist ('the leading figure' in the New York Theosophical Society according to Dunlop) that prompted him to take up extensive research into the esoteric significance of the zodiac. Percival (who, it seems likely, had chosen this name as a pseudonym at an early stage in his life) was born in the same year as Dunlop and died in 1953. Early on in the year 1893 he had undergone an experience of spiritual illumination which had been of decisive significance throughout the rest of his life. One year previously a newspaper article had drawn his attention to the existence of Mme Blavatsky and the Theosophical Society, and as a result he became an ardent member of it. Percival's experience of enlightenment (which, remarkably enough followed chronologically quite close on Dunlop's visionary experience in Dublin) consisted essentially in a process whereby he suddenly became 'conscious of the Presence of Consciousness', as he himself later put it. From that moment on, in the middle of the New York traffic where this consciousness dawned on him, Percival recognized 'the great worth of being conscious of Consciousness', in the fact 'that it enables one to know about any subject, by thinking!' And by 'thinking' he meant 'the holding steady of the Conscious Light within, on the subject'. This was the method Percival later made use of in order to produce the contents of his principal work *Thinking and Destiny*.

It is possible that Dunlop had already got to know Percival at the theosophical convention held on 26–27 April 1897 in New York. Between 1904 and 1905, in a magazine called *The Word* of which he was the editor, Percival published a series of editorials on the zodiac. They evidently had a profound impact on Dunlop's own occult-cosmological views. In 1912/13 he was to reprint them in his own magazine *The Path*[58] along with certain transcripts of lectures he had given himself; in them he takes up Percival's ideas and develops them in a concrete way. The substance of these thoughts became flesh and blood to Dunlop, and as late as 1918 he concluded the introduction to one of his books with the following reference to his friend: 'Credit is due to Mr H.W. Percival, editor of *The Word*, published in New York, for his original work on the philosophy of the zodiac, and I acknowledge my indebtedness to him.'

Let us now take a look at those occult principles embodied in Percival's cosmology of the zodiac which came to find a permanent place in Dunlop's thought. The following conception of man, established by Percival and developed by Dunlop during the following years, has nothing to do with the usual forms of astrology. On the contrary, whilst the latter, as it is generally promulgated today, appeals again and again to the hopes and fears of the *personality*, this cosmology, by contrast, is able to throw light on the origins, nature, and evolutionary goals of the *individuality*. Certainly the goals the individuality sets itself cannot be realized without the personality, but the latter is only to be considered as an instrument and not as an end in itself, particularly, as we have already noted, where any form of occult development comes into question. In the article entitled 'The Path of Evolution', for instance, we read:

> The Zodiac is the plan according to which all things come into existence from the beyond, pass through their periods of development, reach final attainment and pass again into the beyond. And this is a process which we human beings do not yet comprehend in full self-consciousness. It is, however, comparatively easy to understand this process intellectually and to follow the ramifications of consciousness depicted in the Zodiac in all their details and varieties. But what is the value of a clearly thought-out scheme of evolution unless it is possible to see the place in it of the life of to-day and the next step that awaits man? When we understand the plan of the Zodiac we must then place ourselves in it and learn the art of living and the science of life involved in it, and suggested by it.[59]

To begin with, a distinction is made between two spheres of existence in which this plan becomes reality: the spheres of 'involution' and 'evolution'. Involution comprises, as far as the human being is concerned, all the processes in the supersensible world which prepare his incarnation right up to the moment he enters into existence as a physical being. This path of involution runs, cosmically speaking, from the sign of Aries ♈ to that of Libra ♎. The path of evolution, on the other hand, runs from Libra (♎) to Aries ♈ and describes the human path leading from the *personality* to the attainment of self-consciousness as a *cosmic individuality*.

In another article Percival goes on to distinguish, with regard to the potential spiritual development of the human being, between an 'occult, spiritual Zodiac of the Heavens' and a 'zodiac of man':

> The Zodiac of the Heavens is shown to be a circle, but when related to man it is represented as a straight line and the twelve signs are assigned to the different centres in man's body from his head to his feet. Students are often puzzled by this apparent contradiction. There is, however, no inconsistency in this, but, on the contrary, a congruity inherent in the nature of things. For one state of consciousness is best symbolized by the circle, another by the straight line. Man's form was circular before he came into the physical world, and he broke through this circle in order to come into the physical world. In his present state, therefore, he is so to say a broken circle, or a circle extended to a straight line. This line begins with Aries (♈) at the head and ends at the feet with Pisces (♓). Thus that part of the line which, in the circle, was above Libra (♎) and symbolized the most godlike part of the form, the head, is now connected with the earth; or in other words, the signs which were *beyond* Libra (♎) in evolution are now really below Libra.
>
> The hinge or turning point of both the circle and the line is Libra (sex), and by means of it all the signs from Scorpio to Pisces fell *below* this middle point, the balance sign of Libra. At the present stage of his evolution man lives in an animal body of sex and has developed and preserves the organs and parts of the body which are necessary for the reproduction and preservation of the animal body. And those centres in the body, which in his circular form stood for mental and spiritual powers, are now used for physical needs and their higher functions are atrophied because of long disuse, except for locomotion in the physical world. So we see that the straight line seems to symbolize the going out or down into the denser, physical aspect of life, and it is this that we name the zodiac of man.
>
> But man still has within him the circular zodiac, which is the occult, spiritual zodiac, and though he does not use it in the occult, spiritual sense, still he has it, though latent and atrophied, and may learn to use it, *through thought*, when he earnestly desires to enter the inner and upward path of the zodiac instead of going downward and outward into the world of the senses and desires. This circular, spiritual and occult zodiac descends from the head down the fore part of the body by way of the heart and lungs, alimentary and reproductive organs of the body to Libra, the sex parts; then, instead

> of going outward, it enters its upward course at the gland of Luschka, then ascends through the terminal filament, spinal cord, medulla, pons, to the soul-centres in the head. This is the path for those who would lead a regenerate and spiritual life. The path is in the body.[60]

It would be to misunderstand both Percival and Dunlop entirely if we were to imagine that this means concentrating human consciousness on the centres along the spinal column in order to obtain spiritual results of some kind. That would be equivalent to the yoga breathing technique which is no longer adapted to our times, at least in the West—a fact that Dunlop himself points out in an article, 'By-Paths in Occult Progress'. It is much more a question of activating the relevant spiritual functions so that the corresponding physical centres may subsequently enter consciousness in rather the same way as a person who is walking becomes aware of his legs simply by *using* them.

Therefore, this attempt to understand the 12 great cosmic principles in their relationship to the human being involves above all the discovery of potential spiritual functions and of corresponding spiritual organs which have become atrophied during the course of evolution. These functions and organs have their correlations in the physical body, and both the spiritual function and the physical correlation are 'prefigured' in the occult, circular zodiac. These 12 cosmic principles or spiritual functions (together with their physiological correlatives either in the 'zodiac of man' or in the 'occult zodiac') can be found on page 78 in a schematic drawing. They are frequently represented in this form in Dunlop's later works and lectures.

From the preceding it will have become clear that the turning-point itself, Libra,[61] is of particular importance, for it marks the beginning of the evolutionary path. But it is for Sagittarius, the principle of cosmic thinking, to make the final decision as to whether this evolution is to turn outwards or into the inner world. For this reason the last quaternary (from Sagittarius to Aries) is called 'the mundane or divine quaternary'. Let us now take a closer look at this 'turning-point'.

> The sex organs of the body are the representative of the sex principle.

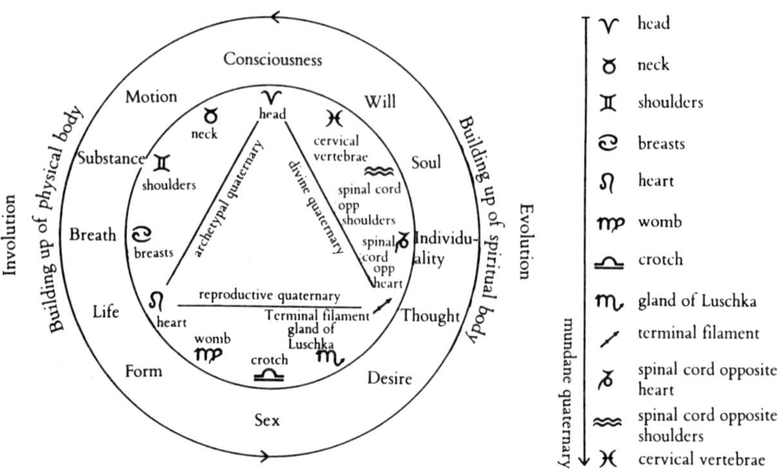

The 'Occult' and the 'Human' Zodiac

Here 'sex' is made evident, and here it is determined whether the life, form and desire shall pass downward—outward into the world—and so make of the zodiac an extended line, or whether they shall turn the gate of balance (♎) and pass inward and upward along the path of the spine, and complete the circle of the zodiac. It is through the sex organs that all bodies enter the physical world, and sex is therefore the medium by which bodies and entities are related to each other, as distinct bodies of desire. Sex thus represents the 'lowest' point of experience in separation and in duality, in the 'thine and mine' aspect of life. But it is also the point from which one rises when he travels inward and upward to the divine. Sex is to the ego as birth and death are to all bodies, for by it he is born and dies to many experiences. It is the hall where invisible beings clothe their forms in physical bodies and enter this physical world. And it is the initiatory, trial gate where one is tempered, for he must die to sex who would enter and consciously live in the inner, immortal world.

These are not words spoken in favour of some form of false asceticism; the only requirement here is that the ego-personality be capable of freely detaching itself from the sexual element *during* the journey 'inward and upward' (and of course no human being can pursue this journey *incessantly* during earthly incarnation). Now among human desires it is sexual desire that appears, to begin with, as the most intense and the most decisive one in edifying the *personality* (♎) upon the *outward* path of evolution. If, however, the personality is able to give up at times all identification with this form of desire (which is what is meant by 'dying'), then the force of human desiring itself can assume a higher form of existence and actually deliver the impulse needed to embark upon the *inner* path of evolution. It unites itself with the cosmic principle of thought and thus becomes a drive towards knowledge, the 'desire for knowledge' in the best sense of the term. This higher form of desire is characterized, amongst other things, by the fact that it becomes less and less dominated by the personality which is so strong at the beginning, finally arriving at a point where its sole aim is that the universal world of human thought (with its objective, conceptual content—depending upon nothing but itself), as well as the *individuality* active within this sphere, should come to ever intenser and clearer expression.

Percival summarized all the results of his research up to this point as follows:

> We have suggested in previous articles that it is possible for man to build a bridge from the physical world to the spiritual world by following the path indicated by the signs of the Zodiac. Such a bridge spans the so-called 'psychic world', that realm of man's experience which is dominated by desires and sensations. He cannot enter the spiritual world until he crosses this chasm. The physical world, the world of form and sex, is the basis of man's life and on it must rest one sustaining pillar of his bridge to liberty. In it is embedded true consciousness, but, so far, man has not discovered this and uses the physical world to increase desires and sensations instead of recognizing the possibility of springing into the formless world of consciousness by means of the same force which has made his physical world. His evolution comes to a stop unless he learns the way out—the door of escape from attachment to form. To enter consciousness, *self-conscious*, is man's goal, according to the ancient symbols of the Zodiac and the physical world is a means to this, not a hindrance.

> Man's body is the path and the way, as we have said before, and its centres are the doors of entrance to the different levels of being. It is along the spine that man raises pro-creative functions to spiritual powers. It is along this path that he builds a bridge from the physical to the spiritual world, across the psychic world.[62]

And at the end of the third essay of the series on the zodiac we find these words:

> Thus we may pass upward to complete the circle of the zodiac or the pathway of consciousness not yet trodden by humanity. This is the meaning of the zodiac as related to our life today.[63]

Initiatives

What was it, we may ask, that was to be erected on the basis of these cosmic 'foundations' we have glanced at in the last chapter? From now on we will be witnessing and following what might figuratively be described as the construction and realization of two edifices or 'buildings'; the two, though clearly distinct, are nonetheless in several respects cross-related to one another. Above the entrance of one of them the word 'Esotericism' is to be read, above the portal of the other 'Exotericism'. In one of these 'buildings' work was accomplished for the few who had managed to find their way to this place and cross the threshold; in the other, in collaboration with many, plans were being worked out for a project that was soon to find its realization on a world-wide scale. The first edifice was dedicated to the founder of the modern Theosophical Movement and named the Blavatsky Institute (the monthly magazine *The Path* being a kind of extension of it); the second was going to be called BEAMA or, in unabbreviated form, British Electrical and Allied Manufacturers' Association. Both of them, with their affiliated constructions, demanded years of work and preparation.

On a list of delegates to the thirteenth Annual Congress of the British Section of the Theosophical Society in 1903, we find D.N. Dunlop registered as President of the London 'Battersea Lodge' founded two years earlier. In the meantime, he was living with his family at Wandsworth, strangely enough in Killarney Road, as if determined to keep the Irish link! The General Meeting of this convention in London was visited by Rudolf Steiner, General Secretary of the German Section since 1902.

Between 19 and 21 June of the following year, Dunlop visited the 'International Congress of the Federation of European Sections of the Theosophical Society' in Amsterdam, and here Rudolf Steiner was again present, this time holding a lecture on mathematics and occultism. About six hundred delegates attended the different lectures and cultural events taking place within the various assembly rooms. After this congress Dunlop travelled, for the first time in his life no doubt, right into the heart of Germany. In the course of a description of the impressions that this journey made on him he speaks with great enthusiasm and admiration of the prevailing mood in the Thüringer Wald, of the minnesingers, of Wolfram von Eschenbach's Grail story and the mystic Meister Eckhart. This enthusiastic report is to be found in *The Theosophical Review*, a magazine edited by G.R.S. Mead and Annie Besant, to which D.N. Dunlop was to contribute many articles during the following years.

The next years indicate ever increasing theosophical activity on the part of D.N. Dunlop. In 1905 he wrote an introduction, rich in spirit and content, to the detailed booklet presenting the programme of the 'Second Annual Congress of the Federation of European Sections'. Here he calls upon the participants not merely to consume the light of theosophical truth and vision for their own personal well-being, but also to use it to illuminate the paths of all those 'who have fallen far behind, and lie, in hopeless apathy, on the barren road'. The main lecture was given by Annie Besant. The 'Dramatic Committee', to which Dunlop also belonged, organized a performance of *The Shadowy Waters* by W.B. Yeats who himself came to watch it.

On 10 July, Rudolf Steiner, also present at this congress, gave a lecture on 'The Occult Foundation of Goethe's work'. An exhibition accompanying the congress displayed, amongst other things, paintings by a certain 'Russell'. In a letter dated 23 July

1905, to Günther Wagner, a longstanding member, Steiner referred to these paintings as follows: 'There were, besides some rather less significant works, some truly remarkable things to be seen. Let me just mention some symbolic pictures by a painter, Russell. He tries to characterize the processes that take place within the human soul by putting them into symbolic colours on the canvas . . .' And Steiner observes that he was 'satisfied by this effort which, after all, a painter of some talent, has undertaken'. There can be no doubt that the 'painter of some talent' was that same friend of Dunlop's youth, George William Russell.

Before we take a closer look at the two 'edifices' mentioned at the beginning, one question still remains to be answered: where and when did D.N. Dunlop first perceive Rudolf Steiner in a conscious manner? In his autobiographical sketch, Dunlop himself makes the following remark concerning this point: 'I had seen him about the year 1906 in a crowded Convention of the Theosophical Society.' This might well be a reference to the 'First International Congress' which took place from 3 to 5 June 1906 in Paris. It will hardly be possible now to ascertain which one of the three congresses Dunlop was referring to when he dated their first meeting 'about 1906'. But this is of secondary importance. What is far more important is that even on this occasion Rudolf Steiner's 'face and bearing made an unforgettable impression' on Dunlop. (DS) This was about the time of Dunlop's second 'moon-node' (or shortly before it) and this 'unforgettable impression' must be counted amongst the most influential impulses to be engraved upon his soul at that time.

*

Now let us take a look at Dunlop's first 'exoteric' initiatives after the turn of the century.

Westinghouse Electric had in the meantime set up a large plant at Traffords Park, just outside Manchester, and in 1908 Dunlop and his family moved to the nearby town of Hale.

We have already described the precarious situation in which the British electrical industy had come to find itself at the precise time Dunlop began his work as assistant publicity manager at the English subsidiary of the American Westinghouse Electric Company. Several years were spent by searching for solutions to the industry's problem, and finally it was decided to build up a comprehensive association based on the principle of co-operation. And so, in 1911, the BEAMA (British Electrical and Allied Manufacturers' Association) came into existence with Dunlop as its first Organizing Secretary; in 1917 the post was renamed Director—what Dunlop had been *de facto* from the beginning.

As early as 1911, the year of its foundation, an old friend, Charles Weekes, had joined Dunlop as legal advisor to the undertaking. Weekes was to be active within the BEAMA until Dunlop's death. He maintained a fairly regular correspondence with AE and thus Dunlop, too, remained indirectly in touch with the friend of his youth. Despite the external separation, AE for his part continued to count 'Dan' amongst his 'lifelong comrades'. Indeed, in 1913 he dedicated his *Collected Poems* 'To D.N.D.—in memory of the household'. But an extract from a letter to Charles Weekes in 1914 gives an even clearer idea of the beautiful way in which AE remained inwardly attached to his closest friends: 'I want information about your pilgrimage. Though curiously I feel I know all about you by some inner certitude, just as I feel about Dan and some other friends of my youth.'[64]

*

In a short historical review of the BEAMA published in 1933 Dunlop himself outlines the motives present in the founding of the organization and the far-reaching goals connected with it. This he does without so much as mentioning his own role in the building up of the organization. In fact one can almost have the impression that the following description stems not from the actual founder of this organization but rather from a friendly-disposed and sober-minded 'outsider'!

> The British Electrical and Allied Manufacturers' Association was founded in 1911 in the belief that voluntary co-operative action

would go far to meet the economic difficulties which, at that time, were proving a severe handicap to the development of electrical and allied engineering in Great Britain. This brochure is a brief review of the work undertaken during the first twenty-one years of the Association's existence; it is, too, a record of an industry which has grown from strength to strength and is today one of the world's three largest exporters of electrical goods, with an unsurpassed reputation at home and abroad for efficiency, reliability and technical initiative. Members of the BEAMA manufacture ninety-seven per cent of the total value of electrical machinery and apparatus produced in Great Britain, so that to all intents and purposes the BEAMA is the organ of the whole electrical and allied manufacturing industry. The work carried out by the Association has been very varied. The BEAMA has been at once a means of introducing order in the commercial relations of members with their customers, the voice of a united industry before Government and Legislature, and a centre from which have been promoted far-reaching policies of research and standardization benefiting not only the electrical industry, but engineering in general. Co-operation without the sacrifice of individual initiative has been the principle behind every one of the Association's activities. The BEAMA has not only co-operated with other organized bodies in the commercial and industrial fields but has been the means of linking together the manufacturing interests with the leading professional institutions in the engineering industries, to their mutual advantage and to that of the position and prestige of the individual engineer.

The present world wide depression only emphasizes the value of the Association, and work of even greater importance lies before it. Co-operation between all engaged in the work of efficient production and distribution is the only certain road to order and progress.[65]

How was Dunlop's own contribution to this Association evaluated in economic circles at the time? In an obituary which appeared in the *Electrical Review* we find the following assessment:

Mr. Dunlop is credited with the original conception of the B.E.A.M.A. organization as it has subsequently developed, carrying its influence in innumerable directions affecting electrical science and industry. He was prominently identified with the Electrical Research Association and the Electrical Development Association, and all movements connected with electrical progress, education, research,

> standardization, & c. He found himself as time went on a member or chairman of a host of committees. He believed in committees heart and soul, and his tactfulness and conciliatory influence in this connection are common knowledge among B.E.A.M.A. members and their representatives.[66]

The writer of these lines could hardly have known anything about the 'esoteric' edifice behind all this or of Dunlop's activities therein; the exclusive appraisal of his external activity thus appears all the more exceptional. However, the writer of this obituary does seem to have *sensed* something of Dunlop's background for he also adds:

> Mr Dunlop was sometimes described as a Scotch metaphysician; and his private philosophic studies are held to have engendered in him a detachment of mind enabling him to face delays and opposition with patience and equanimity.

It is also clear from another obituary in the economic press that Dunlop had provided major incentive for the electrification of the London suburbs in general as well as the railways in particular—as well as for the drafting of legislation for all this.

So much, then, for our first glimpse of the 'exoteric' edifice which was, as is yet to be described, to find its completion in the World Power Conference, that world-wide organization which still exists today under the name of World Energy Council and has its central office in London.

*

Even before the BEAMA came into existence Dunlop had already embarked on another initiative of a more 'esoteric' character, namely, the foundation in Hale of the Blavatsky Institute, which opened its doors with solemn celebration on 5 November 1910.

The Institute was lodged in a simple but spacious building in the middle of a quiet and gently undulating landscape. In his opening speech, Dunlop outlined the specific goals of the institute and also warned against false expectations. He wanted the Blavatsky Institute to be dedicated to the Mysteries of the Spirit, stressing that 'those who sought the psychic realms instead of the realm of the true Psyche would be disappointed'. This whole objective was evidently intended by him as a counterbalance to the innumerable centres of pseudo-occultism which flourished at that time as, indeed, they still do today. This was to be a place where people could learn 'what the sacrifice of the personality really is'.[67] And what Dunlop intended was that the work accomplished in this institute should help spread all those truths 'which are always in danger of being swamped in the lower astral waters at certain critical periods in man's evolution'.

The institute arranged one-day courses, presenting the foundations of the theosophical world-view. For those living further afield special correspondence courses were organized. Dunlop himself[68] gave regular courses of lectures at the weekends right up to October 1912 when he moved back to London. Although next to nothing is known in theosophical circles today about the activities that took place within the institute (in spite of the fact that Annie Besant herself did visit it once, thus sanctioning the undertaking by her presence), it is nonetheless possible to obtain a fairly accurate picture of Dunlop's role therein as many of his lectures were also printed in the magazine *The Path* inaugurated by Dunlop and his friend Charles Lazenby during the same period. This publication is very hard to come by today. But when one glances, in the British Museum Library for instance, through the pages of the four substantial yearly volumes of this magazine, one is instantly struck by the grandeur and comprehensiveness of its conception and by the multitude of authors and the variety of subjects treated in it. Along with articles by Annie Besant, poems by AE and Yeats, short essays by Eleanor Dunlop, the wife of the editor, and the already mentioned essays on the zodiac, we discover, for instance, a series of articles on the tarot by the Russian occultist P.D. Ouspensky.

Both the magazine and the Institute tried to steer clear of any kind of sectarianism: ' "T.S.", we learn in the opening article, also stands for "The Servitors".'[69] And with reference to the growing conflicts inside this society these words are to be found:

> Every split and sectionalizing of our ranks is only so on the outer plane. There is a continuous Theosophical Society which moves down the centuries appearing and disappearing from age to age, and always under the guidance of the Masters of Wisdom. Apparent strife is one of the most effective stimulants to thought, and since the main thing the Theosophical Society exists for on the outer plane is to encourage free and clear thinking, these differences seem necessary to quicken loyalty and definiteness of outlook.[69]

A truly courageous and positive stance in view of the impending rifts—the worst ever in the history of the Theosophical Society. For in 1911, Annie Besant was to back a special order which would lead to the exclusion of the German Section *en masse* two years later and thereby indirectly give rise to the Anthroposophical Society. We are referring to 'The Star in the East' which was called into existence in order to serve and propagate the universal mission of the young Krishnamurti who was proclaimed to be the 'reincarnation' of Christ.

As can be deduced from an interview in December 1911, Dunlop regarded the new order with some scepticism in so far as it set out to promote certain rather sectional interests inside the universal Theosophical Society. And it is clear from the following words that he wanted to keep the movement free of the religious interests of any particular group:

> Mrs. Besant has lately launched a movement which has for its principle object the preparation for 'The Coming Christ', and in the minds of a great many people this is identified with the Theosophical Society (Adyar). Even in the publications of the Theosophical Society one repeatedly finds this confusion . . . I regard the Adyar Theosophical Society as being only *one* of the organizations within the Theosophical Movement.[70]

In view of the ever-increasing promulgation of the so-called 'World-Teacher', supposed to be the Christ Himself, Dunlop insisted once again in July 1912 (in *The Path*) upon the greatest possible vigilance in this matter. He drew attention to another point concerning the return of the Christ, that this reappearance should not be sought in the physical world but in the *sphere of the living*:

> I feel that the way in which the subject has been introduced is a dangerous innovation around which dark shadows may gather. The preparation for a bodily appearance overshadows the presence of the Real Christ . . . The wise course is to live the life which brings us into touch with the Living Christ . . . *A wise discrimination is more necessary now than at any other time in our movement.*

The 'Treasure' of Individual Freedom and the Turn of the Century

Thus Dunlop maintained all along a certain detachment with regard to the internal developments and crises inside the Theosophical Society. It was a position which led him to incur at times the displeasure of Annie Besant and C.W. Leadbeater and their followers. His consistently individual and independent attitude, which could not bow down to any kind of 'party' interest, might perhaps also be considered in the light of another human face and figure, the one he had already set eyes on round about the year 1906 and which had left an unforgettably deep impression on him, much deeper than any that he had experienced within the ranks of leading theosophical personalities up to that time.

In the first number of *The Path* we find a few remarks concerning the problem of excluding individual members or even whole sections from a society such as this. In view of the situation in which D.N. Dunlop was later to find himself within the Anthroposophical Society at the end of his life, these thoughts are of special significance, for they throw a clear light on his basic attitude towards this question.

> We recognize the individual freedom of mankind as a great treasure, and as a society we strive to give that individual freedom a platform for its expression.
>
> The members of the society may believe anything or nothing in

> regard to religion, but their joining a society of this kind is a pledge of their absolute tolerance for the opinions of their fellow men, no matter what those opinions may be. There is no formula or creed to be observed or accepted, and no member has a right to speak for the society in a matter of belief. No doubt there will arise in the ranks of the society, strong individuals who will draw many after them and their ideas, but the society as a whole will never be pledged to any teaching or any specific religion.

And now come the following words which seem to foreshadow *in nuce* the whole of the dramatic and to some extent tragic events that were to unfold inside the Theosophical Society and, later on, within the Anthroposophical Society as well:

> If any council or group of members at any time arrogate to themselves to expel from the society any human being who is a member, in that very decree they will have banished themselves, and although they may retain the name, the life and power of the Masters of Love and Compassion will go with those they cast out, and will not remain with those who scorn and turn from their midst the less developed or less righteous man.
>
> Only those in the coming century who are strong in sympathy and tolerance for a growing mankind, and believe in the freedom we have attained by a long struggle, and who are determined not to give up that freedom which allows each man to think honestly for himself—only these will ultimately stand the shocks brought to bear upon the Society by the opposers of human development, both within and without our ranks, only these will form the Society at the close of the twentieth century, and they indeed will have formed a nucleus of the universal brotherhood of mankind, without any distinctions whatever, of race, creed, sex, caste, or color.[71]

These are clear and unambiguous words which reach far into the future and we shall have cause to think on them again.

Spiritual Striving and the Creation of Community

The Path not only provides us with a wealth of information concerning Dunlop's activity as a lecturer during the pre-war years, it also gives us access to regular reports on theosophical conferences and other events of that period. A theosophical yearbook records Dunlop as having been a 'pioneer of the Summer School idea'—in fact he was *the* pioneer, for he actually launched the idea in a letter published in the *Vahan* in June 1909. Advance notification was given of any summer schools that were due to take place and, afterwards a detailed assessment was made of them in *The Path*.

One has only to read one of these evaluations subsequently printed in *The Path* to realize just how deeply Dunlop felt himself committed at that time to the real spirit of H.P. Blavatsky; and furthermore the reader will be able to perceive the spiritually *practical* attidude Dunlop adopted towards such meetings between striving theosophists by the way in which he considered their spiritual potential in real *concrete* terms. For by creating a 'social body' so to speak on the psychic and spiritual level, a higher spiritual being was offered the possibility of working into it, of permeating this body with the inspiring force of its 'Nirmanakaya', i.e. its own spiritual body. A description of this process is to be found in one of the issues of *The Path* reporting on a theosophical summer school which had taken place in Weybourne Springs from 4 to 7 July 1910:

> The teachings of Theosophy are reiterated over and over again, and yet when a practical demonstration of the truths is presented, even old students are surprised. We are accustomed so often to the saying of the Master of Judea 'Where two or three are gathered together in my name, there am I in the midst', that we have lost all sense of its meaning, and yet it is the simplest statement regarding all Nirmanakayas. When any group of comrades meet together and put all carping criticism of each other out of their mind and unite in thought of mutual love and sympathy, they form by this very unity, a body into which a great invisible being may enter, and connect Himself for the time with the group who have formed this body for His use . . . The spiritual body interpenetrates the whole assembly, and unconsciously every mind present enters into and is coloured by the glory of His presence within it.
>
> 'What is happening?' we ask in bewilderment, what is this

> wonderful upwelling within us, why does the world and our comrades appear so beautiful, what is this far sweep of consciousness into worlds of which we never dreamed? . . . The Nirmanakaya is waiting and His love to us rushes forth to strenghten our love and sympathy for each other. So it was at Weybourne Springs.[72]

The sceptic might deem such a description to be nothing more than the product of wishful thinking. However, that would be to overlook an important fact: that we are dealing here with something that can only be accomplished if certain conditions have been fulfilled. These conditions are twofold. Firstly, the idea of the existence of higher beings capable of permeating a human community must be truly living in both the minds *and* hearts of the participants; secondly, the participants must be ready to put aside any negative personal elements in their relationships to one another for the time being and that means above all any attitudes based on harassment, criticism, vanity, feelings of antipathy and so on. At the end of the report it was made perfectly clear once again, that such elements as these had by no means been lacking—at least at the outset. There had been 'many diverse elements, many strong idiosyncrasies, many firm preconceptions of personal antipathy, but with all these there was in every heart the desire to learn truth and devotion to the Masters of Wisdom and Compassion'. And so, 'within two days the antipathies had melted, and love and comradeship shone forth'.

Although Dunlop had originally planned a summer school in Penmaenmawr for the year 1911, in the final instance another locality was decided upon; thus this particular place was so to speak 'preserved' for a later occasion—the first Anthroposophical Summer School (organized by Dunlop himself in 1923). Indeed, Rudolf Steiner was later on to highlight the choice of this spot as having been a particularly fortunate 'sleight of hand'. Let us note in passing that Dunlop was not only to retain his original intention of organizing a summer school at this particular place but also to carry over into the years of his anthroposophical activities his attitude and approach to the possibility of creating true forms of community on the basis of genuine spiritual striving. Twelve months later, Dunlop organized a summer school in Torquay—another place he was to return to later with his anthroposophical friends, just one year after the Penmaenmawr Summer School of 1923.

The lecturers present at this fourth International Summer School included, amongst others, a certain Mrs Cook, the author of *Light on the Path* and other inspired works who had become known under the pen-name of Mabel Collins, and perhaps it was due to an appreciable extent to her presence there that 'the lectures reached a higher standard than at any previous Summer School', as Dunlop observed, even if 'it was more difficult to build a body for the "Nirmanakaya" of the group'. Once again he emphasizes in his commentary on this summer school (in the September 1912 issue of *The Path*) the idea of building a truly spiritual community:

> Under such conditions all our ideals may be projected in a common ideal, and our most sacred aspirations invoke the 'mysterious visitor' who will express them in the miracle of love in which all personal elements are absent. Here the fragments of the bread of life will be gathered in baskets to feed the multitude. May we all learn to be obedient disciples of the Great One, to mount on the eagle wings of the imagination, to run with winged feet His errands, to walk with steady feet the path of light, and while in the wilderness of life, to faint not by the way.

Naturally much more could be said concerning the significance of these international summer schools as founded by D.N. Dunlop, and strictly speaking this is a subject which needs, and indeed deserves, to be treated in its own right. Let us at this point merely refer to one of the fundamental aims of the summer schools as defined by Dunlop himself. In connection with the fifth International Summer School at Peebles (1913), which was accompanied by a multitude of artistic presentations, we find, in the September issue of *The Path*, the following words:

> Intelligence requires contact and fusion to recognize and finally know Itself; this is man's psychological need and the *raison d'être* of the Summer Schools. But Intelligence is baulked in its operation between

men and women when it is met by personal motives of insincerity. The *sine qua non* of a real school of learning is just the atmosphere which the members made at Peebles, where no one had a special teaching nor a personal 'axe to grind'.

We have already made an attempt in the section entitled 'The Occult Path and the Zodiac' to gain some insight into Dunlop's vision of the 12 cosmic principles which constitute the basis of our physical, psychical and spiritual existence as such. Contenting ourselves with a cursory glance at these principles, we had to leave the reader to reflect further or develop for himself the basic ideas encountered there.

It seems appropriate at this point that certain other subjects of current interest should now also reappear in their original form, i.e. as Dunlop treated them at this period in his life. What is more, the reader may even discover in Dunlop's attitude something of that vast life of the zodiac present in the background and permeating his thoughts even when he is treating quite other matters.

In the following chapters we shall concentrate on three themes which are of central importance. They are specifically related to the individual as a thinking, feeling and willing being. Given the fact that a time was soon to come when he would no longer give so many lectures, nor, indeed, write books or essays, it seems all the more essential that Dunlop be allowed at this point to speak freely and at some length in order to be given the opportunity to express himself, freely and extensively. As regards the style of the following two sections, it should be noted that they were based on summaries and notes taken from lectures.

The Function of Mind[73]

In beginning the study of a subject like this, it seems to me probable that those of you who are unfamiliar with the theosophical classification of man and those who find some difficulty in understanding the nature of man, will first ask 'What is man?' Now man is identified with a Sanskrit word *manas* (mind), which is probably the root of the word *man*. Man is a thinker, and it is essential to make the distinction betwen man, the thinker, and the various bodies which he uses. Most of the confusion of thought in our modern days is due to the habit men have of identifying themselves with the forms they use, and with the characteristics of the forms, *viz.*—poverty, health, success, disease, happiness, etc. Questions affecting the temporary life engage the earnest thought of men and women, and quite rightly too; but they have obscured the fact that man is an immortal being. Therefore I ask you to make the distinction between that part of you which is essential, immortal, and that which passes away with the passing of the physical body; between the immortal life, eternal, everlasting, and the life of form. In making that clear at the beginning, you will solve more easily the problem of the mind as it arises in experience, for if you identify yourself with your name as, for example, John Davidson or Tom Jones, you limit the area of your thought; you limit the universe to the problems of your personality; and the great field of consciousness as it plays through nature, and the races of man, is circumscribed so that it has no particular relation to you as a thinking being except as a matter of passing interest. You know that you are English, Irish, Scotch, etc., and that perhaps affects you because you are living in that particular environment; but when you associate yourself with the immortal part of your nature you begin to identify yourself with the race as a whole, you begin to feel that life which moves through all the races—red, black, white, yellow. And when you identify yourself with that, life begins to assume new aspects; you commence to act more spontaneously from your own nature. The affairs of the personality do not colour your life so much when the wider field of consciousness is contacted; all the circumstances of life begin to take their place in a field of consciousness which is absolutely universal. The failings to reach the ideal, the yielding to desire, depression, fits of the blues, the losing of your temper—all these things affect you less because you are thinking in a larger life.

It is well to keep in mind this great distinction between man as an immortal thinker and the temporary bodies which he uses for the purpose of gaining experience.

Dunlop subsequently develops these two aspects of the human being in more detail. He speaks of a 'spiritual body', a 'mental body', and a 'psychic body', showing how these bodies correspond to the 'shadowless light', the phenomenon of electricity and that of magnetism.

But we can also decipher certain principles of the zodiac in the background here. First of all there is the cosmic principle of *human thought*. If thinking as such is experienced not merely as an offshoot of the personality but as a cosmic principle then it becomes possible to grasp the universal character of the other principles as well. This means first and foremost in the present context that we can come to an understanding of the principles of *life* and *consciousness* which permeate all things. These three principles correspond to the triad Sagittarius, Leo, Aries. Furthermore, *within the thinking process* it is possible to bring the individuality as such to manifestation. This is the step from Sagittarius to Capricorn. Thereby the individual becomes a *true* individuality on the one hand whilst the thinking process becomes truly *individualized* on the other.

However, thought can equally be exploited to satisfy our *desires* or 'prostituted' as Dunlop points out: 'And it is this prostitution of the mind to satisfy desire that is the cause of all the suffering of humanity.' Making use of the function of the mind in this way is equivalent to taking a step backwards from Sagittarius to Scorpio and continuing beyond this point into the world of the senses where *sex* and *form* predominate. If, on the other hand, we choose to tread the path which leads from Sagittarius to Capricorn man in this case stands 'in the middle of his being, realizing the beauty of his spiritual nature, feeling himself the centre, the sun of his own universe, he will see the whole of life passing as a panorama; he will know when he acted under the influence of desire, of self-indulgence, of selfishness, and he will be able to make a daily, an hourly judgment of his actions'.

> And when there is a 'day of judgment' in a man's life every day, none will be necessary after death. When you are able to see yourself standing in the centre as a thinker, you will attach a true, discriminating judgment to every act of the day. You will feel the vibration of immortality in your own being which nothing can shake. With practice you will be able to see that which was foolish and small

and petty, and that which is pure and lovely and full of peace will also be clearly revealed. I have tried it a little and I know I am talking of something which every human being can realize for himself. This is the kind of life men and women want to begin to live; they want to enter into that calm, penetrating, peaceful state of the mind. When you begin to judge yourself that way life is robbed of many of its fears. My friends, face it! Look life straight in the face! Only then will you understand what it is to live without fear, and to let the world crash around you. Only then will you see that the first result of penetrating into your own life by your own mind will be a joy which is unspeakable. To realize yourself as immortal, to realize that the passing things of the body have not stained that stainless self, is in itself a wonderful feeling.

*

Let us turn now to another central theme—the will. Here, likewise, we should not overlook the fact that 'will' is also one of the 12 spiritual principles (corresponding to the sign of Pisces). And if the will is considered not as a personal but as a cosmic principle then in reality it is absurd to speak of a 'strengthening' of the will; it would be much wiser to talk of all those traits within the personality that should be eliminated so that this cosmic force can begin to unfold its activity without let or hindrance.

Perhaps the reader will create within himself the right mood for what is now to follow, if he recalls at this point something in total contrast with it, namely, that ceremonial form of magic which Dunlop had witnessed as a spectator so long ago—the master of the ceremony and its central figure being none other than a certain W.B. Yeats!

Ceremonial Magic in Meditational Form[74]

This subject is one which interested me by virtue of a very small incident—namely, that I read in a book a statement to the effect that theosophists are individuals who read about magic a great deal, but who never for one moment consider it desirable to practise it.

Personally I have always had a very strong desire to be a magician, for I believe that we need more individuals who have first-hand knowledge and information on magic, instead of being able to give only the testimony of others.

There is no school so valuable as the school of experience, and here you find working all those men and women who are really helping the world. It is from this school that the Masters choose their disciples, from among those who are interested in the history of the life of the planet and not merely in the history of one small society or brotherhood. When you enter the school of the Masters you begin to look at the life of mankind in terms of the whole and not in the terms suggested to you by the particular idiosyncrasies of one little sect or society. You are concerned rather with the great events behind the smaller movements of mankind. And, more than this, you begin to direct your movements and interests impersonally in relation to the planetary life. Whether you look at life from the point of view of the artist, or of the scientist or of the mystic, if you are to enter the field of practical magic you are of necessity bound to exercise one great function, and that is the function of the Will. The man or woman who wants to achieve something along the path of inner development must regard as sin anything which misdirects energy or draws the mind away from the object in view. Whatever you have made up your mind to do in relation to your spiritual growth and development, is necessary for you and for collective humanity. Therefore you must necessarily regard anything as sin or weakness which turns you from that self-appointed goal.

Remembering that symbols are the outer expression of inner principles, we will turn to the particular ones I have chosen for consideration. I will refer first to the *Circle*. To deal with its symbolism exhaustively is impossible here, but the particular meaning to which I wish to draw your attention is this: I shall assume that all are interested in *achieving* something, not interested merely in *reading* about spiritual growth; that all realize the presence of an eternal principle overshadowing our various bodies. This being so, you must realize that it is possible for you to achieve what any occultist or mystic has achieved, if you will undertake to tread the thorny path to wisdom step by step for yourselves. It is necessary to begin and walk along that path yourself. Now the Circle in this connection indicates the definition of your task. You are not to stray outside the limits of the circle you have made for yourself, and all intruding influences must be rigidly excluded. Nothing must interfere with the circle which is indicative of the limits of the work you have in view. You stand at the centre and as the centre is at equal distance from any part of the circumference, this position is symbolical of the fact that you have become for the time being perfectly poised and balanced, a difficult but necessary task. In the moments of meditation which precede action you are one-pointed, and intend to maintain the perfect balance. Picture yourself entering an inner room. Create an imaginary circle. You have put a definition before you. You are in the centre of the magic circle, across the threshold of which you will allow nothing which will overcome you. If you are to be successful in your task, you have to surround the circle with those necessary elements which in all ceremonial magic have been found essential for accomplishment. Around the magic circle are placed lighted candles, sometimes nine, and sometimes seven; nine (with yourself in the middle as the tenth) being the most complete. If you will think for a moment you will see how very striking is the symbolism here. The material of which the candle is composed is a certain substance which involves the slaying of an animal; the light which you will use will be derived from the substance of the 'animals' in the shape of thoughts of selfishness and pride, and of all the undesirable elements in your personality which you have slain. From the slaying of these things you extract their energies and they become the very light which protects you, for this light stands as witness to the world of the fact that you are engaged upon some task of a spiritual nature. The light is at the same time your service for humanity and that which you erect for the helping of mankind is likewise your protection. The particular arrangement of the light is symbolical of the fact that certain conquests have been made over elements within yourself. The light is the result of those things of a personal nature which you have destroyed.

At the centre of the circle is to be found the *Altar*, which each of us must erect for ourselves; for the external altars are only symbolical of certain states of consciousness. I am assuming for the sake of this discussion that we are all desirous of being members of that mystical Church which forms the Christ-body in humanity, and every Church whether mystical or physical, centres around the Altar. This altar you erect in your meditation has to conform to certain rules and regulations. Its height will vary in accordance with your height—the height you have attained in spiritual evolution, the point of consciousness you have reached on this path. On it, and within it, is kept everything that you are to use in your magical operations. There, permanently before you, will be your obligation to the Highest you can conceive, so that when you look upon the Altar you will be reminded of that obligation which you have voluntarily undertaken, perhaps in ages gone, to commit your life and energies to the service of humanity in some way or another. It is probably fairly true to say that at the present stage of development there is no one who takes an interest in such a subject as this who has not, ages long since, in some form or another, pledged himself to the service of the human race.

On the *Altar*, within reach, are three important elements symbolized by certain instruments which will have to be used in your progress. The *Scourge*, the *Dagger* and the *Chain*. The Scourge is used for a specific purpose and is symbolical of the fact that you have at sometime or other deserted your aspiration, that you have wandered away after some personal interest and you are consciously aware of it. You use the scourge to bring yourself back to the centre and also to eliminate from your magic circle undesirable elements which you know perfectly well are not for one moment to be allowed to remain there. The *Dagger* symbolizes the fact that you will use it, if necessary, to sacrifice your personal life in the cause which you consider paramount and is indicative of your willingness to remove all personal considerations which hinder the carrying out of your obligation. This does not of course mean your physical life, but those personal considerations which limit your attention to your own immediate interests and which prevent you from looking at life in terms of humanity. In the Christ drama the *nails* take the place of the *Chain*, but the symbolism is identical. You will chain yourself to your obligation as the Christ was nailed to the Cross.

On the Altar is also the *Oil*, compounded as a rule in magic of four different kinds of oil—myrrh, olive, cinnamon and galangal. These oils have this peculiar and significant characteristic, that they will not combine into the right oil unless they are all perfectly pure. The oil is a symbol of aspiration which has to be sprinkled over everything you do. Every work must be anointed with this oil and if it is not so anointed then you may know that is has to do with your personal aspirations only and not with the larger plan of mankind.

Another very important instrument is the *Wand* symbolizing Will, and it is of no use if it wavers. There must be established in the centre of your being a certain polarity which is undeviating in every circumstance of life. Remember too in this connection, that the most dangerous obstacles which the practical magician has to face are never the most obvious ones. Humanity imposes ordinary conventions; moralities change and vary in different countries. These are not the things about which you have to take great care, but certain subtle dangers which become more powerful according to the height which you have reached. A very usual form is that of pride. You perhaps succeed in certain directions where others fail, and you feel self-satisfied and pleased with yourself. In order that the Will may be effective it must be rigid, and if it has to 'touch the stars' it must be firm and stable at the base. Everything must be subordinate to the spiritual will. There is only one Will in the universe and we in our ignorance put our personal will against the Universal Will. The Will is only concerned with universal principles. We all know it; if we withdraw from personal considerations great peace falls over us like a garment of beauty. When you take every personal interest you can conceive of, and lay it on the altar and say in that moment 'Thy will, not mine be done', then it is that the whole universe is yours. Egoity is obliterated and Death itself is obliterated. We feel the pain of death because we have the fear of the loss of 'me and mine'. Cultivate the habit of overcoming obstacles all the time; have a strong and fixed determination to accomplish that which you have set out to do, and fan the little ember of will within you until it becomes a great energy able to carry you through every difficulty. Many people have strong impulses today and cancel them out tomorrow. Strength and weakness alternate in us and that is why we are so ineffective. Do not adopt any formula which suggests that you aim to accomplish the task of becoming a magician at once, but say to yourself, 'I will establish a current which will last through the ages so long as consciousness requires a form to sustain it.' At the moment when nothing in life matters a little bit to you there will awaken that slumbering will which you have established when the chasm seemed almost impassable. Even an elementary acquaintance with the occult path will show this.

The *Cup* is a symbol which suggests various interpretations. The artistic imagination is drawn always by this very beautiful symbol. It evokes so many ideas of beauty; the cup in which the symbol of the blood of the Christ is presented to the communicant; that cup of intoxication which when drunk by the mystic opens the gateway to the eternal glory and beauty; the thousand-petalled lotus which blooms at the midnight hour when the Soul in agony cries 'My God, my God, why hast Thou forsaken me?'—at the hour of supreme initiation when the life-blood of the initiate is spilled in order that the essence of that life-blood may penetrate through the life of the planet and make the work in which the inhabitants of the planet are engaged a little lighter. Then there is the Cup of the Holy Grail, full of the blood of many lives spent in the service of man. The lotus flowers—the cups—are to be found at every centre of the body; for instance the cup at the heart which receives those great energies which can be transformed into spiritual vitality in the body. There is a legend to the effect that the old Venetian glass workers made cups of glass so skilfully that they changed colour if poison were put into them. That is wonderfully suggestive of the nature of this mystic cup of which I speak, for you have to see that no poison enters because its nature is sacramental; and when the disciple is able to drink the cup which contains the full understanding of life his personal life is no more. This mystic Cup is constantly being replenished by the Dew of Immortality, but man more often uses these waters to feed his animal nature instead of his soul.

Next comes the *Sword*, but this is a 'baby-chela's' instrument and by-and-by you will lay it aside, for it is not required in the marriage-chamber. It is an instrument of magic which you are allowed to use only in the name of the King; to use it effectively you must wear the *Crown*, that is—be initiated. It has its uses, however; it is the symbol of logic and reason and analysis, and if you are to understand complexity you must use analysis. But 'those who live by the sword shall perish by the sword'.

The *Pentacle* is the body, the result of past 'karma', and it represents the field of action.

The *Lamp* is always hung in the centre of the circle from the roof, above all the instruments, lighting the whole field of operations, and if you look at it everything else is obliterated. Your consciousness is focused on the Light 'which lighteth every man coming into the world', and which shines equally in every particle of substance through which consciousness has been operating.

The *Oil* in the lamp is the oil which was in the widow's cruse and which replenished itself miraculously. Suppose that in the conflict of life you are overcome in some form or another and forget your aspiration and obligation. Perhaps you have gone on forgetting for years and years and you are inclined to think that you are so depraved that it is no use making any more attempts. Just at the moment when you are inclined to give up altogether the oil of aspiration will bubble up in the lamp, and the light will become bright again.

The *Crown* is the symbol of completion and is worn by the King, the man who has attained. When you have trodden the weary path to the very end, you finally realize that those joys which come to you through the avenue of the senses are evanescent and that the initiate is the only man who knows what real joy is, for real joy can only be understood and realized by the man who has conquered himself. The crown rests on a piece of red silk. This colour is a symbol of the glory of life. The crown rests upon the life; it is impossible to pretend you have the crown if you have it not. You cannot pretend to be a King, that is, to have entered the circle of Initiates who understand Life and its principles fully. The crown of thorns is a crown of radiance; the rays of light appear as thorns to the uninitiated.

The *Robe* which the Initiate wears is symbolical of the aura and also of the silence and mystery in which his real work is enveloped, of the isolation of every mystical life. The true communion always takes place in the inner chamber and there that seamless robe of glory is worn which is the garment of the true initiate.

Then there is the *Lamen*, the breastplate of righteousness. It is worn over the heart as protection and it has in it many jewels which are called 'perfections'. The lamen indicates your work and also the stage you have reached in your inner life.

The *Book of Life* represents your Karma for this incarnation. Everything you do, every struggle, every aspiration has a cumulative effect, and the writing in that book goes on unfailingly up to the very last page.

The *Bell* rings at important points in the struggle and is a symbol of hope. In deep meditation when you have attained to any point of real concentration there is undoubtedly a bell-like sound that gives forth a wonderfully harmonious vibration of peace. The bell may be taken as indicative of a certain state of consciousness attained by you when 'the song in the heart' sounds forth. It signifies peace and power over all the disturbing elements.

The *Magic Fire* is symbolized by the incense which is burned in a censer on three legs which are emblematic of the triple flame, the three higher principles in man. Everything you have acquired, all the powers for which you have fought, have to be burnt up at the end, and only then will the imperfect elements which were put into the censer at the beginning be transformed into the perfect. Remember that if you seek to retain one single power for personal ends the struggle has to begin all over again.

We have briefly glanced at these symbols and we come back to this point: how can men and women become practical magicians? It is absolutely necessary that they should do so if the world is to be transformed, the chemical elements transmuted. I am no pessimist in regard to man and his possibilities. I have had glimpses of a deeper vision and I know if we are faithful to these enduring principles of life and consciousness that some day the golden age will dawn for mankind, the Earth will marry the Heavens and humanity's purpose on this planet be accomplished.

*

Let us turn finally to our third theme. Here again we are going to let Dunlop speak for himself; all the more so because we are dealing with a subject which had preoccupied him intensely since his earliest youth. Nor must we forget again that the following pages are composed of *notes* made of a lecture; they have a somewhat fragmentary character and are not so rounded off as is generally the case with Dunlop's other essays and writings.

The Christ Drama According to St John[75]

We are, as Mystics, concerned very largely with the symbolical interpretation of the great Scriptures of the world, and we shall not take the purely exoteric view-point which sees in them no more than historical records of physical happenings. I do not say for a moment that they have not an historical basis, but it is not that which makes them of value to the student of the mystery teachings. It must also be borne in mind that it is very difficult indeed to find any evidence at all for the existence of Jesus as an historical figure. So skilfully did He conceal His personality that two thousand years after His death no authentic proofs of His existence can be produced . . . The Gospel of St. John is a book of spiritual magic, and those who come to the study of it with unprejudiced minds will undoubtedly find a key which may be used to solve some of the problems of life and consciousness. The Gospel begins in a wonderfully effective way, with a kind of Cosmic Prologue, which contains, for those who have eyes to see, a recital of the order of the emanations. 'In the beginning was the Word, and the Word was with God, and the Word was God.' *Word* implies vibration, sound, resonance, intelligence; all nature is an expression of the thought of God. The manifested universe is an outbreathing of divine consciousness, and everything that is to come into being is already in the thought of God. The Word 'in the beginning' includes the great primeval Trinity of Consciousness, Energy, Substance, which necessarily precede all manifestation, and the 'light that shineth in the darkness' is the light of intelligence which polarizes the chaotic elements of a previous planetary system and brings into them the state of order and balanced relationship necessary in the unfoldment of a manifested universe from the elements held in solution. The light of consciousness and of intelligence precedes differentiation and 'nature' is the image of the divine mind . . .

It is one of the sayings of occultism that we all live in the midst of the 'dead ones', and the meaning of this is that we live associated with bodies in which the spiritual centres have, to a great extent, become atrophied. It is the purpose of the mystic and occultist to waken these slumbering centres into life and activity, so that he may make manifest in the world of flesh the consciousness which he possesses in the three worlds, and into which humanity at the present stage enters during the period of deep sleep only. There is a good reason why the spiritual consciousness should have been shut off as far as the ordinary waking consciousness of mankind is concerned. It was necessary for the purpose of evolution that full attention should be paid to the physical world, that from the mineral, vegetable and animal kingdoms the life of God should be liberated and finally attain the 'human' stage. It is our function as 'human Gods' to perform this task, for there is not a single sleeping spark of intelligence in the mineral or the vegetable kingdom which does not receive some of that wonderful solar energy which can be transmitted and manipulated by man in providing for human needs. Even though it was necessary in the past that a veil should be drawn over full spiritual consciousness, the time is coming again when that veil must be lifted. We have explored the lands and oceans of the physical world and we are beginning to awaken our earlier vision into activity, and, consequent upon this to realize that in the spiritual worlds there are whole continents of wonderful beauty and mystery waiting to be discovered and explored. We will be helped in this by the keys to understanding which a magical book like the Gospel of St. John puts into our hands.

The particular interpretation which I am going to put before you very briefly may be called the psycho-physiological rendering of the allegory, and we shall see how the countries and places in which the different events take place have each their special significance. *Galilee* represents the head, the spiritual consciousness; *Samaria* the heart centres, the psychic nature of man; and *Judæa* the material world, the *Dead Sea* being symbolical of the sea of generation. The *Jordan* is the spinal cord, the sacred river of the body, where the magnetic and electric currents flow between the head and the other centres in the body.

After the Cosmic Prologue to the Gospel to which I have alluded, there is a sudden drop from the Macrocosm to the Microcosm—'*There was a man* sent from God whose name was John.' John in this particular interpretation is the psychic self, the soul bearing witness to the light of the Spirit which 'was in the beginning'. The psychic self is the Messenger, the forerunner of the true light, but not the light itself. The psychic self prepares a path through the wildernesses of life which later the Master Consciousness will tread, and this function is recognized by the Soul. Certain individuals came to John asking him 'Who art thou?' and he answered quite simply: 'I am the Voice of one crying in the wilderness—prepare ye the way of the Lord.' That is a beautiful lesson for us today. The voice of the soul is to cry in the wildernesses of our Nature, 'Make straight the ways of the Lord in the three worlds, from Galilee, in the symbolic sense right down to Judæa.' I have sometimes thought that John's reply is rather in the nature of a rebuke. Many are found in our midst anxious to know on what authority such and such a statement is made, and we become involved in the consideration of past incarnations and the part we personally played in them, which really does not matter at all. What does matter is that we are here, and that by every magical message we are referred back to the light of the spirit in ourselves.

The psychic man baptizes in water, and here again the symbology is perfect. Water is always taken as a symbol of the psychic world, of the turbulent waters of emotional life in which we so often lose ourselves, and its purification must be accomplished before the baptism by fire can take place.

The Marriage in Cana or Galilee and the turning of the water into wine is full of significance. Wine is symbolical of that spiritual intoxication which at times seems to break over the whole being, and once that is experienced you can never be quite the same again. It is of the nature of love, outgoing, fiery, irresistible. The work of spiritual alchemy must begin in Galilee—that is in the brain, the organ of spiritual consciousness, and the 'water' in the six centres (represented here by the six stone jars) must be transmuted into spiritual qualities and inspiration (wine). It is obvious that after this transmutation must follow the cleansing of the temple of the body. It is said that Jesus went down into Judæa, to Jerusalem, and drove out of the Temple the 'money changers', and those who sold 'oxen and sheep and doves'. Spiritual illumination vitalizes and cleanses the whole body and 'health' arises from using the bodily organs no longer as centres solely for the functioning of animal consciousness, but for the expression of the spiritual energies, to which the chemical atoms respond readily after adequate preparation.

Next there is the conversation with Nikodemus. Until we have drunk of the wine of spiritual inspiration which liberates the soul of man we cannot fully understand the meaning of the 'birth from above'. Neither could Nikodemus understand the mysteries of the spiritual teachings. He was a 'Judaean'.

The next incident in the drama is that of the woman at the well, in Samaria, which represents the middle region, the psychic or heart centres. The woman, symbolical of the more intuitional side of the psychic nature, is said to have had five husbands. They are associated with the five magnetic colours visible to clairvoyant vision around the heart centre, the sixth not functioning in the majority of humanity. It was said to the woman: 'He whom thou now hast is not thy husband'—the sixth magnetic 'colour' had not been brought into activity as yet. You have here the assistance given by the spiritual consciousness of the Master; the whole life of the woman was changed by the purification of the heart centres, and she went back into the city and called the people to 'come and see' the man who had worked this spiritual alchemy within her.

The healing of the 'little lad' at Capernæum refers symbolically to the purification of the throat centre. When your inner development makes you able to sound the note appropriate to each element, all must of necessity respond to you. At this stage the disciple is able to speak to every man 'in his own language', to utter the word of power.

There is next the healing of the sick man at Jerusalem. The various purifications confer the power to master, thence to heal the body. Following the exercise of the control which has been won over the functions of physical life the disciple is able to control the forces of nature, represented in the drama by the miracle of the loaves and fishes.

At this stage the past misdeeds of the personality are forgiven and blotted out, and to the woman taken in adultery is spoken the benediction 'Go and sin no more.' In the Master consciousness there is no room left for condemnation, for the actions of the personality under the attachment of desire will teach their lessons naturally in the working out of karmic law. When the illusions of material life are overcome, sight is given to the man born blind. The final triumph, the complete mastery over the psychic world, is represented by the raising of Lazarus from the dead.

We come now to perhaps the most beautiful part of the whole drama, to the incidents connected with the Crucifixion. The wisdom of the material world condemns the Master to death. Now that is what happens literally in the life of every man who takes up the obligation of treading the spiritual path. He must die in the personality to reach liberation as a God. After his condemnation he takes up the great burden of the world and of humanity and the Cross which he must bear is placed upon him. And then we are told how the Master stumbled because of the weight, and how He met His mother, and the women who mourned. On the path towards Golgotha human love is a necessary consolation, strong to help and uplift right to the very end, and the bearing of the Cross by Simon of Cyrene illustrates the necessity for human co-operation in the carrying of the burden. The incident connected with Veronica is illustrative of the loving receptivity of humanity in its more spiritual aspect towards one who is treading the path. The stripping of the garments, which are symbolical of the silence and mystery surrounding every truly mystical life, is an incident which touches us very closely. No one can know our inmost experiences, but it very often happens that the most sacred incidents in the life of those who are bearing the greatest burdens are given over into the hands of enemies. Skill in action comes only from long experience. The Master is nailed to the Cross; that is, He is bound by love to the world and no longer is it possible for Him to leave humanity, for He becomes one with the planetary life. The darkest hour, from the point of view of the personal self, is the moment of supreme triumph for the Spirit and it is said that the Initiate is born at the midnight hour, when the 'earth' is enshrouded in silence and mystery. The body is first laid in the arms of His mother, returning to the elements out of which it originated, and is then laid in the sepulchre until 'out of the corruptible' rises 'the incorruptible'—and this body is transmuted into one of vitality and light.

'The Philosophy of Co-operation'

We may well want to ask: what about the realization of such profound insights and aspirations on the *external* level?

Two months before the outbreak of war, publication of the magazine *The Path* ceased. The Blavatsky Institute had already closed its doors. In these circumstances what would happen inside that 'exoteric edifice'?

In the preceding notes on the Christ Drama, reference was made at the end to Simon of Cyrene. This figure appears as a kind of archetype representing the necessity for human beings to work together.

At the beginning of 1915 Dunlop, as *de facto* director of the BEAMA, brought out a magazine of the same name. In the course of the first few numbers he wrote a series of articles for the first edition, under the title 'The Philosophy of Co-operation'. This was certainly a curious way of inaugurating a magazine which was apparently meant to serve purely technical and economic interests. After Dunlop had worked them over and expanded them, these essays reappeared in 1916 in the form of a book entitled *British Destiny*. On the basis of his wide experience in the technological and economic field, Dunlop draws a number of conclusions in these essays culminating in the idea of extensive co-operation in just this area. The way this is done can leave us with no doubt whatsoever that, in the meantime, he himself had acquired that faculty whereby, to a remarkable degree, he was able to speak to each man 'in his own language'. Another idea expressed in the notes on the 'Christ Drama' which also comes to external fruition in this context is 'skill in action'. Translated into the terms of Rudolf Steiner's *Philosophy of Spiritual Activity*, this would be equivalent to 'the faculty of moral technique'.

Dunlop writes:

> A man, or a firm of large interests, may stand out against co-operation and declare that he sees no advantage in it, because he does not wish to give others the advantage of his co-operation. And he will not voluntarily adopt it until he sees that *his* advantage is tied up with the advantages of others, until he really learns somehow or other that the interest of others *is actually also his interest. It is not possible to get beyond self-interest*; what is possible is an enlargement of intelligence to perceive how extensive self-interest really is. Petty, personal self-interest learns expansion through experience. In its narrow, self-seeking aspect it is revolting to intelligent persons, and is as ugly as an ostrich with its head buried in the sand. But it is a stage in the process by which we all evolved.[76]

What is expressed here in clear and generous tones is an attitude which Dunlop was to adopt up to the end of his life, not only in 'anthroposophical' matters but also in what might have appeared to be purely 'business' affairs as well.

In the background of Dunlop's life it is possible to decipher a steadily evolving, constantly renewed ego-experience. Therefore it would be quite erroneous to imagine that an individual marked by this kind of experience would be ready to put a 'Philosophy of Co-operation' into practice at the expense of the individual—on the contrary: 'The strongest and most valuable associations . . . are always composed of the strongest individuals.'[77] For Dunlop the strongest individuals possible should serve as pillars; and a strong individual, according to him, could only be one who has become aware of his spiritual connection with the universe.

In his eyes, England offered a particularly fertile soil for such associations to thrive upon. Such associations should never be thought of as mere 'temporary measures' expressing nothing more than the criteria of the subjective personality. Dunlop's description of what makes a statesman, philosopher or thinker 'truly great' bears this out:

> History does not preserve the memory of any statesman, philosopher or thinker who is not really great; their fame does not survive the centuries unless they have enunciated and endeavoured to carry into practice those immortal Principles which inhere in Man and characterize the race. If they identify themselves with what is eternally true, they become part of the tradition of their country, and even of that of all countries, when their insight has been especially profound. These eternal Principles are the causes of existence, the source of all life; they are everywhere in operation; they are partially explained by mathematics and science, and are revealed to men when they begin to think impersonally and universally; they are that in which we live and move and have our being, and are secure even though continents become submerged.[78]

As we have already observed there are, according to Dunlop, essentially 12 cosmic principles. These can all be grasped by one of their number, the equally cosmic principle of thought—provided that the activity of thinking assumes a really universal and individual nature (i.e. Sagittarius and Capricorn) instead of being used in a partial or personal manner exclusively to interpret the world of the senses linked to time and space with a view to dominating it for purely egoistical purposes.

> History shows, without doubt, that the highest civilization, in any period, prevailed in the nation, or nations, who most nearly interpreted the principles which have been variously translated as justice, liberty, law, beauty, balance, order, etc. These are forgotten when the people become engrossed in outer things, in personal gratifications and ambitions; degeneracy and decay ensue, and 'supremacy' passes away to other nations who express more accurately the real ambitions and desires of humanity. But wherever the fundamental laws are firmly rooted in the consciousness of a nation, a just war will strengthen the convictions of the people and nerve them to preserve their existence through which their ideals are realized and made manifest.[79]

If the practical institutions which Dunlop had hitherto sought to establish (and indeed would continue to do so in the future) appeared to be 'external' and adapted to specific conditions, they were nonetheless and to an equal extent born from a philosophy rooted in such principles as these. Another important idea contained within this book is that relating to the cyclic return of ideas, wishes, and constellations of events—a law the knowledge of which must be of inestimable value to all those who believe themselves to have a 'practical' attitude towards life:

> We have observed only those cycles which obviously affect our physical bodies; our observation has not extended to the recurrence of moods and ideas. Most persons, however, have their periods of depression and elation, of 'dryness' and inspiration of action and introspection; and the same is true of nations and of the race as a whole. These cycles are facts in nature, they are the evidence of laws . . . which may be understood. Energy flows like the tide and the wise man knows when the ebb or flow is on . . . He understands, because he has developed within himself a knowledge of the Principle corresponding to that which universally operates, viz. Intelligence, and which functions in men as Mind . . . Man need not work in the dark, associated only with 'matter'; it is possible for him to work intellectually in the Light, associated with energy. He is a Mind-Being, and, as such, should enter with understanding into the processes of Life. His responsibility is rooted in this fact . . . There are times for action and times for inaction. The 'dark period' is the opportunity for the thinker. In such an age when inertia is coming upon the people, due to the ebbing of energy, the philosophers and artist-thinkers withdraw with the current, and, in the world of ideas, they speculate upon the meaning of life, they study the laws of existence and learn to understand polarity, the relation of energy to mass, etc. Thus they generate ideas and prepare for the turn of the tide when these ideas may be carried out into expression by statesmen and leaders of men in the affairs of the world. In the lives of individual men these times of activities and withdrawal are also to be observed in shorter or longer cycles . . . It has happened often in the history of the world that periods of activity have not forwarded human evolution, because the function of the thinker has been divorced from that of the actor; revolutions, miscarriages of justice, cardinal errors in administration have resulted when unthinking men have entered the field of action as leaders. With the cycle of returning energy all the various elements in human nature are thrown outward, passions and sectional interest become rampant and are often in excess of impersonal, intellectual powers. Deep understanding and a desire to

assist evolution in its true direction are necessary in those who come upon the scene at the flood-tide, if a *renaissance*, a rebirth, of consciousness is to take place. Human progress depends on human beings, and if thinkers refuse to act at the right time, they but delay their own evolution as well as that of the whole race. The opportunities of a man's life pass; his 'period' comes to an end. So also terminate the opportunities of nations and of races. In this sense we each have our 'change'. But an unintelligent man never knows his opportunity when it arrives; and it requires great skill in action for enlightened men to overcome the inertia and ignorance of the mass of the people at crises in history . . .

'When the law of periodicity is understood,' Dunlop concludes, 'men will use appropriately and intelligently the condition of each period.'[80]

We can hardly fail to recognize that Dunlop makes the same demands with regard to immediate circumstances and solutions in everyday life, as Rudolf Steiner puts forward in his *Philosophy of Spiritual Activity*. They concern the revelation and expression of the *whole of human nature* in the highest sense: 'We have distinguished between the knower and the doer,' Steiner says, 'and have left out of account precisely the one that matters most of all—the knowing doer.'[81]

In every human being a certain feeling for the totality of individual existence on the one hand can coexist with the appreciation of humanity as a unity on the other; to the extent that these two perceptions awaken within each man . . .

. . . scientists, philosophers, artists, educationalists and industrialists (employers and employees) will all recognize the respective functions of each, they will see the necessity for their intelligent co-operation in order to produce a better civilization, and they will apply their combined energies to the solution of the social problems about which men continually speculate and theorize . . . The thinker will realize the essential function of the manufacturer and will understand that he constructs the forms without which no ideas can find adequate embodiment. At the same time the manufacturer must also realize that, in their nature, forms are impermanent and constantly change, and the bases of these passing forms are ideas . . . Without Letters, without Science, Art, Philosophy and Religion, Commerce would have no *raison d'être*, as it is merely auxiliary to all these. But without Commerce, scientific and philosophical ideas would not have the means of embodiment necessary for their realization by men; without Commerce, Literature could not be printed and circulated, Art could not be produced. All man's experiences depend, in the last analysis, on the multifarious operations of Commerce, and the basis of it are the toilers in the fields and factories without whom all man's highest ambitions would never be attained.[82]

Richard St Barbe Baker and the 'White Lodge'

British Destiny is indeed a remarkable book. Whilst certain pages seem to be directly aimed at economic and industrial specialists (with details concerning prices, taxes, quality of goods, etc.) others are immediately full of the most striking and meaningful observations concerning the spiritual essence of the human being. This spiritual essence is seen as the foundation of all intelligent and responsible actions man can accomplish in this world. From this same conception of man an infinitely comprehensive and generous 'breath of inspiration' issues forth, pervading the whole of this book written as it was in the middle of the war period. Dunlop adopts a positive and totally unchauvinistic standpoint, observing that the British people have an important task and future provided they continue to spread the 'eternal' principle of voluntary co-operation as the basis of a world-wide, future civilization.

The ideas are clearly outlined and, for any really thinking person, must have had a thoroughly constructive and stimulating effect appealing as they did to the forces of free initiative. During the war and just after it many an aspiring and discerning individual must have found new energy and insight here. We even have a moving account of one such case.

Richard St Barbe Baker, founder of the organization 'Men of the Trees', and previously a forester in Kenya for many years, describes in his book *I Planted Trees* how he was wounded on the Western Front during the third year of the First World War.

With a number of other supposed 'fatal casualties' he was about to be transported to a mass-grave for burial when a sergeant noticed that the 'corpse' was still bleeding.

> I woke up three and a half days later at the Duchess of Westminster Hospital in the Casino at Paris Plage. I was dragged back to life and eventually returned to the Front. I was smashed up again, and finally invalided out in April, 1918.
>
> In hospital I had read a book called *British Destiny*, which made such an impression upon me that I wrote to the author, Daniel Dunlop, to thank him. In reply to my letter he visited me in hospital and invited me to go and stay with him as soon as I was allowed out. It was at the White House at Wimbledon that I met so many of his interesting friends. His wife, I discovered to my delight, had been a great friend of Walt Whitman.

St Barbe Baker then describes how Dunlop opened his eyes to certain things, indeed, how the meeting with this man had opened up entirely new horizons for him:

> Talks with Daniel Dunlop opened my eyes to the fact that we were losing more lives through the ignorance of health in our great cities than we were on all the fronts put together. War slew its thousands, but preventable disease its tens of thousands. Inspired by Dunlop, who himself had been largely responsible for organizing the Federation of British Industries, I called on industrial magnates, captains of industry, and so forth, and urged them to appoint welfare officers, and create sports grounds to be run in connexion with their factories and workshops. I worked hard for the British Institute of Social Service, which helped to pave the way for the Ministry of Health. As soon as the Ministry came into being, I felt it was time for me to return to my forestry studies and Cambridge.[83]

After his studies in Cambridge St Barbe Baker was Assistant Conservator of Forests from 1920 to 1923 and then for six years in Nigeria. He travelled thousands of miles around the USA, Canada and South America, surveying the vast forest areas. When he founded 'Men of the Trees' in Kenya in 1922 it was at first regarded with some scepticism. However, the movement spread over the whole world and in 1979 the present Prince of Wales became its patron. In 1950 St Barbe Baker undertook the first ecological survey of the Sahara. The obituary published in the *Daily Telegraph* concluded by saying that he 'spent his life in a single-minded campaign which stressed the essential importance of the part trees play in people's well-being.'[84]

A few years before his death in 1982, St Barbe Baker gave a lecture in Rudolf Steiner House in London. In the meantime he had immersed himself in the study of anthroposophy. David Clement reports how, on this occasion, 'he began his lecture with a panegyric on Dunlop. He had been to him as a father and shown him the way to his life's work.'[85]

The Inner Path

Let us now take another look at the reverse side of the coin—a glance into the inner workshop of the 'esoteric building'.

In the same year in which *British Destiny* came out, Dunlop published another work dealing with a subject apparently quite opposite in nature. The book, entitled *The Path of Attainment*,[86] reproduced three lectures given during the autumn of 1915 in the Blavatsky Lodge, London. They were 'hurriedly revised' and printed at the 'urgent request' of those who had heard them. The first lecture deals with the problem of 'Adepts, Masters and Mahatmas', a question of considerable importance in theosophical circles at that time. This is followed by a careful consideration of the conditions and goals of spiritual development. A chapter on initiation forms the conclusion of the book.

The first chapter is illuminating in so far as it gives us a clear picture of Dunlop's attitude towards the true nature and manifestation of the so-called 'Masters'. And it was indeed in connection with this very question that the greatest problems of all had arisen within the Theosophical Movement and Society. There was certainly no lack of 'Masters' ready themselves to put pen to paper, to send letters to the leading personalities of the society, or to make manifest themselves by some other means; nor was there any shortage of exponents, both inside and outside the

Theosophical Society, ready to challenge (and often rightly so) the authenticity of such documents.[87] For if, as Rudolf Steiner confirms, certain individualities who had attained a degree of development far surpassing anything the human being normally acquires had indeed inspired the Theosophical Movement in its original phase, it is just as true that, in the times that followed, large numbers of credulous members fell prey to illusion and deception when confronted with the problem of the 'Masters'. As Dunlop had been in a position to follow these developments very closely, it appears that he had an impulse to provide many of these individuals (dubbed *Freiherren von Unterscheidungsvermögen* by Rudolf Steiner on account of a certain natural talent to take liberties when it came to making clear distinctions) with ample opportunity for making a differentiated assessment of the matter.

Dunlop's words leave no doubt whatsoever as to the illusions both potential and real that had come to the fore with regard to the manifestations and 'inspirations' of the 'Masters':

> You will probably find hundreds of persons who have seen the vision of a body representing the state of consciousness equivalent in their minds to the person of a Master. They have seen a thought-form; but that does not necessarily mean they have actually seen and come into conscious communication with a Master. Such appearances are frequent in the astral world, where symbolic images and forms of many Adepts and Masters may be found. These appearances are deceptive; they are less than the shadows of realities. The play of the thought-energy of many thousands of people upon these images may set them in motion and cause them to become objective. Messages and definite directions as to work may even be given, and the 'voice of the Master' parodied . . . Most of the forms of Masters are thought-forms temporarily visible by increased vibration. The path leading to the Master involves a distinct knowledge of noëtic action in a high grade of substance. The 'Presence' cannot be described in terms of the senses.[88]

What Dunlop wanted above all to make clear to his listeners and readers was that there was another question far more important than that concerning the manifestation of the 'Masters', namely: what steps must one undertake in order to be adequately prepared for the spiritual body of a Master? Dunlop unequivocally asserts that the first step consists of developing the faculty of pure, sense-free thinking, for to begin with 'there is only one thing that reaches the ear of the Master, and that is *thought*'.

As for mediumistic and spiritualistic practices, here again, Dunlop is perfectly clear about these things: 'Those who frequent *séance* rooms and circles, and take part in necromancy of any kind by raising the psychic shells of the dead,[89] are placing obstacles in their path of discipleship.'[88] Once the pupil has decided to tread the path of knowledge there will be numerous trials awaiting him; these will be arranged under the auspices of his own Higher Self—not by any other authority:

> Whatever position the disciple is in, this inevitable test is being made by his inner nature, trying him this way and that, to see what stuff he is made of . . . It does not matter what happens to you while you hold this attitude; if you lose your reputation, your place in society—if you have ever had a place—if everything tumbles about you, your task is to stand undismayed. As one teacher very pregnantly says, you may put yourself in imagination into some of these positions, and just imagine how you would feel if everything were gone from you, if whatever little reputation you have amongst your friends, whatever little place you fill in society—if all that were gone, would you stand unafraid before His Will and not mind the destruction of a million Universes? I do not think any of us would . . . Nevertheless, that is the goal, that is the object: . . . the evolution of a self-conscious, self-poised being who, standing at the centre of his nature, will be able to look out on life from that centre, and direct his energies wisely in accordance with the plan which he now sees and partially comprehends.[90]

It is perhaps just as well at this point to recall that for Dunlop 'individuality' is one of the 12 spiritual principles—in fact the first to be attained as a result of the cultivation of a truly pure (i.e. universal) form of thinking.

An important recommendation is made to the pupil upon his path of spiritual development: to permeate the whole of his inner being with the conviction that it is entirely useless to spend time regretting things. This is by no means a recipe for thoughtlessness or 'sinning' with a good conscience; it simply draws attention to the futile, inevitable sterility of all thoughts which would have the past, in some way or other, different from what it in fact *is*: 'Regret nothing. Cut all doubts with the sword of spiritual knowledge.'[91]

By the control of thought the disciple 'learns to overcome all the elemental desires . . . until his desires reflect true thought as it is in the archetypal world.'[92] There are four precepts from the ancient mysteries that he should have at heart to help him orientate himself upon this path: 'Watch, Pray, Hope, Be Silent.' The first word points to the *constant* watchfulness that must be kept over the lower nature and the mind; the second is a 'demanding and realizing power' directed at higher beings—it is the power necessary to govern both the lower nature and the mind. 'Hope' means 'aspiring to the highest'. 'Silence' is the means by which 'the personality may listen and may hear the Voice of the Divine Self'.

Now it was the last word in particular that played a central role in all the ancient mysteries. Indeed, it is precisely on account of the strict adherence to this fourth rule that little or nothing of relevance has been passed on to us on an exoteric level concerning the actual procedures which took place within the mystery temples. Thus, on an exoteric level little is known, for instance, about the real initiation rituals which took place within the 'Greater Eleusinia'.

The Eleusinian Mysteries continued to exist until the Gothic invasion led by Alaric I in AD 396; the 'lesser' mysteries were celebrated in February, the 'greater' mysteries in September in the magnificent temple of Eleusis.

The Eleusinia must have been of especial interest to Dunlop. Indeed, in one of the first numbers of *The Path* in August 1910 we find an extensive calendar listing the nine days of festivity of the greater Eleusinia—nine days of initiation from 2 to 10 September. They 'began in public as a pageant and festival in honour of Demeter and Persephone; but the secret purifying rites were celebrated in the secrecy of the temple, to which none but the initiates were admitted. Every initiate was bound by an oath of inviolable secrecy; hence, nothing of any importance is known concerning the initiatory ceremonies'.[93]

The next remark that Dunlop makes is particularly illuminating in the context of this biography: 'However, there is good reason for believing that in the Eleusinian ritual the Zodiacal symbols were employed, and that some of the instruction was given in the form of dramatic representations. The symbolism of the Zodiac was really a cryptic language in which certain facts concerning the inner nature of man were expressed.'[93] The initiatory rites 'were designed for moral purification, the development of spiritual faculties, and the attainment of conscious immortality'.[93]

Dunlop explains how these rites covered four stages or 'degrees':

> The first of the degrees covered the whole field of the inductive physical sciences, and they were concerned with investigating the phenomena of external nature. The second degree embraced exoteric religion and all phases of blind belief, and these two degrees—pertaining to the lower mind—comprised all the knowledge available to those whose consciousness does not transcend the illusions of the material world. The third degree related to speculative philosophy, which sought to arrive at first principles by the effort of pure reason. The fourth degree was the direct apprehension of truth by the clear, calm mind, independently, practically, of any reasoning process whatever. And these two degrees pertained to the higher mind, as we understand it, in theosophy; they represented the field of knowledge open to those whose consciousness rises to the world of spiritual reality.[93]

The true esotericist does not rely exclusively on the senses and the mental faculties but aspires, through intensive self-evolution, to gain 'conscious control of his hidden potencies which are the immediate cause of his individual evolution'. He seeks to master that 'fontal essence within himself, which is the primary source of all elements and powers and being, of all that he is, has been, and will be'.[94]

Initiation and Occult Centres of the Human Body

No doubt it will already be clear to the reader from the preceding chapters how much emphasis D.N. Dunlop placed on the occult-physiological basis of all spiritual development; indeed it seems as though Dunlop was intimately acquainted with the occult mysteries of the physical body—which is, with good reason, said to be a 'temple of the gods'.

For Dunlop the physical world and consequently the physical body is, in certain respects, the most important one. He sees in it the crystallization of three other worlds connected with the occult elements of water, air and fire. These three worlds are active together within the physical. 'Initiation or spiritual re-birth,' Dunlop explains in the last chapter of the book *The Path of Attainment*, 'results from the quickening in man of that divine energy which evolves through upward direction of the creative energy into the deathless spiritual body.'[95] This upward movement is made possible by the 'Jordan' of the spinal column. This is what Dunlop attempts to make clear as he interprets some of the more central scenes described in the book of *Genesis*. It is an attempt which is all the more fascinating for being undertaken by one who, from his ninth year onwards, had become ever more intimately acquainted with the Holy Scriptures.

The 'divine energy' Dunlop mentions is the force pertaining to the so-called Serpent, the 'good serpent' of ancient symbology sometimes represented with an egg—the 'auric ovum'. It was known in ancient India as *kundalini*. In Greece it was called *speirema*. Dunlop describes it in the following terms: 'Semi-latent within this ovum is the light of the Logos, which, in energizing, becomes what we may roughly describe as living conscious electricity of incredible voltage, and hardly comparable to the form of electricity known to the physicist.'[96] By means of this force a 'spiritual body' of an immortal nature can be fashioned by the human being. In an undeveloped person this body is nothing more than a potential organ which never assumes its true form of reality. '*The giving birth to oneself as a spiritual being, the creation from the concealed essence of one's own embryonic nature of a self-luminous immortal body, is the object of initiation, the great theme of all the mystery dramas of the ages.*'[97]

This primordial 'electricity' is expressed in the images of Genesis:

> In the third chapter of the book of Genesis it is symbolized as the serpent, 'more subtle than any beast of the field which the Lord God hath made'. Eve, according to the story, when this force stirred within her, was tempted to its misapplication. Directed downward through the lower physical centres, 'unhallowed by a consciousness of responsibility to God and the incoming soul, the serpent force brought knowledge of evil'. Directed upward toward the brain for regeneration, the formation of the spiritual body, it brought knowledge of good—spiritual knowledge. Hence the dual operation of this solar force is symbolized in the story as the tree of the knowledge of good and evil. The curse of the Lord upon the serpent, 'Upon thy belly shalt thou go, and dust shalt thou eat all the days of thy life,' makes reference to the fact that during a certain period of human evolution man shall remain in ignorance of the law governing this solar force, and during that period it will manifest in man's earthly vehicles misgoverned by the human mind. 'And I will put enmity between thee and the woman, between thy seed and her seed; it shall bruise thy head, and thou shalt bruise his heel.' During this cycle of evolution—the *kaliyuga*, as it is called in the East—in ignorance of the law governing this divine force, man continually directs it downwards or bruises the serpent's head, while the serpent fire, thus misdirected, from the point of view of spiritual evolution, bruises man's heel, heel here being regarded by many authorities as a euphemism for that part of man nearest the earth, that is to say, the lower emotions and the mortal mind. And the Lord said: 'Behold the man has become as one of us, to know good and evil. Now, lest he put forth his hand and take fruit of the tree of life and eat and live for ever'—here the tree of life symbolizes the upward play of this solar force for the creation of the immortal body. Hence the meaning is, lest man should learn the law governing this force, and by directing it upward become immortal before he has learned sufficiently the necessary experience under the bondage of matter . . . This force, once liberated, begins immediately to displace the sluggish force, the sluggish nervous energy, and to open and perfect those nerve centres or minor brains atrophied by disuse, and which, when regenerated,

reveal to man super-physical states of consciousness and knowledge of his lost sovereignty over nature. This force manifests on the physical plane by passing through the ganglia of the sympathetic nervous system, and thence up the spine to the brain, where its currents unite to build up the deathless body. In its passage from one ganglion, or chakra, to another its voltage is raised, and it awakens and is augmented by the power peculiar to each ganglion which it dominates. These centres are the 'concave mirrors' whose property it is to concentrate the fire of the world, or divine solar energy which proceeds from the Sun behind the sun. In the cerebro-spinal system there are many centres awaiting regeneration. Hence the spinal cord is the relaxed string whose pitch must be raised by the exaltation of the element of fire which is in us. Knowledge as to the development of this power or force has been sacredly guarded in all ages, lest man through ignorance should employ it to his destruction. The soul who renounces the 'world', i.e. all personal ambition, and who seeks by selfless service of his fellow-beings to obey the divine spirit within, may, without external teaching or assistance, evoke this flame and achieve unaided a knowledge of nature's secrets and mysteries. He who seeks divine knowledge will surely find it, for the God in man ever strives to render unto him his lost birthright. No sincere effort to solve this mystery passes unheeded by the 'silent watcher' within. But unless with selfless purpose and governed by the spiritual principle within, this fire will intensify the lower passions and cause the man to become a destructive force, working contrary to the law of nature.

The philosophers hold that man is fourfold in nature, having four bodies corresponding to the four elements. The physical body is interpenetrated by a body of finer matter, vibrating at a higher rate, in which emotions and passions register, as I have said already, called the 'water body'; the earth and water bodies are interpenetrated by a body composed of still finer matter, vibrating at a still higher rate, the mental body in which thoughts register, called the 'air body'; and informing these three bodies and engendering them is the divine spark, the potential solar body or God in man existing, as it were, in embryo, awaiting the evolution of the earth, water and air bodies, to sustain the flow of the solar force which shall stimulate and perfect its divine unfoldment.[98]

Referring to human aspirations towards 'conscious immortality', Dunlop repeatedly evokes two other organs—the pineal and the pituitary glands. He describes their functions as follows. The pineal gland, situated behind the third brain cavity, 'is the organ of divine thought *per se*, and, when touched by the vibrating light of kundalini, it becomes the centre of spiritual intelligence and illumination'.[99] The pituitary gland on the other hand 'is the organ of psychic vision and . . . it should be the servant of the pineal gland'.[99]

In a slightly different context, Dunlop points out that philosophers of ancient times considered the pineal and the pituitary glands to be the seat of the spirit. He explains how this spiritual force creates a kind of bridge of light along the vertebral column, running from the gland of Luschka, through the terminal filament, spinal cord, medulla, arbor vitae, pons, reaching right up to the two cerebral glands.

Naturally the esoteric pupil can very easily succumb to a kind of spiritual materialism if consideration of physiological and occult-physiological correlations becomes too one-sided. This may well be the reason why Rudolf Steiner, whilst himself frequently referring to such correlatives at an earlier period, in his later lectures and works rarely paid much attention to them.[100] The first priority is to grasp the spiritual in its own right, irrespective of the phenomena which may accompany it on the physical level. Only then can it become clear that the 'accompanying phenomena' are also of a 'spiritual' nature. Consequently it becomes possible to free oneself from the illusion of interpreting them in a purely material sense.

However, it can certainly be of great value to take a closer look into the secret alchemical processes unfolding within 'the temple' during the 'divine service'. This must be especially true for those who have embarked upon the spiritual path of Anthroposophy. For the expression 'temple of the body' becomes full of meaning to anyone who has freed himself from the above-mentioned illusion. It was this consideration alone which could justify the preceding expositions concerning the function of the various physical organs. Of course, when considering the relationship between the two we should never forget that 'function precedes organism' and that at all events the first task which has to be undertaken is to purify the thought process for 'when the thought is pure, desire is likewise pure' and this results in 'the purification of the temple'[101] as a natural consequence. Indeed the correct assessment and the most practical use of knowledge concerning these occult-physiological correlatives can only be made if this purification has already to a large extent been achieved.

Dunlop himself is all too aware of the fact that this direct 'path of the body', as one might term it, can only be trodden without danger when quite specific conditions are fulfilled. And the fundamental condition presupposed here is that the pupil has, from the very outset, spiritualized his relationship to all that is of a bodily nature. Thus, once the word 'temple' has been integrated into our understanding and attitude to life then 'no act of the body will be profaned, but inspired by the strength and beauty of the divine consciousness . . . Personal considerations must be transcended, and everything done "to the glory of God". Alas! how meaningless the beautiful mystery-language has become!'[102]

This last emphatic exclamation almost has something of a lament about it. It is illuminating for us in this context as it hints at an important fact concerning all these descriptions of the 'path of the body': they are firmly rooted in the mystery culture of ancient times. And, indeed, the circumstance that Dunlop is not merely evoking external tradition here but speaking out of the deepest wellsprings of his own experience is itself a matter which will be developed later in this book.

The dangers of this path of initiation, in so far as it is a 'path of the body', are outlined by Dunlop himself as follows:

> The subtle connection between the higher brain centres and the generative organs, through the spinal cord, and the sympathetic system, clearly indicates the dangers and difficulties to be undertaken in the work of regeneration, and suggests to the student why so many mystical schools have been wrecked on the rock of phallicism. The three vital airs (sushumna, pingala, ida) are controlled and guided by will, or its reflection—desire. The airs must be 'cool', otherwise the delicate and sensitive organs in the brain are in danger of being 'scorched', and disease results in some form. The Leyden jar of the

> divine fire cannot be discharged with impunity. To the daring soul, however, the 'witness' is always present to guide, and the warnings, so gently given when personal desire 'heats' the 'airs', will lead, if they are promptly heeded, to safe exercise of power, and 'the door of Brahma'.[103]

Whether such signs are heeded at the crucial moment is, however, the question which is raised upon this path, today more than ever indeed.

In 1916, Dunlop's simple diagnosis of the catastrophic conditions of his time was already this, that 'it is surely obvious that the present confusion of caste and all the blighting conditions of human life can be attributed to misuse of the god-given energy within the body . . . The power of the holy paraclete cannot be exercised by man while he is gross and sensual, when his mind is constantly filled with images of impure desire.'[103] Consequently at the end of this chapter on initiation Dunlop states clearly that for most people the occult centres in the body can (and should) only be *indirectly* activated, i.e. only after or *via* the purification of the thought and feeling life. 'Spiritual forces, for the majority of humanity, can only be awakened by introspective meditation, by control of thought, by the ability to concentrate the mind upon abstract conceptions to the exclusion of irrelevant ideas.'[103] It is only *after* this that 'the action of the Paraclete conquers the life-centres.'[103]

'Drinking of Oblivion'

Let us mention another small work of Dunlop's at this point, entitled *The Path of Knowledge*. No indication is given of the year of publication but apparently it did not come out before 1919. It is a light volume of about 70 pages, dedicated 'To my friend AE' and in one of its footnotes we find the first reference to one of Rudolf Steiner's works, *Occult Science*, which by then had been translated into English.

The quality of numerous passages to be found in the two final chapters of this book gives clear evidence as to the degree of certainty and independence with which Dunlop's individuality already seemed to have covered considerable distances on the path of occult knowledge. Here again he refers to the necessity, at the beginning of the path, of developing thought that 'transcends all sense perception'. Once this has been attained to some extent it is possible to enter 'the mental world'.

But for Dunlop it is of fundamental importance that personal independence and individual initiative be totally preserved in the process. For the human being has to make his own way across the 'trackless spaces' of another world and leave his *own traces* behind him there. Furthermore, 'the light of the mind becomes the Sun of the mental cosmos and the currents of the thought of other minds are seen as roads which have been made by the world's great thinkers. These currents of thought are the tracks of the mental world along which the minds of men have moved.'[104] And at this point a surprising reference is made to the need for independence and powers of spiritual initiative on the part of the aspirant to initiation:

> *The aspiring mind, however, must turn aside from these beaten tracks*. It must soar upward and still upward and by its own light illumine the path and thereby create other currents of thought for the assistance of lesser minds who follow it.[104]

Whilst access to the mental world is gained by means of 'thought *per se*', one can only enter the 'spiritual world of knowledge' (for the two are evidently not identical) by true discovery and 'realization of the Self'. For 'when a man knows who and what he is, he discovers the world of knowledge.' In terms of the previously outlined cosmology, this corresponds to the transition from Sagittarius to Capricorn.

Once he has become 'a conscious light' he can begin to 'shine through this heavy, dark physical body'[105] and as such he is more and more able to shine through his various bodies, becoming 'conscious of the world which each represents; he impresses on the materialized life-matter the signature of his true Nature and causes it to be stimulated and to reach out towards the light. Man shining through his form perceives its unreality, and realizes that it had previously deluded him into identifying himself with it.'[105]

In this way man is able to attain what Dunlop calls 'conscious immortality'. And in the human being who has found the way to the very core of his true individuality 'invulnerable love and power' are born. As an 'immortal' he 'sees the heart of each thing, and *is* that thing completely.'[106]

As Rudolf Steiner was to point out several years later in Penmaenmawr, in 1923, the mystery teachers of ancient times had the task of bringing the unconscious knowledge and experience that every human being possesses, whilst he is asleep, to consciousness; for the modern mystery teacher, however, it is not a matter of bringing that nocturnal knowledge but rather the subconscious prenatal knowledge that every human being bears within himself, into the sphere of waking consciousness. Rudolf Steiner observes that in this sense spiritual science does not want to bring anything 'new' as such, but 'only' to be there as a stimulant, that we may reactivate our capacities of memory concerning that prenatal knowledge which has since become unconscious.

But where and when, we might well ask, was this prenatal knowledge extinguished and how was it obscured from human consciousness? Was it during the embryonic phase or earlier? Once again a somewhat surprising insight comes to us from the cosmology based on the zodiac, with which Dunlop was so intimately acquainted. At the beginning of the chapter on initiation in his book *The Path of Attainment*, he connects this state of forgetfulness of prenatal knowledge with a certain fixed-star constellation. And this is how he describes the processes which take place during the incarnation of the human being:

> The starry cup, placed between Cancer and the Lion, is a symbol of this mystic truth, signifying that descending souls first experience intoxication in that part of the Zodiacal heavens through the influx of matter. Hence oblivion, the companion of intoxication, begins silently to creep into the recesses of the soul; for, if souls retained in their descent to bodies the memory of divine concerns of which they

> were conscious in the heavens, there would be no dissension among men about divinity. But all, indeed, in descending, drink of oblivion, though some more and others less. On this account, though truth is not apparent to all men of the earth, all exercise their opinions about it, *because the defect of memory is the origin of opinion*. But those discover most who drink least of oblivion, because they easily remember what they had known before in the heavens.[107]

Dunlop himself seems to have been one of those who had drunk least of oblivion and for whom true 'spirit-recollection' was easier to attain than for those who had emptied the cup and drunk full measure.

4

THE MEETING WITH RUDOLF STEINER

The first meeting brought instant recognition: here is the knower; the Initiate, the bearer of the spirit to his age. D.N.D.

Prelude

D.N. Dunlop had first 'set eyes' on Rudolf Steiner in 1906 or thereabouts. At that time few of the latter's lectures and works had been translated and made available to the English public. Dunlop, who mastered little German at the time, could only have begun a methodical study of Rudolf Steiner's thought some few years after this.

In December 1912 Baron Walleen, a long-standing pupil of Rudolf Steiner, was invited to give two lectures in the 'Light on the Path Lodge' in London. During this period the German Section of the Theosophical Society had begun to grow apart from Annie Besant's Adyar-centred lead on account of the 'humbug' concerning the 'Star in the East'. So Walleen chose precisely this moment to try and clear up certain misunderstandings. He did this by presenting his listeners with a detailed picture of Steiner's view of evolution and especially of his Christology. On both occasions D.N. Dunlop acted as chairman, introducing Walleen to the public and speaking himself at some length after the lectures. Deeply moved at the end of the second one he asked Walleen 'to tell Dr. Steiner that in England we are ready to receive this teaching with open arms . . . to discuss it freely and consider it . . . find out what there is good in it and take that and incorporate that into ourselves . . .' These words bear beautiful testimony to the great openness he felt towards Rudolf Steiner's ideas with which he could then have been scarcely acquainted. We have seen that in the appendix of his book *The Path of Knowledge* Dunlop refers for the first time to Rudolf Steiner's *Occult Science*. This book was no doubt among the first that Dunlop 'put to the test'. Perhaps the photographic portrait of the author repeatedly drew his attention in between readings—as was certainly the case with George Adams.

However, Dunlop had already been afforded amply documented experience of error and deviation within the Theosophical Movement and above all within the Theosophical Society. He was therefore in no hurry to arrive at a final assessment of Rudolf Steiner's work and personality. For 'the manifest absurdities and trivialities filling Theosophical literature, above all from the year 1907 onwards, gave rise to a natural caution when Rudolf Steiner's work first came into my hands.' (DS) Dunlop was quite determined not to be overruled by any spontaneous feelings of natural agreement. The lessons he had learnt inside theosophical domains were all too present and fresh within his mind. He had indeed soon registered the clear sensation that Rudolf Steiner's writings were, in contrast to everything that he had met with up till now within the field of theosophical literature, 'utterly different in tone and content'. However, he also had the definite feeling that 'they must be approached with reserve and balance'. There is something in Dunlop's attitude that reminds us of the mountain-goat ('Capricorn') that only ventures to jump off its rock when it is inwardly sure of its new ground; for years he looks over the anthroposophical terrain, then, one day, he steps out onto it with a firm, decisive tread and not the slightest trace of ill-considered hastiness. For whoever has entertained within his soul certain thoughts and feelings of eternity will know how to *take his time*. And whoever, beyond the reach of time, actually *has time* will also know the secret of the 'right moment' and how to grasp it when it comes.

Alongside, and despite his numerous business engagements and responsibilities, Dunlop continued to work untiringly during the years from 1918 to 1922 for the theosophical cause. In 1918 he published another book, *The Science of Immortality*. It contains several revised lectures, some of which had already been printed in *The Path*; other chapters are concerned with the immortal soul as well as with the function of the senses in their relationship to particular spiritual faculties. In the last case exercises are proposed for the development of certain spiritual capacities, and Dunlop gives his assurance that 'by engaging yourself in these exercises with the object of developing, through mind, your powers as a spiritual being, you may attain spiritual knowledge and get rid of the desire for psychic experiences and new sensations'.[108]

And with regard to the earlier-mentioned problem concerning the 'Masters', Dunlop has this to say: 'By practice of the exercises which develop man as a thinker, as a centre of pure Intelligence, you will come in time to the knowledge that the Master is to be found nowhere outside your own heart.'[108] In view of Dunlop's imminent meeting with 'an Initiate in the physical body', it is important for the overall picture to understand the significant role of just this last aspect. And if we also recall the final image which presented itself to him during his decisive visionary experience in Dublin it becomes quite clear just how 'well-prepared' Dunlop was as he went towards his meeting with Rudolf Steiner. At any rate, it is only to be expected from a human being who has found the 'Master' in his own heart, that he will be able to meet an initiate on the external plane in an entirely different way from one who, if he seeks a 'guide' at all, looks for him exclusively in the world outside himself. The latter is much more likely to give up or suppress the further development of his inner independence, even to be misled perhaps by some form or other of misconstrued 'devotion'.

In 1918, an anthroposophical study group appeared with Dunlop at the head of it. The 'Human Freedom Group', as they called themselves, met every week in order to study Rudolf Steiner's works and lectures. Now by this time Dunlop's professional activities had become remarkably wide.[109] So it was only 'in the midst of many business concerns' that he consented to give an opening lecture at the annual conference of the Braille and Servers of the Blind League on 31 May 1919. The theme he chose to speak of was 'duty'. He developed it in a very simple yet profound manner by trying to make clear to his audience that 'duty' is nothing other than 'crystallized karma'. The whole lecture can be condensed into two ideas expressed by Dunlop in these terms: 'Every single man in the world at any given moment knows what his duty is,' and, 'Be, in each moment, ready to perform the duty of that moment.' In the printed version of this rather beautiful lecture Dunlop explains why he choose this subject: 'I wanted to lift the idea of Duty away from the rather pious atmosphere with which it is often associated and to restore some of the ancient inspiration which saw in the daily round of tasks accomplished the fulfilment of Divine Law.' At the very end of the lecture Dunlop includes a personal anecdote which, in its simplicity, is truly moving, revealing that besides his many other qualities he also possessed that of simple kindheartedness. 'I remember once, when I felt the skies were as brass, the world empty, and everything seemed to conspire against me, that a little child in trouble came across my path. In trying to make that little child happy, the skies became clear blue and the joy of life broke over me again like the rising of the sun over grey hills.'[110]

To see the great and eternal things of human existence, even in the smallest duties of everyday life; not to let oneself be prevented, even by serious maladies or infirmities, from remaining inwardly flexible, mobile and lively: such, it seems, were the thoughts, feelings and impulses that Dunlop wished to impart to those particular listeners in order to help them on their way. In 1920 another little book came out: *Nature Spirits and the Spirits of the Elements*. It contains the third 'Blavatsky Lecture'—an annual address which had been instituted two years previously as a result of an idea emanating from Dunlop himself—which was delivered at the annual convention of the English Section on 22 May 1920. Both lecture and book must have been received with great enthusiasm for only one year later it ran into a second impression. In this lecture the term 'nature-spirit' is used to describe elementary beings in the widest sense. The term 'elemental being' on the other hand designates those beings especially active within the human body.

The basic tenor underlying the whole of the piece can be expressed in the occult maxim: 'Everything that exists, is, has been, or will be Man.'[111] Thus 'the most advanced of the lower Nature-Spirits look forward to the time when man will perform for them that which they most desire, that is, the imparting to them of his immortal nature, and when they can in exchange render him service of which he will be conscious.'[112]

Having thus set out the theme Dunlop goes on to describe the action of the elemental beings in the human body. These beings are guided and controlled by the 'human elemental' who is in touch with the body via the nervous system. In the final instance all natural processes are of a 'magical' kind. They only appear to be 'natural' to the human being because he is surrounded by them, or rather their physical effects, every day of his life. Thus, to speak of 'natural laws' (if one does not bear in mind that these 'laws' exist and work as essential powers in nature) must, on a deeper level, appear as pure thoughtlessness. If the human being desires to enter into contact with the 'nature-spirits' then he must first get to know the laws concerning the activity and function of the 'human elemental' within himself. However, it must be noted that, whilst all the organs in the human body are connected to one another by means of the sympathetic nervous system (where a kind of interaction between 'inner' and 'outer' elemental beings takes place), the human mind works through the central nervous system. Of course, in an undeveloped individual the conscious mind hardly manages to penetrate further than the central nerve of that part of the spinal cord where the cervical vertebra are to be found. But in order to enter into conscious relationship with the elementals (both in one's own body and in nature) the human being must be able to extend his consciousness throughout the whole of his central nervous system. It is only then, we learn, that thinking assumes a constant and continuous form and the human being becomes able to truly grasp both his vocation within nature and the significance of this vocation for nature and her beings as a whole.

Dunlop then goes on to touch upon the function of the elementals within medicine. He observes at the very outset that medicaments are very often ineffective for the simple reason that, generally speaking, medicine is not yet a really exact science. Thus 'vegetable drugs are gathered irrespective of the elemental influence prevailing at the time of gathering'. However, this latter has to be taken into account by reason of the fact that all medicinal effects are produced by bringing about an interaction and direct contact between nature-spirits on the one side and elementals in the sick organ, or organic system, on the other. For 'the medicine does not make the cure; it simply allows the Nature-Spirits to come into touch with the Human Elemental and through that into touch with the organs or systems in the human body. By setting up this reciprocal action, the adjustment is made between nature and man. This is the basis of the science of Homoeopathy.'[113]

And now Dunlop develops one particular motif which he has already touched upon: the purpose of this collaboration between the human being and the elementals is 'the preparing of the human elemental in order that in another planetary incarnation it may reach the human stage and become endowed with mind.'[114] However, this goal can only be reached when a high level of moral development has been achieved simultaneously. So long as that is not the case the occult laws, under whose governance the nature-spirits stand, must, for the greater part, remain concealed. For,

> . . . what would happen if one man or a Government should be able to operate forces which are at least as far above those working in the present aeroplane, submarine, mortar guns, poison gas tubes and gas bombs, as these instruments are above a simple club and a stone? What would become of human civilization? *One great air Elemental, with its hosts of lower spirits, could wipe out an army of men, destroy a countryside, efface factories and institutions*. Formal declaration of war is not necessary to start the destruction. One man could do that in the midst of peace, merely to vent his spleen or reap the fruits of his rule of terror.[115]

Certain aspects of black magic and alchemy, as well as the phenomenon of possession, are also touched upon in their relationship to the elementals. Once again, at the end, Dunlop comes back to the task incumbent on the human being—to release the elementals from their 'bewitched' state. This means not only the hosts of beings that flow through the human senses, but also all those connected with his various moods and states of mind—his indolence or assiduity, his optimism, pessimism, etc.

The overall vision that is given here is, then, of a great

complexity of interactions between the human being and the ocean of elementary life—'the waters under the earth', as the Rosicrucians called it.

The motif of deliverance or redemption, which is again alluded to and further developed at the end of the book, will doubtless remind any reader who is well acquainted with Rudolf Steiner's works and lectures on this theme of the second lecture in the cycle he gave in Düsseldorf on the Hierarchies.[116] It seems that now, at the very latest, Dunlop has reached the phase in his testing of Rudolf Steiner's thought where he can incorporate what seems plausible to him into his own thinking and even into his public functions and activities. In this particular case, he does not refer explicitly to Rudolf Steiner; however, only ill-will could possibly interpret this as cloaking some form of partial plagiarism. One has to be quite clear about the circumstances in which this lecture was given—only seven years after the exclusion of the German Section from the Theosophical Society. Seen from this angle one is bound to marvel at the skill Dunlop employed in putting forward to these theosophists certain thoughts perfectly concordant with those of the greatest 'apostate' of the Theosophical Society!

Thus, this little book possesses something of a Janus character. On the one hand the subject is treated on the basis of personal experience (employing sources more or less easy to recognize and locate). On the other, shining through all this, we perceive quite clearly, and for the first time, thoughts stemming from Rudolf Steiner's Anthroposophy. Finally, and this is again in itself well worth noting, it is the last extensive piece of writing of a spiritual-scientific nature that Dunlop was to publish during the whole of his lifetime.

*

On 14 December 1920, D.N. Dunlop applied to become a member of the Anthroposophical Society. The person he chose to sponsor him was Harry Collison. They had known each other for quite a long time already and had learnt to mutually respect their somewhat different appreciation of Theosophy as well as their individual approach to Anthroposophy. On 31 January 1917, we encounter Collison in London, in the premises of the H.P.B. Lodge of which Dunlop was soon to become President. According to the lecture/programme published in *The Vahan*, on that particular evening Collison had chosen to speak about 'The Occult Philosophy of Dr. Steiner'. He had probably been invited by Dunlop himself who, in his characteristic open-mindedness, had already given a warm welcome to Baron Walleen at the 'Light on the Path' Lodge several years before. In the meantime, Collison had withdrawn from the Theosophical Society on account of the official exclusion of the German Section on 7 March 1913 and become a member of the Anthroposophical Society which had been founded shortly before the expulsion. He had translated several of Rudolf Steiner's works into English, including the Mystery Plays. The configuration Dunlop-Collison, which now meets us on the face of Dunlop's application form, marks a new stage in their relationship—a new collaboration within the Anthroposophical Society and Movement, and one which will not be altogether without certain difficulties and even tragic elements at times.

As one would expect, Dunlop still retained his membership of the Theosophical Society. Indeed, a good year afterwards, on 1 April 1922, when he was elected Treasurer of the Theosophical Society, he still felt he could accept this post. He did not believe in rash confrontations or changing fronts on the spur of the moment. On the contrary, his external actions were always subordinated to the principle: do what is possible wherever it is possible. And in the long term it will not have been without significance for the Theosophical Movement that a personality like Dunlop did not immediately break off all ties but maintained, above all, the human relationships which he had made.

'I had always longed to hear of the cosmic mysteries connected with Christ and His incarnation,' Dunlop wrote in 1935 in his brief autobiographical sketch. This desire, voiced by the 66-year-old man, had its origins in the experience on the Isle of Arran. In the first part of this book we saw him there, as a 9-year-old boy, proclaiming the Logos in enthusiastic tones to his 12 young friends. Or we may call to mind the commentary on *The Gospel of St John*, especially the Prologue, which was given in the last part of this book. 'Here, in Anthroposophy', Dunlop writes, 'was the first indication that rang true.' (DS) 'Rang true'? There is no question here of spontaneous conviction and immediate acceptance but only a serious consideration of something new—and nothing more. Indeed, during this period he was again beset by all the former reservations he had had towards the one-sided and too often dogmatic attitudes he had encountered in the exponents of theosophical doctrines. 'Was Anthroposophy, after all, based merely on the assertions of psychic faculties as yet unproven?' And he had great reservations as to whether 'room would be left in Rudolf Steiner's teachings for the exercise of that "healthy human reason" which now seemed to have deserted so many thousands of Theosophists'. This is an obvious allusion to the Krishnamurti affair—which in both its preceding history and after-effects brought all the obscurities, confusions and absurdities within the Theosophical Movement to a certain point of culmination, especially with regard to the interpretation of the Christ-event. Furthermore, Dunlop's demand that 'healthy human reason' be seen as thoroughly applicable within the sphere of occultism demonstrates an important point: he belongs to those who, beyond any kind of one-sided leaning to intellectualism on the one hand or to mysticism on the other, want to tread the path of the *active spiritualization of the intellect*—that path which is in keeping with the scientific training and general disposition of modern Western man.

One criterion of vital importance concerning Dunlop's assessment of Anthroposophy remains to be mentioned—*its practical applicability*. This is the criterion *par excellence* of a Westerner: as soon as he has accepted an idea, he will want to know immediately: 'how can it be put into practice?' In Dunlop's words: 'Was this new spiritual teaching capable not only of theoretical but also of *practical* application to human life and activity, to art, to science, in all its branches, to therapy, education, religion, economics, industrial and social life?'

However, even if all these great questions could be answered positively, another one would still remain, itself the most imperative: 'And Rudolf Steiner himself?—that was the greatest question of all!'

No amount of studying, even over years and years, could have brought him the answer to *that* particular question—all the more so since 'the overwhelming wish' had been born in him during his studies of Blavatsky's works (in the company of AE and his other Dublin friends) 'to meet an Initiate in the physical body, to be able to recognize, here on Earth, a *knower* of spiritual truth, and then to take my share in spreading this truth for the "well-being of humanity".' It is significant that Dunlop's motivation was not born of any kind of impatient mystical curiosity, but inspired by spiritual knowledge—the conviction that there are indeed 'Masters', individualities, who have evolved far beyond the normal degree of human evolution and accomplishment. Hence the desire to meet one of them *incarnate*. This wish was of that rare kind described by Rudolf Steiner in his book *Knowledge of Higher Worlds—How is it achieved?* Education of the life of wishes is especially necessary in the process of occult development. This does not mean that we should have no wishes; we must wish for anything that we are to attain, and a wish will always tend to be fulfilled if backed by a particular force. This force is derived from right knowledge. 'Do not wish at all before you have recognized what is right in any particular domain—that is one of the golden rules for the pupil. The wise man first learns to know the laws of the world and then his wishes become powers which prove their efficacy.'[117]

Dunlop's desire to meet an initiate in the physical body was, from the very beginning, linked to a particular motive: to be able to serve both his fellow men and the world as a whole in a more effective manner. And it was precisely this element, standing beyond all personal considerations, which would sooner or later inevitably attract its fulfilment. Thus, the needle of the inner compass had already been pointing for some time towards a meeting with Rudolf Steiner; the whole orientation of Dunlop's deepest aspirations demonstrate this point. However, several years were yet to pass before the time was 'ripe'.

The very manner in which Dunlop advanced, step by step, and with the greatest possible calm, towards this meeting, is a sure sign of his spiritual maturity. The following comment is revealing: 'I knew that really deep acceptance of a new form of knowledge must always be an act of will—not only of mind and feeling.' Thus speaks the esoteric pupil of the *West*. We have already seen, from a previous chapter concerning a meditational form of magic, just how much importance Dunlop attached to this kind of will-element permeated by spiritual knowledge. It was this selfsame force which enabled him to approach this meeting as though it were a wonderful kind of experiment. From studying the works of Rudolf Steiner he had formed an idea of the essential nature and being of this individuality; this meeting would *show* him whether it corresponded to reality. For Dunlop realized 'how easily human beings may be carried away by the glamour of a great personality'. In his theosophical phase he had had ample opportunity to observe this fact. 'I was studying Rudolf Steiner's works continually, but I knew that no final decision was possible for me until in his actual presence I could perceive whether the undoubted greatness indicated by his seership expressed itself too through him as an human being, as a man among men.' And a final word sums up the basic tendency of the Westerner: 'In the West we want to "see for ourselves".'

A Remarkable Meeting

W.J. Stein and E.C. Merry both reported the description Dunlop gave them of the first meeting. George Adams spoke of it too on one occasion, adding a few important details.[118] Finally, Dunlop himself described the meeting in the short sketch he gave of his life in 1935 with that significant succinctness so characteristic of his manner.

George Adams places the meeting between D.N. Dunlop and Rudolf Steiner in the spring of 1922. For the first time since 1913—

the long period of absence was due to the war—Rudolf Steiner was once more staying in England during that spring. The immediate reason for his visit was an invitation from the 'New Ideals in Education Committee' in the context of the Shakespeare Birthday Festival in Stratford-upon-Avon. Both before and after lecturing in Stratford, Rudolf Steiner also spoke in London. The first occasion was on 14 April 1922 after another lecture in the Hague on the previous day.

According to both Stein and Merry, the businessman and leading industrialist Josef van Leer acted as intermediary and interpreter on this occasion—at least this was the role he believed he should play given the fact that Rudolf Steiner spoke hardly any English and Dunlop very little German. Van Leer 'tried to explain in a long speech who Dunlop was. But it seems that Rudolf Steiner had already made up his mind about his vis-à-vis.' (St)

At this moment, unobtrusively—for van Leer evidently perceived nothing at all of this—Rudolf Steiner grasped Dunlop's hand from under the side of the table and held it fast 'for many minutes'. (DS)

Dunlop must have experienced this as a kind of liberation from a long period of prudent reservations and patient trial; at least one can sense from his own account that he felt a kind of relief and release within his inner being:

> But the first meeting brought instant recognition: here is the knower, the Initiate, the bearer of the Spirit to his age. The human relationship was established immediately: a clasp of the hand which lasted for many minutes; a conversation which while it took its course in ordinary language seemed to lie in a realm of understanding infinitely deeper, and was filled with an undescribable sweetness and warmth. I felt as though the meeting had been—as indeed Rudolf Steiner himself once hinted—of the nature of a re-union after years, maybe lives, of wandering and seeking. I came away from that first meeting, and from others, with my heart on fire with thankfulness that a quest had found fulfilment. (DS)

In order to appreciate the peculiar stamp and signature of this encounter it is advisable to visualize this scene again and again; one will then perceive how something of the unique character of this human relationship already comes to expression in the very first meeting on the physical plane—in all its extraordinary circumstances and details.

*

On 1 April 1922, Dunlop had taken up the office of treasurer entrusted to him by the English Section of the Theosophical Society. At the beginning of May he resigned this office and withdrew from the Theosophical Society. The two events were separated by the period between 14 and 24 April when he met Rudolf Steiner for the first time. This constellation of dates and events raises certain questions. Is it possible that the same man who, in his innermost being, had always been opposed to any kind of change of allegiance, who knew, furthermore, from years of experience in the Theosophical Society 'how easily human beings may be carried away by the glamour of a great personality' (DS) could have suddenly lost his head on meeting Rudolf Steiner? Was he himself, for the first time, 'carried away by the glamour of a great personality' that he should thus from one day to the next have turned his back upon the Theosophical Society? Given the image of Dunlop that has emerged from the preceding chapters of this book and judging on the basis of the biographical facts encountered there, there is nothing whatsoever from a characterological point of view to justify such a deduction. So then what happened? Let us attempt to gain a somewhat clearer image of this constellation of events. To do so we shall have to take up the few facts that have come to light since then and combine them with that spiritual faculty which Goethe described as 'exact imagination' (*exakte Phantasie*). For here we are dealing with one of those symptomatic phenomena that the historian often comes across. If he is a purely pragmatic type of chronicler then he must pass over all such points in silence. The true historian, however, will also undertake to illuminate precisely the areas *between* certain facts by means of an exact form of 'historical imagination'.

The first days after his meeting with Rudolf Steiner must have left Dunlop in a deep state of shock—shock resulting from knowledge. Like a thunderbolt the recognition must have come to him: this was the man Annie Besant excluded from the Theosophical Society just 10 years ago! She sent away the most significant Initiate that had ever come to work in this Society! 'I disagreed with the action by which she (Mrs Besant) robbed the Theosophical Society of the invaluable co-operation of Dr. Steiner.' These are the words we find in Dunlop's letter of resignation, as quoted in the British monthly *Theosophy* of October 1922. And he continues: 'How much the Theosophical Society has suffered from her action, it is impossible to estimate.' Dunlop had certainly disapproved of the president's action at the time, but now after his first meeting with Rudolf Steiner, it suddenly became clear to him what this had meant for the Theosophical Society—spiritually speaking it had been left out in the cold!

No doubt the newly appointed treasurer of the English Section had already told his theosophical friends about his meeting with Rudolf Steiner; and no doubt he had done so with that characteristically powerful enthusiasm which he felt towards everything worthy of veneration and respect. Had it not been a serious mistake to have excluded Dr Steiner, he might have remarked to his friends. Would it not be sensible and indeed vital to attempt to win him back again—or at least to recommend most warmly the study of his works to all serious theosophists? The man *has* most definitely got something to say!

But by and large among his theosophical friends Dunlop will have met with complacent and even scornful rejection of Rudolf Steiner's teaching and person. 'We are ready to receive his teaching with open arms and to discuss it freely,' Dunlop had asked Baron Walleen to tell Rudolf Steiner 10 years before. But now he had to concede that the vast majority of theosophists, when faced with the proposition, at least inwardly, turned their backs on him. According to a candid report published in the June 1922 issue of *The Canadian Theosophist*, Dunlop pointed out in his letter of resignation that 'the field of service of free and independent members is restricted in every direction by the attitude of those who use their "freedom" to circumscribe every influence but the one'. In this context 'the one' can only refer to the Besant-Theosophy proceeding from Adyar. And in the same report these words concerning Dunlop are to be found: 'He leaves the Society because he thinks, in spite of official declarations, freedom of opinion is not permitted, and that even the leading members of the Society are unwilling to have anyone think otherwise than as they dictate. He says this in direct fashion and uses names.' If Dunlop's *complete* letter of resignation ever comes to light we shall probably be able to learn a few more details about what actually happened. But none of these will possibly give a more essential explanation of Dunlop's motivation than the one given in a letter to the members by Emily Lutyens (published in *Theosophy*, July 1922). According to Lutyens, Dunlop explicitly referred to the '*false teaching of the physical return of the Christ*'.

The encounter with Steiner had spontaneously persuaded D.N. Dunlop of the necessity 'to seek a new spiritual impulse in fields other than the Society which was once the repository of such high promise'. The Theosophical Society suddenly appeared to him to be like a 'shell', and the living substance which had once resided in the great soul of her who had founded it had now, in Dunlop's eyes, passed on to Rudolf Steiner.

Everything points towards the conclusion that Dunlop held his withdrawal from the Theosophical Society to be in full accordance with what Helena Petrovna Blavatsky would have wanted—as pursuing her real interests and *present* intentions in fact. Indeed, it is almost as though he heard her whispering to him from the other side of the threshold, 'Let the dead bury their dead—I have moved on! And I live on there, where Rudolf Steiner leads the way!' Or should we assign it purely to the work of chance that this long-standing, ardent admirer of H.P.B. and her mission in modern times should have chosen to make his withdrawal from the Theosophical Society *on 8 May*? For this is the very day, 'White Lotus Day', that for the previous 30 years had been celebrated the whole world over as the commemoration day of the founder of the Theosophical Society. It is the anniversary of the death of Helena Petrovna Blavatsky.

*

In the late autumn of the same year Rudolf Steiner was already back in England. He spent a good week in London speaking on the following subjects: 'Experiences of the Human Soul During Sleep and After Death in the Spiritual World'; 'Exact Knowledge of the Supersensible Worlds According to Anthroposophical Spiritual Science'; 'Christ from the Point of View of Anthroposophy'; and 'Questions Concerning Education and Teaching'[119]—a very wide spectrum given the relatively short space of time. There was a period of three days (between the first and second lectures in London) in which Steiner gave no lectures at all. It would probably have been during these days that he visited the sick and bedridden Dunlop at his home (as he recalls in the closing words of the lecture-cycle at Penmaenmawr on 31 August 1923). During this visit Dunlop acquainted Rudolf Steiner with the seeds of three ideas he was nurturing at the time. They were profoundly characteristic of his nature and also of his future contribution to the Anthroposophical Movement as a whole. Rudolf Steiner recalls how Dunlop 'was at that time completely filled with the idea, in the midst of all that had been achieved in such an admirable way for Anthroposophy, also to put forward before the whole world what actually constitutes the core of the Anthroposophical Movement as such. And he also told me that it was his particular idea to hold a Summer School in which the content of Anthroposophy, as expressed by the spoken word, together with what emanates from Anthroposophy as eurythmy, might be placed before the world.

'And he also expressed a third idea; however, as it was too great to be realized at the first attempt, it could not, of course, be put into practice immediately.'[120]

Penmaenmawr—Airs of the Mysteries

Dunlop's third idea had been to organize a number of public anthroposophical world conferences in various capitals of the world beginning with London. This could not be put into practice immediately; in fact it was only realized for the first time in the summer of 1928 and, indeed, in *this* form it has never since been repeated. So whilst this project had to wait Dunlop began making preparations for the realization of the two other impulses immediately after his talks with Rudolf Steiner in November. He had already gained a certain amount of experience in realizing projects of this kind pioneering the summer school idea during the period of his activities within the Theosophical Society. Part of the preparation consisted of choosing a *place* where the conference could be held. Choice was made of Penmaenmawr, on the Welsh coast not far from Anglesey, a rather insignificant-looking spot today, but at that time quite well visited. Penmaenmawr was, in a certain sense, 'well-prepared terrain' for as we have noted Dunlop had already envisaged this locality in connection with a theosophical summer school 12 years earlier.

Despite the catastrophe which occurred in Dornach at the turn of that year when the Goetheanum was destroyed by fire, Rudolf Steiner kept to his promise to participate in the planned summer school. Having finished the teacher training course at Ilkley, he arrived at Penmaenmawr on 18 August 1923 and began a new cycle of lectures on knowledge and initiation (later to be published in English under the title *The Evolution of Consciousness*).[121] It dealt with 'The Spiritual and Physical Development of the World and of Humanity in the Past, Present and Future from the Point of View of Anthroposophy'—a truly magnificent thematic complex entirely corresponding to Dunlop's explicit desire for the 'core' of Anthroposophy. In the first words of his opening address Rudolf Steiner referred to his 'particular joy and satisfaction' that 'Mr Dunlop's choice of theme' had afforded him. 'For,' he continued, 'it gives me the opportunity of connecting what Anthroposophy has to say concerning the present and near future with the very oldest wisdom and most ancient spiritual life of humanity.'[122]

Many are the remains of Druidical places of worship that can still be found today in the surroundings of Penmaenmawr and on the Isle of Anglesey. But this was not the only factor which enabled Rudolf Steiner to make a link with 'the oldest wisdom and most ancient spiritual life' of humanity. Another element which he emphasizes, both in the closing speech of this cycle and in a written report on this tour subsequently published in *Das Goetheanum*,[123] was the spiritual, atmospheric quality of this special place and its surroundings:

> If one looks here not only on the weavings of the outward materialistic atmosphere, but also on the prevailing soul-atmosphere, which permeates the air just as the human soul permeates a man's body, then in Penmaenmawr we find that this soul-element in the atmosphere is different from elsewhere. I will give just one example to make this clear.
>
> Suppose that in a certain region of the earth Imaginative cognition exerts itself . . . to call up Imaginations of what is really going on there. These Imaginations may be more or less easy or difficult to hold on to, for the possibility of retaining or quickly losing an Imagination in consciousness varies in different regions. Here we are in a region where Imaginations continue for a remarkably long time and so are able to grow intensely vivid.[124]

Rudolf Steiner draws attention here to the fact that it was precisely on account of this peculiarity that the Druids had sought out these places, and continues:

> Therefore, even from a spiritual viewpoint, one can find differentiations over the Earth. A map might be drawn painting in those places where, for Imaginative consciousness, there is no difficulty in holding Imaginations. Those regions where they soon pass away could be given a different colour, and we should get an extraordinarily interesting map of the Earth. We should need a particularly strong colour for the prevailing character of soul-atmosphere here . . .
>
> So I fully believe that those taking part in this lecture-course will be able to perceive here something of what I would call an elementary esoteric mood. It looks in at the windows, meets us on our walks, in fact is present in a quite different way from anywhere else.[124]

We should recall at this point that even during his theosophical phase the idea of a summer school had for Dunlop always been inseparably linked to another motive—that of creating true forms of spiritual community; in this respect too this elementary esoteric 'mood' must have been of importance for all those taking part.

Rudolf Steiner was therefore able to take up 'the most ancient spiritual life of humanity' in a very special way and add something to it. Of course this method of working with given realities pervaded *all* Rudolf Steiner's activity as a spiritual scientist—it was merely the other side of the fact that the elaboration of spiritual science itself is due entirely to the spiritual forces of the *individuality*. The two aspects are intrinsically and reciprocally related to one another. For if spiritual science were *exclusively* to work with the given realities of the past and present, it would scarcely be able to do more than retain or warm up old traditions. If, on the other hand, it were to be developed exclusively out of the recesses of the individuality then it would find no access to reality, or at least its spiritual content would have to be propped up everywhere from outside. Rudolf Steiner always sought to place the seed for the new within the old. This was possible now in Penmaenmawr to such a degree that the lecturer himself was deeply moved and full of gratitude. He even attached special importance to this cycle of lectures as occupying a pre-eminent place within the whole perspective of anthroposophical endeavour:

> So I am particularly grateful to the organizers of the course for having chosen an area where the esoteric may be said to meet one at every turn. It does so indeed elsewhere, but not with the same ease and directness. I am exceptionally grateful for the choice of this place, out of many possible for the holding of a course such as this. From the point of view which I have just expressed, this course may be said to take its place, in a wonderfully beautiful way in the whole evolution of the Anthroposophical Movement.[124]

The 'Core' of Anthroposophy

In the autumn of 1922, D.N. Dunlop had 'requested' Rudolf Steiner to expound on the central part, the core of Anthroposophy. This request found organic correspondence with one of the basic motivating forces behind Rudolf Steiner's activity during the whole of the following year. One need for instance only recall his lectures in Stuttgart in February 1923 in which he urged his listeners again and again not to forget the 'mother' herself—Anthroposophia[125]—out of sheer enthusiasm for the daughters. In the closing speech of the summer school, he took up this thread again:

> Whoever is capable, in a deeper sense, of understanding certain aspects of the human soul; and, more precisely, whoever is capable of verifying in a deeper sense the relationships that exist between a movement such as the anthroposophical one and everything which can arise from it within the world at large: for any such person it is clear that all other off-shoot movements can be correspondingly effective in the world only if that which is *central* to Anthroposophy really comes into its own . . . Never could I any more assure someone that it might happen with inner truth in the world that by bringing the educational movement into the front line this educational movement, as it has grown out of Anthroposophy, could itself be completely understood . . . The right thing in the truest sense of the word must be the opposite: that precisely through Anthroposophy itself, by cultivating the most central part of Anthroposophy, a real understanding for what has grown out of Anthroposophy arises, and specifically for the educational movement which is so important for the world. That is why Mr Dunlop found a straight path to my heart at the time when he said to me that the most important thing was to set out what must be the source of everything, and to put that before the cultivation of the 'daughter'-movements. This is what touched me in his words. I am bound to say, when I think back on just that conversation, that when one stands as I do, within the spiritual-scientific movement (which now happens to be called the Anthroposophical Movement), when one stands in it in the way I have to, then one can only impart that which one is able to give if and because it has been *requested*—that is requested in the right way.[126]

We cannot undertake to give a detailed report here of the way in which the 'core of Anthroposophy' came to expression in the various aspects of this summer school; nevertheless, a few essential points might be worth mentioning. From the very first lecture onwards the reader will no doubt be struck by the freshness and directness with which Rudolf Steiner so to speak 'grasps his spade' and digs straight down to the real base, the *methodical* foundations on which all the following results of spiritual-scientific research are built. Starting with a succinct description of everyday consciousness he describes the conditions for the development of an 'Imaginative' form of consciousness: the first step consists of 'finding the transition from a purely passive form of thought to an inner activity of thinking'. On this first step towards imaginative cognition everything depends upon 'never coming out of the energy which seeks the way over to this activity in thinking'. In this way, 'by dint of one's own activity', one's own thinking can gradually become 'an organ of touch for the soul . . . so that one may feel oneself inside it, as if one were thinking in the same way that we walk, that we grasp or touch; so that one knows one is living in a real being, not just in ordinary thinking which merely creates images, but in a reality, in the soul's organ of touch which one has oneself totally become.'

Here we have a basic characterization of the 'core' of Anthroposophy: it consists less of assimilating (or promulgating) certain highly significant or 'central' *contents* of anthroposophical knowledge than in energetically training the will in the use of the instrument of cognition itself. What is essential is not only that these contents are 'anthroposophical' but also that they be grasped and worked over as such by a thinking that is as active and as truly individualized as possible. This is, in fact, the only way of preventing the results of anthroposophical research from becoming dogmatized with time and turned into a kind of ideology. It is not merely a matter of assimilating something *different from* everything we have hitherto known but also of permeating it with a form of thinking which itself gradually becomes something different—more active. This leitmotif—the very *core* of Anthroposophy—runs through the whole of Rudolf Steiner's life and work. It already finds a paradigmatic form of expression as early as the year 1894 in a book which is often misguidedly thought of as being 'pre-anthroposophical': *The Philosophy of Spiritual Activity*. However, this title, which Rudolf Steiner himself suggested for the English translation of his book, bears unequivocal witness to this inner continuity and to the essential importance that this element had for him from the very outset.

In Penmaenmawr Rudolf Steiner was able from a thoroughly sound basis to take his listeners into vast distances. If on the one hand his bold and generous attitude, the directness and freshness of his approach were in part due to the fact that here something had been 'requested in the right way', another factor may also have played an important role, namely, the fact that the attitude of English-speaking peoples, once they have decided to take an interest in matters of a spiritual nature, calls for a direct and concrete approach. This is a characteristic of which Marie Steiner makes special mention in the preface to her edition of this cycle of lectures which was published in 1927.

Between Main Events

Naturally enough during those two weeks numerous discussions and encounters took place between Rudolf Steiner and various participants of the summer school. A very beautiful and impressive account of such an experience between the main events is given by Guenther Wachsmuth who was invited one day by Rudolf Steiner to accompany him on a walk to the Druid circles above Penmaenmawr: 'In keeping with the spiritual atmosphere of the place, the conversation centred on the Mysteries of the Druids and their opposite pole in Europe, the cult of Mithras, by which the southern Mysteries were contrasted to the northern ones.'[127] Before Rudolf Steiner's spiritual eye the ancient Druid culture came to life upon the spot: indeed he himself seemed to change into a Druid priest, speaking with intimate knowledge and understanding as he began to explain to his astounded companion the arrangement and the function of the stones, 'a unique and strange picture, as now in the loneliness of this lofty plateau Rudolf Steiner entered into the midst of the Druid circle. He told me to lift my gaze above the stones towards the mountain peaks surrounding the plateau, and described to me, with an intensity in his retrospect as if the event were occurring at that moment, how once the Druid priests, through viewing the signs of the zodiac passing along the horizon in the course of the year were able to experience the spiritual cosmos, the beings working within it, and their mandates to humanity.'[127] In this way Wachsmuth was able to experience something that left a deep impression on him—*elementary instruction in the transformation of history into present reality.* Indeed, it is a truly wonderful scene that has been recorded for us in the beautiful 'Druid Sketches'.[128]

In accordance with a certain occult law Rudolf Steiner would always wait until he was asked a question 'in the right way' before launching a new kind of activity in a definite direction. Only then could he respond. In this way his activity in Berlin had been motivated by a question Marie von Sivers had put to him some 21 years before Penmaenmawr; the educational movement, eurythmy, and many other initiatives had come into being in this way.

So too, here in Penmaenmawr, a truly significant and far-reaching 'Parcival question' was put to Rudolf Steiner by Ita Wegman, perhaps after the lecture he had given for those participants at the summer school who were active within the medical profession. Dr Wegman asked: 'Would it not be possible to found a form of medicine based upon the mysteries?' Rudolf Steiner replied: 'The fact that you pose this question is of very great significance.' He promised to make a start upon it as soon as he returned to Dornach, and in autumn 1923 he started writing the book on medicine with her.'[129]

It was also in connection with just this conversation between Rudolf Steiner and Ita Wegman at the end of the summer school that, as she herself noted, their mutual past karma was 'completely revealed'.[130] This revelation already prefigures one central impulse of the Christmas Conference three months later and of the whole final period of Rudolf Steiner's activity thereafter, namely, the complete and utter disclosure of actual historical karma.

Thus, 'in between' the main events at Penmaenmawr, many other things were taking place and, not perhaps by chance, amidst this exquisite landscape endowed with a special atmosphere of 'time'. All these 'subordinate' motifs and impulses (which, however, are of the greatest importance) owe their existence to the fact that 'at the time' this course had indeed 'been asked for in the right way'. And as though to emphasize further the exemplary nature of the Penmaenmawr initiative Rudolf Steiner observes with regard to it: 'In point of fact this law should be recognized much more than is presently the case: true occult science can only be imparted when it has been asked for in the right way. At that time it was indeed asked for in the right way.'[131]

Nevertheless, the first foreshadowings of difficulties to come within the Society also began to waft around. . . Rudolf Steiner had spoken of D.N. Dunlop on this and various other occasions, characterizing him in such a way that it must have been clear to any unprejudiced observer how deeply he felt and appreciated every meeting with this man. But it was also this very fact which gave rise to a certain amount of intrigue and petty jealousy on the part of such as felt themselves displaced. E.C. Merry relates that, even during the summer school, 'there was a good deal of disagreeable talk going on about DND, behind his back. I asked Dr. Steiner why it was that there seemed to be so much suspicion and dislike of DND and he replied: "When there is anyone whom I love as I love Mr Dunlop, then there are always jealousies." '[132]

*

Another 'in between motif' *par excellence* to which attention may be drawn, though indeed it was present on every occasion that Rudolf Steiner came to Britain, was the fact that the lectures had to be translated; for of course most of the audience were far from being able to master the German language. Consequently Rudolf Steiner had twice to pause during every lecture whilst George Adams-Kaufmann made *clear* to the English friends what up to this point most of them had only been able to *sense*. . . Adams had developed his own personal form of shorthand consisting of ordinary notes, drawings, and various kinds of symbols. He never gave a word-for-word translation of the lectures but reproduced their content in a free and yet conceptually exact manner. So, at the end of this cycle of lectures, Rudolf Steiner addressed these special thanks to Mr Kaufmann (as George Adams at that time still called himself) for his devoted work and self-sacrifice:

> Whenever I work for Anthroposophy in England it always means that the audience's patience is going to be taxed: they have to spend twice as long here because everything has to be translated; however, from a certain point of view I do not regret this circumstance at all in so far as it has brought to light something of an extraordinary nature: it has brought to light Mr Kaufmann's extraordinary art of translation. He is also going to have to translate what I am saying now so I shall ask him as always, not to leave out these last words otherwise I must threaten to call on Dr. Baravalle in order to translate these words! . . . I am indeed deeply gratful to him . . . For what would I have done if Mr. Kaufmann had not been there to communicate all that I so much wanted to communicate to you!'[133]

Old Paths Meet

It is possible to obtain some idea of just how highly Rudolf Steiner rated the potential effect of the Penmaenmawr cycle on the whole of the Anthroposophical Movement from the following words which he pronounced in his final address:

> And so I can say that, in my opinion, precisely from this Summer School in Penmaenmawr an exeedingly fruitful impulse can emanate to the whole of the Anthroposophical Movement and its ramifications in England. For this reason we may look back on the time we have been able to spend in Penmaenmawr with such satisfaction. And I am expressing both Frau Dr. Steiner's and my own gratitude when from the bottom of my heart I thank Mr Dunlop and those others who together with him brought this about—making it possible this once to present the core of Anthroposophy and the eurythmy that has grown out of it; and all of this to such a friendly audience as the one which was here present.[134]

We can almost hear the relief within Rudolf Steiner's soul. He is able to breathe freely—he too had been able to experience something of great value here by dint of the fact that this course had been asked for 'in the right way'.

*

The year 1923 saw the founding of various national societies (*Landesgesellschaften*) within the Anthroposophical Society, amongst others that of the Anthroposophical Society in Great Britain, founded in London immediately after the Penmaenmawr conference. Harry Collison, a long-standing active member, was elected first General Secretary of the national society; he was the one who, in Rudolf Steiner's words, had 'done the most work in translating and spreading anthroposophical literature in England and in the colonies'.[135]

However, Rudolf Steiner's address to those present at the Foundation Meeting General Assembly in London on 2 September,[136] in the course of which Collison was elected, presents us with a certain enigma when regarded in the light of a remark he made to Ita Wegman[137] (presumably still at Penmaenmawr): that D.N. Dunlop 'was the right man to lead the Anthroposophical Society in Great Britain'. So what happened?

Let us view the circumstances immediately preceding Collison's election; these were as follows. After he had been proposed by several members for the post of General Secretary some other members came up with the objection that Collison was a Freemason![138] At least this is how Collison perceived the situation when he spoke of it to Rudolf Steiner.[139] Therefore, in his address at the Foundation Meeting, Rudolf Steiner found himself obliged to refute once and for all the total irrelevance of any argument of this sort, bringing to bear the point of view he considered to be right in such matters. If someone 'is a good Anthroposophist then that is what matters for the Anthroposophical Movement. Whether or not he is, in addition to this, a good, bad, or mediocre Freemason, is of no concern to the Anthroposophical Society at all'.[140] And so the following words which he also spoke during that meeting have to be understood in this same respect: 'As far as the other questions are concerned: it seems to me that nothing in what has been here discussed can present the slightest obstacle to Mr Collison's having the very best of qualifications for the post of General Secretary. I cannot see anything that speaks against this.'[141] However, despite the high esteem he obviously had for Collison, we can by no means conclude from all this that Rudolf Steiner had not seen other qualities, in someone *else*, which *positively* predisposed this person to be 'the right man'.

At all events his remark to Ita Wegman shows that he, himself, would have preferred Dunlop. In contrast to Collison, however, Dunlop had *not* been proposed by the members of the British Society and so Rudolf Steiner would have been obliged to make a formal counter-proposal; this he would for obvious reasons have avoided. After all, had not he himself, a few days earlier, drawn the attention of these very people to the fact that occult, spiritual science can only be expounded when it is *asked for* in the right way? Now Rudolf Steiner was bound to assume this kind of occult, esoteric standpoint even in the face of such apparently exoteric matters as the constitution of a society or the election of a general secretary within a given country; this is made evident by the fact that the General Anthroposophical Society (which was to be founded at Christmas in order to unite the various national societies) was given an explicitly esoteric council under Rudolf Steiner's own direction. Evidently no member of the British Society had undertaken to ask Rudolf Steiner *his own* view as to who might be 'the right man' to direct the Society in Great Britain.

Thus this choice, and the whole 'election-situation' in which D.N. Dunlop was indirectly involved, presents us with a perfect example of Rudolf Steiner's attitude in such matters—his careful respect for individual freedom. It may also inspire us to exercise a corresponding degree of discernment in our subsequent efforts to investigate and clarify any enigmas of this kind.

*

Now one would have expected, after the fruitful outcome of those late summer weeks, that D.N. Dunlop would also have gone to Dornach and witnessed how the meditational 'Foundation Stone' was sunk into the hearts of the members. At least Rudolf Steiner had hoped he would be there. Fried Geuter reports how at the

Christmas Conference he 'saw Dr Steiner walking among the members asking "Where is Mr Dunlop? Where is Mr Dunlop?" '[142]

On 30 December, when the conference was already drawing to a close, Mrs Merry communicated Dunlop's apologies thus making perfectly clear that he would not be coming at all. Thereupon, as though to fill out the painful gap which his absence on this occasion had created, Rudolf Steiner improvised a very affectionate and light-hearted characterization of his Scottish friend.

'You see, my dear friends,' he exclaimed, 'we expected to see Mr Dunlop in Stratford, in Oxford, once even in London, and here in Dornach as well, so that I got the definite impression: Mr Dunlop is the man who is always said to be coming—and who then doesn't come. And now he *did* come to Penmaenmawr! And it went extraordinarily well, so well that I wish he were here today so that we could personally thank him again in a really heartfelt manner. But this time I really did believe Mr Dunlop would be here for he said to me in London before I left that the next time he would do it the other way round: he would not say that he was coming, but then he *would* come. Now, he didn't say in London that he was coming—but he *still* hasn't come!'

These words reveal how glad Rudolf Steiner would have been to have seen this man, whom he had met with such evident joy, amongst the participants; and no doubt not least for this reason: Dunlop, with his truly spiritual vision and attitude to community, would have brought a beautifully strengthening element into the whole of the conference. In the section entitled 'Spiritual Striving and Formation of Community', we attempted to draw the reader's attention to the essential elements of this approach; along with the many other qualities inherent in this individuality it would not have remained long hidden from Rudolf Steiner's eyes.

There is, however, a more serious and objective side to Rudolf Steiner's description; indeed one that even sheds light on the future orientation of the Anthroposophical Movement as such. It comes to expression in the following words:

> My dear friends! I have often in various places drawn your attention to the exceedingly satisfactory outcome of the Summer School in Penmaenmawr. And perhaps I can still add this to what has already often been said: that I really believe it will mean an extraordinarily significant step forward for the whole of the Anthroposophical Movement if over the next few years, all those developments of the seeds laid at Penmaenmawr which Mrs Merry has just now referred to here, come to full fruition and practical realization. We may also have confidence that the very best forces are present in order to bring the work of the Anthroposophical Movement forward in this direction; for it was with an extraordinary strength of will and inner, I would say esoteric, insight that Mr Dunlop took this particular Summer School at Penmaenmawr in hand; indeed I should say it was an esoteric accomplishment. For, from the very beginning certain conditions were fulfilled in Penmaenmawr which we have never seen fulfilled elsewhere and which were necessary for the success of Penmaenmawr.[143]

Once again it is clear from this description just how highly Rudolf Steiner estimated the significance of this summer school because 'from the very beginning certain conditions were fulfilled which we have never seen fulfilled elsewhere'.[143] These words bear tremendous weight given the fact that at that time the Anthroposophical Movement already had a good 21 years' experience behind it.

But what exactly were these conditions which had been 'fulfilled' here from the very beginning and which had never been fulfilled elsewhere?

If we take another look at the whole genesis of this summer school, we can identify the following points of major importance:

1 Rudolf Steiner was actually asked to expound the *core of Anthroposophy*—'which has to be the source of everything'. This means that 'from the very beginning' of the enterprise something is brought to the Initiate from outside that, from the very beginning of his anthroposophical activity, had been deeply anchored in his own being, namely the insight that 'all the other offshoot movements can only be correspondingly effective in the world if what is *central* to Anthroposophy really comes into its

own'. This is a vital necessity and one which Rudolf Steiner particularly stressed in his last speech at the summer school.
2 The choice of this particular locality allowed Rudolf Steiner in a quite unique way to connect the new with the old—to bring his new contribution into relationship with what already existed; a principle that he had always been at pains to uphold right from the beginning of his Goethe studies.
3 This summer school was held at a *time* of radical review, a moment of internal reorientation of the whole Anthroposophical Movement. It was the phase which saw the constitution of the various national societies and, at Christmas, their unification within a general World Society. This phase covered most of the year 1923, and Rudolf Steiner's urgent request runs through it like a silver thread: With the 'daughters' of Anthroposophy—now growing up strong and fast and attracting much attention—do not forget what is central to Anthroposophy, the mother—Anthroposophia.

Thus, what we have here is a triple congruence of external and internal (we could also call them exoteric and esoteric) factors such as had never before been realized. Similar congruences will also be found in Torquay.

*

After his impromptu characterization of Dunlop, Rudolf Steiner bade Mrs Merry once again convey his personal thanks and those of the whole assembly to him 'for the inauguration of such an exeedingly significant movement inside the Anthroposophical Movement—one so rich in prospects through the Summer School in Penmaenmawr'. Not only was she to communicate these significant thanks but also Rudolf Steiner's request that Dunlop 'might continue to take such work as this strongly in hand, for in his hand it will certainly succeed.'[143]

One may well ask oneself *why* Dunlop did not go to Dornach; however, as no documentary statements regarding this point appear to exist, we can only conjecture what the real reasons may have been. One important factor would undoubtedly have been the first World Power Conference (described in the next part of this book); this huge undertaking, which demanded first-class organizational skills, was due to take place in July 1924. The conference had been planned a long time before and numerous preparatory discussions, meetings, etc. were necessary in order to bring the plan into actual effect.

Another consideration may have been that at this particular moment Dunlop deemed it wiser (after the success of the summer school had been followed by the election of Collison, who now had the task of representing the British Society in Dornach) to remain in the background for the time being. After all, 'when there is anyone whom I love as I love Mr Dunlop'—we have already quoted the complete sentence so we can leave it at that. Furthermore, Dunlop was not only 'far-seeing' but also endowed with 'clear and delicate perception', as Rudolf Steiner had once characterized this aspect of his being.[144]

*

Since Dunlop himself did not come to this gathering let us use this opportunity to take a closer look at E.C. Merry, the person charged with bearing the fair words of this important message to her anthroposophical friend. In several respects she is to play an important role in the events of the following years.

Eleanor Charlotte Kynaston was born in Eton on 17 December 1873. 'From my earliest childhood,' she relates in her short autobiographical sketch, 'two things dominated my conscious life. One was a passionate longing for knowledge and the achievements of knowledge, and the other was a never-ceasing need for occasions of hero-worship. Up to about the age of fourteen the latter need had many opportunities for its fulfilment; and after that time it transformed itself into a sort of habit of expectancy, of waiting for some crowning event that should satisfy or should be connected with—I could not guess how—my overmastering desire for knowledge.'

Her parents had an extremely liberal attitude towards education: the 13-year-old girl was spared any further regular school attendance on account of circumstances pertaining to her father's profession (in 1886, he was appointed Canon of Durham Cathedral). So it was that she came to spend the following years of her youth in the beautiful atmosphere of the cathedral precincts. And it was here that the deeply reflective future historian was born in her: 'for there reading in the monks' library, being allowed to handle priceless old manuscripts, wandering through the cloisters and galleries of the Cathedral, feeling the powerful thrust and weight of its gigantic Norman pillars, I had a glimpse of real history—that came to me as something utterly different from the history of school-books.'[145]

The numerous encounters with scholars and theologians in and around her parents' home helped to widen and deepen all the spiritual inclinations and needs that had awakened so early within her. The next years were spent studying music and fine arts with the aim of becoming a professional singer. This was followed up, in 1895, by a lengthy visit to Vienna where she underwent a spiritual crisis (predominantly atheistic in nature), but also managed to assimilate a fundamental knowledge of the German language. In the next year she married the distinguished Oxford surgeon Dr Merry, and from then on devoted all her forces to assisting him in his profession.

It was at the outbreak of the First World War that E.C. Merry came into contact with Theosophy. Without the slightest hesitation she got down to studying Blavatsky's *Secret Doctrine* which had been sent to her by someone she did not know—an anonymous friend. Afterwards, she read books by Besant and other authors as well. Her interest in theosophical thought soon began to focus on a central question of the Theosophical Movement and: 'From all that I read one outstanding realization began to colour all my thoughts and feelings and actions. It was that there were actually "Masters", "elder brothers" of humanity, who were seers and adepts, who had trodden the path that I was longing to discover, *and whom it was possible to meet*—either in or out of the body. My childhood's capacity for hero-worship saw itself suddenly transfigured . . .'

We find striking parallels here to D.N. Dunlop's own development: an intense interest in *The Secret Doctrine* and in the true nature of the Masters as well as the ardent hope and desire to meet with one such individuality. After the war one of E.C. Merry's friends drew her attention to Rudolf Steiner's book *Knowledge of the Higher Worlds—How is it achieved?* His portrait, which was included in the original English edition, again and again caught her attention. 'What is he? Who is he? I thought. Can I trust him? I cannot possibly know unless I meet him face to face; and then I shall know finally and completely. And I longed to meet him. But all the circumstances of my life seemed to point to that as being utterly out of the question.'[145]

Then the year 1922 arrived; it was to be perhaps the most eventful and significant year perhaps in the whole of her life. For early in that year her husband died of pneumonia after a few days' illness. 'And then quite suddenly, and entirely unexpectedly, I found myself free to go where I liked and do what I liked.'[145]

*

One evening in January she met the man whom she 'really loved and really knew'[146]—an individuality she was henceforth to speak of only with deep and lasting reverence: D.N. Dunlop. On the evening in question he was reading one of Rudolf Steiner's lectures to his anthroposophical study group in the studio at Camden Hill. We can imagine him there, his fine, strong voice expressing the keenest attentiveness. Of course, as far as the content was concerned, he would have already thought it through very carefully, 'put it to the test' in his own particular way; now the moment had come, to awaken, with inner calm and clarity of thought, the enthusiasm of others.

We can discern three stages in Dunlop's approach to any newly published lectures or works by Rudolf Steiner. 'I remember him telling us,' David Clement relates, 'how when a fresh lecture cycle came out he would read it like a detective novel, scarcely stopping to take breath, and then with his pencil in his hand would go back to the beginning and slowly work his way through.'[85] First attain an overall view of the subject-matter; then work on it in detail; finally pass it on to others: this is perhaps how one could characterize the three successive stages.

As Dunlop read out loud and E.C. Merry followed with rivetted attention, a singular inner vision mingled with her experience of these readings. 'Without describing this in detail,' she writes in her reminiscences on D.N. Dunlop, 'it is enough to say that it represented the ascension of a soul *rising to a vision of Isis*. Not long after, I was able to describe this to D.N.D., and he replied: 'Yes, that is something that belongs intimately to my whole life.' (MD)

Let us recall at this point the fundamental characterization Rudolf Steiner once gave of the Isis figure: 'Isis was the epitome of all the deepest thoughts the Egyptians were able to form about the archetypal forces working in nature and in human existence. If the Egyptian was to look up to the great mysteries in his surroundings, then he had to look up to Isis.'[147]

'The great mysteries in his surroundings' . . . Remarkable here how the Isis theme seems to touch on that zodiacal cosmogony which we met in an earlier chapter of this book. And indeed the new form of the old Isis legend which Rudolf Steiner sketched out for our times is in part characterized by this very fact: that it is related to a spiritualized cosmogony.

> And in contrast to Osiris whom Typhon sunk into the Nile, subsequently burying the dead remains in the earth . . . it is into the wide spaces of the world that the *murdered being* of Isis, the divine being of wisdom has been projected; she has been buried out in the ocean of the universe. As we look out into this ocean and see the relationship between the stars as mere mathematical lines, the force that spiritually permeates the universe is actually buried there . . . We . . . must . . . rediscover Isis! . . . And what we then attain, thanks to this new discovery of Isis, is something that we must be able to place before ourselves in a living way so that it spiritually becomes the whole of the heavens for us—the cosmos . . . We must realize the fact that . . . we have to find an inner astronomy, one that shows us how the universe emanates from and works within the power of the Spirit . . . Ah, my dear friends, the soul will be able to come to unique

> sensations if it feels the duty to experience the new Isis legend within modern humanity. The killing of Isis and the transference of her body into the cosmic spaces which have become a mathematical abstraction, or the grave of Isis; then the search for Isis, the discovery of Isis through the activation of the inner force of spiritual knowledge, which places into the lifeless sky that which stars and planets reveal out of inner life, so that they appear as monuments of the spiritual powers that surge through space.[148]

In the section entitled 'The Occult Path and the Zodiac', we have already encountered 12 such 'monuments of the spiritual powers'; and indeed the whole of this Isis theme as such, especially in Rudolf Steiner's modern rendering, seems to unite harmoniously with that cosmology of the zodiac upon which Dunlop had drawn from ancient western sources.

The first personal conversation between E.C. Merry and D.N. Dunlop took place in May 1922; presumably it *preceded* their exchange concerning Isis. Only a few weeks earlier Dunlop had met Rudolf Steiner for the first time; he would still have been overflowing with the gratitude and inner joy of knowledge at the happy outcome of his 'experiment'—'In the West we want to "see for ourselves".' E.C. Merry relates in retrospect: 'The first time that I had any private and personal conversation with him . . . he surprised me very much by seeming to take for granted that I knew quite a lot of occultism; and he took a piece of paper and a pencil and made various drawings of the Zodiac, showing their connection with the spiritual and soul qualities of the human being.' (MD)

So it was that E.C. Merry received her first elementary instruction in spiritualized cosmology—we could also describe it as elementary instruction in the new Isis legend.

Something similar to what had taken place between Rudolf Steiner and D.N. Dunlop now took place between the latter and E.C. Merry: within seconds of meeting, the personal nature of the relationship was established. And just as Dunlop had experienced his meeting with Rudolf Steiner as a reunion (a sentiment confirmed as fact by the latter at a later point), so now with this meeting between himself and E.C. Merry: 'When he said goodbye, he kissed my hand with a sort of reverence,' she writes in her reminiscences. 'This was in May 1922. We clearly knew that we were not meeting for the first time.' (MD)

But it was not only D.N. Dunlop and E.C. Merry who met here. During the few days in question E.C. Merry began to feel Rudolf Steiner's 'presence' more and more clearly. His shape assumed sharper contours in her mind, for Dunlop described the wonderful experience to her—how he had made the acquaintance of Rudolf Steiner. And E.C. Merry saw through Dunlop's eyes, above all through his soul which was still overflowing with joy; she saw that outstanding figure before her and the meeting for which she had for so long been yearning seemed suddenly to become a real possibility. Free to go wherever she liked and to do whatever she wanted, she set out that same year for Oxford in order to participate in a conference where Rudolf Steiner was due to give a course of lectures on 'Spiritual Values in Education'. The short description she gives of their first meeting is illuminating:

> My first meeting with Rudolf Steiner was a sudden and unexpected one in the midst of a dark narrow passage in an ancient Oxford building. He passed me without speaking, but pausing for a second and looking at me with a penetrating glance. In the gloom of the passage his black clothes, the extreme pallor of his face framed by his dark hair, the piercing brilliance of his eyes, the rapid firmness of his gait, made an extraordinary impression. If any words can be found to describe it they would be these: *He knows where he is going.*'[145]

Later on, at tea, Rudolf Steiner was introduced to Mrs Merry and they exchanged a few words; but inside E.C. Merry's soul it was something like a trumpet-call that she experienced on this occasion: 'I knew without the shadow of a doubt that the central point and meaning of my life had arrived.'[146]

Here again we encounter the unmistakable signature of destiny: a preliminary encounter *en passant* where no words are spoken as the two approach one another; the signature of the will is clearly to be read in this encounter and indeed not long after it the first fruits of deeds were soon to become manifest.

After the lecture-course had been concluded Rudolf Steiner

proposed that Mrs Merry be appointed secretary, in England, of the new movement in education; this occasioned some surprise and even disapproval among certain older members, for Mrs Merry herself had only become a member a few months earlier. On hearing her own objections—she had no notion of education and surely someone else, more suited to the job, could easily be found!—he merely smiled and said, 'You will do it very well.'

Dunlop, who did not himself go to Oxford, will have listened with great joy and deep interest to E.C. Merry's description of her experiences there, especially of course the portrayal of her meeting with Rudolf Steiner. As for Mrs Merry herself, from that time in Oxford onwards she 'had no greater ambition than to serve the cause of Anthroposophy'. And the first great service she rendered to this cause, apart from her activity within the new movement in education, was to help organize the first Summer School in Penmaenmawr.

*

Perhaps something else will have struck the reader from the description of these events. Since the meeting between E.C. Merry and D.N. Dunlop and the meeting of these two with Rudolf Steiner and those most close to him, something begins to happen. Threads of karma, which seem to stem from millennia past, begin to interlace with one another. We are dealing with 'conjunctions' in the highest sense of the word—with a melting of the ways and of the various motivating forces of individual destiny. Furthermore, Rudolf Steiner himself did much to try and bring such forces as these into the sphere of waking consciousness. This is clear from a remark he made to E.C. Merry in Penmaenmawr concerning Dunlop, perhaps immediately after mentioning the 'jealousies'. At any rate the effect this remark had on E.C. Merry was similar to that which the meeting itself had had on her: it was an awakening call from deep within. 'Rudolf Steiner said to me,' E.C. Merry writes in her reminiscences about Dunlop, 'that he was connected with all the ancient mysteries'—an affirmation of tremendous import and one that throws light on much of what has already been considered up to this point whilst remaining equally enigmatic in itself. (We will come back to it later in the final part of this book.) After he had made this profoundly significant statement about D.N. Dunlop, Steiner added this equally significant piece of advice: 'Make the bond with him as strong as you possibly can.' (MD)

Paintings in an Exhibition

Conversations and experiences such as these call for deeds, acts of gratitude and sacrifice. It would then have been in January 1924 that Dunlop received Rudolf Steiner's message from Mrs Merry, to 'continue to take such work as this strongly in hand', that is to say, to organize another summer school. Even if the inauguration of the First World Power Conference, with all the preparatory organization that this entailed, stood high on his agenda, Dunlop would hardly have lost a moment in giving his inner assent to this. Twelve years after the fourth theosophical summer school at Torquay, he now again chose this resort for an anthroposophical summer school which was to be held in August of that year. The course theme had probably already been discussed with Mrs Merry in Dornach during the Christmas Conference. A group of English members had expressed their concern at 'the rapid spread of spiritualism in England, and I asked him,' so Mrs Merry reports, 'on behalf of the Society, to make its dangers and mistakes known to an English audience, and this he consented to do.'[146] Since those days in Penmaenmawr where, amidst his many activities, Rudolf Steiner had also found time to introduce E.C. Merry to a new technique in painting, she had been practising it with great enthusiasm. While sojourning in Paris in May 1924 she told him about her efforts and, as she intended to exhibit some of the paintings which she had produced in the meantime, she expressed the view that it might be a good idea for him to see them beforehand. Mrs Merry describes Rudolf Steiner's reaction:

> He replied: 'I have seen your paintings,' and I said, 'No, Herr Doctor.

> You haven't seen them; they are all in London.' He said again, 'I have seen them.' I contradicted him, and for the third time he repeated that he had seen them, looking at me with his intense dark gaze. Then, for the first time, I realized that he had indeed seen them, but not with earthly sight . . . Never again could I doubt that in spirit he could be at any moment present with his pupils, no matter where they were.[146]

We can imagine how Mrs Merry, with her trust in Rudolf Steiner's occult powers deeply confirmed, was able to return to London and, with new wings of inspiration, get down with D.N. Dunlop to the task of organizing the summer school.

Torquay—Spirit and Matter in Unison

So it was that, on 11 August, in the town hall at Torquay, Rudolf Steiner could begin a new cycle of lectures at the opening of the second International Summer School. The lectures had been announced by Mrs Merry under the title 'True and False Paths in Spiritual Investigation'[149] and were held in the morning. It was George Adams who translated them 'in the most devoted way'.

Here again it is not our intention to give a detailed systematic summary of the lectures given during this second summer course (in which 'newcomers' to Anthroposophy also took part) but rather to touch in an aphoristic manner on a few aspects of particular interest in connection with D.N. Dunlop's initiative and presence on this occasion.

In the first lecture Rudolf Steiner immediately strikes one of the basic chords of his highly varied theme. He explains the illusory character of the kind of vision which experiences nature as a form of matter devoid of all spirit and contrasts it with the aspirations of the ancient Mysteries which tried to come to grips with the reality of the human being as such: 'In all the ancient Mysteries men felt this urge to discover the reality of their inner being, whereas all the transient phenomena of space and time were felt to be an expression of the Great Illusion. And so, in order to arrive at an understanding of man's being, they looked towards something other than what the external senses have revealed. And one felt this something as a spiritual world.' He subsequently describes two fundamental deviations from the path which leads to this spiritual world. One consists of maintaining the same attitude of naive realism towards the spiritual world as one had previously adopted towards the physical world and which had precisely led to an illusory experience of nature; this is the way to ever greater deception. The other consists of simply preferring to 'sense' and 'believe' certain things instead of attaining knowledge; this leads to ever-increasing ignorance. The subsequent lectures show how these two one-sided attitudes can be avoided and a true way found into the spiritual world. Before this goal is reached profound mysteries are revealed concerning the connection between the metals and the various states of human consciousness, and clear light is shed on mediumistic practices and the phenomenon of possession.

And one deep note resounds throughout the variations on this theme; it is the observation made at the beginning of the first lecture concerning the unity which exists between the physical and the spiritual:

> Wherever the external world confronts us we are in no doubt that it is both spiritual and physical; behind every physical phenomenon will be found in some form or other a spiritual agent which is the real protagonist. And there is nothing spiritual which, just to dally in the world, pursues an existence without substance or effect, but everything spiritual which can anywhere be found, will also work right into the physical at some time or some place.

For Dunlop, who arrived in Torquay immediately after the successful conclusion of the First World Power Conference, this fundamental and all-embracing truth must seem to have raised him from the depths of his own soul. For all his previous thoughts and aspirations had basically been permeated by this vision. Perhaps it had been most obviously rooted in his cosmology of the zodiac, where the circle as a whole contains the forces of two apparently opposing processes—those of *evolution* and *involution*. For whilst 'involution', according to this cosmology, designates the process by which the spiritual is rendered physical, 'evolution' leads to the spiritualization of the material world.

If one compares the 'leitmotif' of the Torquay lectures with that developed in Penmaenmawr the previous year, we can see that Rudolf Steiner is taking as his point of departure the world of material substances in order to illuminate the relationship between the human being and this world. Thus, for instance, he shows how certain metallic substances were legitimately used in ancient times in order to produce a certain state of consciousness.

Humanity at an earlier stage had in a very real way experienced such a form of unity between the spiritual and the physical. Rudolf Steiner illustrates this point with the example of the Chaldeans and subsequently refers to the teachers of the School of Chartres in order to characterize the vision of nature prevailing in the Middle Ages in which multifarious traces of spirituality could still be found. This vision did not yet speak of abstract, 'natural laws', as was to be the case as soon as the modern natural sciences began their ascendancy; instead, it spoke of a being that permeated and determined all of nature's manifestations—the goddess Natura. She was portrayed as a transformation of the Greek Persephone who had already inspired teachers and pupils at Ephesus.

Thus the listener and the reader alike are presented with a wonderfully concentrated tableau of the development of human consciousness. And indeed this constitutes, as we shall presently see, a 'Michaelic' leitmotif of the very first degree.

The Shining, Fiery Truth of Reincarnation and Karma[150]

On the second day after the opening of this course in Torquay Rudolf Steiner informed members of the impulses created by the Christmas Conference. Here again it is the unity of the physical and spiritual which moves into the foreground of the events, for since this Christmas Conference no distinction was henceforth to be made between the spiritual stream of the Anthroposophical Movement itself and its earthly counterpart or reflection in the Anthroposophical Society.[150] 'Since Christmas the opposite holds good. The Anthroposophical Movement is now one with the Anthroposophical Society; the two are no longer to be distinguished from one another . . . The whole Movement, flowing through the Society as it now does, must have an esoteric character.' One of the first effects of this impulse will be that 'our conception of history must be quite different from that prevailing today'. Such an attitude to history will be based on the fact that the idea of karma and reincarnation has been really assimilated and is seriously applied to historical facts. 'For when one takes the idea of karma seriously then history is resolved into human acts and the movements of human lives flowing into the present from a distant past and continuing on into the future.' Thus, on the second day after his arrival in Torquay, Rudolf Steiner pronounced the 'shining, fiery truth' concerning reincarnation and karma: 'Just as we sit here, so we are in this life—in the repetition of previous earthly lives. We have brought with us from previous earthly lives into this one the results of previous earthly lives.' Concrete examples of karmic-historic relationships were subsequently given here in Torquay as they had been in other places.

On 14 August, in the evening lecture, Rudolf Steiner took up the 'karma motif' once again and developed it further. E.C. Merry and D.N. Dunlop would have been keenly attending. Indeed, it must have been a deeply impressive and significant moment for everyone when Rudolf Steiner, at the end of this lecture, spoke out in the boldest and most unreserved manner concerning an event which he was later to term 'the Michael Prophecy':

> Because of the particular form which the rulership of Michael assumes, there will be many deviations from the laws determining reincarnation in the case of those persons whose karma and connection with the rulership of Michael leads them into the Anthroposophical Movement. For they will appear again at the turn of the 20th/21st century—therefore in less than a century's time—in order then to carry to full and culminating effect what as anthroposophists they are able now to do in the service of Michael's rulership.[150]

It requires both an unprejudiced and profoundly serious attitude to understand what kind of momentous impulses such words must have awakened in the souls of those listeners—especially as some of those present had from the very outset brought with them into the Anthroposophical Movement a very far-sighted vision.

Rudolf Steiner made it perfectly clear that he was not speaking *in general* about all those souls connected to the Anthroposophical Movement, but rather about the *possibility* that existed for each and every person present to enter into a relationship with this Michael Prophecy. It remained a possibility because there was a condition that had to be fulfilled before any such person could enter into the sphere of influence of the said prophecy. It was this: that interest and understanding be freely forthcoming for these given ideas of karma. It is of the greatest possible importance to consider this point most carefully, otherwise it might seem impossible to solve a certain problem which this prophecy raises: is not Rudolf Steiner—here and wherever he spoke about reincarnations of anthroposophists at the end of the century in the course of 1924—influencing the individual destiny of these people by revealing and as it were sketching out in the 'future indicative' their immediate karma? Would not such an act as this have the effect of a kind of 'psychological imperative' within the soul of the listeners and rob them of the possibility of freely shaping the immediate circumstances of their lives?

It would, however, only be possible to see even the mildest infringement of anyone's freedom here if one were to fail altogether to notice that Rudolf Steiner is in a certain sense not really revealing anything radically new but 'only' drawing the attention of his listeners to the effects which would be given by a certain *free act of understanding*, with regard to karmic revelations, should this act be forthcoming. In as far as any of those present might freely choose to develop an intense enough interest in these things he would then enter into the sphere where this prophecy comes into effect. It does not possess anything of that deterministic, or even fatalistic nature so characteristic of everything that is generally described as 'prophecy', *for the condition necessary for its fulfilment is a real act of freedom*—to *will* a real act of understanding of practical karmic realities. Thus, the peculiarity of this prophecy is not that it reveals the karmic consequences of certain external facts or occurrences but rather those of free acts of understanding. It is therefore impossible to find anything that might infringe upon the individual's freedom here. In order to make this aspect of the Michael Prophecy perfectly clear, two words within the following quotation, the whole of which continues on from Rudolf Steiner's words above, are printed in italics: 'The urge to be a true Anthroposophist expresses itself in the interest that *can* be taken in matters of the kind of which we have been speaking—provided the interest is sufficently deep. The very *understanding* of these things gives rise to the impulse to return to the earth in less than a century in order to give effect to what Anthroposophy wants.'[151]

Tintagel—The Birthplace of European Civilization

As at Penmaenmawr the year before so now too during Rudolf Steiner's stay in Torquay it was possible to visit one of the most important Mystery-centres of the human race; on the Sunday after the first week of lectures, a small party gathered for an excursion to Tintagel.

When at a very early hour Mrs Merry came across Rudolf Steiner in the hotel corridor, he was already dressed for the journey. She asked him apprehensively if, given the state of the weather, he still intended to go. Outside everything was covered by thick mist and the rain was coming down in torrents. Rudolf Steiner answered confidently: 'A few minutes after 8 o'clock the rain will stop.'[152]

At ten past eight the small party of travellers, consisting of Mrs Merry, D.N. Dunlop, Rudolf and Marie Steiner, Mrs Cotterell,[152] Ita Wegman, Elisabeth Vreede, Guenther Wachsmuth, Mr and Mrs Scott-Pyle and Mrs Pease, met at the hotel entrance to take stock of the weather in typical English fashion. It had stopped raining, the mist had dispersed and the sun was trying to show itself, albeit somewhat reluctantly. They set out immediately on their 50-mile journey across the heather-clad landscape of Dartmoor using one private and two hired cars for the trip. Mrs

Cotterell relates how Rudolf Steiner spoke of 'mischievous pixies and nixes' appearing during their journey and making 'long noses' as they passed. Most of the way 'small fragments of rainbows seemed to descend to the sides of the road and hovered about us as though to make our journey a triumphal progress.'[152] At Tintagel the last remains of the rainbow bridges disappeared completely and the sun drove away the last traces of mist. The sea was raging. The small party stood there in silence absorbed by the wonderful view before them. Then they experienced something quite extraordinary: Rudolf Steiner, standing upon the rocky promontory amidst the ruins of what had once been Arthur's castle, pencil and writing-pad in hand, speaking of the Arthurian knights 'who experienced, in this external struggle of the forces of light with the elements of the earth a reflection of their own inner battles.'[153] Just as in the previous year, there now again took place before the eyes of the spellbound onlookers a wonderful example of 'pictorial instruction', of 'history brought into present reality'. Mrs Merry recalls some of the details of Rudolf Steiner's description:

> 'Here,' he said, 'were the Kitchens, and over there the Knights' quarters.' Presently he said, 'A Knight is approaching us . . .' I looked in vain, there was apparently nothing there. He described the Knight, who, I think, was not riding but walking. He wrote other notes about the Knights' quarters and perhaps the banqueting hall; but for the most part he was silent and absorbed, though at the same time very positive and aware of everything.
>
> Presently, most of us—and Dr Steiner—set out to scramble up the stony path of the opposite cliff, where there were more ruins. He said these had been the servants' quarters, and also the stables . . . As we descended the cliff we went into what is traditionally called Merlin's Cave. Inside it there was a wonderful natural structure in which one had a good view of the shadowed rays of the sun.[152]

In *The Life and Work of Rudolf Steiner*[153] Guenther Wachsmuth also gives a summary of this memorable visit. He adds that Rudolf Steiner spoke about 'Merlin's teachings'. (According to Mrs Merry mention was made in this context of Richard Wagner, Rudolf Steiner thereby alluding to the mystery of the 'Entelechy', whereby some of the karmic background of this particular individuality was being revealed.)[154]

The innate quality of such moments makes them exemplary of a new attitude towards karma, not only with regard to the activity of the esoteric teacher in unreservedly revealing specific facts concerning karmic history but also with regard to the attitude of those whose task might be to assimilate and integrate this knowledge in the right way. For 'these things may not be taken lightly; one has the right only to take them up if one has the necessary respect for them',[150] as Rudolf Steiner had emphasized in the first lecture to members at Torquay.

A few days later, in the next lecture to members, Rudolf Steiner returned to this most significant excursion. He spoke at some length of the spiritual mission of the Arthurian knights and most importantly of their relationship to the being of Michael. Intelligence as such used to be a cosmic principle which Michael 'presided over'; gradually during the first centuries after Christ it became more and more individualized. However, whilst the individual increasingly began to form his own abstract thoughts, the Arthurian knights retained something of a more conservative element. 'This was actually the community which worked longer than any other to ensure that Michael should retain his dominion over the Cosmic Intelligence.' How did this peculiar relationship to intelligence as a solar-cosmic entity express itself? One could say, referring to Rudolf Steiner's indications on this subject, that it found its principal form of expression in the way creative intelligence, or as it were beings of pure intelligence, were experienced as present everywhere within the elementary and natural environment. The knights of this community 'did not feel a personal intelligence within themselves'. They did not say: I form my thoughts, my intelligence-filled thoughts myself. They experienced intelligence as *revealed*. One can picture to oneself the kind of 'revelation' it must have been, for Steiner says the following: 'If with the eye of the spirit one stands on the site where once the castle stood and gazes over the stretch of sea which a cliff seems to divide into two, there, in a comparatively short time, one can perceive not only a wonderful interplay between the light and the air, but also between the elemental spirits living in light and air. One can see how the spirit-beings which soon pour themselves onto the earth in the rays of the sun are soon mirrored in the shimmering-flowing, fluid downpour and catch their mirroring; one can see what underlies the sway of earthly gravity appearing in the air as the denser spirit-beings of the air.' Rudolf Steiner speaks in this context of a form of 'pagan piety' that can be experienced here; 'Pagan piety is a surrender of heart and feeling to the manifold spiritual beings working in the processes of nature.'[155]

However, in order actually to 'take hold' of 'spirit-forces working there in nature' so that they could be effective on a social level a group of men was necessary, 'one of whom felt himself as the representative of the Sun at the centre, and whose twelve companions were trained in such a way that in their whole temperament, their disposition and their whole manner of acting, all of them together formed a twelvefold whole—twelve individual men grouped as the zodiacal constellations are grouped around the Sun. Such was the Round Table: King Arthur at the centre, surrounded by the Twelve, above each of whom a zodiacal symbol was displayed, indicating the particular cosmic influence with which he was associated'.

The importance that this Arthurian and Michaelic movement held for the development of Europe is evident from the following statement made by Rudolf Steiner during this lecture: '*European civilization so to speak proceeded from this place.*' At first sight these words might appear strange or even alarming. Do we not look on ancient Greece as the cradle of European culture? However, that is just the point—to distinguish clearly between *culture* and *civilization*. What is to be understood by 'civilization' here can be deduced from Rudolf Steiner's description of the task of the Arthurian knights: 'It was here that King Arthur and his Twelve Knights drew into themselves from the Sun the strength wherewith to set forth on their mighty expeditions through Europe in order to battle with the wild, demonic powers of old still dominating large masses of the population, and drive them out of men.'

Thus it was the Arthurian knights who actually had to create *the prerequisite conditions for European culture* as such. This they accomplished by 'battling for outer civilization', and in order to develop the 'impulse of civilization' they 'imbued themselves with the Intelligence'.[156]

One can easily imagine with what devoted interest and attention D.N. Dunlop must have followed this truly illuminating characterization of the very essence of the Arthurian knights. And once again it is actually a motivating factor in his own life that is touched on here and developed in a new context. Had not he himself been the bearer of such an Arthurian impulse, of a great impulse of civilization, forever acting on the external level in such a way that the construction of the BEAMA and especially the organization of the World Power Conference were the resultant fruits? Had not he, as a modern-day Arthur, fought relentlessly 'for external civilization', 'intensifying the struggle the moment European culture sank into the abyss of the First World War and all but disappeared?

Taking into account Dunlop's previous achievements as well as his future activity within the external, economic sphere it really seems as though, here in Tintagel and Torquay, he was initiated into a *modern* type of Arthurian knighthood—modern in so far as he was fighting for civilization in a manner totally adapted to the twentieth century. His broad and comprehensive impulses centred on co-operation, and co-ordination in the economic and technological fields were the means by which he sought to drive out the 'demonic powers' of irrational behaviour and short-sighted egoism.

A Significant Caricature

Rudolf Steiner expressly pointed out that the name 'Arthur' should not be understood as being applicable to any particular historical personality; on the contrary it designates a degree of spiritual development in rather the same way as the names 'Dionysios' and 'Percival' do.[157] Of course that does not exclude the possibility that, at some time or other, a real historical figure as well might have borne one of these names as well.

From this point of view, then, it would be totally absurd to assert that 'King Arthur was ... a Roman general named Artorius, protégé of a commander called Ambrosius'[158] who, after having defeated the Saxons on several occasions, finally turned the tide of battle in AD515. However, this is the assertion that is to be found in a potted biography of Rudolf Steiner put together some years ago by Colin Wilson and one that constitutes the basis of his criticism of Rudolf Steiner's occult research and the degree of reliability that can be accorded to it.

Furthermore, the castle which Rudolf Steiner had visited—clearly defining the various parts and functions on the spot—is, according to recent archaeological research, supposed to have been built round about the year 1140. *Ergo*, Wilson concludes, it must be nonsense to speak of Arthur and 'his' castle in the same breath. (Though of course the question still remains as to whether such an archaeological estimate itself is even chronologically exact or valid or to what extent the castle which Rudolf Steiner was describing was the one whose medieval ruins can now be seen.) One might easily be tempted to take the view that such a superficial assessment as Wilson's is hardly worthy of serious attention and would be better left unmentioned in the present context. However, let us leave for a moment the author of this attempted biography of Rudolf Steiner and pose the following question. At a time when there is growing interest in the legendary and mythological heritage of all the different peoples of the earth, is it possible that certain deeper-lying motives have come to the surface here? From this point of view the matter can acquire a symptomatic interest for us. The fact that in the book in question there are, indeed, certain intentions on a deeper level of reality than that which meets the eye is borne out by the way in which the author, on account of this alleged historical error, makes 'short shrift' of *everything* established by Rudolf Steiner on the basis of spiritual research concerning Arthur and the 12 knights of his company. The idea that when Rudolf Steiner spoke of 'Arthur' he may have had one or several personalities in view, other than the aforementioned Artorius born about the year 470 is a possibility that is not even considered in any part of the book; instead the reader is served up with the apparent conclusion that 'all this leaves no possible doubt that Steiner's "spiritual perception" of King Arthur and his twelve Knights of the Round Table was pure imagination'.[159]

Thus this arbitrary identification of Arthur with Artorius, which Rudolf Steiner himself had never asserted, leads to a deliberate misrepresentation under the apparently innocuous guise of an intellectual exercise. However, the attentive reader will discover even more significant and deeper-lying intentions than these in the succeeding pages of the book.

During a lecture he gave on 10 September 1924,[160] Rudolf Steiner spoke of the 'later campaigns of Alexander' in connection with those that the Arthurian knights had undertaken within Europe. According to his spiritual-scientific research the real motivation behind Alexander's campaigns was to spread the Aristotelian impulse of intellectual wisdom into Asia. Wilson lights on the figure of Alexander the Great and contends that there is good reason to suspect 'that Steiner was inventing another myth that was pleasing to his imagination'.[161] And here, all of a sudden and before he is aware of it, the reader finds himself in the very midst of the practical results of Rudolf Steiner's karmic research. Then, as though he were travelling on a ghost-train, he is whisked past figures like Livy, Walter von der Vogelweide, Strindberg, Marx, Eduard von Hartmann, Nietzsche and their earlier or later incarnations. In the meantime it apparently becomes 'self-evident', as we advance along this ghostly track, that everything Rudolf Steiner says about these various incarnations is to be regarded with an equal degree of scepticism. Of course the previously-mentioned Michael Prophecy would fall into this category as well . . . Rudolf Steiner spoke of 'anti-Michael' beings which are violently and unreservedly opposed to the revelation of the karma-mysteries which are, in fact, Michaelic Mysteries.[162] It is true that the activity of these beings was paralysed by the impulse of the Christmas Conference[163]—at least in so far as Steiner's own work and influence were concerned. However, that does not mean that the revelations of practical karma that have been irrevocably placed before the world are thereby protected for all eternity from the attacks of such beings. The above excerpt serves to illustrate by means of a concrete example just how such attacks may manifest themselves in our present-day world.

One might find several elements in Wilson's 'biography' which indicate a certain empathy with Rudolf Steiner's work and person; however, if such trends such as are characterized above become apparent in the treatment of such essential areas of Anthroposophy as those concerning the mysteries and revelations of karma, then we are certainly not doing Anthroposophy any favours by overlooking the fact that, despite the author's apparent or real 'positiveness', such trends are to be traced back to those sources that are absolutely and unreservedly opposed to the karma impulse of Anthroposophy. Whether the author of this purported biography of Rudolf Steiner consciously drew his inspiration from these sources or simply allowed himself to be inspired more in the manner of a medium is a question which does not in any way affect the matter at issue.

New Light on H.P. Blavatsky

The reader will no doubt recall the significant role that the person and work of H.P. Blavatsky had played in the spiritual development of D.N. Dunlop and E.C. Merry. For both of them the study of her *Secret Doctrine* had been an act of decisive importance which had set them on their path. This book had not only given Dunlop access to the theosophical forum in which his own spiritual activity could gradually unfold, but had planted also a special seed within his soul—the desire to meet an incarnated Initiate. As for E.C. Merry, she was actually led, some 12 years later (in quite a different and more direct manner) to the person and work of Rudolf Steiner himself.

It must therefore have been of the greatest interest for both of them when, two days from the end of the Torquay course, Rudolf Steiner came to speak of H.P. Blavatsky. He gave a description of her particular methods of acquiring spiritual knowledge and made, not for the first time, a carefully differentiated assessment of *The Secret Doctrine*: 'One must only distinguish what is right from what is wrong,' Rudolf Steiner observes, 'but then tremendous truths are to be found in the *Secret Doctrine*.'[164] It may have been words such as these that inspired E.C. Merry to convey to him what she had experienced in connection with this book, for these experiences must at times have confronted her with deep riddles. She writes in her autobiography:[146]

> . . . a parcel arrived. It was the *Secret Doctrine* of Mme. Blavatsky. Why had it come? I had not ordered it, and actually I never found out why, nor if anyone had sent it, nor if it was a mistake of the book shop, but I kept it. It was a second-hand copy, and did not cost much. It fascinated me entirely, and I felt myself wholly familiar with 'H.P.B.' and her ways of writing and expressing herself. I had, of course, heard of the Theosophists, but knew little or nothing about Theosophy itself. Anyhow, I read the book. And then an odd thing happened. When a passage puzzled me, I used to pause and think, and then it was as though my soul asked a question. At such times an inner voice—a thought—but also a real voice, would find utterance; it was as though I heard 'see page so-and-so, in volume so-and-so'. I would look up, and there was my answer! Or if not my answer, an indication of where the answer could be found.
>
> What was this? I thought it must be 'H.P.B.' herself speaking. But I was sceptical; no, it is no disembodied ghost; it is I myself who subconsciously knew the answer! At the same time I saw—not with my physical eyes . . . a hand that lay on the page of the book. A living hand it was, not a dead one. I knew it was Blavatsky's . . . it was a kind hand; it would lead me on. This did not occur very often, but it did occur, and when I ultimately met the great leader, Rudolf Steiner, I asked him about it, and he said, 'Yes, it is true; she led you to me.' There was more than that, but I cannot tell it yet.

What conclusions can be drawn from Rudolf Steiner's remark in this particular situation? Of course it will have been of great importance to Mrs Merry *personally* (in so far as it would have enabled her to transform her hesitant inklings about the true character of her experience into certain knowledge); but apart from this it seems to have been a reference to a very far-reaching and objective *fact*.

From the very earliest period of Rudolf Steiner's activity within the Theosophical Society right up to the summer of 1924, his lectures are punctuated by countless references to H.P. Blavatsky and her work; these appear most frequently, and in the greatest detail between 1915 and 1916, during the First World War.

H.P. Blavatsky was born in 1831 and died on 8 May 1891. At the time when Rudolf Steiner was most concerned with her life and work (or at least at the time this preoccupation came to expression within his lectures), Blavatsky had already spent a considerable period of time in the spiritual worlds—in fact more than the span of a third of her life on earth. According to indications given by Rudolf Steiner, the discarnate soul has at this point, under the regular law of human existence and evolution, passed through that phase after death which is concerned mainly with soul-realities and is generally called the 'Kama Loka' period; it has discarded all personal aspects of its past earthly life and is ready now to enter into the spiritual world as such.

In the autumn of 1915, in a lecture course entitled *The Occult Movement in the 19th Century*,[165] Rudolf Steiner goes to some lengths to distinguish between various aspects of H.P. Blavatsky's nature and being—her destiny, occult imprisonment, and the mistakes she made. If we consider Rudolf Steiner's spiritual preoccupation with particular human individuals in the light of the remark he made to Mrs. Merry, we may be able to conceive to what extent this preoccupation can be classified as a practical act dealing with concrete realities; and the tremendous importance it must have had for the persons concerned in the future shaping of their destiny—especially if they were no longer incarnated and had already passed through Kama Loka. The light which Rudolf Steiner was able to throw upon the lives of numerous individuals by dint of his spiritual research will have been to many of them of the greatest assistance in their own spiritual development. From this point of view it seems almost impossible to estimate the value of all the karmic revelations Rudolf Steiner made in 1924 on the basis of his spiritual-scientific research. They must have had tremendous significance for all those souls concerned! In practical terms we may surmise from the remark to Mrs Merry that, after death, the individuality who had incarnated as Blavatsky spiritually received some assistance from Rudolf Steiner in coming to an understanding of her own unique and very difficult destiny. His spiritual research will have been in a certain sense a source of instruction for her and, however startling the idea may seem, she will have recognized in Rudolf Steiner her true successor—the one who would continue and expand her pioneering work. Thus she will have freed herself, in a relatively short space of time, from the one-sided attitudes and conditions of her activity on earth. A profound and truly wonderful metamorphosis appears to have taken place soon after death. Any tendency to cling to her own past work or activity seems to have been replaced by the desire of her own spirit to help whoever is attracted to the works she left behind to go beyond them and discover the great human individuality whose pupil she herself had now become. 'Do not stay fettered to the letters of my works, for they are dead,' the individuality of Blavatsky seems to call out to all those who, past or present, might take an interest in her works. 'If you would join me not only in my accomplished works but also in my continuing spiritual activity and endeavour, then embrace the works of the great individuality who has come into the world in order to complete the work that I began.' We have already seen how D.N. Dunlop seemed to have listened to such 'words' from the ever evolving individuality of H.P.B., when placing the date of his exit from the TS precisely on 8 May.

Spiritual Alchemy and the 'Weaving' of Karma

Rudolf Steiner had a huge working agenda in Torquay. Apart from the morning course and the three evening lectures for members he also gave lectures on education for the teachers of the new English Waldorf School between 12 and 20 August. In addition to this there was both a lesson of the 'esoteric class' and a considerable number of individual conversations. He also gave addresses in the town hall on several occasions when Marie Steiner organized public eurythmy performances.

The flames that had already destroyed the building of the First Goetheanum on New Year's Eve 1922/23 had undoubtedly consumed something of the life-substance which its creator had invested in it. In the ensuing period, especially following the Christmas Conference, his condition seemed to polarize itself in the following way. On the one hand, his state of health was visibly deteriorating on account of the increasing pain and difficulty he had in absorbing food; on the other, his lecturing activity intensified in both number and quality, thereby *strengthening* and *rejuvenating* his weakened physical body that was now being influenced by forces very different from those that govern purely physical conditions. Several people, amazed or deeply moved, realized that Rudolf Steiner was in this respect undergoing a series of tremendous metamorphoses. Emil Bock reports that after he returned from his trip to England in September Rudolf Steiner 'could get out of the car and move to the rostrum only by means of the greatest physical exertion'.[166]

Yet how little did Rudolf Steiner's 'illness' actually have to do with anything that is normally associated with this word! This becomes unequivocally clear from the following episode which took place between Rudolf Steiner and D.N. Dunlop in Torquay.

'Only a few weeks before his last illness,' wrote Dunlop in his autobiographical sketch, 'I spoke to him during the Summer School at Torquay of my fears for his physical health. Firmly, but with infinite gentleness he drew me aside and conveyed to me that ordinary conceptions of illness should not be applied to his condition. Those few words of explanation revealed to me far more than their ordinary meaning.' (DS)

Now we would certainly not wish here to make any presumptuous attempt to clear up the entire mystery of Rudolf Steiner's illness, but at least let us consider one aspect which, generally speaking, is not adequately appreciated in this connection.

Earlier, we endeavoured to illustrate how one factor was actually linked to the 'Michael Prophecy' that is not normally included amongst the elements capable of shaping human karma, but in this particular case becomes just such an element. We are referring to the factor of free understanding, where results of spiritual scientific research are concerned, especially those pertaining to practical karmic connections and realities. Rudolf Steiner wanted to make clear to those sitting in the audience that their understanding of these revelations of concrete examples of individual karma would work itself into the same sphere of the will in which karma is wrought and fashioned. Over-riding certain laws of reincarnation and karma that normally hold sway, this would lead to a new reincarnation on the earth soon afterwards. Again and again after the Christmas Conference Steiner emphasized that his decision to assume the presidency of the General Anthroposophical Society carried with it very serious 'possible consequences': that the spiritual beings behind the Anthroposophical Movement might not so to speak 'co-operate', in which case the results of spiritual-scientific research would no longer flow in such rich abundance as they had done before. However, after the conference he also repeatedly emphasized the fact that the opposite of what he had feared had actually occurred. Thus on 18 July he explained to his listeners in Arnheim[167] that 'it may now be said that this'—the withdrawal of the inspiring powers of spiritual beings, after his decision to take over the presidency of an external, World Society—'did not happen, but the contrary is the case: these spiritual powers are responding with an even greater measure of grace, with even greater bounty, to what is streaming through the Anthroposophical Movement.' As we have already noted, this is primarily a reference to the fact that knowledge concerning practical cases of individual karma was flowing even more abundantly and without restraint.

However, in this connection Rudolf Steiner also speaks of a 'pledge' to the spiritual world: 'In a certain sense a pledge has been made to the spiritual world. This pledge will be unswervingly fulfilled.'[167] Only a vague indication of the content of this pledge was given by Rudolf Steiner himself. He evidently intended that it be left to the attentive listener—or the attentive reader today—to investigate the matter entirely on his own initiative.

This 'pledge' certainly presents a great riddle. However, the degree of 'understanding' or 'comprehension' seems to constitute a key factor both with regard to this 'pledge' as well as with regard to Rudolf Steiner's illness. For if Rudolf Steiner drew attention to the fact that, at least where the Michael Prophecy was concerned, the *act of understanding* could become a means for the individual to shape his own karma, it seems extremely probable that this would also be the case concerning a certain *lack of understanding* as well. A real lack of understanding in this context would mean that one merely takes cognizance of the various revelations concerning practical karma without thinking them through in such a way that one's whole feeling and willing become directly involved as well.[168]

If this point of view is accurate then we come to the following conclusion: 'those Powers in the spiritual world that lead the Anthroposophical Movement'[167] were indeed ready, after the Christmas Conference, to allow an even greater wealth of spiritual wisdom to flow through Rudolf Steiner's research, but only on one condition—that he be willing to *make himself accountable for the karmic consequences that a lack of understanding of these practical karmic revelations by those who might be there to receive them would necessarily produce.* In other words, while the *understanding* of such revelations would have significant karmic consequences for the members and all those present at the time, any possible *lack* of understanding would have karmic consequences for him, i.e. the spiritual teacher himself.

From this point of view Rudolf Steiner's 'illness' and death appears to have been the direct result, the karmic consequence of a lack of understanding on the part of the membership and therewith the tragic 'unswerving fulfilment' of that 'pledge'.

Several statements made by Ita Wegman seem to point in this direction. In a letter to all members, dated 4 October 1925, she had this to say about Rudolf Steiner's state of health during the period in question, i.e. autumn 1924:

> Would it not have been wiser to take more of a rest after the journey to Torquay and London which had only just taken place? But this

would be a limited, pedantic way of thinking. In the Spirit there was another point of view. 'These lectures,' said Rudolf Steiner, when we begged him to forbear, 'do not tire me at all. It is the lectures that keep me in good health. What is tiring are the dead thoughts that approach one; it is the incomprehension, the lack of understanding in men that maim one's forces.'

But there was a still deeper reason why these great exertions were made during the Michaelmas season of last year. It was as though Rudolf Steiner still wanted to make every effort, to attain something of what could be attained. It was as though he would protect himself and ward away the influences of illness. One could see it with one's own eyes; the body, often so tired at the beginning of a lecture, grew more and more fresh as the lecture proceeded, and stood at last before us seemingly strong and rejuvenated. We experienced with him every time this metamorphosis proceeding from the Spirit. This was his therapy.[169]

The mysteries of karma are Michael Mysteries *par excellence*. For this reason, once they have been openly and unreservedly revealed, as was the case with Rudolf Steiner, they can only be fruitful and have a beneficial effect if they are taken up with free and energetic understanding. Otherwise, the anti-Michaelic, demonic beings break through the 'meshes' of the intellect, the power of human understanding, and sweep down on these revelations—to caricature them and, if possible, to wipe them off the face of the earth. An example has already been given to illustrate how this can happen in reality. And further light is shed on the background and the spiritual abyss connected with this lack of understanding, by another remark Rudolf Steiner made to Ita Wegman. She mentions it in the same letter in order to illustrate the effect and influence of those demonic beings that can come to power thanks to the lack of human understanding, thereby pointing to deeper levels of reality connected with the enigma of Rudolf Steiner's illness: 'One day Rudolf Steiner told me how mercilessly the anti-Michael demons were setting to work to destroy and prevent the rise of the work of Michael . . . These anti-Michael demons, to whom Klingsor and his hosts also belong, were hard at work, and threatened derisively to come into their own if the Michael-impulses that had begun so strongly, should not be able to break through.'

Now, whether a 'break-through' of this kind can succeed or not depends, in the age of Michael, solely on whether adequate *understanding* of the Michaelic Impulses is forthcoming or not. That is the crucial question: is there sufficient understanding of these impulses or does the lack of understanding so to speak 'outweigh' it, so that these demonic beings can hinder the 'break-through' for the time being?

Ita Wegman continues: 'It was my anxious question: "What then will happen if the Michael-impulses do not succeed in breaking through?" And his answer was: 'Then Karma will hold sway." '[169]

From the whole context the karma in question here would appear to be first and foremost that produced by the listeners' and members' lack of understanding—a 'karma of the lack of understanding'. But it was also a karma which, since the Christmas Conference, and by means of an 'irrevocable pledge', *had entered into the active sphere of Rudolf Steiner's own karma.* 'And karma did hold sway,' Ita Wegman observes, 'on and on, inexorably. We all know how painfully events unfolded. Karma required the sacrifice of death.'[169]

There is of course no intention here of trying to identify any particular persons so as to make them responsible for this lack of understanding. As we have already pointed out, it is not simply a question of understanding something in an intellectual sense but rather of being ready to permeate one's entire feeling life with such understanding, to take it so seriously into one's willing that it actually leads to inner or outer consequences. And who can honestly maintain that he has never understood something one day only to leave it aside the next and not take it really seriously any more? Indeed, the word itself also points to this inner relationship between true *understanding* and the will—expressed externally in a physical activity of the limbs.

We have here to some extent anticipated the coming events. But it seems impossible to make any kind of approach to the enigma surrounding Rudolf Steiner's death without at least touching on such thoughts as those exposed above; for he himself explicitly declared that no ordinary conceptions of illness should be applied to his condition. Perhaps we may now find a more specific meaning in these words. In a normal case of illness the malady is rooted somewhere in the individual's personal karma as such; here, on the contrary, we have to look for the cause in the entire group of human beings to which Rudolf Steiner had bound himself through the Christmas Conference, in a way that he had never done before, and in this group the lack of understanding evidently proved to be *too great*.

If we consider Rudolf Steiner's death in this light then there is an important and urgent lesson to be learnt from it today. His death is a sacrifice that stands before us and the whole future as a kind of warning; it reminds all those who desire to link themselves to Anthroposophy of the necessity for an unceasing striving towards a true understanding of spiritual science, the kind of understanding that can reach down into the heart and even into those depths of will where destiny is formed. Lack of understanding for his teachings had, and indeed still has, its consequences for the founder of this movement.

But let us return to our point of departure—Torquay. For D.N. Dunlop the whole of the scene in question was imbued with presentiments of further knowledge to come. During his conversation with Rudolf Steiner he was able to fathom some of the depths of what Ita Wegman describes above as 'therapy'. Dunlop himself had this to say about it: 'I felt then, and afterwards, that the veils of mysteries connected with the transmutation of the physical organism itself may sometimes be lifted, and a spiritual alchemy made manifest.' (DS)

These moments of intense experience in Torquay must have stirred, or at least brought to the surface, a deeply held interest and predisposition that Dunlop had always had for a spiritual vision of medical affairs. Indeed, it may even be the case that Rudolf Steiner's illuminating words concerning the non-applicability of ordinary concepts to his own condition were also accompanied by a mild innuendo of this kind: to strike in him a faint chord—one that he had long since recognized though it had been scarcely audible till now—so that it might finally vibrate with sound. In any event, one gets the impression that there is a definite link between this conversation and Rudolf Steiner's request a little later that Dunlop take on the medical work to which he had personally dedicated himself in collaboration with Dr Ita Wegman; and also that Dunlop should see to it that the book on medicine[170] which he had compiled with Ita Wegman's collaboration would be published in English translation.

So for Dunlop, too, some significant threads of destiny began to weave together in Torquay, connections with anthroposophical medicine and Ita Wegman—threads which would grow stronger and stronger in the years to come. Before the year 1924 was out Dunlop had founded the British Weleda Company, and as for his work with Ita Wegman, who often stayed in England after Rudolf Steiner's death, a wonderful kind of collaboration continued between the two of them—right up to the moment of D.N. Dunlop's death.

Recorded in the Golden Book of the Anthroposophical Movement

On 22 August 1924, at the end of the Torquay course, Rudolf Steiner gave a farewell address in which he looked back on the happy outcome of the summer school.[171] This address may be considered as a special kind of legacy given the fact that Rudolf Steiner's death, which followed on 25 March 1925, meant that the Torquay course provided the main content of the last summer school during his lifetime. In the course of his speech he once again alluded to the fact that he had only been able to deal with certain subjects here because, from the beginning, certain prerequisite conditions of a spiritual nature had been fulfilled by the persons organizing the conference. Indeed, this had even been so to the extent that certain aspects of the lecture-hall which, 'from an occult point of view, were not very sympathetic in nature, nor artistically inspiring' had been as it were 'paralysed'. And once again it is clear that he found something extraordinarily fulfilling in the harmony and concordance between what he was confronted with as external conditions and circumstances, and what he bore within himself and actually wanted to achieve on an anthroposophical level.

'In these Summer Schools,' he observed, 'it has been possible for the first time to develop things which needed their ground to be prepared in a certain way. One could put it this way: both Summer Schools were organized in such a manner that one felt in an occult sense "at home". Indeed, it seems to me, looking back on everything that could be felt during the time of this Summer School, that the initiatives of our friends Mr Dunlop and Mrs Merry stem from a background which is clearly perceptible to feeling—from a genuine source of spiritual scientific striving.'

In some of the preceding sections we have attempted to throw a little light on this background.

> This year, and the year before as well, one felt so to speak in an occult sense 'at home'. We were able to be in environments which speak out much of primordial significance. Indeed, it is on account of all that has been preserved of primordial significance, that the surroundings still speak to us today in a spiritually exceptionally significant way. In such an environment and milieu the very words and spiritual forms which would like to approach the adherents and sympathizers of the Anthroposophical Movement are also set free—that is, to those who are ready to take up in themselves and actively represent that all-embracing form of anthroposophical will and aspiration which must now enter into the present and immediate future in accordance with the signs of the times. This anthroposophical aspiration stems from those spiritual worlds to which during this course of lectures we have repeatedly referred. And so it was possible here to feel in a certain sense a kind of growing together between what flows through the Anthroposophical Movement as such and what has here been prepared as a kind of framework for it by our dear friends, above all Mr Dunlop.

In the closing words of his farewell address Rudolf Steiner summarized the overall significance of both summer schools in these terms:

But in conclusion I would like to assure your souls once again that the memory of the Conference which we spent here in Torquay will live on in the same way as that of Penmaenmawr. *It will live on in the sense that everything that has come to us here from loving hearts, from souls really permeated with Anthroposophy, all this will be regarded as something which can be recorded in a very special way in the Golden Book of the Anthroposophical Movement.* For precisely in this Anthroposophical Movement much depends on whether or not a real element of an occult, spiritual-scientific, anthroposophical nature comes into what is being organized—into what comes to pass; and the presence of this element will accompany us hereafter in memory like a brightly shining light from the past. I would hereby give you the most heartfelt assurance of this!

A Leave-taking in London

After Rudolf Steiner had completed the Torquay course, he spent a few days in London before returning to Dornach. Speaking out of the spirit of the Christmas Conference he wished to inform the members of the impulses that had given rise to it.[172]

The three lectures Rudolf Steiner gave for members are in the present context of quite special interest to us because they were to be the last that D.N. Dunlop and Mrs Merry would hear. In what follows we will single out one or two points which seem to be of importance in relation to Dunlop's presence at these lectures.

Once again we come across a kind of 'leitmotif' concerning the right attitude towards karma—the necessity of 'taking karma absolutely seriously', and thereby also that 'true and authentic way of looking at history' which arises 'when one sees the background of human destinies against the foreground of the events which meet us on the external stage of history.'

Rudolf Steiner described to his London audience how the impulses inherent in the Christmas Conference represented a kind of return to original spiritual intentions which had been powerfully present in all of his anthroposophical activity right from the very beginning. However, the theosophists had not wanted to know anything about them at the time; they had received a 'terrible shock' when confronted with the 'concreteness' of these realities.[173]

In a similar way, although on a larger historical scale, the form of spiritual consciousness that from now onwards we are to develop is equivalent to a kind of 'return'—though of course on the higher level of fully waking consciousness—to a form of consciousness experienced by prehistoric humanity. For, as Rudolf Steiner described in the first of his London lectures, the concrete vision of karma was something which still played into the sleeping consciousness of human beings at that time.

One aspect of this lecture which Dunlop would have found particularly appealing is the way in which Rudolf Steiner indirectly leads up to the faculty of karmic vision as it has to be attained in the future, first of all by describing what clairvoyant vision encounters behind the mineral, plant and animal kingdoms, in order to show how 'behind all the mysteries of the world there lies, in truth, the great mystery of karma for the human being'. For in the final instance, 'behind all that appears there as a foreground, there then appear the overwhelmingly sublime manifestations of karma'. Such considerations would have struck a particularly deep chord in D.N. Dunlop who, since his Dublin days, had been intent upon 'awakening people to the wonders surrounding them'.

In the second lecture Rudolf Steiner gave more concrete examples of how karma works in history. Here again Dunlop will no doubt have been deeply moved by the way in which the lecturer approached Voltaire and Ignatius of Loyola, bringing the cosmic-planetary aspect of karma into the very forefront of his considerations. And it must have been of gripping interest to Dunlop when, in the same lecture, Steiner went on to depict *Emanuel Swedenborg* and *Laurence Oliphant*,[174] two historical figures not mentioned by him in any other of the karma lectures. For had not Dunlop some 35 years earlier found a close connection with the Swedenborgian seer Harris and then shaken off his influence just as Oliphant had done? We might also recall in this context that in Dunlop's eyes what was valuable in Oliphant's work could mostly be traced directly back to Harris. It will therefore no doubt have come to him as something of a revelation when Rudolf Steiner spoke of Oliphant, even in his opening words, as 'an exceptionally interesting personality, a personality who, if one studies his books, at once . . . strikes one as very significant.'

In addition to this Dunlop will also have been deeply grateful for the allusion to Ovid's karma—especially in relation to Brunetto Latini and Dante. Ovid had been 'a guide in the spiritual world for many initiates'. These revelations shed new light on the figure of Laurence Oliphant. And what is more, Dunlop seems to have had a strong connection to the epoch of Dante as well. (An external manifestation of this connection can be seen by the fact that he had met his life-companion, Eleanor Fitzpatrick, at a lecture on Dante.

In the third lecture, given in London on 27 August, Rudolf Steiner again took up the Arthurian theme, this time bringing in new aspects connected with the Christ impulse. It is also clear from what he expounded in this context that the most intense period of King Arthur's influence reaches right back into the centuries before the Mystery of Golgotha, stretching over a total of a thousand years or more.[175] He describes how 'in the play of nature between sea and rock, air and light, the Event of Golgotha was as it were played out in spiritual reflection.' Furthermore he alludes to the *Hibernian origin* of the Arthurian impulse and speaks of a 'science of the higher graduates' among the Arthurian knights and also of 'exercises' which 'were concerned above all with the Mysteries of the Zodiac'. The polar relationship between Grail stream and Arthurian stream is also touched upon once again:

> The other stream, rooted inwardly in the hearts of men, which later on became the Grail stream, is to be perceived more in the South, coming from the East. It bears the actual, true, real Christ. The stream coming from the West, the Arthurian stream, brings a cosmic image of the Christ to meet it.[176]

At the end of this lecture Rudolf Steiner focuses once more on the Michael impulse. He describes the relationships of those souls belonging to the Michaelic stream who, since the blossoming of the school of Chartres in the twelfth century, had received a grandiose form of cosmic instruction in the supersensible worlds, in the 'School of Michael'. Their principal instruction had consisted of a magnificent retrospect in which 'review was given of all the ancient mysteries', but also a 'vista of the future was opened up' to them. At the very end of this last lecture for members, this 'vista of the future' leads into a renewed proclamation of the 'Michael Prophecy'. Rudolf Steiner obviously wished to plant it deeply into the souls of those anthroposophists present at the time who would 'feel a strong urge to come down to the earth again very soon'.

Dunlop would certainly have engraved the following words deep within his soul; they are words which, in their fiery concentration, call on the vigilant will to awaken to fully conscious action and activity; they portray the historical necessity of a turning-point in time, brought about by a great intensification of activity in the Michaelic sense:

> Every Anthroposophist should be moved by this knowledge: 'Here I stand. I have in me the impulse of Anthroposophy. I recognize it as the Michael Impulse. I wait and am strengthened in my waiting by true activity in Anthroposophy at the present time in order that after the short interval allotted to anthroposophical souls in the 20th century between death and a new birth, I may come again at the end of the 20th century to promote the Movement with a much more spiritual power. I am preparing for the new Age leading from the 20th into the 21st century.' This is what a true anthroposophist says to himself. Many forces of destruction are at work upon the earth! All culture, all civilized life must fall into decadence if the spirituality of the Michael Impulse does not so lay hold of men that they are capable of uplifting what in civilization is hurrying downhill.
>
> If there are to be found truly anthroposophical souls, willing to bring spirituality into earthly life in this way, then there will be a movement leading upwards. If such souls are *not* found, decadence will continue to spread. The great War, with all its attendant evils, will be merely the beginning of still worse evils.
>
> Mankind stands today before a great contingency: before the contingency of either seeing everything which forms civilization going down into the abyss, or of raising it by spirituality and

promoting it in the sense of the Michael Impulse which stands before the Christ Impulse.

*

Rudolf Steiner made his departure from London. By this time the clock measuring the hours of Dunlop's life already pointed to the imminent accomplishment of his third lunar-node cycle. A more favourable biographical constellation than this is hardly imaginable, for it provided the most fertile terrain for the Michael Prophecy, a prophecy which inflames the spiritual depths of will. This was one of those 'moments' when certain 'windows' are no longer closed and our world 'opens . . . onto another world'.[21]

Let us recall how D.N. Dunlop had made the acquaintance of AE in Ireland round about the time of his first lunar node and had thereby begun to clarify certain substantial aspects of his previous spiritual experiences by connecting them, quite concretely, to the idea of reincarnation, and how the subsequent conclusion of his second cycle of lunar nodes had brought in Paris a marked impression of Rudolf Steiner's person. At the completion of this, the third phase of his lunar nodes, both of these threads of destiny are united and increase in significance in a totally unexpected manner: in Dunlop's experiences of the Michael Prophecy.

Now the exact focal-point of these lunar nodes coincides with the end of September. However, we can also take into account the months before and after it as they belong to the temporal 'aura' of this extremely significant biographical 'moment'. Thus we can speak, with regard to these lunar nodes, of a phase stretching over a period of about six months. It was out of this phase that, apart from the Michael Prophecy, two other events of great significance had also emerged; one of these was the whole Torquay Summer School course; the other was the opening of the World Power Conference in London, which will be described in the next part of this book.

*

Although Rudolf Steiner had been pursuing his own spiritual research into the Celtic stream long before these summer schools, Dunlop succeeded in bringing him into a special kind of relationship to it. By leading him to Penmaenmawr and Torquay, he enabled 'the bearer of the spirit to his age' to meet a real need for spiritual knowledge, for 'a spiritual "cosmogony" in which he recognized the true and innate tendency of the Western spirit'.[177] Dunlop had known how to 'ask for' this from the very beginning in the right way and had also possessed an acute sense of the cosmopolitan and universal dimensions of Rudolf Steiner's mission. Whilst the imaginative experience of his youth on the Isle of Arran had coincided with the dawning of the Michael Era, it was during the two and a half years of his personal acquaintance with Rudolf Steiner that he had become a fully conscious servant of Michael. It is in this sense that we must interpret the words that Rudolf Steiner spoke at their parting as he held Dunlop's hand between his own, just as he had done during the very first moments of their initial encounter, three words that expressed his joy and gratitude at their meeting as well as a rare acknowledgement of spiritual maturity: 'We are brothers'—that is, brothers in the service of Michael.

5

THE IMPULSE OF THE WORLD POWER CONFERENCE

The eternal is discovered most fully in what appears to hide it most effectually. D.N.D.

A Congress in Cannes

In Cannes, on 5 October 1986, the French president, François Mitterand, opened the Thirteenth Congress of the World Energy Conference which lasted until 11 October. The World Energy Conference* is a *permanent* international organization which meets at a different venue every three years.

On this occasion about five thousand participants from all countries of the globe were gathered in the huge congress building situated on the French Riviera; approximately three thousand of them were specialists from the closely interconnected branches of energy research, production and technology. The theme of the 1986 conference was 'Energy—Needs and Expectations'. Although preparations for the Congress had already begun two years earlier it took place in the wake of the recent Chernobyl disaster whose multiple aspects and consequences were examined during the plenary discussion.

In May 1986, Eric Ruttley, then Secretary-General of the World Energy Conference (which has its headquarters in London), gave a short résumé of the history and the development of this organization pointing out at the beginning that it had been founded in the year 1924 under the title 'World Power Conference' by 'Daniel Dunlop, a theosophist and anthroposophist'. Ruttley described the founder as a 'visionary', for 'it was his vision that created this organization of power engineers'. By bringing together more than two thousand technicians, 'the men who were going to build the power houses of the world in coming decades,'[178] he had given expression to a universal desire of

* *Author's note:* The name of the World Energy Conference was changed to World Energy Council in 1990.

humanity after the destruction brought about by the First World War. In the information brochures handed out to journalists on the spot we again find a mention of Dunlop, and similar traces of the founder of this organization appeared also in Montreal in the autumn of 1989 when the Fourteenth Congress was held.

The fact that this organization, which remains an essentially private institution even though, in its modern form, it embraces some 80 member countries, still betrays clear signs of D.N. Dunlop's past involvement is in itself already reason enough to examine somewhat more closely the circumstances and intentions connected with its foundation and the evolution that it has since then undergone.

On 30 May 1986, the anniversary of Dunlop's death, a new edition of the constitution of the World Energy Conference was reprinted for the Congress in Cannes. Under the heading 'Objects' we find the following definition of the purpose of the organization, unchanged since 1924: 'The Objects of the World Energy Conference are to promote the development and peaceful use of energy resources to the greatest benefit of all, both nationally and internationally.'

The Prince of Wales Lends his Prestige

On 30 June 1924, the First World Power Conference was inaugurated by the then Prince of Wales (later Edward VIII) under the auspices of the British Empire Exhibition in the presence of over two thousand delegates from some 40 different countries.

'Not many years after the War, he conceived the idea that the engineers and scientists, whose inventions had been so powerful in destruction, should lend their great talents in the rebuilding of the world.' These words appeared in Dunlop's obituary in *The Times* on 5 June 1935. The idea at the root of the World Power Conference was in complete accordance with Dunlop's comprehensive 'Philosophy of Co-operation'. The aim was to create a forum in order to facilitate the free flow and exchange of information concerning the production and technological use of energy throughout the world; and this exchange was not in any way to be limited or hindered by political or ideological considerations. The technicians, engineers and scientists gathered to this end were to establish a kind of inventory of the world's total energy resources—a task certainly showing far-reaching vision, especially for that time. The survey was to show to what extent these resources were already being used for practical purposes and to indicate the technical problems encountered in connection with their exploitation. Finally, the participants were to take the first steps towards organizing an extensive international framework for collaboration and research into new sources of energy and to formulate the economic, political and cultural questions inevitably linked to such an undertaking.

The Conference took place entirely on Dunlop's personal initiative (brought by him in 1922 before the Council of the BEAMA and fully endorsed by that body). It is also noteworthy that this was the first international conference after the First World War to invite and indeed to be attended by not only Russian but also German delegates. 'If you think along the line of facts,' Dunlop told Stein some time afterwards, 'you will find that no international Conference on technical subjects would be complete without Germany.' The invitation to Germany was called for simply on the basis of a 'feeling for reality and a sense of justice'. (St)

Calling on Germany to participate (just after she had been placed in the international pillory at Versailles) was not the only bold step Dunlop took on this occasion. C.H. Gray, whom out of 40 different candidates applying for the post Dunlop appointed Secretary of the International Executive Council of the WPC in 1929, stated in his retirement speech: 'It was Dunlop who had the courage to name the 1924 Meeting "The First World Power Conference" at a time when only his faith gave any grounds for thinking that it would not also be the last World Power Conference.'[179]

It is indeed characteristic of Dunlop's farsightedness that he should have planned things in such a way that, from the moment the project was launched, a potential continuity was bound up with it. Thus, in the realization of this project we encounter not only an exceptional faculty of moral intuition but also a corresponding capacity for exercising farsighted moral phantasy as well as a skilful mastery of moral technique.[180]

A further illustration of Dunlop's exceptional faculties of moral imagination and finesse can be seen from the following. Shortly before the conference was due to begin it was still uncertain who should actually inaugurate it. Of course Dunlop could have done this himself but in his eyes this would not have demonstrated very much 'skill in action'. It would certainly be far more effective to win over someone whose name would find the greatest possible resonance on an international level; not in order to create an artificial or exaggerated interest in the undertaking. Dunlop's purpose was simply to draw the attention of the general public to it from the very start. In the circumstances this might even add substantially to both its impact and its ability to survive, especially given the deeper-lying intentions connected with the First World Power Conference.

One day, as Dunlop later explained to a circle of his close friends, whilst he was sitting in his office with this open question,

> the Prince of Wales came to his mind. Time being short, he immediately telephoned St. James's Palace. He spoke to the Prince's secretary. After stating what he wanted there was a pause and then the secretary said: "His Royal Highness is here now and if you will come straight round he will see you." So, just as he was, having little idea how he should behave in the presence of a Prince, he jumped into a taxi. At St. James's he was shown straight in to the Prince of Wales, who was by nature sympathetic to such ideas as Dunlop put before him: To organize the power resources of the world so as to make them available to all peoples. And so it came about that the inaugural meeting of the World Power Conference was opened by the Prince of Wales, which Dunlop obviously felt was the best beginning it could have had.[85]

For the Prince of Wales, then aged 30, delivering inaugural speeches of this kind belonged to his routine duties. It is to be presumed that the basic concept of his speech grew directly out of this conversation with Dunlop (that is, if the latter did not compile the greater part of it himself). In any event it seems that the Prince was by no means lacking in a genuinely cosmopolitan and liberal attitude. He began his opening speech:

> It is with great pleasure that, as President of the British Empire Exhibition, I now welcome the delegates who are assembled in session to discuss the many vital problems connected with the first World Power Conference. I feel this to be an occasion of great importance, for it may prove the beginning of a series of conferences, whereby the combined knowledge and judgment of the world may be devoted to the solution of the many difficulties confronting, not only science and research, but also economic progress throughout the world. We have become accustomed to the idea of an international clearing-house for many things, and in the League of Nations, with its Labour Office and International Court of Justice, have seen international co-operation at work in political and labour questions and in law; but the deeper questions connected with industrial progress and equipment, with natural resources, with the conservation of energy and of fuel, with standardization in design and manufacture, have hitherto, I believe, been examined by each country in isolation, with results that are apparent to everyone. In this effort to create for industry, and especially power, what the League of Nations intends for politics, lies I think, the true significance of the World Power Conference, and in the belief that something more fundamental than merely technical discussions will result, I extend a cordial welcome to the distinguished representatives here today.[181]

In his later memoirs, looking back at his various activities during this period, the former Edward VIII describes the purpose of these duties: 'When, in the preparation of these memoirs, I had occasion to thumb through my old calendars, I was surprised at the variety of things that I did . . . The job of Prince of Wales, as I tried to interpret it, was first, to carry on associations with the worthy causes outside politics and clothe them with the prestige of the Prince's high position; and second, to bring the Monarchy, in response to new conditions, ever nearer to the people.[182] However well the Prince of Wales may have succeeded in achieving the first of these goals, the second certainly seems to have been his undoing—if in this respect one considers his marriage to a divorced American woman which brought him after the first few months of his reign into the cross-fire of British politics and led to his abdicating in December 1936. Nonetheless, the simple fact that he had sensed the future significance of the World Power impulse in so far as he predicted a potential functioning of this international forum along parallel lines to those on which the League of Nations was functioning at that time reveals just how much he was motivated by an attitude which, in the long run, might even have brought his influence to bear beyond the well-defined interests of the British Empire.

'International co-operation!' the Prince emphasizes at the end of his speech, 'may emerge from the realm of the ideal, into the realm of practical utilization, as the result of your deliberations and I sincerely trust that full success will attend them.'

Already some time before this congress national committees had been formed; during the conference its own establishment with the status and constitution of a *permanent* institution was now also carried out. We have already noted how Dunlop went to some lengths to present this conference in such a way that from the start the character of potential continuity should be imprinted upon it; now let us consider the reverse aspect of his intentions here. Supposing, as indeed was the case, that an organization defined as a 'conference' were to be successfully transformed into a permanent institution, then the danger of fixation and stagnation that threatens every institution from its very birth would from the outset be forestalled. Therefore the fact that it was called a 'conference' meant that, once this had been accepted, the public (upon whom very much depends in the effective spreading of such an impulse) would be much more likely to retain an impression of something new and fresh—perhaps even something in the process of being born. During the conference, which lasted 13 days, *The Times* printed extensive daily commentaries on the proceedings. Behind some of the articles which appeared it is possible to discern, directly or perhaps indirectly, the hand of D.N. Dunlop at work. For he was unlikely to have missed any opportunity for giving the occasional newspaper reporter a few useful indications, or even of providing the press with the odd article which he himself had written—anonymously of course. Thus, on the third day of the conference, we find a long article entitled 'The World's Power House', in which the expression 'World Power' is used in such a way as to lead us to suppose that there may have been deeper-lying intentions behind *this* choice of words as well:

'As a rule . . . the term "World Power" is used in connection with military armaments, for purposes sometimes of national defence, sometimes of national and territorial aggrandizement. At the Wembley Conference its meaning is something very different. It embraces all the different kinds of power latent in Nature.'[183]

Thus, the word 'power', with its strong political connotations, is in a sense completely 'turned round' and consciously integrated into an impulse concerned with the economic and technological sphere. It is as though, even in the choice of name, Dunlop wanted to arouse a certain feeling within the public at large: after the disasters of the World War the idea of individual power, or power in party-political terms, must give way to more urgent considerations concerning the use of the power inherent in nature as a whole, power which does not belong to any single individual or party but which has to be used in the most reasonable way for the good of all mankind. That is the real power problem facing the whole of humanity today, a problem that can only be solved by an attitude of brotherhood that is able to transcend all personal and national points of view. Such considerations as these might well have inspired Dunlop to make this choice of name. At all events it is the reason for our choice of the title which appears at the beginning of this part of our book—a part in which this aspect of Dunlop's life and work is to be considered as fully as space permits.

Broader Aims and Perspectives

The first conference in London in 1924 was just as meticulously prepared as all the subsequent ones have been to this day. Long before its beginning many of the intending participants had already sent in written versions of their contributions; copies had been made and sent off to other participants so that they could look over them beforehand. A few months after the conference, the wealth of contributions reappeared in a more visible and tangible form in the 'Transactions' of the copies. However, Dunlop attached considerably less importance to these copious volumes than to the fact that, in an atmosphere of expert knowledge and experience on the one hand and of tolerance and trust on the other, a host of international as well as eminently personal contacts could be, and indeed were, established.

Naturally Dunlop had, during these times, become acquainted with Rudolf Steiner's ideas concerning the threefold social order. A translation of *The Threefold Commonwealth* had already come out in 1920 and the impulse he had received from and since his first meeting with Rudolf Steiner in 1922 played a significant role in his conception of the World Power Conference, the foundation of which had indeed first been proposed by him in that very same year. And two years later, after the Torquay Summer School, Steiner had himself visited the British Empire Exhibition at Wembley, where the World Power Conference had been inaugurated a month earlier, and had discussed with Dunlop its aims. And Dunlop had certainly also followed Steiner's social activities with keen attention and perceived how the latter's attempts immediately after the War to realize the idea of a new social order on European soil had initially been unsuccessful as insufficient impact had been made on the leading figures in the political sphere.

Thus, Dunlop's intentions in founding the World Power Conference were more all-embracing than might at first meet the eye (even of the practitioners of the World Energy Conference today). This is made evident not only from the Prince of Wales's speech in which he evokes the idea of a potential parallel functioning of this international forum with that of the League of Nations, but also from a statement Dunlop made on one occasion to Walter Johannes Stein. Stein recalls that in 1924 Dunlop 'founded the World Power Conference. In reality he wanted to found a World Economic Conference. In this connection he said to me: "I could see clearly that it was impossible to bring together politicians, and as all the important economic decisions are in the hands of politicians, it was hopeless to found an international economic body as a first step. But it was possible to bring together human beings in the field of technical questions, and so I started there. But I always had in mind the idea of enlarging this body of engineers to a body of experts of all branches of industry and agriculture. I wanted not only to include the producers and distributors but also the consumers and consider their point of view.' (St)

*

Undoubtedly one of the essential sources of inspiration for the World Power Conference can be found in Rudolf Steiner's new social ideas mentioned above, which are rooted in the basic idea of a *threefold social order*. Steiner tried to introduce a new consciousness within the social organism. The constituent elements (or rather 'members') of this organism currently interpenetrate each other in a totally chaotic fashion; in the future the cultural, judicial and economic spheres must function as three autonomous bodies within it. Just how profoundly this idea is anchored in the development and conditions of modern civilization has been explained by Rudolf Steiner in a variety of contexts. One of the most significant aspects of this development is to be found in what he termed *the unconscious process whereby mankind as a whole is passing over the threshold of the spiritual world*.[184] However, if individual consciousness does not activate itself in accordance with the Michaelic nature of our times in order to lift this transition more and more into the realm of clear awareness, then the only outcome from this process will be a growing number of pathological cases and caricatures of spiritual states of consciousness. In this connection man will have to become conscious of another factor inseparably linked to the crossing of the threshold: the fact that the three activities of the human soul—thinking, feeling, and willing—have broken free from the chaotic bond of unity that once held them together and, in effect, served as a model for the unity of nation-state. Since these forces are thus becoming ever more independent of one another, it is from now onwards the task of the truly spiritual ego within the human being to bring them into a new relationship and to create a free form of interaction between them. Considered from this point of view the expression of this need for a threefold social organism appears as a direct response, on the social level, to just this aspect of the evolutionary conditions of modern-day humanity.

What Dunlop tried to do in the technical and economic field was to make a really dynamic contribution towards realizing this idea of a threefold social order. He brought new impulses into this field and directed them towards the formation of a world-wide, autonomous economic entity, free from all restrictive and destructive influences stemming either from the sphere of politics or from the domain of various kinds of 'ideology' (as our spiritual and cultural life must be termed so long as it remains unfree and in a thoroughly dependent state).

Behind this impulse to establish a world economy, the inspiring activity and influence of that Being which has become the dominant Spirit of the Times since the year 1879 can be felt—Michael. Indeed, perhaps it is not mere coincidence that the notion of world economy as such (in contrast to that of national economy tied to the unit of the nation state) was first expressed by the English economist Marshall[185] in that same year, 1879. Neither does it appear to be pure coincidence that at about the same time before and after this decisive year Dunlop himself, who was so intimately connected with this cosmopolitan impulse in and for the economic world, underwent two experiences of fundamental importance for his life and, although belonging to another dimension, equally inspired by the Spirit of the Times in that they helped to give birth to his *own spiritual independence*.

Even if such underlying aspirations as those that Dunlop had associated with the founding of the World Power Conference remain to this day unrealized, we shall nevertheless do well to keep them in mind in the following pages, which describe the ensuing developments and evolution of this organization. For these aims are manifestly inherent in the World Power Conference from the first breath of its existence right down to the truly practical form that this organization has assumed today, without as yet, however, realizing its full potential.

'The Order of the Starry Heavens Reflected on the Earth'

As Chairman of the International Executive Council, Dunlop suggested that the next conference should be held as early as 1926. It was to take place from 30 August to 8 September so as to coincide with an exhibition in Basel based on 'Inland Navigation and its Relation to the Utilization of Water Power', and to be the first so-called 'sectional meeting' of the conference.

This second international conference was organized by the Swiss national committee and attended by about six hundred representatives from about 40 different countries. The following themes were on the agenda: the utilization of water power; inland navigation; exchange of electrical energy between countries; and railway electrification. The opening of the conference was also marked by a musical event—the performance of part of *My Country*, Smetana's cycle of symphonic poems.

In his opening speech[186] Dunlop alluded to the way in which culture and commerce (i.e. the economic sphere in general) were necessarily linked. Switzerland, and especially Basel as its oldest university town, was a very good example of this. He pointed out that it was not only in the field of electrical industry that Switzerland was in the first rank. She was also in an outstanding position thanks to her seven universities, her schools specializing in commercial and technical instruction and her system of education as a whole; she finally distinguished herself by the inherent love of peace of her population. All this made Switzerland a specially predestined home for international movements.

The speaker moved on from these historical considerations of the immediate environment and turned the attention of his listeners to the events connected with the First World Power Conference and thereby also to present tasks:

> The success of the First World Power Conference was due almost wholly to the fact that the main principles behind the Conference fitted into a powerful international tendency which had not yet found expression. For a moment, the idealists might have envisaged a Parliament composed of members of all the nations, intent on bringing the science and economics of power development and utilization into a single grandiose scheme capable of embracing the whole world, but such ideals are not realized in a day or even a century. The work of classification and research is immense and can only be carried out effectively as a result of many conferences devoted to special aspects and finally to large problems. The First World Power Conference gave the broad outlines but left the elaboration of the various parts of the picture to further Conferences and Sectional Meetings such as this now held at Basle. It may be possible in the future, when all the details are mastered, to view in complete perspective what will be ultimately the perfect fresco. Meantime we must continue our deliberations in the knowledge that the cause of international co-operation in the field of power at least, is being advanced.

The participants were subsequently led over four stages of questions concerning the ground to be covered during this conference: **1.** What were the overriding goals of the first Conference? **2.** What results had been achieved? **3.** What were the next steps to be taken on the basis of these results? **4.** How can these steps be reconciled with the all-embracing goals posed at the outset?

Dunlop then goes on to discuss concrete details and problems connected with the technological exploitation of energy. He proposes that in every part of the world where nature supplies the necessary resources power zones be created in order to raise the economic and industrial standard of development and he expresses the opinion that international co-operation in *this* field can facilitate co-operation in other spheres as well.

After considering various facts and figures for both Europe and indeed elsewhere he makes it quite clear to his listeners that the economic unit in world trade is no longer the nation as it was in the nineteenth century, but the whole world. On the basis of his assessment of modern conditions and trends Dunlop develops the idea of a world economy which is here to stay. By so doing he draws the attention of his listeners to an important change in the economy as an inherent part of the threefold social order.

These words bear no resemblance to the fine self-satisfied utterances we may be accustomed to hearing from the president of a conference; nor is there any trace of fanaticism or over-anxiety to be found in them. On the contrary, they betray the presence of a very generous form of idealism—one that knows how to take its time, centuries if necessary. They witness a profound trust and confidence in the positive and productive forces of human nature. It was this idealism and confidence that Dunlop wanted to awaken in his listeners, for without such a basis as this even the very best and most comprehensive exchange of information was bound to remain totally external and completely ineffective with regard to other social spheres. For 'the key to the happiness of the world does not lie in a return to standards of fifteen years ago, but in our capacity to learn from each other and to act in such a way that confidence will be established among men. Along this line, which is the path of peace, of prosperity and of progress, lies our duty to our fellow men'. Thus it is clear that Dunlop wants to speak to the *hearts* of his listeners. It is certainly not his intention to inflame their interest in some external form of Utopian progress. He even points to the dangers of an interpretation of progress based exclusively on technological criteria and evokes certain visions of a one-sided technological civilization of the future—visions expressed in the West, in Middle Europe and in Eastern Europe by three well-known authors of the time:

> If we consider the successive stages in the history of civilization, we cannot fail to see that such stages are closely connected with the discovery of the means of utilizing the resources of Nature effectively, but the last hundred and fifty years have seen an altogether amazing speeding up of the progression of material development. Wherever we look, we see the most remarkable instances of this, and even while we look, scientists in all countries are dreaming of future conquests of Nature's secrets. But here a word of warning may not be out of place. Samuel Butler envisaged a race of

> men dominated by machinery, Anatole France conceived a series of civilizations which by their irrational development of power, sowed the seeds of their own decay. And recently Karl Capek presented the world with a terrifying conception of mechanical robots.

Given the world-wide scepticism of the population at large that was aroused by the Chernobyl disaster, the doubts concerning the trustworthiness of an atomic industry governed by economic interests and power politics, the next words of Dunlop's speech seem now to express a quite contemporary sense of urgency: 'It is quite obvious that the lay mind entertains not a little secret fear regarding our dealings with natural forces.' The Chernobyl disaster brought this fear into the consciousness of the *general public*—that is the only difference. That even at that time Dunlop did not believe such fears should be ignored or smothered (a tactic that many 'practically-minded' people still consider today to be the only realistic line to take in such circumstances), is clear from his next words. For suddenly, as though *en passant*, he weaves into his thoughts an entirely new but yet well-prepared theme: 'These fears can only be overcome satisfactorily by the cultivation of a free and independent cultural life, the influences from which will flow into the economic and political spheres with beneficial effect.' Skilful allusion is here again made to the need for a threefold social structuring of society, this time with the accent on the spiritual, cultural life as one pole of it—purely from examining the relevant factual context and without employing any kind of vocabulary that might be only half understood by the participants or in any way 'weighted'. It is in just such a case that we can observe how in a given situation Dunlop was able to weave into matters under current consideration various background themes and to create an atmosphere of trust on the basis of an objective, thoroughly unprejudiced and comprehensive approach, so that here and there the seeds of much more comprehensive ideas could be sown.

The climax of the speech, both in terms of rhetoric and content, comes right towards the end and is in marked contrast to the three gloomy prospects of the future outlined above: 'The key to unlock the forces still latent in matter lies in the heart of man. When man wills the good, then the tempest of national and international jealousies will be stilled and the order of the starry heavens will be reflected on the earth.'

Of course at first glance these words too might appear to be nothing more than beautiful rhetoric aimed at creating a good general atmosphere. However, as we have already attempted to illustrate earlier in this book, it is really not only a matter of *what* is said. What is far more important is *who* is saying it and what his intentions on a spiritual level may be—in other words: 'to what spirit they belong'. Behind all words there is always a real human being with all his individual experiences and attainments and the predominating quality of his particular intentions. So that in this case whoever is prepared to take an overall view of all that we have brought forward up to this point in our attempt to throw light upon the individuality of D.N. Dunlop and the development of his personality will no doubt come to quite different conclusions and feelings when contemplating such words as these.

Perhaps the principle of an all-embracing will appears most clearly and profoundly in Dunlop's meditation on the 'Symbols of Magic', especially with respect to an external activity placed in the service of humanity. For Dunlop 'good' can only mean that which advances the universal goals of man; and in the 'stilling' of 'the tempest' it is possible to feel something of that elementary power of the will which can subdue all the contrary forces. Even behind such expressions as 'the order of the starry heavens' . . . 'reflected on the earth' it is possible to sense certain scenes and condensed experiences from his life-story. The same phrasing which, for someone who only pays attention to the wording, must sound like poetical and metaphorical clichés can take us back to that scene in Dunlop's youth where, as a 9-year-old boy, he sought to communicate the meaning of the Universal Word to his 12 comrades . . . It can also take us back to Tintagel where Dunlop, under the full impact of Rudolf Steiner's 'on-the-spot' discoveries and his enlightening observations a few days afterwards, had as it were received his 'Arthurian initiation'.

Thus a keen eye may see through such utterances into the

background where real spiritual forces and impulses are at work. Dunlop's aim was not to reap fame and recognition but only to act, in the fullest sense, according to what he himself had recognized as being good. It would have been entirely superfluous to speak of a 'threefold social order as envisaged by Rudolf Steiner' or of a 'magic will', or the 'principle of the Round Table as the impulse of modern civilization'. In such situations what matters is *to act* in accordance with these impulses—and with as much 'skill in action' as possible. The secret of their effectiveness is that a certain spiritual force is to be found behind such harmless-looking metaphors.

So then, what *was* the effect D.N. Dunlop had upon his non-anthroposophical public as a speaker? According to one of the press notices: 'He was the fortunate possessor of a voice which, while appearing to be scarcely raised above the level of ordinary conversation, yet carried every syllable which he uttered to the opposite end of a hall as large as the Session Chamber of the Houses of Parliament in Copenhagen. The sincerity and simplicity of his speeches did much to foster that atmosphere of practical idealism most favourable for the carrying on of the work of the Conference.'[187]

As can be deduced from the conference programme and from various newspaper reports, a cheerful note was added to the proceedings by a variety of shared activities including banquets, excursions, visits to exhibitions, etc. The Basel Theatre arranged 'A Special Performance in Honour of the Sectional Meeting of the World Power Conference': Richard Wagner's opera *The Flying Dutchman*. An inspection of the power works in Andermatt also gave an opportunity to make an agreeable trip through the Swiss mountains. The enthusiastic newspaper reporting on this part of the conference at times almost reaches heights of rapture:

> At about eight o'clock the second 'train spécial' left Basle—an endless chain of saloons and dining-cars. The morning mists were rising from the valleys and the autumnal woods and alpine meadows began to smile in the light of the sun. The stolid villages of the Basel district went rushing by. Then suddenly the horizon opened out: the

'Mittelland' of Switzerland. In the distance the peaks of the Alps rose up like spectres from the vaporous mists. The foreign visitors were peeping from their windows. Cries of admiration rang out in thirty languages through all the carriages. The Pilatus Massif was a sure sign of the not-far-distant 'Lake of the Four Forests' (Lake Lucerne) and sure enough its rippling waters could already be seen gleaming from afar, embedded in the mountains' ageless magnificence and majesty.

The admiration of the on-lookers increased to loud delight and wild enthusiasm . . .[188]

One could almost imagine this as being an enthusiastic group of young art students, travelling on to wherever.

*

A good example of the magnificent way in which Dunlop was able to sum up the general proceedings really comprehensively and to draw from them an interim conclusion can be found in the final part of his speech; on the last day of the conference, he ends on a truly warm, friendly and humorous note:[189]

The World Power Conference is an Institution—shall I say—that will take time to solidify its programme, and to concentrate upon those essential matters which are of the greatest importance from the more or less immediate point of view; but I think, as a result of our meeting in Basle, we can feel that the World Power Conference has taken a great step forward. We feel that all the detailed aspects of the programme put before the conference have been dealt with in a masterly manner. I have never attended a conference which has been so excellently organized in every detail. [This comment is very illuminating given the fact that Dunlop had already organized numerous theosophical and anthroposophical conferences in addition to the First World Power Conference.] I think a great tribute is due first and foremost to our Chairman Dr Tissot and also to the Organizing Secretary, Dr Hübscher, who has so energetically and with such ability assisted in the arrangements for this conference and the carrying out of its details, and, of course, to our good friend Mr Zangger, who, as technical secretary, has been, as you have all seen, so busily engaged throughout the whole conference that I do not

> think he has had time to take food or to sleep. (*The speech was enthusiastically honoured*).

At the official opening of this conference, speeches had been made by the President M. Tissot and the Chairman of the International Executive D.N. Dunlop, as well as by M. Chuard, member of the Swiss Federal Council and the mayor of Basel, Herr Aemmer; the conference was concluded with the corresponding official ceremonies.

'Very pleasant sociable activities and excursions . . . followed on after the official completion of the Programme,' the Basel *National-Zeitung* reports.[190] 'The Swiss Federal Railways were kind enough to lay on an extra train which steamed over the Bötzberg pass, thus providing the travellers with an opportunity to observe the work being done on the electrification of the railways.'

A review in the German press is particularly illuminating in so far as it highlights the supra-national character of this impulse and its attempt to unite the various peoples of the earth. In the *Abendblatt der Frankfurter Zeitung*[191] we find the following words: 'One day before the significant Plenary Meeting of the League of Nations in Geneva, in which Germany has been granted a seat and vote, the *World Parliament for the Management of Energy*, the sectional Meeting of the World Power Conference in Basel, concluded its deliberations.' This coincidence of timing reminds us of the official opening of the first conference when the Prince of Wales spoke of the World Power Conference as potentially operating on a parallel basis to that of the League of Nations. The following lines, written by the same reporter, illustrate how unusual and welcome it was for German delegates to find themselves fully recognized at this sectional meeting: 'Not only English and French but German too was accepted as a language for negotiation . . .'

A Comprehensive Survey of the World's Energy Resources

On the occasion of the 1928 Fuel Conference in London (which treated questions related to the production and conservation of fuel), Dunlop proposed that a further step towards international collaboration might now be taken and thereby one of the most important fruits of the World Power Conference began to ripen. It must have been the first time in the whole history of the production and application of energy that a comprehensive survey was to be made of the *Power Resources of the World*, to use the title of the monograph which Dunlop subsequently published.[192]

It is difficult today to imagine what immense preparatory work was at the time required for such an undertaking as this to succeed. For in order to embark upon a detailed international survey of the world's energy resources a uniform method of calculation had first of all to be worked out, one that would make it possible to compare all the information streaming in from the different corners of the earth—otherwise it would be of no practical value whatsoever. Apart from this political barriers had to be surmounted, for if information were withheld for political reasons it would not be possible to establish an adequate overall picture of the real position, even if a uniform method of calculation had been found. From these two considerations alone it is easy enough to see that the monograph published at that time could not hope to aspire to any kind of perfection—rather it was published in order to communicate the impulse of applying *world-criteria* to the analysis. These are the only criteria that can do justice to the technical development of present civilization which has, *de facto*, reached the stage of *world-economy* even if human *comprehension* of this development often lags behind the facts.

So when Dunlop suggested that the international sources of energy be documented, he attached great importance to this first attempt to establish a *global image* of the world's energy resources. Since then, at about six-yearly intervals, the World Energy Conference has brought out several such volumes concerning the world's energy resources. When a few years ago President Carter commissioned another comprehensive study to be made (the results of which were published under the title *The Global 1000 Report to the President*), the authors of this survey stated that to a large extent they had based their own research on estimates made by the World Energy Conference, as these are still considered to be authoritative.[193]

The basic idea at the root of Dunlop's proposal to carry out an international survey in this sector might be summarized as follows. If industry and commerce are to free themselves from the limitations imposed on them by an outdated form of national economy, which is always kept in check by national and political interests, then no economic activity will be practicable or can even be contemplated without being established on an exact knowledge of the sources of energy existing in various countries as well as the real scope for their utilization on an economic level. However, although the 1929 publication was an important step towards gaining a practical, overall picture of the world's energy resources, the next step—and Dunlop certainly had no illusions about this—was going to be a good deal harder to make. For it consisted of working, on the basis of this fundamental and overall view of things, towards a *permanent* form of collaboration, co-ordinated on an international level and in such a way that political and economic forms of narrow-minded egoism (whether individual or nationally 'collective' in kind) would come to have less and less significance within this sphere.

In 1929, only two years after the conference in Basel, which had required an enormous amount of preparation, two more sectional Meetings of the World Power Conference were held, one in Barcelona and one in Tokyo. (The late C.H. Gray, former secretary of the IEC, believed that the arrangement of *two* conferences in the same year was perhaps the only mistake Dunlop ever made as chairman in view of the pressure the preparatory work for both conferences was put under because of the shortage of time.)

Berlin 1930—a Ghost-like Stage for the WPC

The Second Plenary Meeting of the World Power Conference was held in Berlin in 1930 and focused on 'The Distribution and Use of Energy'. Approximately four thousand representatives from about 47 countries arrived in Berlin in order to take part. A reception was given in the Reichstag before the official opening of the conference, which took place in the opera-house in the presence of Reichskanzler Brüning. In his greeting to technological leaders from all over the world he read out a special message from Reichspräsident Hindenburg. The conference was presided over by Oskar von Miller, founder of the Deutsches Museum. Dunlop, 'the spiritual father of the Conference'[194] was prevented by illness from attending it, the chair beside the president being left vacant to mark the fact. He was replaced by Eduard Tissot, who was an exemplary organizer and whom we have already encountered at the sectional meeting of the World Power Conference in Basel.

After the Reichskanzler had welcomed the participants Tissot expressed his thanks and the hope that the whole world 'would unite more and more in an effort to create a peaceful form of collaboration in all fields of human activity'.[194]

A strange feeling comes over one when looking back upon this scene from the present historical distance: those well-meaning words of peace uttered by Tissot from within the opera halls; and then the presence of a Reichskanzler behind whose back another figure had already begun his climb to power—one who was about to drag the whole of Europe into the abyss. Indeed, this creepy feeling may become still stronger if one listens to the words of a reporter describing the half-hour speech which followed. It was by Albert Einstein who, shortly before, had been hailed as 'the greatest of living men' at the Zionist Conference in Zurich. Had one been able to sense the disaster that was threatening humanity from behind the political scenery of those Berlin opera-halls, one might also have sensed the same latent danger in the growth of modern science and its industry, as Einstein climbed onto the stage. At that time he was director of the Kaiser-Wilhelm

Institute for Physics in Berlin although before three years were out he was to be dismissed from this office and obliged to emigrate to the United States of America. Einstein had extended Planck's quantum theory to a photon theory of light, thus supplying the world with one of the essential foundations of atomic physics which was soon to 'celebrate' the first of its fatal triumphs in the course of the Second World War. As the theme of his address during the opening ceremonies of this conference, Einstein had chosen 'Physical Space and the Problem of Ether'. The following impressions were recorded by a newspaper correspondent in Berlin:

> The scholar reads from a sheet of paper. However, he always looks up after a few sentences and improvises, making one or two remarks to illustrate something he has just said. At one point there is an unfortunate interruption on account of the brazen audacity of certain film camera-men and photographers who, not content with using all the theatre-lights throughout the proceedings, have also erected a sharp spotlight in the wings, bathing the speaker in wild, violet light and making him appear, with his hair all on end, like some strange phantasy-figure from another world . . . The house exploded with applause.[195]

So here on the one side is a German Chancellor who two years later lost Hindenburg's confidence, and four years later emigrated to the United States of America, with already the phantom figure of a maniac moving up behind him; and on the other is a scientist whose theoretical works were soon to be misused in the most hair-raising manner—for war by the very country to which he had been forced to emigrate. The appearance of these two men standing before the curtains of yet hidden dramas, one before the machinations of national politics already heading straight for the abyss, the other before the distortions of a modern science which, by bowing to national politics, was forcing all humanity towards the same abyss—looking back on all that has since happened, do not these two indeed appear as figures 'from another world'?

Despite these catastrophic trends already present behind the scenes and which, in the following decades, were to enter into the full limelight on the stage of world history, this conference was, in the eyes of the participants and press, a total success. The *Neue Zürcher Zeitung*[196] concludes:

> . . . the most important achievement of the conference was the fact that so many experienced people from all over the world have made new and personal relationships . . . One of the main tasks of the conference has been to demonstrate the means by which the price of energy can be reduced by cutting the running-costs of plants involved in energy production and its distribution, as well as by the more permanent exploitation of these plants . . . The conference has also shown that to provide the world with machine-power, light and warmth must ultimately lead to less unemployment. It has opened up entirely new perspectives in the fields of science, technology, economics and sociology. Some of the most important lectures were especially aimed at illustrating how we have entered into a new age which, after taking us through widespread specialization, will bring a *new and unified spiritual culture* . . .

*

Whilst Dunlop was unable to attend this the Second Plenary Meeting of the World Power Conference, in the course of the following year he did manage to visit Berlin in order to take part in a gathering of several hundred bankers and businessmen. The event was reported in the press. On 29 September, the *Deutsche Allgemeine Zeitung* gave the following account:

> *President of the World Power Conference in Berlin.* The well-known English industrialist Mr Dunlop, Chairman of the World Power Conference, is at the moment visiting Berlin . . . The opportunity was taken . . . for a meeting at the premises of the Hotel Kaiserhof between various leading personalities in order to deal with major world-economic questions of the present day. Dunlop himself explained that it had been Rudolf Steiner's book *The Threefold Commonwealth* that had given rise to his decision to establish an alliance within his own field of work between certain cultural and spiritual forces of the world by creating the World Power Conference. He had been delighted at the positive response this idea

> had met with and the way all nations had joined together in order to collaborate in this sphere.

The report of this meeting, which was concerned with Rudolf Steiner's new monetary theory, is of interest to us not only because it contains an explicit reference to his ideas in connection with the impulse of the World Power Conference; it also demonstrates how Dunlop applied himself to preparing the ground within the financial and economic sphere for the practical realization of the far-reaching ideas of this impulse. But however full of promise and potential this step forward into the financial and economic sphere appears to have been, it was to be the last attempt of this kind which Dunlop would make on German soil.

'Can you use my services?'

In the year 1933, just as the 'Monster of Unreason', that personified form of political madness, rose to power and the outlines of disasters on a global scale began to show themselves quite clearly to those with eyes to see, Albert Einstein set off for America and another exile, intimately connected with our story, also took permanent leave of Germany. Walter Johannes Stein, then in his forty-second year, had a certain amount of Jewish blood in him from his mother's side and had already noticed at the beginning of the twenties the attempts, mainly concentrated upon German territory, to spread over humanity a 'unified *anti-spiritual culture*' (as we might recoin the phrase used by the press as cited on page 223). He had been in Munich in early 1922 when certain groups of Nazis had tried to assassinate Rudolf Steiner who, after this, made no more public lecture tours in Germany. Stein had been working as a history and German teacher in the first Waldorf School in Stuttgart since 1919. In addition he was frequently active as an anthroposophical lecturer. However, by the early 1930s he came to realize that 'teaching was no longer free', as he relates in an autobiographical account in 1941:

> Historical research was no longer possible. Every lecture advocating

> freedom of mankind, or democratic principles, was broken up. The students of the universities found pleasure in storming every platform where freedom of mankind was mentioned. In Göttingen I had to face two thousand students with trumpets and drums and the lecture ended in fighting. When Hitler came to power our time was over.[197]

Besides both this unhappy constellation of the times (whose 'eruptions' appear as distortions of the genuine impulses of the century given by the true Spirit of the Time) and the mortal danger in which he suddenly found himself owing to certain components of his ancestry, W.J. Stein had other important reasons for leaving the continent—they will be touched upon in this book. For the time being, however, let us follow him upon his path, against the general background of these historical events, as he steps onto British soil through the door of the World Power Conference, with Dunlop as its guardian. For however significant and illuminating these background elements may be, the *decisive* factor in his taking the radical step of emigrating was his link with D.N. Dunlop and his keen interest and desire to participate in the healthy growth and evolution of Dunlop's 'favourite child'—the World Power Conference.

W.J. Stein had made Dunlop's acquaintance in the late twenties, presumably on the occasion of one of the conferences in England which Stein had attended after Steiner's death (perhaps during the World Conference on Spiritual Science in London in 1928 at which he had been lecturing. A wonderful bond of friendship had begun to grow between the much younger man (always ready to widen the horizons of his own experience) and his older acquaintance who, already of mature years, was then at the peak of his public activity. The World Power Conference, and its future goals, had certainly been the subject of one or the other conversation between them on various occasions—for instance, during March 1932, when Stein spent several weeks in England lecturing at different places, as extant correspondence shows.

At the end of March 1932 (as Stein relates in a letter to his wife) Dunlop founded a World Economic Association.[198] Next to nothing, however, is known about the nature or real object of this organization, though there are good grounds for assuming that it was primarily destined to serve ends similar to those discussed in Berlin one year earlier, i.e. to penetrate into the financial basis of the economy and permeate it with new ideas and impulses such as could be practically realized in the spirit of Rudolf Steiner's idea of a threefold social order. At least we know a little more about Dunlop's plans concerning a 'World Economic Conference' which no doubt was connected to the World Economic Association. It is clear from a letter he wrote to Stein on 4 June 1932 that Dunlop had already discussed with him specific details of the conference during those weeks in March. Initially they had thought to hold this particular meeting in Rome and to arrange for Mussolini to call it via the Italian National Committee. In order to bring this about Stein was to enter into contact with the Italian Consul, providing him with a complete list of the members of this committee; such a list, Dunlop observed in the same letter, would 'impress the Italian Consul'. In his exuberant enthusiasm Stein wanted to enter into direct contact with Mussolini himself and communicated this intention to Dunlop. The latter wrote straight back on 9 June to the effect that in accordance with the constitution of the World Power Conference he would himself have to contact Mussolini via the Italian National Committee.

'My feeling is,' Dunlop hurriedly concludes at the end of this letter, 'that your letter could go quite soon, but should indicate that I meet at Paris the representative of the Italian National Committee at end of this month and will discuss details with him before writing.'

All this reveals the interesting fact that at that time Dunlop still considered Rome and Mussolini as a possible context for the World Power Conference (the latter's political slide to the extreme right only becoming totally manifest in the years that followed). But these two letters and the rest of the Stein-Dunlop correspondence also illustrate that Dunlop could, in a given case, whilst actively encouraging a colleague's initiative simultaneously correct it if this appeared to be necessary. Stein will have been extremely grateful for any indications or 'tips' of this kind. For they permitted him to learn much of importance in the perfection of his own moral technique, and this on ground where his older friend was already operating with natural virtuosity.

*

It was then early in 1933 that Stein suddenly found himself (not for the first time in his life) without either financial means or any practical prospects of a new career. In the years immediately after the First World War, Rudolf Steiner had charged him with the task of promulgating the impulse of the Threefold Social Order and putting it into practice, and subsequently Stein had often set about this by means of either the spoken or the written word. After Rudolf Steiner's death he had made the acquaintance of the one human being whom he hoped would, despite the coming eclipse in Middle European politics, still be able to work in accordance with the necessities of the economic and social life—and this in thoroughly practical terms. Thus, rootless and desolate though he was, he took courage and sent a telegram to Dunlop. In it he simply asked his older friend, 'Can you use my services?' Dunlop's reply completely changed Stein's fortunes. As he later observed, 'it was this letter that brought him to England'.[197] The letter, dated 8 June 1933, was directed to an address in the Hague where Stein had already been staying for some time. Dunlop's answer was as direct as Stein's question had been:

> Dear Dr Stein,
>
> With reference to our interview[199] I confirm what I then told you that for some time I have been awaiting a suitable opportunity to start a Research Bureau in association with the World Power Conference for the collection of data and statistical information in relation to World Economics, with the twofold object of:
> (a) Preparing for an International Conference, and
> (b) Publishing, in a suitable form, conclusions arrived at based on the data and information collected. I hope it will be possible for you to come to London at an early date, so that your services may be available in the initial stages. I do not anticipate any difficulty in

receiving the necessary permission for you to come to Englind for this work of international importance.
Looking forward to seeing you and your family in the near future,
I am,
Yours sincerely,

D.N. Dunlop,
Chairman.

As the letter was obviously typed by a secretary the personal nature of their relationship is concealed by the neutral businesslike style; however, it is all the more evident from this that Dunlop was in the process of taking another decisive step forward in the realization of his concept of a World Power Conference. He needed a research bureau for statistical information and had already started making other practical arrangements for a World Economic Conference (for that is what was envisaged in the first of the two objectives set out in his letter). At all events at this particular moment in the evolution of Dunlop's plans Stein's estrangement from German soil appears as a very fortunate 'sleight of hand' on the part of destiny.

In anticipation, let it be stated at this point that the World Economic Conference which Dunlop intended to inaugurate has to this day not been brought about. The main external reason for this was his own death, which occurred scarcely two years afterwards following a long period of illness. There had not been anything like enough time to prepare for such an undertaking, in comparison with which the organizational feats of the other conferences could only be regarded as preparatory exercises. However, it is equally true to say that the darkness which gradually spread over the whole of the political scene also substantially contributed to thwarting the realization of Dunlop's plans.

The Magazine *World Survey*

By 21 June of that same year, 1933, Dunlop had already sent Stein the official visa (limited to begin with to a period of one year) which was necessary for his entry to and residence in Great Britain. So a few months later Stein found himself in London, sitting in a newly established Research Bureau in Bloomsbury Square.

When some time before Stein had asked Dunlop whether the World Power Conference would agree to an extension of its *objects* in the sense outlined above, his friend had replied:

> 'I hope so, because even in the first publication issued by the World Power Conference it is indicated.' And he took the membership list in his hand and opened the first page. He showed me the paragraphs under the heading 'Objects' of the World Power Conference and I read:—the establishing of a permanent World Bureau for the collection of data, the preparation of Inventories of the World's Resources, and the exchange of industrial and scientific information through appointed representatives in the various countries. (St)

As is clearly visible from the heading of one of the letters Stein addressed to Dunlop, the latter, as chairman of the International Executive Council, also figured as director of this small 'Institute of World Economics'. This is a clear indication of the fact that those aims which ever since its beginning had been inherent in the World Power Conference, over and above the technical problems related to energy production and evaluation, were now advancing to their next stage of fruition.

With genuine, exuberant enthusiasm W.J. Stein plunged into his new work. His first task was to enter into contact with the various economic institutes and their publishing organs scattered over the four corners of the earth. To this end he established a number of new connections to various individuals, as is documented in his correspondence. Furthermore, in the wide-ranging circle of his acquaintances, he already had many friends who were able to help him with his research.

Dunlop always worked to a very tight schedule and consequently was obliged to programme his various activities with a certain degree of precision. Thus he answered the first letter Stein wrote reporting on work in progress by simply writing down any remarks he had to make in the margin of the letter and sending it back to him again. This procedure is characteristic of the whole style of their business correspondence and it shows how the work in the Research Bureau, which at the outset was so to speak a 'one man job', proceeded without any kind of bureaucratic complications whatsoever.

One and a half years later, in April 1935, the first 'conclusions arrived at based on the data and information collected' were indeed published 'in a suitable form', to use the phrases from Dunlop's letter of invitation to Stein in June 1933. This 'suitable form' was the monthly magazine *World Survey* which appeared for the first time in April 1935. It was published, as the title-page indicates, 'under the auspices of the World Power Conference'. Thus, it was not the *direct* mouthpiece of the organization but only related to it in the previously explained sense. Again, this illustrates how very clear and well thought out Dunlop's plan already was when he revealed it to the amazed Stein:

> Then he took a copy of *World Survey*, opened the title page and his fingers rested on the words:—'Published under the auspices of the World Power Conference for the exchange of economic and technical information and the provision of a World Economic Service and International Power and Fuel Bibliography.'
>
> 'You see,' he said, 'that it is not the Journal of the World Power Conference. It is an independent enterprise, but under the auspices of the World Power Conference, and time will decide if what is intended there will continue under those auspices.' (St)

This was an experiment—a skilfully arranged attempt to extend the work of the WPC into the sphere of world economy. Should it succeed then the function of the magazine under these auspices would be confirmed by solid facts and if not, then the extension of these goals would have to be taken *without* the blessing of the WPC. Here again we can identify something of special interest: the way in which Dunlop always incorporated a certain 'flexibility' into his plans; that is to say, he would, already at a very early stage, consider any potential extensions which might have to be made to immediate aims at a later date. Thus he also took into account the possibility that he might have to accomplish his objectives in a different framework from that originally planned.

In the introductory article to the first number of *World Survey* entitled 'World Unity and World Economics', Dunlop immediately puts forward a wide view of the subject to be discussed. Taking the world economic crisis as his starting-point, at the beginning of this article he poses the question:[200] 'Will the close of the great economic depression also mark the end of a distinctive period of economic development?' The 'distinctive period' Dunlop is referring to here is the phase ruled by national economy—one orientated according to purely national political criteria; furthermore, as Dunlop tries to make clear to his reader, it is a phase which has finally come to an end with the conclusion of the world economic crisis. For 'the dominant characteristic of the present situation is the fact that the world has now become so inextricably linked as to be virtually one unit, and if economic problems are now of greater importance than ever before, it is to this fact that we must look for a reason and for the explanation of the inadequacy of purely national remedial measures.' Hence this was 'something that was to be recognized throughout these pages; the contribution which each nation can make to the cultural advancement of the world is fully appreciated and valued as being both individual and peculiar to it, but in the economic sphere such differentiation is losing its usefulness as the world becomes the only relevant basis for analysis. The national economy progressively loses its autonomous character. The analyses and comments therefore of *World Survey* have as their basis an appreciation of the unity of the aims, conduct and progress of economic life, overriding political frontiers and superimposed divisions. Whilst these may distort any particular development, economic activity when examined as a whole possesses an undeniable unity and today is best comprehended as such. This is perhaps the most striking lesson of the great depression, and, paradoxical as it may seem, the very efforts at segregation which it has provoked are themselves witnesses to the ubiquity of these economic trends. The influence of this conception of a world unity will be seen throughout *World Survey*, for in each section an endeavour will be made to deal with world problems and events as a whole.'

In the second article, entitled 'Power—Mankind—Economics', Dunlop discusses the question of how the whole of mankind can make the best economic use of energy resources and production.[201] In another article W.J. Stein deals with questions concerning 'The Problem of Stocks, restricted Consumption and Production—from a new Angle'. Under the heading 'World Economic Service' we are informed about Belgium and the gold standard, the world rubber situation, and we also find an extensive table of World Economic Indices as well as an International Power and Fuel Bibliography.

*

In the third issue of *World Survey*, which came out in June 1935, we find an obituary of Dunlop who had died on 30 May of that year. Certain aspects of his unexpected death will be considered later in this book. The reader will recall from the obituary which appeared within BEAMA circles (see page 414) the impression which people active within the technical and economic sphere had of Dunlop's personality and work. At this stage we only wish to single out a few of the points that were made in the obituary published by *World Survey*, in order to complete that picture.

In this obituary Dunlop's relationship to the World Power Conference is described in the following terms:

> From the beginning he envisaged something much more than a technical organization of the producers and consumers of power and fuel. He saw in it the meeting-place between scientists and engineers, on the one hand, statesmen and economists on the other. He placed an even higher value upon the opportunities for personal encounters which the World Power Conference provided than upon the great technical results enshrined in more than forty volumes of Transactions.
>
> Dunlop was Chairman of the International Executive Council and

> of the British National Committee of the World Power Conference from their formation up to the date of his death. His close colleagues will probably remember him best as the ideal Chairman of the International Executive Council. At the Council's Annual Meetings he showed something not short of genius in presiding with tact and patience and humour over the deliberations of often more than a score of different countries, so that the little group of regular attenders became in the course of years an international family party with a real unity of purpose which no external events could disturb.[202]

Of course Dunlop's death caused a significant interruption in the progress of certain aspects of the World Power Conference. This is particularly evident with regard to his attempts to extend its objectives and activities in the spirit of the overall aims with which it was originally conceived. For by reason of both financial and other difficulties, the work of the 'Research Bureau' was discontinued. On 26 June 1935—scarcely two years after Stein's promising new start on English soil—a letter from the then secretary of the International Executive Council of the World Power Conference, C.H. Gray, informed him of his dismissal. So Walter Johannes Stein stood once more upon the street with a period of one month's notice in which to rearrange his life!

From that letter it is clear that from 1 January 1935 Stein had been employed as a member of the editorial staff of the new magazine. The fifth and last issue was to come out in August, not least, as C.H. Gray stated in his dismissal letter, 'owing to the necessity under which we unfortunately lie of exercising the most stringent economy'. Such measures to cut costs were evidently found imperative. But the sentiment of 'regret that we cannot continue to make use of his services' seems to be sincere and this appears to be confirmed by the extraordinarily high evaluation of Stein's method and work, and of the nature of his person as such. For Gray expressly states that 'Dr. Stein has shown himself to be a most painstaking research-worker in connection with the economic and statistical studies and analyses published in *World Survey*. In addition, his international connections have proved most valuable. Dr. Stein is very hard working and his enthusiastic co-operation with his colleagues can be relied upon.'

The Earth as a Basis of World Economy

This was not the first time that destiny had called upon W.J. Stein to adapt himself with vigour and imagination to an abrupt change in the circumstances of his life, and he showed no hesitation in so doing. He decided to bring out his own magazine. Dunlop had already suggested that another magazine of more generally cultural character could be set up beside *World Survey*. So with very meagre, indeed at the outset thoroughly primitive means, Stein got straight down to work and by Christmas that year the first issue came out. The magazine was called *The Present Age* and continued to appear in print until the invasion of Poland in 1939. As has already been pointed out, Stein's account of Dunlop's life included in the opening number represents a central source for external details of this biography.

It is not our intention here to produce a complete picture of this multi-faceted magazine, however interesting this might in itself be. However, in a special number Stein published a very important piece of writing which had also been worked out upon lines originally suggested by D.N. Dunlop. It is entitled 'The Earth as a basis of World Economy'. As can be deduced from the preface, signed on 30 May, the anniversary of Dunlop's death, Stein himself considered this work to be fragmentary in character and incomplete in many respects. What more than anything else motivated him to publish it was the fact that 'two years after his death . . . his far-reaching plans have been forgotten'.[203] Stein 'resolved to make this uncompleted plan known, in order that future promoters of a World Economic Conference may make use of the foundations which we had worked out together'.[203] Dunlop had asked Stein to think out a plan for the organization of a conference on World Economy[204] and it was as a result of this request that he had undertaken the present study. A single glance at the headings of the ten chapters is enough to show the enormous breadth and scope of everything that was to be embraced within this World Economic Conference. The overall spectrum of subjects to be treated included considerations concerning the cosmological and geological aspects of raw materials and their distribution on the earth; the cyclic evolution of chemical substances; the cosmological origin of the various metals; the oceans of the earth; the air and temperature system of the earth; the influence of the sun and the other planets on weather and climate as a basis for harvesting and fixing prices. The final chapter consists of more immediate considerations concerning world economy.

In Stein's Preface we read:

> If order is to be introduced into the chaos of World Economy, raw materials and the laws of their distribution must be traced back to their cosmological origin. Astronomy, geology, mineralogy, botany, zoology and geography must collaborate. Even palaeontology and the sciences which study earlier conditions of the earth and the universe must be included. This book shows that this is not the dream of a mind remote from actualities, but the practical solution of urgent and topical problems, such for example as that of over production and the distribution of raw materials.[205]

Stein particularly emphasizes the fact that economic life, as part of the social organism, 'is not the result of human activities alone, it is part of . . . the life of the whole earth',[205] an idea of fundamental importance which today is beginning to dawn on general consciousness after a number of minor, and more especially major environmental catastrophes.

Nevertheless there are still various obstacles posed by a materialistic view of nature which prevent this consciousness from really taking root. It is very easy to pronounce the *word* 'organism'; however, to see in reality the *whole of the earth* as a living being similar to the way in which we perceive particular plants or animals—that can only be the result of efforts within the sphere of knowledge leading to the development of 'an apprehending power of judgement' (*anschauende Urteilskraft*), in the sense attributed by Goethe to this term. The sphere of *life* and of all living beings is, of necessity, bound to remain inaccessible to a form of thinking which is chained to the external senses. Here we touch on an important task posed as a challenge to human consciousness by the now rapidly spreading ecological sensitivity to the earth as a 'living' whole. So long as we continue to avoid this aspect of the problem the attitude described by Stein in his introduction will remain true for our time as well: 'It is the present-day tendency to be concerned only with individual nations and groups, and to regard the earth only as the stage on which the action takes place, as the mere provider of raw material.' Stein goes on to develop in more concrete terms the notion of the earth as a living entity:

> To be convinced of the earth's separate life we need simply take a plot of land as an example. In observing the plant life which grows there it is hardly enough to ascribe this life to the plants alone . . . the earth is not simply the supplier of chemical substances for the nourishment of the plants; the soil does not represent mere dead, chemical matter. It is this spurious line of thought that has led to excessive use of artificial fertilizers; for in that procedure no account is taken of the soil as a living organism. Plants and soil together make a living unit in which the life of the one part is balanced by the life of the other. In a garden, the root plant will thrive best when it is grown in near proximity to the flowering plant. In a cornfield we find sainfoin. In the kitchen garden the horse-radish and the potato flourish side by side by reason of the piquancy of the one and the mildness of the other. The same relationship exists between plants and their soil as between one plant and another. Definite types of soil suit certain plants. In the same way as plants, by secreting salts in their roots tend to become mineralized, so does the soil by producing plants become a living organism, going as such through the seasons and taking part in cosmological processes, the seasons themselves being the result of the relationship between the earth and the cosmos. It is not, therefore, sufficient to describe the earth solely from the chemical point of view; it must be described from the cosmological point of view too: for not only the processes of growth, blossoming and fruit-bearing vary with the seasons, but, as it has been experimentally proved, so also do such phenomena as crystallizations. This would imply that the cosmological constellation and the cosmic life are at work on every plot of land.[205]

Now this kind of practical all-embracing concept of life applies to the economic sphere as well; for this sphere too is completely integrated into the living organism of the earth:

> What is true for a small plot of land is equally true for the whole earth, and this is the basis of economic life. The living earth, regarded as the foundation of economic and social life, presents quite a different aspect in the understanding and solving of economic problems, from the earth when looked upon—as it usually is—as a mere object of exploitation.[205]

Furthermore, Stein presents us with a picture of evolution in which man appears at the apex in so far as he is capable of bringing the whole cosmos to self-consciousness within himself; proper appreciation of this fact is the best possible starting-point for the human being to begin assuming *responsibility for the whole cosmos.*

Such considerations as these form the basis of this small work, and on this foundation the reader is introduced to the previously mentioned studies set out in the various chapters. Every step in Stein's expositions is accompanied by a variety of examples which show that what in the final instance he was aiming at was a quite perfectly practical application. To quote but a few examples, Stein depicts the uneven distribution of coal within the earth in relationship to the great geological epochs and the two major belts of mountains that encircle the earth and which, owing to a movement of the earth's crust, covered different areas of the earth at different epochs. The same two principal mountain systems are today situated in such a way that they lie predominantly in the Northern Hemisphere. The shifting of the earth's crust, which enables ever new areas of the earth gradually to become Northern and Southern Polar regions, is caused by cosmological processes. Therefore the science of cosmology will have a decisive word to say if we want, for instance, to find out whether new coal-mines can in future be found ('even should they lie under the sea') and what the possibilities of their technical utilization might be.

Plans for a Second Volume

We cannot here embark on a more detailed discussion of the many perspectives opened up by this book but must rather use the available space to throw a last glance at a *second volume that Stein had planned*. It was to be a comprehensive study of nation-psychology[206] and to serve as a basis for various expositions on this subject within the context of a World Economic Conference. Certain of Stein's preliminary studies are still extant today in manuscript form. From these, as well as from certain chapters which seem, to all intents and purposes, complete, it is possible to establish some kind of picture of Stein's intentions and the manner of his portrayal of this subject. In the introduction to his planned second volume Stein writes:

> This age, more than any other, demands that humanity of the present and the near future recognizes those common problems which concern the whole of the human race. For this very reason we must accept the challenge of the times to recognize each one of us as belonging to a particular nation. The various peoples must come to a knowledge of themselves. Self-knowledge of the nations, that is what is necessary if each nation is to make that thoroughly unique contribution that only it can make towards decisions concerning humanity as a whole.
>
> We have come to know the earth from the point of view of the natural sciences. Thanks to Geology, Geography, Meteorology and Climatology we have an image of the diversity and multiplicity of earthly conditions. However, we cannot regard the earth merely from the point of view of exploitation.

Stein then goes on to consider the activity of real, individual national entities in shaping the conditions of the earth (such an entity is generally described as the 'spirit of the nation' with, however, next to no meaning being implied in the phrase); their real existence can be traced back even to such a misunderstood and misused phenomenon as that of the individual's feeling for his homeland. Other indirect evidence of the real existence of such entities is put forward by Stein in relation to the particular nature of certain regions of the earth which can never be satisfactorily explained as solely external processes of nature: 'Medicinal Geography is well acquainted with the fact that the soil, the geological configuration of the ground itself, conditions with respect to water and air, the climate, as well as an indescribable "aura" that can nonetheless be felt, all this can have a healing effect . . .' The particular character of these regions can change if the peoples that inhabit them, and who are led by a real folk-spirit, move on or are obliged to migrate:

> It is clear from this that vast areas can be modified in character when the territorial effects of political upheavals, conquests and peace-treaties cause the masses to modify certain regions of the earth. Indeed, another phenomenon which seems to point in the same direction is the inner drive of certain peoples at certain times to migrate, thus bringing about a new constellation and interaction of natural and human forces. Just as the human being, by introducing economic activity and intervening in the formation of the earth's substance, initiates a new geological epoch, the *Psychozoicum*, so too the migrations of various peoples inevitably lead to an alteration in the whole natural constitution of one or even many areas.

Stein takes some examples from his new English homeland[207] in order to illustrate how, following movements of mass-migration, the impulses that live in certain peoples can 'become established' in entirely new areas.

> There is a province in England that bears the name of 'Holland'. In this province a number of Dutch legends and stories are to be found as well as . . . windmills which endow it with a Dutch character . . . In Cornwall, the 'English Italy' (which, even in its external form, reminds us of Italy), legends associated with Virgil are to be found in the Merlin Legend; Tintagel is a miniature of Naples; and the Scilly Isles a metamorphosis of Sicily. Thus a comprehensive description of a tract of land is much more than just the enumeration of its raw materials or its geopolitical tendencies to . . . extend its power to other regions. Of equal importance is that particular 'aura', that force which is capable of creating legends and which half hangs over the landscape and half resides within the inhabitants of a given land.

Using the *Gudrunlied* as an example Stein shows how humanity of earlier times was instinctively acquainted with such elemental influences of the folk-spirit (or 'nation spirit'), whilst our time demands that we become thoroughly conscious of such things 'in order that they may become the basis for practical action.' After having thus characterized the more territorial function and influence of the folk-spirit, Stein goes on to consider that aspect of this entity which is more directly related to the human being as such, though this too is viewed in connection with the given conditions of the various territories:

> Each people has its own secret—that which it bears within itself as its own temperament. It is a very different nature that is manifest to us say in the melancholic Russian, or the melancholic and sanguine German, or the phlegmatic Englishman; and in order to develop that nature these peoples need a corresponding geological base. Little research has been done into the relationship of these elements but one should simply study the effect for example that chalk has on people. It is quite different from that of granite. One part of Germany, Swabia, has a population quite different from that of the rest of Germany. Some say that the Swabians are ponderous. Others say that they are religious. All these attributes are correct. Swabia has given birth to many great religious and mystical movements but also to a very well-grounded, and highly esteemed form of economic existence. There is a locality in the Swabian Black Forest called Calw. Calwerstraße is the name of a Dutch street, and it was along this street that wood used to be exported. However it was also along this same street that the religious movements spread. Economic matters are inseparable from those concerning the human soul. *Whoever tries to deduce the economy from mere statistics does not know where the real economy resides*. Human beings are the bearers of all economy—heart and soul. It is the chalk which makes these people ponderous, reliable, solid, but humorous as well; for they have to transcend the chalk. Swabia lies in the Swabian Jura Mountains, a chalk formation. Calcified dragons are excavated there but both the dragons and the chalk continue to live within because people are so easily offended. However, it is so, that the same forces are at work both in a positive and in a negative sense.

In this way the members of a particular nation can find it most illuminating to consider such traits of temperament and personality in relation to the constitution of the ground under their feet. Stein tries to make this clear by giving a description of a 'granite-mentality'—one which is diametrically opposed to the temperament mentioned above. Thus he points out that 'granite makes people lively and fresh and I know how much Vienna owes to its granite pavements. It was thanks to nature, and a very wise human being, that Vienna came to be paved with granite. Such an undertaking is not only of economical significance, it also has an important effect upon the human soul; a population that walks on granite, assumes a fresh and mobile character.' And for those amongst his readers who might be quite sceptical, Stein adds the following remark: 'Little research has been done on these things as yet; but that does not make them any the less true. Our science simply does not have enough humour to consider such things as worthy material for experimentation . . .

Thus the themes sketched out above, which Stein would certainly have elaborated if the book had been completed, may suffice to give us an impression of the direction in which he was moving and how much he had achieved in his efforts to fulfil the task assigned to him by D.N. Dunlop, namely, to make plans for the organization of a conference on World Economy.

The Real and Potential Evolution of the World Power Conference

In the period following Dunlop's death there was no more talk of realizing any far-reaching plans of this kind within the framework of the World Power Conference. There were various reasons for this, not the least of which was the state of crisis in Europe and the outbreak of the Second World War in 1939. Any clear and sober-minded person could see that in these prevailing circumstances it would have been naive and ridiculously Utopian to want to bring about a World Economic Conference based on such all-embracing points of view. Nevertheless, the World Power Conference had in the meantime become not only a well-known organization but also a highly-rated one. From the German side, at the beginning of the war-period, attempts were even made by the German National Committee to have the headquarters transferred to Berlin. It was thanks first and foremost to the negotiating skills of J.G.T. Bakker, the then chairman of the

Dutch National Committee, and also to C.H. Gray that this danger was averted. The latter brought forward the argument that such a transference would have to be decided upon by the International Executive Council which itself could not meet under the present war conditions.

The last Plenary Meeting of the World Power Conference *before* the war took place in Washington in 1936, and indeed its general theme 'corresponded' to an international war atmosphere—'The National Energy Industry'. The first conference after the war was held in London in 1950. In the meantime the status (still valid today) of advisory committee had been conferred upon the organization by the UN. Six years later, Vienna played host to the fifth Plenary Meeting of the Conference. Certain aspects of this conference are of special interest to us both with respect to Dunlop's person and with regard to the problem of atomic power stations—a question which has of course become even more urgent since the Chernobyl disaster.

'World Power Conference Dampens Atomic Optimism—Soviets also cautious with their plans'. These headlines of the report on the conference in Vienna appeared in a German newspaper in 1956.[208]

According to the article, the same thing happened here in Vienna as had already occurred at other conferences, namely, 'the expulsion of the bogeyman spreading the fear that energy supplies would be exhausted'. On the other hand, however, 'not a little cold water was poured over exaggerated expectations of the possible achievements of atomic energy.' The English president of the conference, Sir Harold Hartley, then chairman of the International Executive Council, 'therefore warned against exaggerated hopes with regard to atomic power stations. Not to mention the difficulties connected with protection against radioactivity, which clearly alarmed the German delegates much more than their Soviet-Russian colleagues.'[208]

Hartley, who had been present at several conferences whilst Dunlop was still alive, included in his opening speech a few remarkable sentences about the founder of the World Power Conference. They are remarkable by reason of showing the

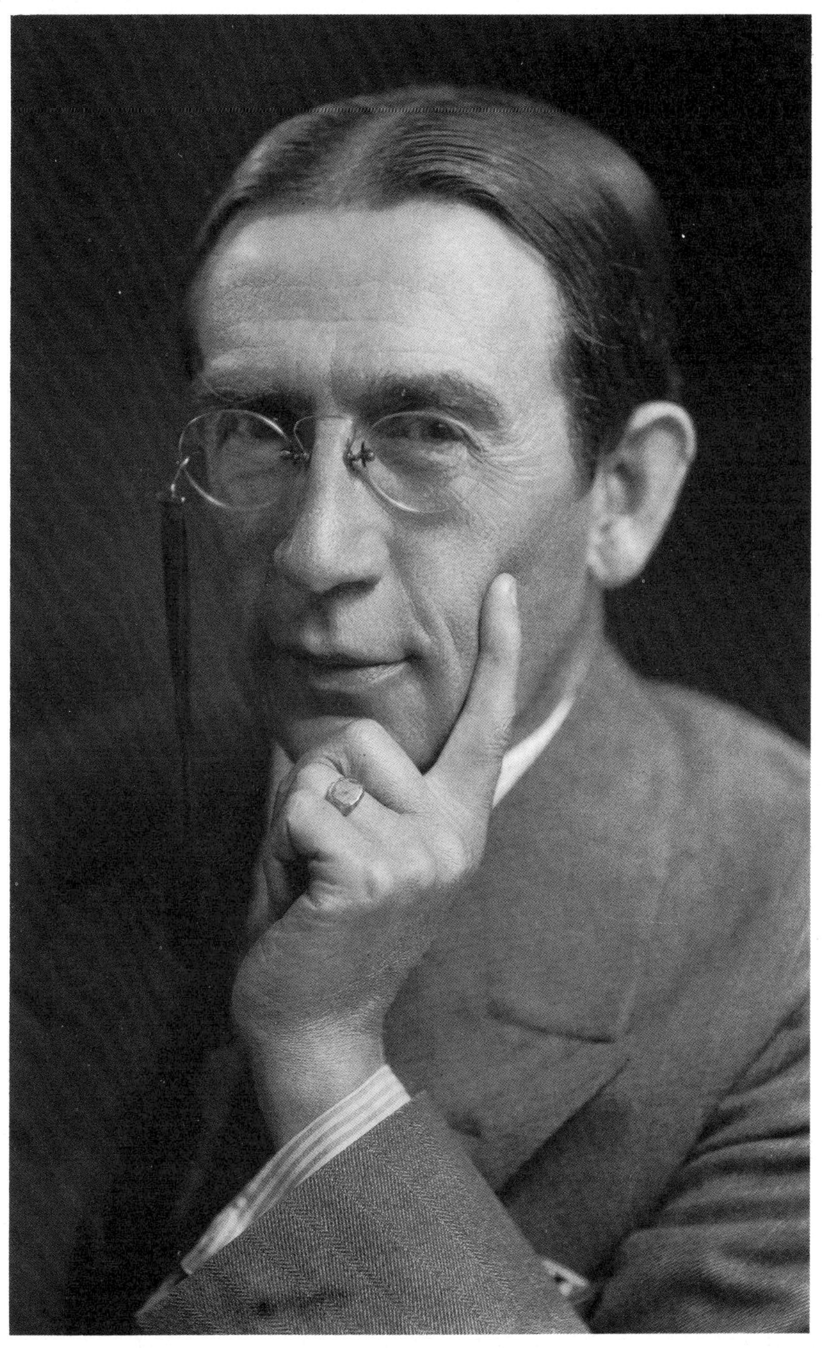

*1. D.N. Dunlop c. 1930**

**Where no credits are given illustrations stem from the author's own archives.*

2. *Standing stones on Arran*

3. *George William Russell c. 1890. From: John Eglinton,* a Memoir of AE, *London 1937*

4. W.B. Yeats as a young man, BBC Hulton Picture Library, London

5. D.N. Dunlop. By kind permission of David Clement

6. Eleanor Dunlop. From: Edith Young, Inside Out, *London, 1971*

7. *Helena Petrovna Blavatsky*

8. James Joyce in 1938, BBC Hulton Picture Library London

9. Rudolf Steiner in 1907. © Verlag am Goetheanum

10. D.N. Dunlop c. 1920. By kind permission of Edith Young

11. *Rudolf Steiner in 1915. Foto Rietmann. © Verlag am Goetheanum*

12. Stone circle above Penmaenmawr. By kind permission of Frank Teichmann

13. Rudolf Steiner visiting Anglesey in August 1923, with Harry Collison and Marie Steiner

14. *The 1923 Summer School at Penmaenmawr. Foto Gmelin. © Verlag am Goetheanum*

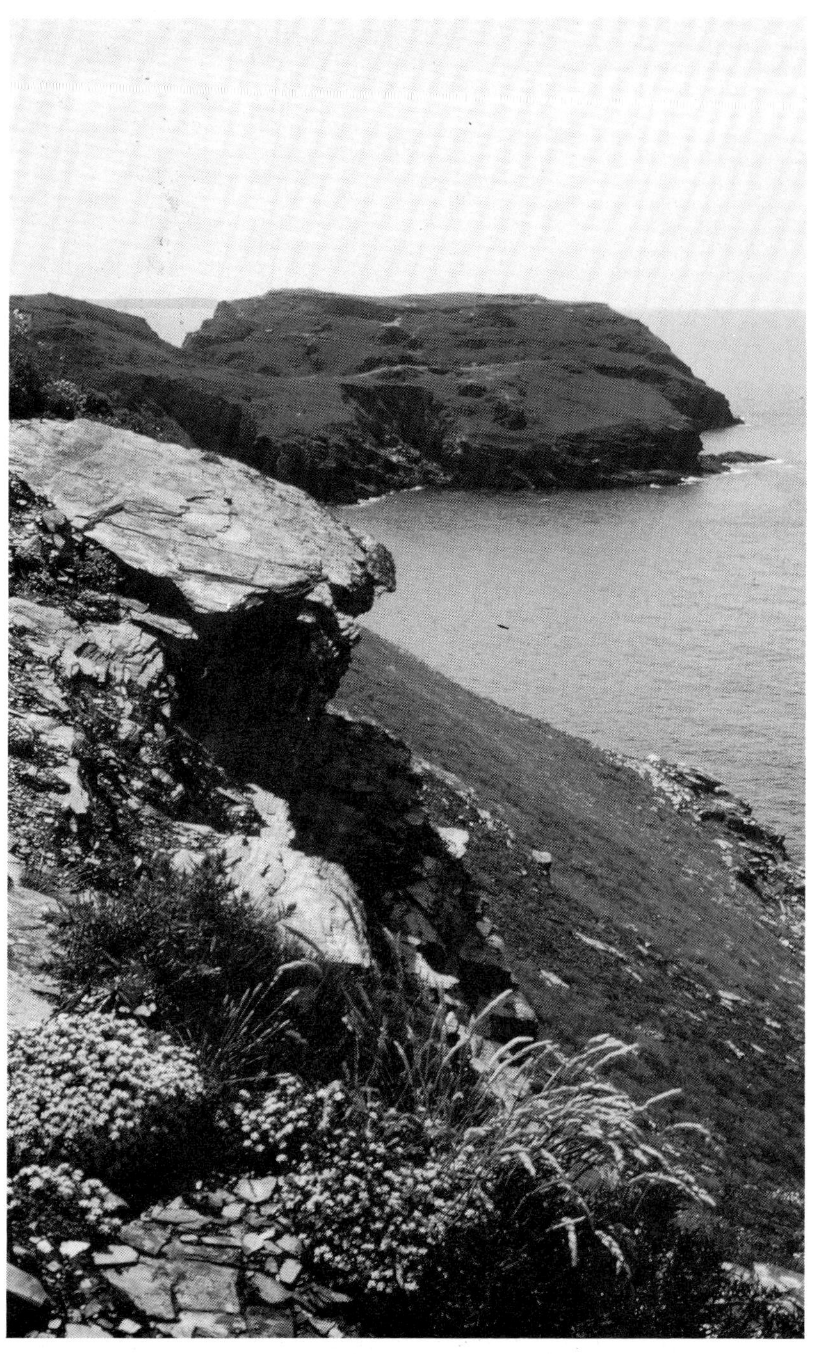

15. Tintagel. By kind permission of Frank Teichmann

16. D.N. Dunlop. From: Edith Young, Inside Out, *London 1971*

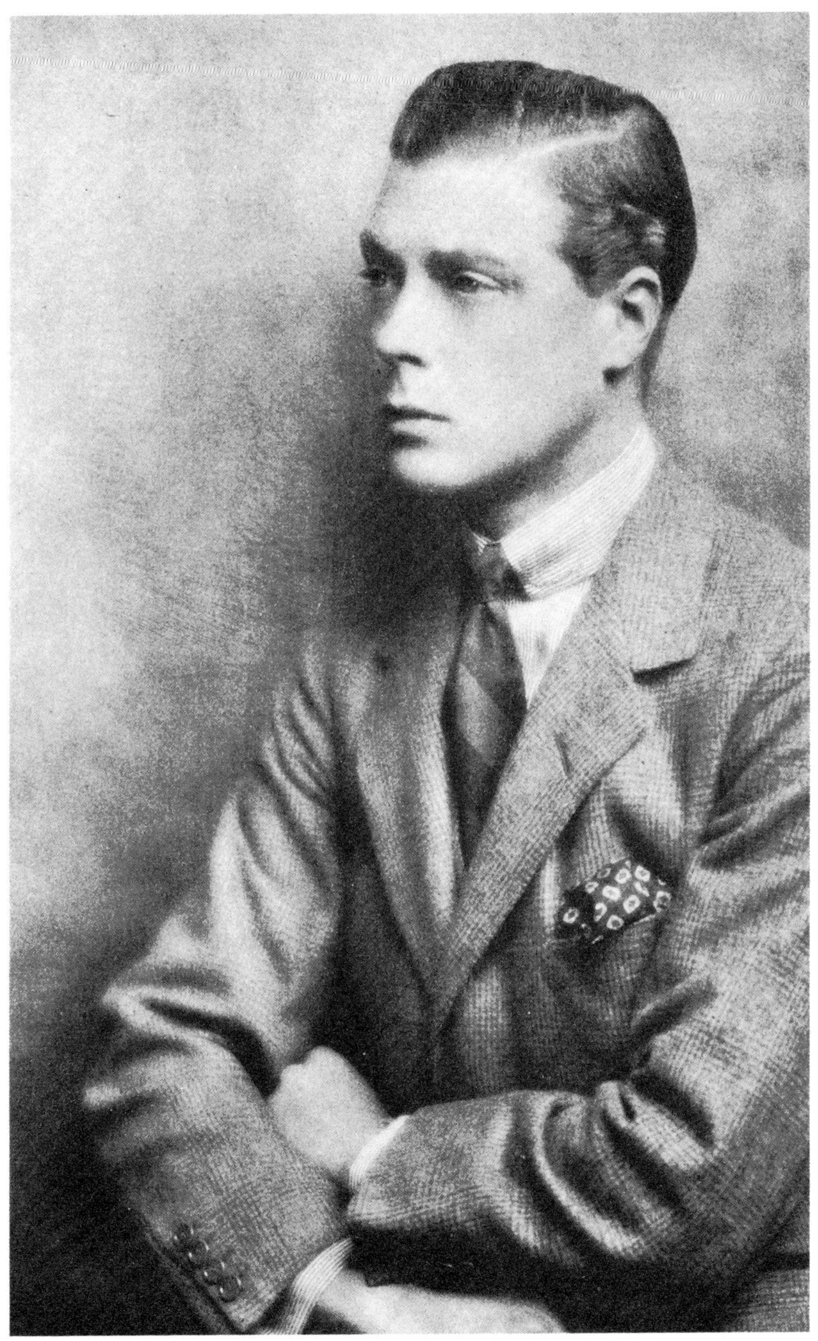

17. *H.R.H. Edward, Prince of Wales*

18. *Executive Council of the World Power Conference*

19. W.J. Stein c. 1931

ANA
IA
CANADA
ON

CHILE
CHINA
COLUMBIA
CZECHOSLOVAKIA
DENMARK
DUTCH EAST INDIES
ESTHONIA
FINLAND

FRANCE
GERMANY
GOLD COAST
GREAT BRITAIN
GREECE
HOLLAND
HUNGARY

INDIAN EMPIRE
IRELAND
ITALY
JAPAN
JUGOSLAVIA
KENYA COLONY
LATVIA

LITHUANIA
LUXEMBURG
MEXICO
DOMINION OF NEW ZEALAND
NORWAY
NYASALAND
PERU
POLAND

ROUMANIA
RUSSIA
SOUTHERN RHODESIA
SPAIN
SWEDEN
SWITZERLAND
UNION OF SOUTH AFRICA
UNITED STATES OF AMERICA

RLD POWER CONFERENCE

INTERNATIONAL EXECUTIVE COUNCIL
Chairman:
D.N. DUNLOP *Great Britain.*
Vice Chairman:
ED. TISSOT *Switzerland.*

Telephone: HOLBORN 5802.
Telegrams: WORPOWCON, HOLB., LONDON.
Cablegrams: WORPOWCON, LONDON.

Central Office
63, LINCOLN'S INN FIELDS,
LONDON, W.C.2.

DND/JJC

8th June, 1933.

Dr. W.J. Stein,
The Hague,
Holland.

Dear Dr. Stein,

With reference to our interview I confirm what I then told you that for some time I have been awaiting a suitable opportunity to start a Research Bureau in association with the World Power Conference for the collection of data and statistical information in relation to World Economics, with the twofold object of:

(a) Preparing for an International Conference, and
(b) Publishing, in a suitable form, conclusions arrived at based on the data and information collected.

I hope it will be possible for you to come to London at an early date, so that your services may be available in the initial stages. I do not anticipate any difficulty in receiving the necessary permission for you to come to England for this work of international importance.

Looking forward to seeing you and your family in the near future,

I am,
Yours sincerely,

D.N. Dunlop

CHAIRMAN

20. Letter from D.N. Dunlop to W.J. Stein dated 8 June 1933

21. C.H. Gray in later years. By kind permission of the World Energy Council

22. D.N. Dunlop c. 1932

23. *D.N. Dunlop in 1925*

24. E.C. Merry in 1927

Telegrams
"PERIHELION, WESTCENT, LONDON."
Telephone
HOLBORN 0502 (SIX LINES).

36 & 38, KINGSWAY,
LONDON,
W.C.2.

16 . VI . 32

Dear Dr. Stein,

I feel very strongly that an Effort should be made during the next year or two to form an

International Association
for the
Advancement of Spiritual Science.

A preliminary prospectus should be prepared to circulate widely in all countries, and when the Foundation is laid a Conference should be called. This should be guided & controlled by Anthroposophists who feel the call & need of humanity everywhere, and who feel how inadequate the General Anthroposophical Society (as it is now controlled from Dornach) has become.

Will you think about it & see if you can get the impulse for a preliminary prospectus & we can speak of it when we meet in London.

Fraternally
Yours
D.N. Dunlop.

25. *Letter from D.N. Dunlop to W.J. Stein (16 June 1932)*

26. *Group photo taken during the Summer School at Westonbirt, 1934. Bottom row, seated, left to right: Nora von Stein, W.J. Stein, Caroline von Heydebrand, Karl Schubert, D.N. Dunlop, Elizabeth Vreede, unknown, Eugen Kolisko, unknown, George Adams, Dr. Hauschka, unknown, Eleanor Merry*

Telegrams
"PERIHELION, WESTCENT, LONDON."
Telephone
HOLBORN 0502 (SIX LINES).

36 & 38, KINGSWAY,
LONDON,
W.C.2.

3 Apl. 35

Dear Dr. Stein,

I may not be able to come to your lecture tonight. So if I am absent you must forgive me; it will be my loss.

Yours Ever
D.N.D.

27. *Letter from D.N. Dunlop to W.J. Stein (3 April 1935)*

28. Ita Wegman in 1935. By kind permission of Emanuel Zeylmans

29. AE in 1935

30. D.N. Dunlop c. 1930

31. *George Adams-Kaufmann and Ludwig Count Polzer-Hoditz during the Harrogate Summer School, 1935*

continuing orientation of the conference, at least with regard to general outlook, along the lines of Dunlop's original impulse:

> Our founder, Daniel Nicol Dunlop, had the vision more than thirty years ago to foresee the need for a forum where the representatives of all those sectors could meet for the discussion of problems of mutual interest in order that the energy policies of the future might be formulated on the broadest front. That is the pupose for which the World Power Conference was founded and it is a great tribute to Dunlop's imaginative conception that the wording of our original charta has remained practically unaltered.[209]

*

A number of celebrities were also invited to speak at the opening of this Vienna Conference. For instance there was the physicist Erwin Schrödinger, who tried to make clear to his audience that the whole world (the same world which was to be discussed in relation to the controversial matter of atomic energy and technical questions concerning radiation) was nothing other than 'a construction of various sensations, perceptions, and memories'. However, the audience had already been 'prepared' for such a precipitous change in points of view—from that of everyday life to that of Schrödinger—by his opening words of greeting: 'Honoured guests! Please forget for a moment that you are gathered here for a World Power Conference. There is not enough time for me to make a long introduction. Perhaps to begin with you would care to follow me along a purely philosophical line of investigation which takes me back thirty years.' Doubtless, there would have been several listeners in his audience who, despite this entreaty, would not have been altogether able to forget that they were assisting at a World Power Conference which had originated—likewise about thirty years ago—in an idea which had been orientated towards the future and firmly rooted in *reality*.

Views may differ as to the merit of the various contributions made by invited speakers who attempted to widen the extent of the participants' interest in cultural and philosophical questions beyond the narrower limits of their own affairs. It was certainly an element, like the music recitals, which gave a certain breadth to the whole atmosphere of the proceedings. Unfortunately this element faded more and more into the background during the years that followed.

In a sectional meeting of the conference in Tokyo in 1966, the then secretary of the International Executive Council, C.H. Gray (whom we have already mentioned on several occasions and who retained that office until this same year), referred to Dunlop as a 'visionary and man of sound Scottish common-sense', whose creation, the World Power Conference, 'remains, in all essentials, today'.[179]

At the next Plenary Meeting of the conference, which took place in Moscow in 1968, it was decided to change the name of the organization to World *Energy* Conference. This modification of the title was desired by the Americans, owing to the fact that, over the years, the expression 'power' had in America become employed almost exclusively in connection with *electrical* energy.[210]

From 1980 to 1983, Peter von Siemens, who died during the first weeks of the Chernobyl disaster, was president of the World Energy Conference. In the present context this figure is of special interest to us, for Siemens, who planned to extend the development of the nuclear power plants, had been trying for decades to turn the light of anthroposophical knowledge onto certain riddles posed by the phenomenon of atomic energy.

In a certain sense this constellation of events is perhaps something of a 'warning'. For if the World Energy Conference were ever to become fixed on the further development of atomic energy, then such factors as the atomic disaster of 1986 might bring the work of the conference into a remarkable conflict with its own, purely humanitarian objectives as defined in the statutes of the organization: 'The Objects of the World Energy Conference are to promote the development and peaceful use of energy resources to the greatest benefit of all.' Strictly speaking this paragraph alone ought to ensure that within the framework of the conference the 'peaceful' future use of nuclear energy will remain, to say the least, a very controversial matter. However, it is also one which might lead to some entirely new and stimulating questioning. Amongst the new questions to be posed would have to be that of the 'Strader-Machine' mentioned in the introduction to this book and especially all the social problems connected with it. By interpreting the 'signs of the times', quite a lot could be achieved or at least prepared in this direction—in the anthroposophical field in particular.[211]

In the earlier-mentioned statement which Eric Ruttley, Gray's successor, made at the press conference just before the congress in Cannes, he emphasized the point that the World Energy Conference, which today embraces some 80 member-countries (including such contrasting members as the People's Republic of China and Taiwan), is *equally* concerned with the industrialized world *and* the developing world, for 'as Dunlop said in 1924, "the progress of even the most advanced nation is clearly seen to be limited by the conditions of the whole".'[178] We have already seen what in the widest sense belonged to this 'whole' for D.N. Dunlop and his special 'emissary', W.J. Stein.

*

'The WPC never deviated from these objectives and at the end of 1984 they are as alive and relevant as in 1924,' we can read in a newsletter 60 years after the founding of this organization. Such references to the original impulse of the World Power Conference, as well as the prospect of future congresses like that planned for 1992, seemed to present a good reason for looking into the entire background of Dunlop's original aims in order to make a generous appraisal of the history and development of his 'favourite child'. It is only natural in such a retrospection as this, which is basically concerned with its *origins*, that certain aspects of the impulse of the World Power Conference should have received special attention even though they have remained nothing more than 'seeds' of a potential reality. However, to the extent that others in the future may take up these seeds and also reconsider what still remains in the way of unexecuted plans, this retrospective view might itself provide a glimpse into *future times*. These are the times already envisaged by Stein in 1937, when '*future promoters of a World Economic Conference may make use of the foundations which we . . . worked out together.*'[203] These same 'future promoters' will doubtless attempt to establish a World *Economic* Conference as a *permanent organization* along lines similar to those of the World *Energy* Conference, that is, *if they really take up the seed of the original intentions*. We have already seen something of the vast and comprehensive nature of the questions such a conference will have to treat. If in the future a World Economic Conference can really start off on the basis of these original unrealized aims this will also mean that full justice will be done to Rudolf Steiner's impulse for the founding of a threefold social order.

6

'ANTHROPOSOPHY FORMED A NEW ORGAN IN ME'

The inspirer of the twentieth century has lived among us, and lives among us still. Is it not for us to work as labourers unto harvest? D.N.D.

A Cosmic Prologue

Now that our reflections on D.N. Dunlop's 'favourite child', the World Power Conference, have brought us up to present times and even to the threshold of certain future perspectives, this chapter of the book will take us back to the year in which we embarked upon these events—the time around Rudolf Steiner's death in 1925. In the preceding chapter we have, naturally, seen Dunlop's activity in the technical and economic field move into the foreground of this biography; now we shall attempt to trace the last ten years of his life primarily from the point of view of his inner connection with Anthroposophy and his active participation and initiative in spreading its impulse in the world, in other fields besides those which the World Power Conference provided.

Of course Rudolf Steiner's death, in March 1925, left a great hiatus in the lives of all those belonging at that time to the Anthroposophical Movement. However, Dunlop had the strong feeling that over and above the tragic element there was another aspect of this death that should never be forgotten: 'For behind the grief that befell us on that March day when the Gates of Death swung open for the spirit we knew as Rudolf Steiner, we could hear the echoes of the trumpets that were sounding for him on "the other side". The hosts of heaven were welcoming him back to the regions which he left for six short decades because he had been mindful of the cries that went up to him from the earth.'[212]

Thus, in Dunlop's eyes, the death of the Initiate did not call for inactive mourning or narrow-minded efforts to conserve the universal wealth of wisdom he had brought into the world, nor did talk of greater 'sacrifices' for Anthroposophy seem appropriate: 'For those of us who knew and loved him there can be no talk of sacrifice in our labours for Anthroposophy. There can only be joy that, at least, our Karma has enabled us to further Rudolf Steiner's work in some small degree.'[212] Such words of deepest gratitude were spoken by one for whom duty and sacrifice went without saying.

D.N. Dunlop knew perfectly well that all attempts to advocate or spread Anthroposophy were bound to meet with powerful opposition, particularly in the West. According to Rudolf Steiner's spiritual science the inspirers of the Western form of opposition are the so-called 'Ahrimanic beings'. He had already drawn attention to this in 1922 when 'he warned that the opposition would be terrible, meaning the Ahrimanic powers would wage a mighty war against the spread of Spiritual Science'.[212] For this reason it was essential in Western regions to work with especially clear insight and unswerving energy:

> Ahriman knows the strength of his weapons; he knows the stupefaction which the senses have brought about in the spiritual life of man; he works consciously in the fear men have in face of concrete spiritual revelation. We should realize that the opposition to Spiritual Science is only just beginning; it will grow stronger and more insidious . . . Therefore for us there must be no compromise with materialism in whatever form it may be; we have to assert a wisdom that is 'not of this world' and therefore in its pure form, inaccessible to the darts of Ahriman.[212]

These words of Dunlop's appeared in the August issue of the magazine *Anthroposophy* which was dedicated to Rudolf Steiner's memory. They are just as relevant today as they were then, particularly his observation that 'there must be no compromise'. This must be taken especially seriously with regard to the external growth and spreading of anthroposophical institutions and initiatives. Rightly understood, it has nothing to do with social intolerance: it merely concerns the question of how to bring about that particular 'pure form' of Anthroposophy which is 'inaccessible to the darts of Ahriman'.

*

Let us illustrate this point with regard to a concrete symptomatic case. The circumstance that Rudolf Steiner's work may today be 'highly esteemed',[213] as one author puts it in a recent collection of quotations by Rudolf Steiner compiled a few years ago for Catholic readers in the German speaking world, does not change the fact that, with regard to the *core* of the Roman Catholic Church, undiminished opposition against Anthroposophy is, as ever, at work. To believe otherwise would only lead one to overlook the insidious nature and character that this particular form of opposition has assumed.

'In spite of all increased consciousness,' we are assured in the introduction to the above-mentioned book, 'this spiritual research remains on the level of immanence . . . Nor does Rudolf Steiner claim that it is possible to advance into the unattainable space of God's transcendence.' An allusion made by Rudolf Steiner to the role that 'grace' has to play in practical occultism is torn out of its context and used to stifle at birth any kind of *concrete* spiritual advance into the manifold, rich and infinitely differentiated domain of 'God's transcendence'. For as far as Rudolf Steiner's spiritual research is concerned, here again 'the precept of "eternal striving" is not the last or even the decisive word to be spoken on this subject.'[213]

Now does it in any way serve the anthroposophical cause if such powerful attempts are made to render Anthroposophy so to speak 'palatable' to a Roman Catholic way of thinking, if its purely spiritual, we could also say Faustian and Michaelic, aspect is watered down or undermined in favour of 'divine grace'? Does it in any way help if Rudolf Steiner is presented to our contemporaries as a somewhat wilful spirit but nevertheless one perfectly compatible with Roman Catholic tradition—as a kind of modern 'prodigal son' who has returned with enough friendliness to leave everyone alone with their old dogmatic beliefs and habits of thought? What is this if not an insidious attempt to create an *appearance* of compatibility?

An even more striking example of a mixture of basic Catholic views and anthroposophical ideas can be found in the late writings of Valentin Tomberg (born in St Petersburg in 1900, died in 1973 in England). After having been a student of Rudolf Steiner, Tomberg joined the Catholic Church in the forties, but continued to adhere to certain anthroposopical ideas. In *Lazarus, Komm Heraus*, one of his works published after his death, he repeatedly stresses the importance of Steiner's *oeuvre* and person. Yet at the same time he claims that Steiner 'unfortunately' (!) chose to present his experiences of the spirit by means of scientific methods and terms. According to Tomberg, Steiner was therefore only able to encompass the 'way' and the 'truth', but missed the third element: the 'life'.

In his book *The Great Arcana of the Tarot* (posthumously published under the pseudonym 'Anonymus d'outre Tombe') Tomberg expresses a striking view of the question of knowledge of evil: 'Of evil no intuition must arise', for intuition requires love. 'Now we cannot love evil therefore evil cannot be known in its essence.'

There can hardly be anything more highly appreciated by any (human of purely spiritual) opponents of Anthroposophy than such an agnostic theory of 'knowledge' with regard to evil!*

In order not to lose one's bearings in personal accusation or polemic against the various opponents of Anthroposophy, one has to view the spreading of all kinds of hostility towards spiritual science in a *spiritual* light, in the spirit of the words spoken by Dunlop—against the background of Ahriman and his hosts, described earlier as 'anti-Michael' beings (page 180). It would certainly be naive to believe that in the foreseeable future such beings could take any pleasure in a science of the spirit, or that, in order to achieve their ends, they would, in the foreseeable future, have any difficulty in finding plenty of 'human recruits' to assist them.

The most important thing is not to wage polemical warfare on

* On the whole Tomberg controversy see the author's book *Die Bodhisattvafrage* (Basel 1989). It goes also into the question of the Catholicized view of the mission of the Bodhisattva of the twentieth century.

this or that recruit (who is anyway more or less 'temporary'), but to come to an understanding and knowledge of the real function and activity of such beings.[214] For whilst human freedom makes it possible for such recruits to place themselves at a future point in time under entirely different spiritual powers, the beings in question here are bound by a higher law and are obliged to pursue the realization of their goals without any freedom at all.

These comments should suffice to illustrate the point of view from which both Dunlop's utterances about this opposition and our own attempt to give some relevant contemporary examples are taken.

'Ahriman,' so Dunlop writes, 'works first and foremost in the fear men have of *concrete* spiritual revelation.' On a human level this can produce the tendency to make spiritual compromises; it can lead to an inclination not to take karmic revelations really seriously—either to reject them or to caricature them (a symptomatic example of this was given in connection with King Arthur (page 178ff).

To refuse to 'compromise' in Dunlop's terms means to take the Michael Impulse absolutely seriously. In the earlier parts of this book an attempt was made to elucidate some of the more *spiritual* aspects of the Michaelic influence; in the present context attention may also be drawn to another aspect more connected with the human *soul*. The Michael Impulse is in itself a very central and complex matter; in the framework of the present biography it seems best just to to let it sound forth at intervals like a musical theme—for that is the way it is woven as a determining factor into Dunlop's whole. It must be left to the reader himself to investigate more systematically the specific details of this particularly important 'leitmotif'. To try and fight against fear is pointless. It can only be vanquished by attaining knowledge, especially by attaining knowledge of those spiritual powers[214] who exploit the fear that seizes men in the face of *concrete spirituality*. A clear, untroubled vision must be gained of the function and activity of the 'negative inspirer' and the spirits in his train. For it is this being that inspires us *not to take seriously* the revelations made to us by spiritual science. Such vision indeed would seem the only way to counterbalance that element of fear which is otherwise exploited by these powers. This means developing a modern form of courage which is absolutely necessary, if Anthroposophy is to be brought forward without compromise. Such courage is the living reflection of a certain aspect of Michael's being shining forth from within the human soul.

It is only on the basis of such courage that it is possible to achieve what Dunlop considered the most important task incumbent upon Rudolf Steiner's pupils after his death:

> The Michael-Wisdom which he proclaimed must now be wrested from the spiritual world and made real in the physical world by us. We must storm the Kingdom of Heaven with our human forces that he made more strong, if his earth mission is not to be in vain. Mighty he was in life, but he may yet be mightier in death if our hearts are strong enough to beat to the sun-rhythm that is his rhythm, if our will is strong enough to embody his will in *Act*.[212]

Once again, these words are not merely written *in memoriam*. They are intended to spur the reader onwards to the future work of harvesting. For they contain the insight necessary to inspire the will and identify its aims. Everything is in them: the 'forlorn' situation of Rudolf Steiner's pupils after his death, the need to bring Anthroposophy into its own in the world without compromising it in any way; the growing strength of opposition to spiritual science inspired by cosmic-supersensible powers, which was not going to stop dead even before the gates of the Anthroposophical Movement itself.

*

Thus everything Dunlop wrote here in 1925 *in memoriam* of Rudolf Steiner seems to mark out the boundaries of all he was himself to undertake and experience in the last ten years of his life. His words indeed constitute a kind of cosmic prologue to all his future experience and action, a prologue in which the human 'Entelechy', fully awakened to its own immortality, has become the principal actor standing between two other figures on the cosmic stage—Ahriman and Michael—and in this drama it is his own acts that will prove decisive.

Something like a metamorphosis of Dunlop's Dublin experience, that moment of great decision, might here be noted—the battle-scene, where the human ego has the decisive role to play, has been widened out into cosmic spheres. And indeed, in the years that followed his meeting with Rudolf Steiner until his death in 1935, the whole drama of D.N. Dunlop's life was played out in this vast context. It was a change which might be expressed as follows: *from a servant of Michael to a champion in his ranks.*

Paving the Way for Others

As Rudolf Steiner's 'brother', Dunlop will no doubt have felt himself as something of a younger brother; on the other hand, in the years following Steiner's death, he was himself able to help and advance many of the latter's younger pupils in a truly brotherly fashion, and as a more experienced friend. Thus more than one of those who had been close to Rudolf Steiner during his lifetime was afterwards helped by Dunlop to make a transition to the new phase in the Anthroposophical Movement—to find the corresponding possibilities for realizing his most intimate goals in life by working for Anthroposophy in accordance with the Spirit of the Times. We have already seen what this meant for W.J. Stein; in a like fashion Dunlop decidedly 'paved the way' for many other people as well. For he had the deeply-rooted faculty of knowing when the right moment had arrived to clear a path for someone else, and with intuitive certainty he always hit the mark. This form of active brotherliness was in a certain sense the inner aspect of that impulse of co-operation which he was at pains to realize within the technical and economical sphere.

In the same way as Dunlop had opened up new avenues of destiny for Richard St Barbe Baker at the end of the First World War, and just as he was destined soon afterwards to help Stein find his way through the 1930s, so now after Rudolf Steiner's death in 1925, he also enabled two young anthroposophical doctors to 'make a start'. Emanuel Zeylmans describes the event in the biography of his father, Willem Zeylmans:

> In 1925 Zeylmans was invited to London along with Dr. Eugen Kolisko to speak to English doctors. The invitation came from Daniel Nicol Dunlop, the General Secretary of the English Anthroposophical Society. For both speakers this was their first English lecture and naturally enough they were both suffering from a certain 'stage-fright'. However, Dunlop as Chairman of the Conference radiated such an impressive calm and met the two young doctors 'from the Continent' with such trust, uprightness, and warmth of approach, and his few words of introduction were so heartfelt and sincere 'that the lectures were already a success before they had even begun' as Zeylmans himself later commented.[215]

This marked the beginning of a deep friendship, especially between Dunlop and Zeylmans who during the following years often stayed on in England for consultations for the further development of anthroposophical medicine in England.

What those two doctors right from the beginning experienced was what Rudolf Hauschka once described as being present in the atmosphere reigning over the work between Dunlop and Stein.[216] It was a 'breath of a wide world, heart-warming' that blew away all timidity. David Clement, already mentioned in this book, also received similar 'provisions' from Dunlop as he embarked upon his anthroposophical 'journey': 'While I was talking with him once, Dunlop strongly advised me against specializing; instead, he recommended that I should study *men*. The world, he said, was full of specialists only too glad to assist you with their specialist knowledge, but there was a sad dearth of people able to draw the strings together with a real understanding of human nature.'[85]

Clement also relates how Dunlop invited Dr Mirbt to England through George Adams and comments: 'and so began the Bio-dynamic work in this country.'[85] Something similar occurred in the case of Fried Geuter, one of the pioneers of curative education. Here again 'Mr Dunlop was also a prime mover in bringing Fried Geuter over and with him the impulse of curative education.'[85] Both Mirbt and Geuter moved to England in 1929, several years before the curative educationalist Karl König settled in this country.

Lastly, let us mention another witness who came to Anthroposophy in 1927 at the age of 23 and who often attended lectures presided over by Dunlop. At first there was nothing particularly close in their relationship. One day, however, this witness recalls, 'I was standing . . . in the entrance to Rudolf Steiner Hall . . . and I saw Mr Dunlop looking behind me. I thought he wanted to speak to somebody standing behind me. I moved out of the way. But there was nobody behind me. He held out his hand to me. He seemed to be looking right through me at some physically invisible part of my being and welcoming me!'[217]

*

Thus, after Rudolf Steiner's death, Dunlop worked extensively to smoothe the way for the impulse of Anthroposophy; he did this by helping those who truly represented it to 'make a start', especially if they were in the early stages or at a critical point of their activity. As can be deduced from the preceding examples, Dunlop could be of assistance on three different levels according to what each person required: the two young doctors felt the flames of his encouragement light up within their *souls*; Stein, Mirbt and Geuter received *will*-impulses working right into external spheres of destiny; whilst in the last example Dunlop addressed himself directly to the higher *spiritual* nature of a human being as though beckoning it on and helping it to be born.

Numerous accounts are to be found witnessing the wonderful way in which Dunlop prepared the ground for other pupils of Rudolf Steiner. But of course he also tried to pave the way directly for Anthroposophy itself, for he was permeated through and through by the cosmopolitan aspect of Michaelic activity in the spirit of what Ita Wegman reports[218] from her conversations with Rudolf Steiner:

> I would like to communicate what Rudolf Steiner felt to be so important for us anthroposophists and which he expressed in

> conversations from time to time: it is the fact that the spirit of the times, Michael, under whose guiding influence we stand today, will increasingly require us to carry Anthroposophy out into the whole world, so that the tendencies formerly appropriate to a Mystery Centre of limiting oneself to narrow horizons will have to be replaced by a truly cosmopolitan spirit.

Of course it is clear from what Rudolf Steiner says on the subject that there is nothing coercive about this requirement; it is more like a gesture, an indication of something that is *possible*. That is precisely what is so special and new about the present stage of humanity's development—the fact that, for the first time, a spirit of the times is exercising its guidance in this unimposing way.

So Dunlop arranged for a third anthroposophical summer school to be held in 1927. This time it was at Gairloch, Scotland, and it was possible to make excursions to some of those legendary islands of the Hebrides. The choice of this locality would certainly have afforded Rudolf Steiner the deepest satisfaction. For as far back as 1909 he had expounded on the mysterious human destinies which had unfolded upon these islands thousands of years ago during the migrations of the Celtic population from Atlantis.[219]

The Medical Section of the Goetheanum also took part in this summer school, and its leader, Dr Ita Wegman, greatly emphasized the importance of developing a *geographical science of medicine*, the outlines of which she attempted to present. In a written report on the summer school she observed that 'this geographical medicine—and it is also the medicine of the Mysteries—must gradually be developed'.[220] At the end of the school many of the participants visited the island of Iona where St Columba had taught and from whence his pupils left for the European Continent imbued with a Celtic form of Christianity. The subsequent excursion to the very different basalt island of Staffa which houses Fingal's Cave also left a deep impression on the visiting-party. 'With heightened feeling we left the island and when we met together again, our souls were the richer by a great experience', wrote Ita Wegman.

Thus, as far as locality and surroundings were concerned, there was a certain continuity in this choice—one could feel how these islands were still imbued with an ancient Celtic and Christian past, so that this summer school followed beautifully on from those previously held at Penmaenmawr and Torquay.

*

Dunlop, however, wanted to pave the way for Anthroposophy in the modern civilized world on a still larger scale and in even bolder terms. When speaking to Rudolf Steiner in 1923 he had suggested organizing a huge international anthroposophical world conference. Rudolf Steiner mentions Dunlop's plan at the end of the Penmaenmawr Conference as the 'third idea' Dunlop had put to him which 'could not, of course, be put into practice immediately'.[120]

Now, five years later and after more than two years of planning, this project could at last be realized. However, it did not proceed without several warning and disapproving voices from within the Anthroposophical Society making themselves heard. Some did not think the Anthroposophical Movement and Society were yet ready to face the public in such a vast and all-embracing manner. It was also objected that the conference would inevitably collide with the opening of the Second Goetheanum, planned for autumn 1928. Far-seeing as he was Dunlop therefore felt obliged to write a few words of explanation concerning the origin and purpose of this initiative. These explanatory comments were published in the anthroposophical news bulletins[221] both in Dornach and in London no less than nine months before the conference. They make it clear that it was not easy for him to appreciate the reasons for any misunderstandings:

'It is naturally difficult for me to realize how objections to such a proposal can be entertained, and explanations seem to be satisfactory only to those who need no explanation,' he writes at the beginning of his article for members; and with respect to the 'experimental' nature of such an undertaking based upon co-operation: 'Such a Conference can only fully justify itself when it comes into being. If it fails to realize expectations it will be due more to a lack of co-operation among members of the Anthroposophical Society than to any other cause.'

The following clarification is particularly significant:

> I discussed the general idea of a *series of World Conferences* in the Capitals of the world with Dr. Steiner on two different occasions when he visited England. He left me in no doubt as to his attitude. He approved the project most heartily and indicated that he considered London the best place to begin. When the new Goetheanum should be ready, he foreshadowed great Seasonal Festivals at Dornach, and suggested that the more that Spiritual Science, or Anthroposophy, was carried out into the world, the more important Dornach would become as a Spiritual Centre. The years 1926/1927 were suggested for the first Conference; but his passing from the physical world naturally made an extension in time necessary.

We can conclude from these words of explanation that what had been envisaged here was, in a way, similar to what had been planned in connection with the first World Power Conference, i.e. a continuous *series* of world conferences to be held on a long-term basis, with London as the most suitable starting-point for the initiative; and there is also an illuminating reference to the balance which Rudolf Steiner considered necessary within the Anthroposophical Movement between the pole of the centre and the work at the periphery. If Dornach was to work more and more intensely as the spiritual focal-point of the movement then the periphery would have to see to it that the anthroposophical impulse found its way more and more effectively into the external life and civilization of the times. To be able to develop fully and without hindrance both functions would, of course, have to be strongly rooted in a healthy reciprocal relationship. However, as we shall see, it was to prove increasingly difficult to establish and maintain such a reciprocal relationship in the years following Rudolf Steiner's death. This is one of the principal reasons why this Anthroposophical World Conference, with its aim of bringing Anthroposophy out into the world on the broadest basis possible and yet in 'pure form', remains to the present day the first and (unlike the World Power Conference) last conference of this kind.

*

At least Dunlop's words of explanation will have helped to make the idea of such a large-scale undertaking acceptable in the hearts of most of those who might have been sceptically inclined.

Dunlop acted as chairman at all the morning events during the fortnight of the conference and, according to a report given by one participant,[222] he opened the conference on July 20 with the words: 'The heart of this Conference is Rudolf Steiner.' A simple glance at the lecturers listed on the programme as well as the themes of the various lectures themselves can give a clear enough idea of what the aims of the conference were: to promote Anthroposophy in many different ways whilst maintaining, thanks to the experience and competence of the main speakers, its 'pure form'. It had not been principally conceived with a view to meeting other cultural movements and their representatives 'half-way' on the basis of some compromise. Uppermost in the minds of its organizers had evidently been the question: how can Anthroposophy be put forward in such a way that people who are not anthroposophists may feel themselves inclined and able *to make their own 'way' to Anthroposophy*?—a subtle and yet essential difference. Absence of compromise and the clarity of this objective had already come to explicit expression in the first of the ten paragraphs stating the 'objects' of the conference. These appear at the end of the programme pamphlet and were intended to enlighten every participant as to the nature of this undertaking. It reads as follows:

> **1.** To examine the present state of the World in its political, economic, industrial and cultural aspects, with the object of removing the prevalent idea that a re-shuffling of outworn traditional methods will suffice to meet the present world-conditions.

First of all therefore, prejudices and illusions had to be dismantled or cleared from the scene; after this it would be possible to develop certain essential aspects of Anthroposophy with much greater clarity. Both spiritually and physically the conference counted on the presence of an international spectrum of participants as is evident for example from the fifth paragraph of the 'objects':

> **5.** To consider and determine . . . the essential Reality underlying SPIRIT, SOUL and BODY, as it is expressed in the divergent characteristics of the Eastern, European and Western Nations.

Summing up in retrospect the 'outcome' of the conference, Ita Wegman observes:[223] 'The first two days ran their course extremely well, albeit with a somewhat exclusive attendance, but from then onwards the public became more and more interested.' Indeed, some events were attended by up to two thousand people totally new to Anthroposophy.

> The lectures and demonstrations were representative of the whole range of anthroposophy and its manifold practical results, and these appealed in ever-increasing degree to the general public, and aroused also the interest of the Press so that many notices and illustrations appeared in the newspapers . . . It is a matter for the deepest satisfaction that such a Conference could be organized precisely in the West; for the West is the guardian of human civilization, and it will only be able to fulfil its task if it can transplant the anthroposophical impulses which are nurtured at the Goetheanum, ever more and more into the processes of life.

And how did the initiator and chairman of the conference, D.N. Dunlop, rate its success? Certain indications regarding this point can be found in a nine-page report published in *Anthroposophy*[224] (a magazine of which Dunlop had in the meantime become the editor); and indeed in many respects these enlightening comments might also be of interest to organizers of similar conferences in the future.

In his introduction Dunlop emphasizes the unifying aspect of the conference with regard to the different peoples attending it: 'It is the *soul* that wakes and greets its brother soul. This mood was apparent throughout the Conference and communicated itself in some degree to every member of the public.'

From the rest of his review it becomes evident that all, in the widest sense of the term, 'practical' applications of Anthroposophy seemed to have 'made a deep impression'. Apart from numerous eurythmy performances this included exhibitions of handwork and painting from Waldorf Schools, toys from the Waldorf Toy Factory, and a display of photographs and reproductions of photographs showing experiments made by Lili Kolisko in the field of capillary dynamolysis, and many other things besides. However, it was precisely in connection with these events and exhibitions, which were visited by numerous representatives of the press, that certain shortcomings were also clearly to be detected in the manner Anthroposophy was presented to 'an entirely unenlightened public'. Dunlop considered it absolutely essential, at any future undertakings of this kind, that lecturers prepare a short synopsis, 'as brief, concise and as simple as possible—which can be handed to any Press representative'. For 'any clear line of connection between, for instance, a toy factory and a spiritual teaching is not in itself sufficiently obvious for correct estimation by a hurried and extremely practical-minded journalist to grasp. Thus great numbers of really splendid opportunities for sound and truthful publicity were entirely lost for lack of material prepared by the lecturers beforehand.' To represent Anthroposophy without any kind of compromise it was not enough, in Dunlop's view, to study 'in the intimate atmosphere of the anthroposophical workshop'. This is clear from the following words: 'If in some respects it may be true that we are not ready to bring Anthroposophy before the public, that is not due to a lack of knowledge of the fundamentals of Spiritual Science but to a lack of knowledge of the "world". And the way to gain knowledge of the world is to rub shoulders with it and to refresh our memory of its language.'

According to Dunlop, anthroposophists could learn something new from this conference, especially with regard to two points. Firstly, with regard to 'practical knowledge of the world' which is a necessary element of counter-balance to the intimate cultivation of spiritual knowledge:

> Dr. Steiner has pointed out how too deep a devotion to the needs of the inner life may tend to introduce an element of fear where active

> initiative is called for: one can become like a bee that is afraid to *sting*—afraid to pierce into the crusts of materialism.

Secondly, anthroposophists might be stimulated by this conference to become more aware of the significance that the geographical *movement* of groups or whole peoples can have for the human soul and spirit:

> To go from place to place is to gain knowledge of the inner life of the Earth, in the sense that one gains experience of what rises out of the Being of the Earth into the soul-life of its people.

In this connection it is important to recognize a certain peculiarity of England as a country. Whilst, as the heart of the English-speaking race, she 'is more than ready to receive the spiritual message of Middle Europe', England nevertheless remains 'blind and ignorant' as to the ways and means. 'England, whose shores are continually receiving the countless ships of immeasurable seas,' as Friedrich Rittelmeyer said in a lecture he gave, must also learn to behold 'those "invisible ships" that were bringing the message of a new spiritual revelation.' Then England, as the threshold between Middle Europe and the West, could also fulfil a very important task on the spiritual level as well.

*

With regard to just this matter it is of interest that Rittelmeyer, himself the Erzoberlenker of the Christian Community, had come to this conference accompanied by Alfred Heidenreich who had undertaken the task of bringing the Christian Community to the English-speaking world. In his reminiscences Heidenreich recalls that at the World Conference he 'met many interesting members of the British Anthroposophical Society, among them its General Secretary, Mr. D.N. Dunlop. Mr. Dunlop was an international figure by that time and a pioneer of economic co-operation in the international field. He gave me a warm welcome and pledged his support to our plans.'

Nor was this by any means the only fruitful contact which the conference brought about. For also Dr Mirbt's lecture on bio-dynamic agriculture so impressed Dunlop that, as we have already mentioned, just one year after the conference he invited Mirbt to come to England in connection with this impulse. Eberhard Schickler's lecture on cancer treatment had similar practical consequences: in the foreseeable future a clinic was to be opened in London to treat cases of cancer. And destiny was later to show that another significant foreign presence at the conference was that of a young Austrian doctor by the name of Karl König, then about to start work at a home for handicapped children at Pilgramshain in Silesia. His lecture on 'The Origin of Man: the Evolution of the Embryo' was described by Dunlop in his report as 'a splendid lecture'. In his autobiographical fragment König wrote: 'In retrospect this World Conference appears to me like a motiv which at first gently sounded out and which I was to take up again ten years later, so as with it to call the Camphill Movement into life!'

*

After turning the spotlight on various other aspects of these very rewarding days, Dunlop sums up the net result with reference to three noteworthy criteria which may perhaps serve to measure the success of any conference of this kind:

> In conclusion: the Conference is past, and one naturally inclines to ask oneself the question, was it a success? But how does one measure success in the sense of Spiritual Science? Perhaps in three ways: by the experience gained; by the degree in which the power of initiative has been strengthened; and by the quality of the spirit which animates the undertaking. The last named guarantees the nature of the result. If the spirit is 'true', if behind the deed there is as great a measure of love for the 'Sun-filled' Earth as we, in our present stage of evolution are capable of giving, then a multiplication of that spirit must inevitably ensue.

Just as the preparation for this conference had been both circumspect and thorough, so too might the exemplary character of this 'follow-up' also be observed by initiatives seeking to emulate it.

A Morning Prayer

Let us try at this point to take another glimpse 'backstage' as it were in order to perceive what it was that stood behind Dunlop's activity both on the anthroposophical level and in the sphere of his economical and organizational achievements. Where did he find the power and strength to maintain such a constant and sustained level of external activity over such long periods? The question might at first appear rhetorical. Is it not plain enough that Dunlop found the essential source of strength needed for his external activity through his meeting with Theosophy and, later on, with Rudolf Steiner and his work? From a general point of view this is, of course, correct. But in such general terms the same thing could obviously be said of countless other pupils of Rudolf Steiner.

Perhaps the reader will by now have noticed how, even during his earliest youth, D.N. Dunlop is connected with what has been termed since ancient times the 'Mysteries of the Father'. These are Mysteries which, in the spirit of the Christian tradition of the Trinity, are intimately connected with the godhead as *Father*—actively ruling and permeating the world of space. We have already seen this indicated in Dunlop's life in the strangely predominant number *12*. Twelve is the number of space *par excellence*. It determined the constellation of his group of youthful friends and later on it became the predominant number in his research into the zodiac. Then again Dunlop's affinity to the Arthurian Mysteries, originally founded in Hibernia, point in the same direction. Of course by this we do not mean to imply that Dunlop was *not* related to the Mysteries of the 'Son' and 'Holy Spirit' as well (many biographical experiences would point to quite the reverse); it is merely a matter of discerning where for a particular individual the emphasis lies. D.N. Dunlop always sought 'to cast his "spiritual anchor" in those spheres where the godhead as Father is ever present and permeating the world of Space', as a friend of his once expressed it.

It is therefore probably not surprising to learn that Dunlop formulated a meditation, in which he actually addresses the godhead of the universe as 'Father'. He called it 'A Morning Prayer'. In printed form it found its way (possibly only after his death) into the hands of a group of friends, and there it has remained alive right up to the present day:

> Father, for me a new day is beginning. Thou hast sent it and Thou canst make me strong for its duties. I pray that Thou wilt suffer no petty cares or great perplexities to draw me from my true rest in Thee. In my sorrow, be Thou Understanding. In my pain, be Thou Patience. In my joys, be Thou Joy. Amid the rude shocks of life, keep me undisturbed and quiet in Thee.
>
> Thou Who hast made me an immortal soul, give me the courage of one who is immortal. Help me to bless by word, or look, or deed, all whom I shall meet this day, and to give them of that same love Thou givest me. Thou Who art the Heart of Love, bless me with love. Thou Who art the Great Servant, teach me to serve. Thou Who didst create me, keep me by that same Power, strong, selfgiving, sane.

Crisis in the Society

For some years now Dunlop had been acting as chairman of various anthroposophical activities. David Clement[85] recalls a series of Christmas lectures in 1928 where Dunlop took the chair: 'Like Jove himself he sat before us—kind, humorous, all-wise.' Of medium height, he always appeared immaculately dressed with a thick black ribbon tied to his monocle. During this period it was only on rare occasions that Dunlop would lecture himself; usually he would introduce other lecturers or speak at the end. On certain occasions his words of introduction would grow into a 20-minute 'lecture' in themselves. This, however, was done out of quite conscious motives which will be discussed later on. But of course not all anthroposophists present on such occasions could fully grasp the need for such extensive introductions and summaries, not only on account of their occasional length but also with regard to some of the subjects touched upon, not to mention the extraordinary warmth of soul with which they were sometimes expressed. After all, most of these events took place on English soil, and under the influence of the English folk-soul people tend generally towards a more reserved manner of expression, even preferring to employ the famous 'understatement'.

At the present time, under the influence of the English folk-soul, something is being accomplished not only individually (as in other countries) but also nationally as well: the development of a certain attitude of soul which seeks to raise itself in full consciousness above the sphere of what is experienced as subjective feeling and sentiment. The constituent of the human soul which arises from such an attitude or tendency is described by Rudolf Steiner as the 'consciousness soul' or 'spiritual soul'.

Apparently, what the Scottish chairman D.N. Dunlop required of his listeners sometimes clashed with a certain aspect of this attitude and consciousness. On one occasion, Mr Wheeler, the treasurer of the British Society at the time, gave Dunlop a broad hint. The net result was that, on the occasion of the next General Meeting, with the treasurer present in the hall, Dunlop commenced by stating that Mr Wheeler had complained to him that he spoke too much of love, which was a subject that the British people did not like mentioned too often. 'Then,' according to David Clement's report, 'to everyone's amusement . . . Dunlop launched forth on what almost amounted to an Address on Love.'

*

Towards the end of the 1920s Harry Collison, who had been elected General Secretary in 1923, expressed his wish to retire from the more active and administrative work which this post involved. So he was then elected President of the Anthroposophical Society in Great Britain, an office which had been left vacant since Rudolf Steiner's death in 1925, and Dunlop was duly elected as his successor in the post of General Secretary. The two of them then worked in collaboration with each other, to outward appearances harmoniously but with increasing inner differences, through the rest of 1927 and the first half of 1928. In July of this latter year Collison was absent from the World Conference through illness. In September, however, it was he who as President travelled to Dornach to represent the British Society at the opening of the Second Goetheanum at Michaelmas. On this occasion, to the consternation of other English members also present, Collison publicly announced the formation of a 'Rudolf Steiner Union in England' as an opposing body to the British Society. When news of this announcement arrived back in England, it led to the immediate calling of an Extraordinary General Meeting of the Anthroposophical Society in Great Britain, which took place just three weeks later, lasting for two whole days, 20 and 21 October. At this meeting a resolution was passed by which the affairs of the British Society were now to be conducted by an Executive Council of 12, to which both Collison and Dunlop were among others then appointed. By a further resolution the offices of President and Secretary-General of the Anthroposophical Society in Great Britain were both abolished. The Executive Council then conducted the affairs of the British Society without these offices for the rest of 1928 and most of 1929. At a further General Meeting in October 1929 the decision was taken to re-establish the post of General Secretary with effect from the following January, when Dunlop was reappointed to this office.[225] Of course, one of the consequences of his appointment in these new conditions was that from then on he was much more intimately bound up with the actions, destiny and sufferings of both the British Society and the General Anthroposophical Society as well.

This whole catalogue of internal complications within the British Society was not just an isolated organizational curiosity but rather represented the particular expression on the British scene of major difficulties which were then afflicting the General Anthroposophical Society as a whole.

For in the period immediately following Rudolf Steiner's death a kind of polarization had begun to take place in the Executive

Council (*Vorstand*) in Dornach between Marie Steiner, Albert Steffen and Guenther Wachsmuth on the one hand, and Ita Wegman and Elisabeth Vreede on the other. This is not the right place to examine in detail the many different features in the background of this phenomenon, but in *essential* terms the divergence was connected with two different attitudes which had begun to materialize immediately after Rudolf Steiner's death. They could be found both in the *Vorstand* which he had himself set up as well as in wider circles of Society members. Those whose sympathies lay with Marie Steiner and Albert Steffen were more of the opinion that the death of the Initiate had created a hiatus it would be impossible to bridge. Therefore their task would now be to promote Rudolf Steiner's work and spiritual influence in the future by cultivating and advancing the works that he had left behind on *this side* of the threshold to the spiritual world. In contrast to this the other two members of the *Vorstand* and those close to them were inclined to think that Rudolf Steiner's work could in the future be continuously cultivated and spread *from the other side of the threshold*; they believed that this could be achieved by dint of courageous spiritual activity accomplished in real spiritual communion with the Initiate's *enduring work and activity* after death. In this sense there were also two fundamentally different attitudes towards the problem of how to direct the Anthroposophical Society and its affairs after Rudolf Steiner's death: one was orientated as it were 'under' the threshold of the spiritual world, the other 'above' it. The second attitude came to expression for instance in Ita Wegman's attempt to follow up Rudolf Steiner's spiritual intentions by trying to extend the *Anthroposophical Leading Thoughts*[226] which he had started to formulate in the last years of his life. This undertaking naturally met with some harsh criticism.

With the hindsight of over 60 years it is possible to appreciate that either one of these attitudes, if not complemented by the other, must lead to a one-sided interpretation and hence to practical and spiritual error. Seen in this light the unity of the Dornach *Vorstand* was a problem of vital importance for the future and destiny of the whole of the Anthroposophical Society.

It was the tendency of the *Vorstand* to polarize itself in two directions which spread out among all the members of the Society and subsequently led to real divisions within it. In the period following Rudolf Steiner's death four symptomatic factors can be singled out as having partly provoked and partly strengthened this tendency (the conflict about Rudolf Steiner's literary estate will be dealt with separately at a later point):

1925: the 'quarrel over the urn', which was based on a misunderstanding between Marie Steiner and Ita Wegman as to what should be done with Rudolf Steiner's ashes.
1925: the above-mentioned attempt by Ita Wegman to 'extend' the *Anthroposophical Leading Thoughts* which was criticized by Marie Steiner and Albert Steffen.
1926: the founding by Willem Zeylmans of a World Federation of Schools to provide a unified basis for all anthroposophical initiatives within the educational field; in the period just before its foundation the misunderstanding arose that it had *already* been founded without Marie Steiner and Albert Steffen having been consulted.
1930: the 'Northern Petition'. In accordance with the desire of a large number of people it was proposed by Scandinavian members that Albert Steffen on his own take over complete leadership 'in order to bring a decisive line of action into the direction of the Society', a proposition which Steffen himself refused.[227]

Of course a number of other 'contributing factors' could in this context also be mentioned and elaborated upon. However, it is *not* our task to present here a history of the Anthroposophical Society *but only to illustrate, by means of a few facts, how the divergence of attitudes began to centre on certain members of the* Vorstand *and their sympathizers* and how, in the years following Rudolf Steiner's death, this increasingly gave rise to certain conditions favourable to personality-cults and struggles for power.

Dunlop took over the official direction of the British Society at a time when these diverging attitudes within the Dornach *Vorstand* had begun to reach a state of smouldering crisis—a crisis that in the following years was to culminate by embroiling the whole Society as well. If we recall in this context what Dunlop's earlier attitude and line of action had been in the face of certain divergences and ensuing rifts within the Theosophical Society, we will hardly expect him, when confronted with similar developments in the Anthroposophical Society, to have reacted in a different manner. He knew that his commitment to Rudolf Steiner, as the bearer of the Michael impulse, was of such a nature as to exclude, from the very beginning, every possibility of 'siding' with any particular faction or group. As is clearly witnessed by the words he wrote *in memoriam* of Rudolf Steiner, for Dunlop the only 'parties' that mattered were those active on a higher plane, those standing behind the development and evolution of the Anthroposophical Movement and Society as a whole.

*

Apart from new tasks as an anthroposophical General Secretary with now full authority, the year 1930 had other things in store for D.N. Dunlop. He had to make extensive preparations for the second World Power Conference in Berlin, described in a previous chapter, which was due to be opened in June; and then there was the 'Kamp Stakenberg' which was due to take place in Holland during August. This was an anthroposophical youth congress, attended by many of the most prominent anthroposophical speakers of the time. Its fresh approach was to awaken a great deal of enthusiasm and to be widely talked about.[228] During the first half of the same year Dunlop underwent a serious crisis in his health. This was no doubt partly due to the enormous work-load he had both in the preceding year and in the present one but also partly to the mighty storm-clouds that were appearing on the horizon of the Anthroposophical Society. Amongst other things Dunlop was prevented by illness from taking part in the Berlin Conference. This whole crisis represented a culmination of a series of illnesses and, according to E.C. Merry, 'brought him to the gate of death'. (MD)

Mrs Merry, who as an intimate friend experienced at first hand the whole evolution of this illness, does not mention in her personal notes anything of its specific nature or causes. However, she records all the more clearly the spiritual and soul-metamorphosis of her friend when he at last emerged after the most crucial days were past. During his triumphant struggle with death new spiritual horizons seem to have opened up before the immortal eye of his Entelechy:

> When, after a day or two, he emerged from the stupor of his terrible fight with death, he seemed entirely changed. I shall never forget the overpowering impression he made upon me. His face was terribly thin, and covered with a dark beard. His eyes burned with a wonderful and holy fire. He told me that he was not the same as the D.N.D. I had known . . . that he had seen Christ's Light beside him. Then he said: 'I *am* Christ.' He meant that he had received Life from Him. Then he went on to speak about the need to found a new Order of the Mysteries—an order of Twelve. They were to be the *new Mysteries of King Arthur.* (MD)

When, a few days later, Mrs Merry asked him about this Order, 'he said he thought he had been looking into the future—that the time was not yet ripe.

'After this illness he was never quite the same. Though he seemed to others to be so. He was obliged to shorten his hours of work a good deal for a time—but later found a way by which he could do as much, or even more, than before. He could not get up so early in the mornings; but he worked far later into the nights. It became more and more difficult for him to *incarnate* in the mornings . . .'

Once again let us think back to that 9-year-old boy on the Isle of Arran, proclaiming to his 12 friends the Mystery of the Logos that became flesh in Jesus. During the crisis this former motif reappears, but in a much more intense form, bringing real fulfilment to the soul. The principle of the 12 now opens up a vision of the *future.* As for Dunlop's experience of the Christ—that Mystery which can only unfold within the individuality, flooding the innermost sanctuary of human experience with new life—we may only touch upon it here. It belongs to a sacred sphere of human life into which even a biographer may not venture.

But what about the Arthurian theme? Is it not strange that it appears in *this* biographical period—just as Dunlop enters into the most intimate bond of destiny with the Anthroposophical Society? Rudolf Steiner had already indicated that the anthroposophical impulse could only be realized in the world if *four times twelve* human beings were found in whom the Michael-thought was active.[229] Does the founding of new Mysteries in Dunlop's vision of the future imply that the new General Secretary had in some way already apprehended that the Anthroposophical Society, now having moved into a crisis-phase, was in need of a new life-impulse, or at least, was going to need one soon?

It is not our intention here to answer this question which Dunlop's vision poses. Even unanswered it may perhaps help to explain why, in the face of subsequent developments within the Society, he was to assume a standpoint above all 'party' tendencies; why, even during the most tragic moments of those developments, he was to remain unmoved in that part of his being where he continuously sought to shape the present in accordance with his vision of the future.

A few lines from a letter which he sent to E.C. Merry during the period of his illness also express, in an entirely different way, this inner invulnerability which in English is so appropriately described by the word 'detachment'. In these lines Dunlop speaks with admiration of the 'Days', pictured as real beings. In order to enter into the substance of these lines the reader may like to recall Rudolf Steiner's expositions in his Helsingfors lecture-cycle[230] where he describes the work of certain nature-spirits not directly active in the elements as other beings are; they are responsible for the rotation of the whole earth, and consequently for the alternation between day and night:

> When I saw the task of the DAYS I was caught up in adoration. They lend their sustenance to all the activities of Man, and cover him in sleep with their amplitude. They reveal the souls of men while they sleep adorning the Heavenly Mantle. They know the secrets of Action and what lies hidden in Action, and they watch, with calm poise, the weavings of Destiny. The DAYS endure like the great

Rocks. Man's work is sustained by them from one civilization to another . . .

'Anthroposophy formed a new organ in me'

On 18 February 1931 Walter Johannes Stein (whom we have already met in connection with the World Power Conference) wrote the following lines to his wife in Stuttgart as he travelled by train from Dover to London:

> I have just had a wonderfully stormy crossing. The waves splashed all over the deck and the wind blew so hard you had to hold your hat on with two hands . . . Lots of people were sea-sick, but not me. Nowhere near . . . The French are a decadent lot. Nobody knows when the trains leave. You can't buy a timetable or find a bureau de change at the station. You have to change your money at the buffet where the waiter demands extortionate rates of interest. People smoke in smoking and non-smoking compartments with total impunity. And there is no restaurant-car in the express train . . . England remains, as always, but especially in contrast to France, the ideal country . . .

That same evening Stein was due to give a lecture in London to members of the Anthroposophical Society. George Adams was to introduce him and D.N. Dunlop to speak some concluding words at the end of the lecture.

'I spoke at some length,' Stein wrote in the continuation of this letter, 'about Apollo and Natura. Natura, and the Seven Free Arts, mirrors Apollo and the nine Muses. Apollo—the astral body; Natura—the ether body. Apollo reveals the Christ descending to the earth as the sheath of the soul—the Grail; Natura, the ascending ethereal Christ, as the sheath of life. I went into all of this in detail, with examples from the Delphic and Eleusinian Mysteries, as well as from the Middle Ages. The audience was with me all the way . . .'

After the lecture Dunlop offered Stein some remarkable words of greeting, thereby in a way welcoming him to his 'ideal country' and future homeland, England. 'Mr Dunlop said afterwards,' Stein went on to inform his wife, 'in that exquisite manner of his: "Mr Stein speaks with such precision that many will say it was Ahrimanic and with such beauty that many will maintain it was Luciferic, but" . . . etc.'

If Dunlop's characterization was as accurate as it was beautiful, what anthroposophical lecturer could hope for a more satisfying evaluation of his lecture?

During a conversation with W.J. Stein at a Dutch Conference in 1922, Rudolf Steiner had already spoken the following words[231] which not only characterized Stein but also helped him to find his path: 'Just because you are able to master so much and work on it with such great mobility of thought you will in the future be personally faced with difficult cognitional tasks. However, you also have the capacity to add something to all this and give your listeners the most beautiful thing of all—the whole of your real self.' Apparently, this is what Stein succeeded in doing at that evening lecture in London: he managed to meet his audience not in a merely one-sided way as a thinking, feeling or willing individual, but with the 'whole of his real self'.

However, if the inner totality of Stein's being found its most beautiful form of expression in the many lectures he gave, in Dunlop's case the meeting with Anthroposophy led to a very different form of expression of *his* inner totality of being. For two things had radically changed since he had become an anthroposophist: he could no longer write any more books as had earlier been the case, nor could he any longer give regular lectures. With regard to his writing we learn the following from Mrs Merry's notes: 'He could no longer *convey the thought*, which he could have put into an article, through his hand, on to the paper. But what he *could* do, and most brilliantly, was to write down quickly and surely, some large content of ideas—such as for instance the *form* of a whole organization or constitution—condensed into a few words.' (MD)

In answer to Stein's query concerning his lecturing, or rather his *not* lecturing anymore, Dunlop replied: 'Anthroposophy formed a new organ in me. *Others* must lecture, but *I must speak afterwards*. People do not like it when I speak after a lecture—they think it unnecessary; *but I have to do it*.' (MD) Whether the expression 'do not like it' was literally applicable may well be doubted. However, the question still remains: to what extent did Dunlop see this as a special task, even a necessity?

According to Mrs Merry's testimony 'what he said on those occasions was nearly always something which *enlarged* the picture—but in such a way that it became more living and more *planted in the earth*.' Dunlop 'did not like things "left in the air".'

> If anyone gave a lecture for example about the inner life—perhaps speaking about details from *Wie erlangt man* etc . . . he would always turn it into simple practical everyday problems. But the *essential* thing in it was the *source* that his words came from: they came from his heart. They were spoken as messages—secret messages—from his heart to other hearts. It was this gift, always being used, which made so many people speak of him as a father and not only among anthroposophists—among even his business friends. He was their 'father' too.

Just as Dunlop engaged himself in the technical and economic field to bring isolated facts into relationship with each other so as to place them in the light of the *whole*, so now he also developed the faculty of 'treating' in a similar fashion the specific spiritual-scientific content of lectures given by others. In a certain sense he left all that the speaker had just developed quite untouched. Eschewing all criticism concerning any particular point, he would instead move around the whole of what had been put forward, *as though on the periphery*, in order to stress some aspect that seemed to him of particular significance, or he would add something here or there in order to balance out the general picture.

How infinitely more productive such an approach is bound to be compared with any form of direct contradiction or criticism which can arise so easily and often simply eliminates a part or all of what might just have been stated! A speaker would have been less inclined to feel himself rejected. Indeed, if one could speak of criticism at all in this context, then it is only in the sense of an indirect correction—one which would enable the speaker to advance in his own development on the basis of a specific extension Dunlop had made to his lecture. In any event, according to Stein's experience, 'there was something about his interest and love that encouraged you to unfold your real self'. (StN) We may with good reason assume that it was this interest and love that was present whenever Dunlop spoke his concluding words. The element of unfolding, which seems to be connected with this new faculty Dunlop was in the process of acquiring, obviously presupposes the full development of another faculty—that of being able to listen intently and with absolute devotion. What is more, it is possible to gauge to what extent Dunlop had already developed *this* faculty and was using it as the basis of his activity as he extended the work of others, helping them to 'unfold' their true capacities. The previously mentioned Willem Zeylmans gives us this description of Dunlop as a partner in a personal conversation:

> Having a conversation with Dunlop was a unique and fascinating experience. At first he would say very little, but instead would listen intently all the time. However, at the end of the conversation he was fond of developing his own points of view, putting them forward on a very wide basis and taking up again all that had previously been touched upon in the course of the conversation. At the very end he often expressed very deep ideas, full of spiritual content which he gave out in a voice that 'sang' forth almost in rather singing ritual tone.[232]

Another, slightly different version of the reasons Dunlop gave for no longer writing books and giving lectures provides us with further insight into the 'new organ' he was developing: 'Since I became a pupil of Rudolf Steiner, I felt very deeply and clearly that I had not to speak and not to write, but to give the proper people the right opportunity to write and to speak. And so I restricted my work to such things as organizing summer schools, producing magazines and speaking as the chairman after someone else has given his knowledge.' (St) So after his meeting with Rudolf Steiner Dunlop increasingly acted as one who prepared the way for others. Earlier in this book several concrete examples were given; now we are attempting to discover the underlying motives for this attitude. His personal aims can be seen to 'disappear' so to speak in the will to help others suited to various tasks to 'break through' and realize their own creative potential. He increasingly identifies himself with this element of the *will*, an element which, transcending all personal considerations, embraces the motives and motivating forces inherent in the action of others. In *this* sense his own action becomes more and more 'peripheral' in nature.

*

Thus the *personality*, as a centre from which personal will-impulses stream out into the social environment, recedes into the background—not only in the field of knowledge but also in the sphere of practical and social action. Dunlop had long since held the individuality to be a cosmic principle; now, it is more and more that same individuality that alone gives birth to the decisive impulses of the will. Moreover, the individuality is not, as is the case with the personality, bound to or centred on the body; it lives in the whole environment or 'periphery', which is to say the whole social environment as well.

Now one of the central components of this new organ that 'Anthroposophy formed' in D.N. Dunlop is that like all supersensible organs it does not represent anything comparable to the 'finished' state of the physical organs but rather it consists of one (or several) *activities* or *faculties*—to derive the motives for what one does and how one acts from a peripheral experience of the whole environment, so that in this way real service can be rendered to humanity.

*

Another aspect of this supra-personal mode of action arising 'from the periphery' can be seen in the way Dunlop sought to solve certain questions and problems in the realm of business affairs, together and with the aid of other human beings:

> He had the greatest reverence for human freedom and working under him in his office, working out his economic ideas with him as my immediate superior, I could observe his method. The ideas would originate with him, but he would give them freely to his helpers to be worked out along their own lines. Then he wanted them written down, but he would not read what was written. He would give it to others to read and watched their reactions to it, asking them questions. Finally he would call together, maybe for lunch, people whose views he valued, and with whom he wanted to have a living discussion about the matter in question. (St)

Just as Dunlop as anthroposophical Chairman would take up what had been put forward during a lecture, pursuing the thread and adding to it, so too as a creative entrepreneur in the business world he would let ideas that had originated in his own mind circulate in the social environment of his colleagues in order to allow them to be extended or enlarged upon. Thus in this field of practical action too, Dunlop acted, in contrast to the more or less centralized, authoritarian style of leadership, from the periphery.

For him this simply corresponded to a certain law which anyone who wanted to organize anything in any field should observe: 'If you want to organize, you have to learn how to use other people's brains. You must learn to think with their thoughts, receiving at last the full truth arrived at as the balanced result of all possible points of view. Wisdom always arrives at the end. But the right beginning is the desire to help in a certain direction.' (St) Stein also referred to the way Dunlop left people free in their work. Here again he gave an example: 'His most characteristic habit was to give one the opportunity of telling him what one thought to be the most important thing to do, and then he would underline some of what had been suggested to him, or he would correct it by saying, "Doing it in that way is not wise, it would give a wrong impression." But he did it in such a way that it left one feeling entirely free. This was his greatest talent, the giving of freedom.'[233]

This example again shows clearly how great a value Dunlop attached to developing a real moral technique effectively concerned with the problem of *how* a certain idea can be put into practice; and it equally illustrates the way in which Dunlop, whilst referring other people to the importance of the *how*, would also observe it himself—so scrupulously in fact, that his partner could take up any allusion or correction that might be made, in total liberty.

We mentioned earlier how Stein had worked for Dunlop over a period of about two years in the newly established 'Statistical Research Bureau'. Whilst Dunlop as director of this Bureau took an intimate interest in everything that went on in the new field of work, Stein, as his employee, nevertheless enjoyed the greatest imaginable freedom. Describing both of these aspects in retrospect Stein writes: 'He always knew, even to small details what was going on in our office, and cared for even the smallest troubles. Very often he mentioned such things when they were at a stage where I was not yet conscious of them. He perceived them *in statu nascendi*. During two years he only entered my office twice, except for a few occasions when he came for the purpose of meeting with other collaborators.'[233]

If Stein esteemed Dunlop's 'greatest talent' to be this ability to leave people free and to bestow freedom on them in such a way as to stimulate creative, individual initiative and 'skill in action', another witness highlights a different trait, intimately linked to the element of human freedom. Rudolf Hauschka, who was also active in the industrial field and had known Dunlop since the year of Rudolf Steiner's death, writes how he 'was fascinated from the very first to see how this man handled the industrial and economic problems of our time. If one came to him confused and narrow-minded, after a short discussion one felt, so to speak, lifted to the top of a mountain with a wide view and an enlarged horizon. This was the characteristic tendency of his life, that he always tried to enlarge the horizon.'[234]

Hauschka also confirms that Dunlop's 'spiritual activity unfolded in the sphere of freedom', and adds that his personal intercourse from man to man 'took place in the sphere of love'. We also owe Hauschka the following illuminating pen picture of the singular atmosphere which reigned in Dunlop's own working-quarters: 'It was wonderful how his activity was always combined with a great goodness and kindness. Sometimes, when I was able to watch him in his office, I was surprised at the benevolence manifest in his manner and decisions. Never and nowhere else could I find that in business. It was a new experience to see how fraternity may permeate economic life in the future.'[234]

Against this background and in such an atmosphere as that described by Hauschka, many a business acquaintance or associate found himself stimulated by Dunlop to consider things from a spiritual point of view. Of course anthroposophical or theosophical terms were not employed in such cases—it was often *en passant* and in a joking manner always adapted perfectly to the way of thinking and mode of expression of whoever he was talking to. Years afterwards he could repeat these conversations in every detail to Mrs Merry. In a very living way he would imitate gestures and mannerisms of speech as he related to her how he had talked to such people 'on many spiritual things, on prayer, or the life after death, or the spiritual evolution of the world'.

But let us return to Dunlop's 'greatest talent', his ability not only to leave people free but also to awaken the free being in his fellow men, encouraging them to develop creative initiative in an individual sense. With regard to this spiritual practice, which was based wholly on personal trust and confidence, a further example from the business-world will serve to illustrate just how far he was prepared to go at times. Dunlop permitted a certain colleague of his not only to open mail and reply to correspondence directly addressed to him during his absence, but even to forge his own, clear signature at the bottom of the letter!

*

After all these examples and illustrations (which, incidentally, could be multiplied further), what conclusions can we draw for the moment with regard to the development of this 'new organ'?

It is of course impossible to give a really complete answer to this question for the simple reason that this new organ is obviously connected to the new *knowledge* Dunlop was gradually acquiring through his acquaintance with Anthroposophy. Moreover, this spiritual extension of his faculties of knowledge cannot be directly apprehended since the most decisive consequence it had for his actions was that he almost completely stopped writing and giving lectures.

To put the right people in certain places, to help others to true, spiritual independence by seeking to address the true ego in each one of them—such were the predominant objectives that entered into the forefront of Dunlop's social activity. Realizing these intentions was equivalent to activating the new organ which Anthroposophy had formed in him. Within this individuality no room was left for an egocentric realization of the self or of the personality, for vanity or complacent enjoyment of one's own actions. The individuality, living and experiencing the social environment 'from the periphery', was becoming ever more the source of all Dunlop's activity. In the spirit of Steiner's *Theosophy* we could equally well say: Dunlop was beginning to work actively and consciously out of the Spirit-Self, and in this work was becoming an awakener of the human Ego.

Looking at Other People and Other Events—A Method in Itself

During his theosophical phase Dunlop had been predominantly linked to the esoteric leitmotif of the *Father* (as is clear, for instance, from his Morning Prayer), with its all-embracing theme *Ex Deo Nascimur*. After his meeting with Anthroposophy it is the *Son* that emerges more and more clearly; we discerned this in a certain change of emphasis in Dunlop's social activity. For is the 'environment' or 'periphery', mentioned several times in the preceding chapter, any other than that in which 'the Christ-Will holds sway', as it is expressed in the central part of Rudolf Steiner's *Foundation Stone Meditation*? And in the complete subduing of all will-impulses founded or centred within the personality, is this not the practical realization of the principle *In Christo Morimur*? The personal is sacrificed on the altar of service to humanity; reference was already made to this in 1914 in Dunlop's meditation on ceremonial magic in which the candles were lit at the periphery of the circle to symbolize this event.

This shift in emphasis towards the periphery during the last years of Dunlop's life explains and, it is hoped, also justifies a certain aspect of the present biographical study. For in this biography, too, we have continually seen how *other* persons and events have moved into the foreground of our story. However, is it possible to proceed otherwise if the *method* of portrayal is to be adapted to the life and evolution of its 'subject'? Must we not draw in such 'peripheral' persons and events in such a way as to 'circumscribe' the subject—precisely from the point of view of *others* and characterize the 'subject' in his relationship to the numerous occurrences and tendencies of the times? In the light of the particular traits which Dunlop's evolution assumed, especially during the last years of his life, it seemed indeed to be an inherent necessity to discuss other people and other events at various points throughout this book. Dunlop himself attempted more and more to help *others* find the right opportunity to speak and write—in fact to unfold the whole of their creative potential. Therefore it seems only appropriate that other people should be drawn into a description of his life—through the medium of their *own* words as far as seems objectively necessary.

*

This leitmotif of the periphery probably constituted the strongest thread of a beautiful bond of friendship between George Adams-Kaufmann and D.N. Dunlop even if they never discussed it as such. This friendship had begun to grow ever since the Summer School in Penmaenmawr, and, during the same years in which this motif came to assume more and more importance in Dunlop's social activity, George Adams was busy working out, albeit from an entirely different point of view, scientific ideas intimately connected with it.

Adams, who had already been encouraged by Rudolf Steiner to take up and develop further modern synthetic geometry, sought to arrive at a clear concept of 'ethereal space' upon the basis of this non-Euclidean, new geometrical way of thinking. This space is present wherever new life is formed but the laws that govern it are very different from those that inhere in the physical, 'Euclidean' space we know so well and in which our physical bodies are located and move around. Perhaps one can best perceive the difference by envisaging clearly the way in which all physical forces in physical space 'radiate' out into the circumference in linear form or as 'radii' from a certain point. One need only think of the force of gravity, for instance, with its central point in the middle of the earth. In ethereal space it is the forces of life that are at work and these forces have their effective source or 'centre' in the whole of the circumference. It is from there that they work, as 'surfaces' into the centres of the germinating life of the physical world. In this sense ethereal forces are *peripheral or circumferential* in nature, and they have their greatest 'concentration' in the periphery.

In 1933 Adams published his ideas simultaneously in English and German.[235] In certain of his later works he showed how the idea of ethereal space with its particular laws was not only of relevance to mathematics and geometry but could also fructify biology and, above all, *Christology*. For it is said of the Christ Being that He works within the surroundings or periphery (*Umkreis*); therefore this is something that only becomes comprehensible to human reason if we have some idea of the laws that are active in this 'periphery'. Instead of speaking of a Being that holds sway in the periphery Rudolf Steiner often speaks of the Christ as working in the ethereal world, also making it quite clear that this Being will begin to exercise a very special influence at the beginning of the 1930s.[236]

The fundamental significance of the periphery of the universe for the life-forces of the world in which the Christ holds sway, this was what George Adams was working out in scientific terms. And do not these self-same forces appear in what D.N. Dunlop had, since his meeting with Anthroposophy, been tirelessly and unceasingly practising in the field of his external activities? We could go even further and ask: were not Dunlop's efforts to decentralize the world economy also accomplished in accordance with the Spirit of the Times and the influence of the *Periphery*?

As Dunlop identified more and more with his social environment, people's affection for him naturally grew. And it was fully appropriate to this that George Adams singled out this aspect in his memorial address just after Dunlop's death (see Appendix). Putting aside all his own personal experiences of Dunlop and assuming the standpoint of those many acquaintances, his first words in this address were to be: 'D.N. Dunlop was *our* friend'.

Friendship as an Art of Living

During the later years of his life, Dunlop's way of awakening the ego in other human beings assumed the character of an all-embracing *art* of life. This can be considered as the ripened fruit of the 'moral imagination' and 'moral technique' he had developed in *all* fields of human life and existence. However, it seems to have been based to an equal extent on a certain mastery of the personality as an instrument for realizing spiritual aims, a faculty which he had developed to the point of virtuosity.

It was particularly in his friendships that Dunlop's individuality seemed to shine through his personality with the most life-giving force and richness of colour. Consequently it is in these friendships that we can best observe the fruitfulness of his manner: how he worked with, or rather out of, this polarity between the individuality and the personality in such a way that any receptive person could thereby advance in the development of his own faculties. Indeed, a spontaneous equilibrium between personal warmth on the one hand and an element completely transcending the personal on the other is a characteristic trait of all his deepest bonds of friendship. At times it is even possible to trace the effects of this polarity right down to certain external details. Thus W.J. Stein mentions in his short obituary how Dunlop would make any observations he might have in the margin of the letters Stein addressed to him before sending them back to him again (see Fig. 22): 'In this way he dealt with business affairs,' Stein tells us, 'but in between he wrote other letters, entirely out of the kindness of his heart.'[233]

The most striking example of the way Dunlop worked with this polarity is to be found in his friendship with E.C. Merry who was as close to him as AE or his own wife Eleanor. How did E.C. Merry experience Dunlop as a friend and awakener of the true 'Ego'? She recalls after his death:

> Over and over again I had to discover that apparently trivial things that happened, quite apparently unimportant things that he said, etc. were the cause—or were connected with—very disturbing experiences in my inner and outer life . . . It was as though they were in the nature of *tests*, quite consciously applied by him—as part of my education. Nearly always he denied any knowledge of any consciousness of that. But in the course of the years I came to see that his real Ego was at work. He had in fact—and not always quite consciously—a *method* of training me. This is also true in connection with other people with whom he was at all closely connected . . . Put in a general way, it was that his mission with human beings was to *waken their Egos*—to place them 'on their own feet . . .' Very gradually certain changes took place. These rather unusual and sometimes exciting experiences grew less and less . . . It was as though he took my hand and said: 'Now walk beside me.'
>
> This was really a greater testing. I had to know his Ego in its 'concealed' state, hidden in 'D.N.D.', I had to observe how it was apparently only a 'D.N.D.' who was going about the world; and the being whose ways and methods with other people, with the Society, and other affairs, was continually criticised, misunderstood. I had to know him as a harrassed overworked human being. But wonderful was the way in which he *now* revealed his real self to me . . . no longer through 'magical' moments, but through his *words*. In our quiet conversations I came to know something of the deep wells of his wisdom, imparted directly . . .(MD)

So in course of time E.C. Merry came to experience the real being of her friend in a variety of different ways—sometimes working through more external occurrences, at others somewhat more hidden behind the veil of his 'personality' or revealing himself directly through his words. All these experiences meant that she had to unfold an intense activity within her Ego in order to grasp the inner being of her friend from various different angles and constantly changing points of view.

The following words of her description bring to light a feature of Dunlop's nature which is of significance for understanding the origin of certain obstacles he was destined to an ever greater degree to encounter in anthroposophical circles. Whenever he put forward Anthroposophy he adopted a totally individual style, at times combined with a certain down-to-earth realism. This seemed to give rise to some serious misunderstandings at times. As Mrs Merry describes, 'this wisdom had a certain quality. I found other people always seemed to expect that an "anthroposophist" must speak out of "Anthroposophy" as *they* conceived it. They liked to find an echo of Dr. Steiner's lectures. And if they could not, they suspected it was not "right". But the quality in his wisdom was that it embodied the whole *art of life*. It was as though he knew the "Depths", the *ground* out of which anthroposophy had blossomed upwards . . . It seemed as if there were no secret of the human soul in its struggles with the world which he did not know.'

The following example illustrates how in a given situation Dunlop was indeed able to practise this art and act out of real knowledge of human nature. David Clement relates:

> In those days, the early thirties, my father-in-law Fried Geuter was, I have reason to think, something of an 'enfant terrible' to the headquarters in London. He was to the core of his being a German Idealist, with Schiller as his special hero (notwithstanding he was half English by birth) and the somewhat quiet and phlegmatic approach of us British was often a thorn in his flesh. I remember him driving up to London breathing fire to be met by Mr Dunlop in his warmest and kindest manner. He was always fond of Fried. To me his master stroke was that he always addressed him as 'Fred'. How could anyone destroy us root and branch as worthless people when called Fred? His fiery spirit did indeed continue to wake us up, but I believe Dunlop made him feel accepted and appreciated in the Society.[85]

But let us come back to Dunlop's individual style in the treatment of Anthroposophy. Referring to the deep insights he possessed into the various 'substrata' of the human soul, E.C. Merry observes:

> . . . he did not express these in any way as though, for instance, he had studied *Knowledge of the Higher Worlds*. He once said 'that isn't my path'. Together we coined a habitual phrase which we used to use, with much laughter, when I used to lose myself in more imaginative speculations about things, or in not quite practical aspirations and ideals; it was: *'Well, can you bring it before the Executive?'*
>
> I can well understand how this 'getting down to brass tacks' was thought by some people to be merely an evidence of his capacities as a business man. In reality it was a holy quest—*the endeavour to place the human Ego, spiritually awakened, into the world, to prepare it for the dawn of Spirit-Self.*

*

In one of the next chapters we shall see how Dunlop's all-embracing art of life came to expression in this perhaps most beautiful friendship of his life. However, for the moment, with regard to the crisis within the Society which was soon to reach its culminating point, we want to consider which aspects of Dunlop's work and personality might have given offence to an increasing force of opposition. What element of his work and activity might those who subsequently misunderstood him have found objectionable? In fairness to his opponents—who were quick to move from criticizing thoughts to acts of condemnation—this is the question we should ask ourselves if we wish to show them the greatest possible degree of human understanding.

In the Face of Obstacles

Apart from that undogmatic, occasionally so-called unanthroposophical style and manner of presentation, as well as a certain dimension of solid realism, there were also, as we can surmise from George Adams's memorial address, a whole series of other elements which must to a greater or lesser degree have given some kind of offence. For over and above his habit of getting to the point Dunlop also expressed himself with an extraordinary warmth, speaking straight to the human heart as though this were the most natural thing in the world. We have already noted this phenomenon on numerous occasions. Thus, if some took offence at the sober objectivity of Dunlop's approach others were shocked by his, in some respects 'un-English', warmth of expression. George Adams, however, associates this warmth in a perceptive way with one particular aspect of the consciousness soul. This aspect was described by Rudolf Steiner in the *Leading Thoughts* shortly before his death, and it can easily be overlooked as it constitutes the *reverse side*, in real spiritual terms, of the consciousness soul (or 'spiritual soul')—the one attitude which trains the soul to observe with cool impartiality. Rudolf Steiner remarks with regard to this constituent of the human being that 'in its true essence the spiritual soul is not cold. It only seems so in the initial stage of its evolution, for it is then only able to reveal the quality of light which it contains, not yet the Warmth of Worlds, from which it in truth springs.'[237] For George Adams, Dunlop's warmth of expression was of *this* nature. To ears that were not so well-disposed, this mode of expression might at times have seemed to represent a kind of lapse into the sentient soul. However, this would immediately raise the question as to the degree of spiritual discernment possessed by anyone making such a judgement.

Another element that might have given offence was Dunlop's *will* which 'at some critical moments would become absolute'.[238] What is meant here by 'critical moments' are certain occurrences within the Anthroposophical Society of which the most significant ones will later be related.

So much then, for the moment, regarding those aspects of Dunlop's personality and modes of action which might have met with the disapproval of those less inclined to take an active and worthy interest.

It is certainly not superfluous to turn the 'spotlight' on such phenomena as these for in the following years more than one of the polemical attacks in anthroposophical circles might have found any of these elements to be a point of attack. After all, it is a well-established fact that all polemical activity is based on an attitude which assesses mainly the personality of another and tends to completely disregard the *individuality* behind it.

As far as the essential background to this polemic is concerned, the reader is reminded of the divergence of opinion within the *Vorstand* after Rudolf Steiner's death which now, in the following years, led to real splits and separations between persons and personal groups. Wherever such processes are set in motion in a spiritual movement there will always be people ready to hound out those 'responsible' and to organize some minor or major 'trials'. The triumphant day of the polemical campaigners had arrived—or rather we should say (in the light of the hundreds and thousands of years by which the development of all truly spiritual movements may be spanned), their *hour* had struck. *Personalities* were now attacked and a spiritual blindness seemed to fall upon the attackers' vision in such a way as to increasingly veil and conceal the individuality of the victim.

*

The year 1932 seems to be one of the most dense in this biography. This is the case both in a private sense as well as with respect to the developments which took place within the Anthroposophical Society to which Dunlop was so deeply and intimately connected. At the beginning of the year in question his wife Eleanor died. Dunlop had made her acquaintance in Dublin at the beginning of the 1890s in the immediate circle of AE's friends not many years before Russell himself had met *his* future companion. And now in February of the same year Russell's Violet also died. It seems almost as though destiny had a hand in this coincidence, as in the whole series of underlying parallels that exist between AE's and Dunlop's lives.

As we have already noted (Chapter 5, page 225), Stein arrived in London in March of that year and stayed there for a month. In a letter addressed to his wife in Stuttgart, dated 4 March 1932, he relates amongst other things the following: 'I have just returned from having lunch with Mr Dunlop. He received me and Mr

Kaufmann [as George Adams still called himself at that time] not at his own home—he is a widower and has no one to keep house for him—but in one of those feudal Clubs which are so typical of London . . .' Soon afterwards, however, Dunlop called on his eldest daughter Edith to come to Chelsea in order to keep house for him.

As for Stein himself, he fell ill a few days afterwards suffering from a disorder of the bile. It is touching to learn how Dunlop and other English friends offered to take over the costs of a hospital examination. On March 13, Ita Wegman arrived in London and according to Stein 'said the bilious problem was an after-effect' of his 'experiences in 1924'. What Stein meant by this was certain fundamental spiritual experiences which he mentions in his *Reminiscences*.[239] 'Apparently Dr Steiner had told her that if I managed to break through to certain experiences I would not be spared a bilious illness of some kind—it was simply inherent in my constitution.'

The next day Stein reported from Bolingbroke Hospital that he had been interviewed by two journalists in Dunlop's office that very morning. 'To my great joy, one of them was even acquainted with all Dr. Steiner's books concerning the social life . . . Mr Ferguson caused me considerable amazement for he even understood some things much better than I did . . . Mr Dunlop has made me a present of a silk dressing-gown and so now I am perfectly equipped.' And Walter Johannes Stein, 'equipped' in this manner, soon found himself on the way to recovery.

Further details which Stein communicated to his wife in Stuttgart enable us to recognize an important symptom of the splitting-up process which was taking place within the *Vorstand* in Dornach. In a letter dated 24 of March 1932 he writes:

> Preparations are being made here for some important changes. I am telling you about this but it is better not to pass it on to anyone else. Frau Wegman, too, considers the situation in Dornach to be untenable and believes that she has fulfilled her duty by agreeing to work seven years under such conditions. Now she is preparing to transfer the centre of her activity to England without, of course,

saying anything officially about the matter. Today or tomorrow a house will be purchased with sufficient space . . . She envisages the possibility of German doctors coming here on an alternating basis, Suchantke, Kälin etc, each one for a certain period of time. All this suits me very well. For there is a real need for something really great and world-wide to be established here.

The 'untenable' nature of 'the situation in Dornach' is a reference to the breakdown of confidence between the various members of the *Vorstand* to the point of erecting barriers which made further co-operation impossible—and the resulting consequences. The 'house with sufficient space' is an allusion to the anthroposophical therapeutical institute, Kent Terrace, which was to open its doors in the autumn of that same year.

*

It was not only in business affairs that Dunlop proved remarkably capable of perceiving problems *in statu nascendi*. This was evidently also the case with regard to these problematic developments within the Anthroposophical Society. In the present situation he did not wait until these schismatic tendencies had become outwardly consolidated. Recognizing the symptoms of these trends he immediately tried to create a counterbalance. In accordance with what Rudolf Steiner had emphasized yet again at the founding of the Anthroposophical Society in Great Britain, Dunlop believed that every genuine spiritual movement had to transcend all sectarian tendencies and to maintain right into the future a universally human and truly international character. For this reason there was only one kind of measure Dunlop could take against these intensifying segregational tendencies and personality struggles: to try and ensure, by means of balanced new initiatives and widening perspectives, that this universally human and truly international element survived. It is against this background that one must understand the initiative he took of founding in Birmingham on 27 March 1932 a 'World Economic Association'.

This 'new Society' was, to begin with, 'orientated on a purely economic basis'. With its head-quarters in London it was, however, as Stein wrote to his wife in Stuttgart on 28 March, 'constituted in such a way that at any moment the new Anthroposophical Society could emerge from it.'

The founder-members included Dunlop, Ita Wegman, Stein and, amongst others, the well-known French journalist and anthroposophist Jules Sauerwein. Stein certainly had the potentially explosive nature of this undertaking in mind when writing with regard to the then 'reigning' *Vorstand* Trio in Dornach (consisting of Albert Steffen, Marie Steiner and Guenther Wachsmuth): 'Dornach will rage' and adding placidly 'but that is all the same to me . . . We will calmly wait and see whether we are thrown out by the General Meeting.' This refers to the Easter General Meeting to be held in Dornach which we will presently consider more closely.

It is doubtful whether Dunlop himself would have held such an 'eruption' as that feared by Stein to have been inevitable and would not have attempted to avoid it. Unnecessary provocation corresponded neither with his impartial and far-sighted vision nor with his practical motto of skill in action; for him it was more a matter of preparing things with a view to long-term developments. Thus it must be assumed that he had indeed gone as far as conceiving the World Economic Association 'in such a way that at any moment the new Anthroposophical Society can emerge from it'. But as to this *possible* transformation of function he would have considered that no words should be wasted on the subject until it proved an absolute *necessity*. For Dunlop there could be no question of any kind of provocation or of competition with Dornach; the founding of this organization was only a prudent and far-sighted attempt to provide for the worst possible outcome; and indeed, precisely this outcome was soon enough to materialize.

The 'ship' of the Anthroposophical Society had sprung a leak; this was something that various symptoms had made perfectly clear to Dunlop. Would it not, therefore, be only sensible to prepare a 'life-raft' in case it foundered altogether—one that could later, if necessary, be used as a 'dock' whilst the new ship of the Society was being built? If the leak could be repaired then the

World Economic Association would remain nothing more than a World Economic Association. In face of the difficulties in the Society Dunlop will no doubt have reasoned along these lines and, on the basis of such quite flexible plans, have called the above-mentioned Association into existence.

On 31 March 1932, at the same time as the General Meeting was being held in Dornach, W.J. Stein wrote to Stuttgart: 'I am curious to know what will happen at the General Meeting in Dornach today. Apparently Boos has put forward a motion to exclude me from the Society. It's all the same to me. My journey to London has given me a great deal of strength. More than ever I know where my true path lies and I will pursue it despite all obstacles . . .'

*

In contrast to Dunlop, Stein had, years before this, already become involved in various difficulties with the Society; he had even given rise to certain difficulties himself. Because of what had happened at the Christmas Conference, and on the basis of certain indirect statements Rudolf Steiner had made, Stein was of the opinion that after the latter's death his will and testament had to be modified: so that whereas Marie Steiner had been designated personal trustee of Rudolf Steiner's literary works, the Anthroposophical Society as a whole should be considered as administrator. In a letter addressed to Marie Steiner[240] many years later, on 30 March 1948, Stein gratefully acknowledges all that he owed to her and, looking back on the new situation that had arisen after Rudolf Steiner's death, makes the following judgement of his own previous actions:

> What then followed was the tremendous task of continuing to direct the Society without the physical presence of Dr Steiner. I had hoped that this would be possible and I thought that the spiritual world would help in the task. I believe you also thought it to be possible. But it foundered on the characters.
>
> What then followed was tragic. This is what I remember: Dr

> Steiner intended to settle certain affairs. But much which concerned you he wanted to settle *personally* with you. I learnt this from Frau Dr Wegman to whom Rudolf Steiner had told this. However, none of this materialized because the car which was to bring you to him was only made available for you too late. Your arrival was delayed and so the decisive conversation never took place. *What subsequently occurred was that Frau Dr Wegman and a few of her friends, including myself, made ourselves advocates of a cause which Rudolf Steiner had reserved for himself.* That is the point, I believe, where Frau Dr Wegman and I were at fault. At least that is how I see it today. We wanted at all costs to achieve what only Dr Steiner's wisdom and goodness could have brought about. Now many years have passed. The conflict still goes on but the people standing behind it have changed. It is a tragedy that later insight cannot today help at all because those who understand are not the same as those who today are acting . . .

Already in 1929 Stein had resigned from the Executive Council of the Anthroposophical Society in Germany on account of his views on the publishing and administration rights applicable to Rudolf Steiner's literary estate. Although during the General Meeting of 1932 he was also to be attacked on entirely different grounds, the preceding expositions concerning the 'Nachlass controversy' and the role he played in it may contribute to an understanding of what happened at this General Meeting, especially in regard to Marie Steiner's attitude towards him when he was attacked in his own absence.

Some of the events which occurred during this meeting not only had a direct bearing on Stein but, *indirectly*, on Dunlop as well. First of all Stein came under fire on account of his activity as a teacher in the Stuttgart Waldorf School. He had explained to his pupils the nature of the nine Hierarchies above the human being and had wanted to illustrate with an example how a reflection of this order of spiritual beings can even be found in such an exoteric institution as the order of military ranks. To this end he wrote down the Hierarchies and the various ranks vertically, in two columns, on the blackboard. On the basis of several main-lesson books that were placed before the meeting, the matter was interpreted as though Stein had proceeded by means of horizontal comparisons, i.e. second lieutenant = angel, first lieutenant = archangel, etc, and had presented his pupils with a kind of profane hierarchical doctrine.

Moreover Stein, whom Rudolf Steiner himself had appointed (among a number of other people including D.N. Dunlop) a 'Goetheanum speaker', was also attacked in his work as a lecturer. Two teachers, Blümel and Baumann, both colleagues of his, tried to balance the scales by putting forward positive elements and George Adams made an ardent intervention on behalf of the discredited lecturer, declaring: 'We have no grounds for dropping Dr Stein.'[241] However, Dr Roman Boos was of the opinion that the Stuttgart College of Teachers 'was by no means an institute for teachers in need of psychiatric treatment . . .'[241]

Elisabeth Vreede, at that time still a member of the *Vorstand*, tried on several occasions to raise the level of the exchanges by drawing attention to the manner in which 'some people . . . keep on attacking others'.[241] But in the prevailing emotional climate this had no decisive effect.

In the meantime Stein had arrived at the Hague where he met Dunlop and Ita Wegman. On 2 April he wrote to Stuttgart: 'I have heard that I have been attacked in Dornach—in my capacity as a teacher as well. Dunlop says as soon as we are thrown out we can come to England. He will give us his country residence in Bray, near London, if need be. I thanked him, said I didn't want to precipitate anything . . . Having London to fall back on is a tremendous moral support. Let them say what they want.'

A week later, back in Stuttgart, another letter went to his life-long friend Eugen Kolisko: 'I have just returned from my journey. In forty-two days I have given forty-two lectures, making Doctor Steiner's teachings known in three different countries. On my return I learn that I have been disgracefully treated, my lectures and teaching activity in the Waldorf School abused . . . Frau Steiner read out that I had made a parallel between an angel and a second lieutenant. *Everything was read horizontally instead of vertically.*' This last phrase of Stein's might appear particularly symptomatic of numerous misunderstandings and conflicts arising during these years—not only in this particular case but again and again things were not always considered from the most productive point of view. As for 'having London to fall back on'—here again we can perceive just how beneficial Dunlop's combined capacity for action and farsightedness could prove on the social level. Doubtless he had realized that developments of this kind, having been reduced to such a personal level, could, to begin with, only get worse.

But even Dunlop himself was not to come through totally 'unscathed'.

Immediately after this inauspicious General Meeting, Roman Boos, one of its polemic participants, instigated what he termed a 'minor purgatorial process'. Under the title 'Protection against Nonsense' it was printed in the thirty-seventh issue of the *Korrespondenz der Sozialwissenschaftlichen Vereinigung am Goetheanum* of which he was the editor. Apart from Jules Sauerwein and, once again, Stein, he also attacked Dunlop. This seems to have been the first uninhibited attack of this kind to be made on Dunlop by a member of the Society who felt himself duty bound to the *Vorstand* Trio. For this reason and on account of the far-sighted plan it was to provoke in Dunlop's mind, we cannot here altogether pass over it in spite of its polemical character and the errors it presents in some points.[242]

In Chapter 5 (page 223), we reported on a meeting of bankers and financiers which took place in Berlin in the autumn of 1931 with Dunlop as one of those present. Boos, as leading representative of the Department of Social Sciences at the Goetheanum (Rudolf Steiner had not founded an official *Section* for this discipline), evidently felt himself to have been disregarded as he had not been informed about this initiative, still less invited to attend: 'On the same day as a certain earnest and worthy celebration was taking place in Dornach in commemoration of that day exactly seven years earlier (Michaelmas 1924) when Rudolf Steiner had for the last time addressed the members of the Anthroposophical Society, an international action was started up in Berlin under the protectorate of the English industrial magnate D.N. Dunlop . . . and the French journalist Jules Sauerwein.' Boos expresses his fears that this event might not be 'merely a passing whim but rather the inauguration of an action on a long-term basis'. He further attempts to place Dunlop's activities in connection with the World Power Conference in a false light by referring without giving any details to certain allegations made by the press, according to which on a certain occasion Dunlop had misused his position as director of the BEAMA. In addition Boos singles out a certain remark Dunlop had made at the centenary celebrations of H.P. Blavatsky's birthday. Dunlop had, in fact, accepted an invitation from the Theosophical Society of Point Loma to represent the Anthroposophical Society in Great Britain at a centenary meeting held in London in 1931. His address on that occasion was subsequently reported in an American theosophical magazine as having ended with the statement 'that there was good will in his heart for every shade of Theosophy'.

On the basis of these two events Boos now delivers the following 'purgatorial' judgement: 'Whoever in economic practice works with such methods and in spiritual matters does not strictly observe the distance which objectively exists between Rudolf Steiner and "every shade of Theosophy" [here we can almost hear an echo of a slogan much used in 1932: '*die richtige Methode*', 'the right method'], cannot be recognized as representative of an international action aimed at realizing Rudolf Steiner's social ideas and impulses.'

At the *end* of a letter he wrote to Stein on 4 June 1932, and almost in passing, Dunlop refers to the attack made on him by Roman Boos. His manner indicates both an ironic detachment on his part as well as a startlingly clear and far-sighted comprehension of the whole situation: 'I see Boos has honoured me with a notice in his latest bulletin along with Sauerwein and yourself. If this goes on, the Goetheanum will be dead in a few years. It is not a living force even now—only a centre for distributing forces of ill-health . . .'

Twelve days later Dunlop wrote a letter to Stein informing him of the counter-measures he had inwardly conceived in the face of these symptomatic developments. Boos and his attacks are not honoured with a single word; it is as though all that were already part of a far distant past; a quite different orientation, pointing to various new directions, was already rising in his consciousness, shining clear over the horizon of his all-embracing plans:

> Dear Dr Stein 16. VI.32
> I feel very strongly that an effort should be made during the next year or two to form an *International Association for the Advancement of Spiritual Science.*
> A preliminary prospectus should be prepared to circulate widely in all countries, and when the foundation is laid a Conference should be called. This should be guided & controlled by Anthroposophists who feel the call & need of humanity everywhere, and who feel how inadequate the General Anthroposophical Society (as it is now controlled from Dornach) has become.
> Will you think about it & see if you can get the impulse for a preliminary prospectus & we can speak of it when we meet in London. Greetings,
> Yours
> D.N. Dunlop

Unfortunately no reply to this letter remains extant, nor has any trace of a 'preliminary prospectus' been found. However, even if this initiative did not evolve beyond an early stage of germination, as indeed seems to have been the case, it nevertheless speaks out in a manner which reveals Dunlop's inner attitude to the growing conflicts within the *Vorstand* and the Society as a whole. Faced with the increasingly exclusive nature of particular trends and group interests Dunlop wished, by means of a generous, all-embracing gesture which would once more widen out the perspective, to create a kind of counter-effect and re-establish a certain equilibrium in the situation as a whole. The original *Vorstand* established by Rudolf Steiner himself had been an attempt to realize, on the basis of a common form of spirituality, a unity between contrasting spiritual elements; we could also say: between polar-opposites which, combined, held a tremendous potential.

This polarity, as it was reflected in an archetypal manner in the *Vorstand* with its carefully chosen representatives, was now threatening to become a *duality without a reconciling principle.* On the one side there was the *Vorstand* Trio (consisting of Albert Steffen,

Marie Steiner and Guenther Wachsmuth) and on the other Ita Wegman and Elizabeth Vreede who in recent years had found themselves more and more marginalized with respect to their own role within the *Vorstand*. The ensuing developments only sanctioned in legal terms a duality which in practice existed.

This duality within the *Vorstand* also went hand in hand with a growing tendency to centralize all anthroposophical activities—the centre being more and more Guenther Wachsmuth, Marie Steiner and Albert Steffen. One particularly negative 'milestone' on this path to centralization was the decision made by these three members of the *Vorstand* to issue an *Anthroposophic News Sheet* for English members in an attempt to supplant the already existing *Anthroposophical Movement*, published in London, which had been founded in 1924 at the request of the original *Vorstand* under Rudolf Steiner himself as the official anthroposophical organ for the English-speaking world as a whole. Now all of a sudden this new upstart publication was undertaken directly from Dornach in the hope 'that English speaking members will look upon it as their central organ and give it their support'. The decision was communicated to the British General Secretary in a letter dated 2 September 1933 and signed by Steffen, Marie Steiner and Wachsmuth. In addition to this, in a printed circular sent to English members—including the General Secretary—it was simply stated that 'English translations of Rudolf Steiner's lectures will in future be confined to this *Anthroposophic News Sheet*.' This meant that the old news-sheet *Anthroposophical Movement*, which had been in circulation for no less than ten years and had regularly published translations of Rudolf Steiner's lectures, was suddenly deprived of this possibility. In a letter dated 14 October 1933 Harry Collison, who held the rights over the English translations of Rudolf Steiner's writings, endorsed this veto in his own name. Dunlop wrote to both Collison and Marie Steiner hoping that the matter would be reconsidered and permission given at least to publish Rudolf Steiner's lectures in the quarterly *Anthroposophy*. However, he received only a formal answer from the former and no reply whatsoever from the latter. In the following month Dunlop decided to publish the correspondence concerning this matter 'for the information of Members of the Anthroposophical Society in Great Britain' in *Anthroposophical Movement* (see Appendix, page 386ff). By the end of the year *Anthroposophy*, the magnificent journal which was edited by Dunlop himself and also reached an appreciative circle of non-anthroposophical readers as well, ceased to appear on account of the atmosphere created by the Dornach veto.

*

In preparation for the General Meeting to be held 27–28 March 1934, a motion was proposed that Albert Steffen be authorized, on the basis of fundamental changes in the statutes of the Society,[243] 'to redistribute the offices within the Vorstand'. What this meant in fact was that an underlying trend which had already begun to affect the real state of affairs was finally consolidated: namely, the move towards excluding Ita Wegman and Elisabeth Vreede together with the individuals and groups close to them, from the general leadership and representation of the Society. Sole authority was further to be given to Albert Steffen to accept new members into the Society. In reaction to the centralizing, exclusive nature of this motion, a group of English, Dutch and German members and officials (including D.N. Dunlop and George Adams on the English side), drew up a 'Declaration of Will'.[243] Objectively, without assuming any kind of polemical attitude, and in a way that demonstrated a certain will, despite the difficulties, to co-operate, they sought in this Declaration to put forward various reasons to justify the existence of groups and initiatives inside the Society which had not necessarily proceeded from or been formed by the *Vorstand* Trio. The signatories declared their explicit intention to hold fast to the statutes Rudolf Steiner had given the Society and its *Vorstand* at Christmas 1923, so that 'decisive measures, proceeding from three members of the Vorstand alone, as has been the case recently, cannot be recognized by us as binding for the whole Anthroposophical Society . . . Consequently we are convinced that the Society can fulfil its task only if a differentiating element is opposed to the centralizing tendency which has now taken root in the management of affairs.' Those who composed and signed the document found this necessity to be expressed in the following guideline given by Rudolf Steiner: 'On a spiritual-scientific ground, one becomes united through the fact that one differentiates, individualizes, not that one centralizes.'[243] Looking back over the distance that history has placed between us and these events this 'Declaration of Will' may now strike us as one of the most clear, reasonable and co-operative initiatives that arose out of the confusion of that period. However, discussion of this document at the General Meeting once again gave way to the surging waves of emotional polemics.

On the second day of the meeting, the morning session ended in turmoil and Albert Steffen left the hall announcing his resignation, followed by Marie Steiner. A member subsequently proposed that Albert Steffen, Marie Steiner and Guenther Wachsmuth be entrusted with the task of reconstituting the Society. Accordingly, on 27 March 1934 Albert Steffen put a vote of confidence to the assembly: 'Is the Anthroposophical Society willing to allow these three persons to continue directing work in the spirit of the Christmas Conference and to consider the decisions they make as binding for the Society?' By an overwhelming majority of votes, the assembly answered in the affirmative the question from the President and also carried the motion.[241]

At the General Meeting George Adams represented that part of the English membership that stood behind the 'Declaration of Will'. Dunlop, whose will George Adams was one day to describe as 'absolute', did not honour this meeting with his presence. After the *Vorstand* had thus been officially amputated we will not be far from the truth in assuming that Dunlop's determination (or 'will') to ensure the continued existence of differentiation and individualization within the Society had indeed taken on an absolute character. Up until this moment he too would seem to have reckoned with the eventuality that Ita Wegman and Elizabeth Vreede, and with them a wide section of the membership, would be able to co-operate with the *Vorstand* Trio on a real working-basis. Perhaps the reason he had waited so long before putting his plans for an 'International Association' into action and transforming the function of the 'World Economic Association' was precisely in order not to place Ita Wegman, with whom he was closely associated, in an even more difficult position; there was still hope.

Now all such hopes had been completely dashed for the time being at any rate. And for Dunlop, all anthroposophical activity from now on would only be able to unfold in accordance with that remarkable phrase contained in the 'Declaration of Will': 'The Goetheanum is active spiritually wherever anthroposophical work is carried out.'[243] Following the majority decision in Dornach the main points of the 'Declaration of Will' were endorsed at an Extraordinary General Meeting of the Anthroposophical Society in Great Britain on 10 June by an overwhelming majority of the English membership. They expressed their 'resolve to carry on . . . work as an independent group of the Anthroposophical Society', and to do so in the spirit of the Christmas Conference, which is to say in the spirit of the *whole Vorstand* set up by Rudolf Steiner, and on the basis of 'the statutes given to the Society by Rudolf Steiner' on that occasion.[244]

As a result of Steffen's stipulation that he could not possibly sign any new membership cards requested by those officials who had put their names to the 'Declaration of Will',[245] it was decided in England, Holland and Germany to issue 'provisional' cards for new members; at the same time, the English membership under D.N. Dunlop's leadership which had given its support to the 'Declaration of Will', was integrated into the 'United Free Anthroposophical Groups'[246] originating in Stuttgart.

However, despite the unshakable determination with which these changes were accomplished, the chairman Dunlop emphasized in his closing speech that 'so far as he and the Executive Council were concerned, the door will remain open for re-union, that the three Members of the Vorstand who have withdrawn their support from this Society and any of the activities for which they are responsible will always be given a welcome to the Rudolf Steiner Hall and House if at any future time they are willing again to co-operate.'[244] Similarly, in a remarkable essay entitled 'The

Present Situation in our Society', George Adams also expresses himself in a manner that is both unequivocal and yet always open to reconciliation. Adams makes it clear that the United Free Anthroposophical Groups was not a newly founded Society, 'for we belong to the Foundation given to us by Rudolf Steiner. We would hold all doors open for renewed co-operation with our friends on the other side. While they maintain their present temper and we our viewpoint, *as things are* now there may seem little hope of this. Yet time is a real factor, the more real, where people are sincere in their conflicts . . .'[247]

For Adams, this highly critical phase of the evolution of the Anthroposophical Society, seen as a whole, was nothing more than a 'Stirb und Werde Process' ('Die and become again'), a death-process with an inherent potential for new life. Of course to begin with it was the death-element, the carrier of conflict and strife, which dominated the stage; indeed, even in England this was the case where, under Collison's leadership, the 'United Groups Branch' was created in the wake of the *Vorstand* Trio.

A few weeks after the General Meeting in Dornach D.N. Dunlop decided to republish a communication Harry Collison had made to English members some ten years before. It appeared in *Anthroposophical Movement*, in an issue dated 31 May 1934, under the heading 'What Mr Collison Said in 1924':

> The following communication was sent to members of the Anthroposophical Society in Great Britain by Mr Collison after Dr Steiner's last visit to this country in 1924. Members will no doubt find it of historical interest in view of what is taking place in Mr Collison's Group today.
> D.N.D.
>
> 46 Gloucester Place,
> London, W.1.
>
> *13th Sept.*, 1924.
>
> Now that our President has left this country, we are, I am sure, wondering how we can best put into effect his message and carry on

the work he has given us to do, so I am writing to ask your hearty co-operation with Headquarters.

Dr Steiner is very pleased with the devoted work and the signal success of Mrs Merry and Mr Dunlop at the Summer Schools; but much greater success would be secured in this country generally if their efforts and the efforts of his representatives in England were supported with more unanimity and enthusiasm; he is disappointed that the Society has not made greater progress in the outer world. He says that if he is to visit us again his meetings must be better attended. He is astonished that there should be any doubt among members as to the necessity for Headquarters in England, and warned us that there were two courses open, either to strengthen and develop the Headquarters here so as to enlarge its scope and authority in the outer world, or for the Society to be left to the literature from Dornach, in which case it would return to the narrow limits of similar movements in the Middle Ages. This latter event seemed almost inconceivable, as the Anthroposophical Society had come to stay.

Conscious of my failure to keep the Society together on these lines, and knowing that Headquarters in England is not actively and sympathetically supported by all English members, I resigned my office; but at Dr Steiner's request have consented to continue a little longer. It is now for the members to decide; and I hope you will all meet me on St. Michael's Day, 29th September, at Headquarters, at 8 p.m., and hear a special lecture of Dr Steiner's and listen to short addresses any members may like to give. May the day chosen be a day of re-union in a great cause!

H. Collison,
Sec. Genl., Brit. Anthropl. Society.'

This seems to have been Dunlop's only official comment on the centralizing decisions taken at the Dornach Meeting of 1934. Though indirect and entirely impersonal, it certainly speaks a clear enough language!

*

'The Goetheanum is active spiritually wherever anthroposophical work is carried out': just as in earlier years so too during the summer of 1934 Dunlop attempted to cultivate such kind of anthroposophical work in a particularly concentrated form—in another summer school. This summer school, the last that Dunlop was to organize, was announced under the title 'The Work and Teachings of Rudolf Steiner' and took place in Westonbirt in Gloucestershire from 21 to 31 August. Dunlop, as usual, presided over it. The opening lecture was on 'Rudolf Steiner and Anthroposophy' and was given by Elizabeth Vreede who, shortly before this conference, had been formally forbidden to lecture[248] at the Goetheanum by the legitimized *Vorstand* Trio in Dornach. Apart from her, we also encounter Zeylmans and Kolisko whom we met earlier as 'young doctors'; the educationalist Caroline von Heydebrand and the curative educationalist Karl Schubert were also present. Fried Geuter (the *enfant terrible*) and Dr Mirbt the agriculturist—both linked to Dunlop by destiny, as has been seen—also held courses during the summer school whilst Ita Wegman was prevented by illness from taking part.

A vast mansion at Westonbirt (normally a girl's school), just opposite the great arboretum containing the finest collection of trees in England, was the site chosen for this summer school which was attended by about 250 members and visitors. Here again the surroundings offered plenty of possibilities for excursions. (One afternoon was devoted to visiting nearby Bath and the Cheddar caves or, for those who preferred, Cirencester and Fairford. Others again made their way to Malmesbury to visit the old Abbey under which the Saxon King Athelstan is said to be buried.)

A brief glance through the very full programme of the school shows that, for early-risers, the day started at 7.15 with projective geometry classes directed by George Adams. The various events stretched over the whole day with a final lecture or music in the evening. The lectures dealt with a variety of subjects including the contribution Anthroposophy had to make to the sciences of medicine and chemistry (Dr Hauschka). There was also a lecture on evolution from a geological point of view—as well as W.J. Stein's group on economics. Great emphasis was put on education, and the arts were well represented both in terms of lectures and practical activities.

Three impressions of this summer school and some of its protagonists may provide us with a glimpse of its character: firstly, Elizabeth Vreede (who took an astronomy class throughout the school), leading her students out on to the lawn after dark to observe the stars and the moon; then George Adams, in one of his main lectures, giving a general introduction to the anthroposophical world-conception which 'was particularly helpful in supplying the School's more specialized studies with a far-reaching background'; finally, 'behind all these varied occupations was the figure of Mr Dunlop, presiding at the main lectures and unobtrusively helping to fit the wide range of the School's studies into a harmonious pattern'.[249]

Indeed, all the efforts of the organizers and participants seem to have been pooled in an attempt, above the clashes of disharmony, to create a sound basis and calm atmosphere for serious, spiritual work. This is also the impression one has looking at the photograph (see plate 26). (Dunlop is seated between Karl Schubert and Elizabeth Vreede.) It certainly seems as though here, in a totally relaxed manner, the Goetheanum was 'active spiritually'—despite the decisions which had been taken at Dornach and without any ratification from that quarter.

In the introduction to this book we have already indicated how this summer school at Westonbirt was also of great importance in quite another respect, for, indirectly, it provided one of the first seeds of this biography.

The invaluable source of information in question came into existence in the following way. During the school the main lecture of the day was given every morning at half past ten. On 27 August, Stein had to speak on a truly comprehensive subject—'The Universe as the Foundation of Economics'. Possibly the choice of this subject had been the result of exchanges with Dunlop, especially as Stein was at that time engaged in working out the preliminary indications Dunlop had given him for a study of 'The Earth as a Basis of Economy' (see Chapter 5, page 234). In any event Stein's lecture was clearly and closely linked to his new field of research in the framework of the World Power Conference. It was on the same day as this lecture, possibly during the midday interval, that the 'interview' mentioned in the introduction took place between Dunlop and Stein. In view of the fact that it brought more biographical facts and references to light than any other source to date, we must consider this moment when Stein chose to pose his questions, even if it appeared to be of no particular significance at the time, as one of the most invaluable and fortunate moments that destiny has ever offered the Anthroposophical Movement.

*

'As crisis after crisis followed one another in the Society, his body was tortured,' E.C. Merry writes in her reminiscences on D.N. Dunlop. 'At first the attacks of the demons still pierced into his soul. But in the last year of his life, both soul and spirit had grown so strong and pure that he seemed to show little or no sign of wounds and injuries in the soul. But the attacks had really been striking into the physical body *directly*. He did not *feel them* in the same way in the astral body. It was more deadly.'

Dunlop's work for the World Power Conference and his other business concerns had also undergone changes as a result of his increasing periods of illness. E.C. Merry makes the following illuminating observation in this regard: 'Since his death I have learned how more and more he conducted all his enormous business . . . by delegation. He became the centre of a great Group Soul that carried out his will.' Indeed, in the last years of his life an ever greater widening of his horizons over and above the apparently narrow sphere of his business affairs seems to have taken place: 'The outstanding impression I had of him during the last two years was the astonishing grasp he had of all world-questions . . . and the most amazing capacity to be continually filled with fresh ideas, renewed will—most far-reaching visions of the future. And at the same time the most delicate handling of every tiny detail. He forgot nothing. He seemed to have mastered the whole world in his thought. And his most tender love for all beings grew more beautiful every day.' (MD)

During this same period Dunlop's position in the British Society became stronger and stronger and, untouched by the difficulties and crises in his innermost being, he was still able to pass on some of the fruits of his ego-awakening art of life. This is witnessed in a particularly beautiful way by a conversation in a park in Torquay between D.N.D. and E.C.M. (as friends called the two of them whenever they were mentioned together). It was in early 1934 and about half-way between that fateful majority vote in Dornach and the summer school in Westonbirt. Dunlop, as Mrs Merry describes, was just recovering from another attack of illness.

Torquay—what memories, what positively beneficial and comforting memories this place must have awakened for the two of them, so many pictures of the past, of the experiences they had once shared here with Rudolf Steiner and other friends! And as these images unfolded in the course of their conversations they must have had an illuminating effect, bringing relief and warmth to heart and soul. So much of the past, present and future had here flowed together, not only in Rudolf Steiner's lectures but also in the many personal encounters. And after the summer school, in a report that was printed in the *Nachrichtenblatt*[250] in Dornach, Rudolf Steiner had characterized D.N.D. and E.C.M. in the same breath: 'Mr Dunlop, the anthroposophist of clear and delicate perception, and with far-seeing purposes; Mrs Merry, untiringly active, lovingly devoted to the Movement . . .' If Rudolf Steiner put down in writing such characterizations as these in order to bring them before the eyes of his readers it was not primarily with the intention of informing them of his own particular sympathies regarding this or that person or in order to reveal a special relationship someone might have to him (though there is no reason why this aspect should not *also* be considered). What seems to be of far greater importance is that, by actually publishing brief or sometimes even more extensive portraits of certain persons, he created a basis for the development of a new social faculty—one which, in a new age of anti-social expression of the personality, has become a dire necessity. It is the faculty of being able to consider other human beings in the light of *their* most productive faculties and qualities, especially if they are seen to emerge from a different spiritual background—perhaps even from a different nationality and language as well. Indeed, one may seriously ask oneself: what Rudolf Steiner had perceived 10, 15, 20 years earlier as the essential qualities of various individualities (subsequently bringing them to characteristic expression in a considerable number of these little pen-pictures), did all this suddenly become irrelevant and invalid a few years later, as the subsequent history of the Society seems more and more to suggest? And is it not possible to sense a gentle warning linked to each one of these sketches: 'take care, in the midst of the worst crises and personality struggles that may arise within the Society, never to forget for a single moment that this or that person can always be viewed and experienced in the light in which I once described them in these miniature portraits'?

But let us return to that park in Torquay. 'It was perfect weather, cloudless sky and dazzling blue sea!' writes Mrs Merry.

> We were in the garden together where every leaf and flower seemed in a sort of ecstasy of beauty; a rose-breasted bullfinch was hopping about at our feet. D.N.D. said something like this: 'What can one do with all this wonder and beauty of Nature—how make it live on in one's soul? Isn't it strong with the power to bestow peace? Or does one just look at it and forget it? . . . Do you think that next time you are weary and discontented and disillusioned with life you will be able to remember just this picture and that it will have the power to bring back all its ecstasy and loveliness? Or do you think it will make no difference?'

*

On 17 March 1935, the agenda of the forthcoming General Meeting was published in the *Nachrichtenblatt*. It contained 'proposals for the exclusion of two members (Frau Dr Ita Wegman and Fräulein Dr Vreede) from the *Vorstand* of the General Anthroposophical Society, for the expulsion from the Society of six other members (D.N. Dunlop, George Kaufmann, Willem Zeylmans van Emmichoven, Pieter de Haan, Jürgen von Grone, Eugen Kolisko), and for the severance from the General

Anthroposophical Society of a number of important Groups, among them the Anthroposophical Society in Great Britain.' In answer to the publication of these proposals the British Society sent an open letter[251] to all members and 'especially to those Members attending the General Meeting at Dornach on 14th April, 1935'.

In this open letter the following observations are made with regard to the Dornach proposals:

> The peculiar wording of these resolutions, which speak of 'actions bearing the character of self-exclusion'[252] from the Vorstand, or of persons 'having ceased' to be members of the Society, cannot conceal the fact that the members concerned are to be expelled against their own will and judgment, from the Vorstand and from the Society respectively. The motions are followed by an explanatory paragraph purporting to outline the reasons for these extreme measures, and making grave and sweeping accusations against those concerned, as of deliberate untruthfulness, or of pursuing for years past, from the responsible positions they occupied in the Society, 'private aims and ambitions of power by every means at their disposal'. Further, a Memorandum bearing on the events of the last ten years in the Society and obtainable through the Secretariat of the Society at the Goetheanum, is announced . . . The truth will only begin to emerge when the two sides of the story are available . . .

Just how one-sided was the so-called *Memorandum*[253] (which was supposed to serve as a basis for making a judgement and for voting on the above-mentioned proposals) is clear not only from the multiple obliquities and distortions contained in it but also from its thoroughly personal and polemical tone.

The total of 12 signatories, including, of course, Dunlop and George Adams, declare at the end of the letter 'that the motions, if passed by the General Meeting, will receive no recognition from us. We shall continue with our tasks for Anthroposophy inspired by Rudolf Steiner's life-work, on the basis of the spiritual freedom embodied in the Foundation Statutes, and we shall continue to regard the Goetheanum as "there for *all* members". In the absence of justice in any procedure, there can be no respect for merely legal clauses. We regard as *invalid* any decision which would make the Foundation Meeting ineffective.'

On 14 April 1935, the motions were carried by 1,691 votes for; 76 against; 53 abstentions. In the whole history of the Anthroposophical Movement this amounted to the most devastating 'amputation' that any part of the Anthroposophical Society believed necessary to inflict upon itself. And even the courageous speech of Count Polzer-Hoditz did not prevent it from taking place.[254]

On to New Fields of Action

Right up to the very last moment and despite all difficulties, Dunlop adopted a stance which, in a truly spiritual yet nonetheless realistic way, always attributed to his fellow men (even those who were opposed to him) the possibility of changing for the better and evolving freely according to creative goals. This attitude perhaps finds its clearest expression in the following words from a letter to E.C. Merry: 'Trust all till you find them guilty. Otherwise you create disadvantageous conditions in the other person.'

The majority decision that had been taken at Dornach now meant that a large number of members had created disadvantageous conditions for *themselves*. Instead of seeking differentiation and integration, to use two mathematical expressions, too many had come to believe that a higher form of productivity was to be found in acts of centralization and exclusion.

Now in order to understand Dunlop's position with regard to the culmination of this ten-year-old crisis within the *Vorstand* and the Society, we need only recall what he had expressed more than 20 years previously in the Theosophical Society in the face of quite similar difficulties and quite similar attempts to find a 'solution'. Down to the last detail his earlier words also apply uncannily well to the situation in spring 1935, the only difference being that the overwhelming majority of anthroposophists who decided to exclude others did not carry out the deed in the name of 'The Masters of Love and Compassion' but in the name of the individuality of Rudolf Steiner. What is more, these words, which were penned as an editorial in Dunlop's journal, are also of significance for the future, for they depict the conditions that a spiritual community will need to observe if it wishes to survive the *end of this century*. In face of the threatened exclusion of the German Section from the Theosophical Society—a threat which subsequently became reality—Dunlop had in 1910 published the following words:

> We recognize the individual freedom of mankind as a great treasure, and as a society, we strive to give that individual freedom expression . . .
>
> No doubt there will arise in the ranks of the society, strong individuals who will draw many after them and their ideas, but the society as a whole will never pledge itself to any teaching or any specific religion . . .
>
> If any council or group of members at any time arrogate to themselves to expel from the society any human being who is a member, in that very decree they will have banished themselves, and although they may retain the name, the life and power of the Masters of Love and Compassion will go with those they cast out, and will not remain with those who scorn and turn from their midst the less developed or less righteous man.
>
> Only those in the coming century who are strong in sympathy and tolerance for a growing mankind, and believe in the freedom we have attained by a long struggle, and who are determined not to give up that freedom which allows each man to think honestly for himself—only these will ultimately stand the shocks brought to bear upon the Society by the opposers of human development, both within and without our ranks, only these will form the Society at the close of the twentieth century, and they indeed will have formed a nucleus of the universal brotherhood of mankind, without any distinctions whatever, of race, creed, sex, caste, or colour.[71]

*

At an Extraordinary General Meeting in London Dunlop proceeded to inform the members of the Anthroposophical Society in Great Britain of the outcome of the Dornach meeting. According to an eye-witness[255] he demonstrated no bitterness or hostility; in all frankness he asked those gathered there, given the present situation, to declare in writing in the course of the next few days which of the two societies they wished to be associated with from then onwards—the exclusive or the excluded one.

All this time E.C. Merry had been a very intimate witness not only to the many external events but also to the far-reaching inner experiences occurring in Dunlop's life. She shared all these in a way that made itself felt right down into her physical state of health. 'It was curious that there was hardly any time when either D.N.D or I were both well,' she writes with reference to the crisis-period in the Society during the early thirties right up to the final expulsion. 'If he was ill then I was all right. If he was well, then I was ill.' (MD)

And now Dunlop's last attack of illness was approaching. As though sensing it in advance he visited E.C. Merry—his call clearly bearing the stamp and signature of a farewell visit:

> The last day he visited me was a Sunday afternoon, a few days before he became ill. Quite unlike his usual ways, he wandered round the room, looking at my books, looking long at the view of London which is so wonderful from this height where I live . . . It was as though he were full of thoughts of it all. Then, when we sat down to talk, neither of us had anything to say. I was shocked—I said to myself: *'We have said all that there is to say . . . we have nothing more.'*

During this same week Dunlop still travelled to the British Industries Fair in Birmingham in seemingly normal health. But on his return to London he fell seriously ill. And on the following Sunday a second, and final departure between him and E.C. Merry took place—it was a spiritual leave-taking.

> Three days after his last illness began . . . he came to me spiritually, and spoke to me from his real Self . . . And he said, with immense weight and meaning in the words: *'Do you quite understand?'* My own Ego replied: 'Yes, I understand everything.' It was as though he felt joy at this, and great relief. I knew then that he meant me to understand that he was going into the Spiritual World, and that it was my task to let him go . . . He sent me no physical message of any kind.

Acute appendicitis had necessitated Dunlop's being transferred into hospital in the last days of May where he had to undergo an operation immediately. In the course of these days Ita Wegman arrived in London and, accompanied by her friend the doctor Hilma Walter, they went together to the hospital. But there they were refused permission to intervene in any way in the course of the treatment.

In those same days AE wrote to Dunlop's friend and business colleague Charles Weekes: 'Dear Charlie, I am sorry indeed to hear about Dan. I hope it may not be as you suggest. But anyhow he, myself and our contemporaries have done our work . . .' The sense of premonition which this letter shows was to prove all too true. For it happened that in addition to the peritonitis from which he was already suffering Dunlop also developed pneumonia. This finally brought about his death on 30 May 1935 at eight o'clock in the evening. He was all alone, no one by him. It was Ascension Day.

*

'Since he died, the elements have been wild and restless,' E.C. Merry noted in her reminiscences. 'They have been *awakened*, as Frau Stein said.' The next day W.J. Stein wrote to the engineer F. Zur Nedden:

> At the crematorium there were so many flowers that it was impossible to bring them all into the chapel. More than half of them lay outside in front of the door . . . Individual friends and corporations alike had sent them. All ages were amongst the mourners and all classes. Two memorial addresses were given by two friends. Dr Zeylmans van Emmichoven, a Dutchman, spoke for friends on the Continent and Mr Wheeler, an Englishman, for the English ones.
>
> Nearly all his employees were there and countless friends. Many of them had come from the Continent. In these speeches again this point was touched on—the fact that he made people feel so free . . .

The whole of nature as an elemental being seems to have responded to the impulse of freedom living in Dunlop's soul. In

Rudolf Steiner's terms we could say that the ethereal body was beginning to be woven into[256] its environment, i.e. into the world of those elemental powers that were now unleashed. Since Dunlop's death there had been 'storms and very high winds, great clouds, and brilliant periods of sunshine'. E.C. Merry remarks, 'I never remember such weather in the month of June.' At the same time there was an earthquake in Pakistan which claimed several thousands of lives. On 31 May it almost entirely destroyed the city of Quetta.

'The Individuality Reigned Here'

Thus 'the wheel has come full circle' and we have returned, albeit from the other side, to the starting-point of this biography—that question posed by a passer-by at Dunlop's funeral who 'paused to ask who had died and what manner of man he was'.

Even if, as we hope will be the case, a real answer to some aspects of this question has been provided, other points doubtless still remain to be clarified. To some readers for instance a new enigma may have presented itself in connection with Dunlop's death: what relationship does it have to the Dornach expulsion measures? In what follows a few points of view are presented which may help to answer this question, or at least to throw a little light on the matter.

A few days after the cremation, Ita Wegman gave a short memorial address for anthroposophical friends in London.[257] All that remains of this speech is the original draft (indicated hereafter as WD), written in English, which Ita Wegman might not necessarily have read out word for word on that occasion. So the following quotations need not be her *exact* words as they were spoken. However, some of the facts and viewpoints that figure in this speech are of such significance with regard to the above-mentioned enigma that quotation of the draft (with Wegman's imperfect English idiom and spellings simply left as they are, and translation of her German words supplied in brackets) seems to be fully merited:

> My dear friends,
>
> It is a long time, since I saw you here in London, I am glad to see you again, but at the same moment very sad that it must be in this time, in which we have lost our dear friend Mr Dunlop. Staying here and not seeing him sitting there on that chair in the corner is for me and I think also for you a great grief. It is not to believe that he has gone away. And still it is so, we have to face it.
>
> The question raises in our mind why it has to be so. Inexorably karma has worked. For a few days he was still healthy, then suddenly an illness came, but so strange in its symptoms, doctors were not able to help him. Although longing to help him, there was hindrance on hindrance as if right help might not be. The spiritual world has so to say led his hands on him, it was her affair, and so it came that our beloved friend passed away though the gate of death, quite alone. He was separated from those who loved him, but it has to be so; this was the language of the spiritual world. (WD)

The impression one is given here is that the doctors found it very difficult to make an exact diagnosis of the illness and that *this* was the reason they were unable to help.

Then Ita Wegman, who had twice visited Dunlop in hospital during the last days of his illness, goes on to recount a significant experience which the latter had communicated to her before his death. She relates it to an inner experience that she herself had had—similar to it and yet entirely different. Such phenomena can throw light on a deep inner kinship existing between two souls. Dunlop had told Ita Wegman how 'he saw R. Steiner at his side before his operation took place' . . . and this reminded Ita Wegman of her own experience:

> I stood myself for not so long time before the gate of death in my serious illness[258] and I also met R. Steiner, who had sent me back to earth life, and here R. Steiner took him with him. A Wiederbegegnung [reunion] has taken place which afterwards was followed by a Zusammensein [being together]. R. Steiner is gathering all those who have finished their task, and judged after our earthly mind it can make the impression, that he has not finished what he has begun, but this is a maya, our higher being will never consent to leave earth if in a higher understanding everything has been finished.

At last of all our higher being is the one who stands above life and death and has to bestimmen [decide] about life and death. Under our consciousness we feel if we have to pass away or to stay and out of this consciousness we can feel or say remarkable things . . . In the morning of the day of his death I visited him; it was my second visit, the first was on the day before in which I found him well looking with a good puls and I was full of hope. But he himself spoke the words to Nunhofer 'it is not so easy, I can't get through'. At the next morning the whole situation was changed. His puls was worse and he spoke once again with much more significance 'I can't get through. I don't understand what the surgeon has done'. I remember exactly my own feelings which I have had in such a moment as I myself was serious ill, the patient knows quite well if the doings and thinking of a doctor is in contradiction of his situation. In my own case I knew that the consulting doctor who has had not much hope in his opinion about my illness was in mistake. In my soul life I had the opposite meaning. I knew I would be recovered after a time and nobody can take away this inner knowledge.

And here I heard Mr Dunlop speaking the words 'I can't get through'. It was also an inner knowledge and he had the feeling of a contradictory doing of the doctor not fit to his situation. We have had both out of our underconsciousness the feeling of passing away or passing to life on earth again . . .

O my dear friends in such moments there is a very great abyss between scientific people and patients, who are already half in the spiritual world. And the greatest abyss is between ordinary nurses, who are not believing in a spiritual world and patients who are passing the gate of death. There is no understanding and not a little bit of help. It must be also one of the tasks of the anthrop. doctor to change such abnormal situations. It will not come so soon, but it will come I am sure.

And so it was his Karma that he, who possessed so many friends was in front of the spiritual world alone; here every earthly feeling was to be stopped. *The individuality rained [reigned] here.*

*

In the light of Ita Wegman's account up to this point let us try to consider the enigma in question. The symptoms of Dunlop's illness appear to be of such a strange nature that the doctors are unable to help him. Now this whole situation only begins to make sense when we apply the idea of karma really seriously not only in its past aspect but also as a future reality. This means looking on the external development of Dunlop's illness and the process of chaos and confusion within the Society *not as the actual cause, but rather as elements providing the 'grounds'* for his death.

Dunlop had spent his whole life fighting to realize goals of a truly all-embracing nature. He had long since arrived at an inner understanding of the obvious fact that any truly spiritual movement had to possess a world-wide and universally human character. Up to the last moment, as General Secretary of the British Society, he had hoped that the General Anthroposophical Society would retain this essential quality or that new possibilities would present themselves to re-establish it in new ways (perhaps via the provisional 'life-raft' of the 'World Economic Association' in conjunction with the 'International Association for the Advancement of Spiritual Science'). However, if Dunlop's hopes to salvage something from the General Anthroposophical Society had been dashed by the exclusive tendencies emanating from Dornach, the other option—of 'moving out' and starting afresh—could not be realized because apparently the right moment had not yet come nor, perhaps, were the right people yet there for it. Besides, how could anyone in 1935 have carried a truly international impulse into the Anthroposophical Movement when the overwhelming majority of Society members at that time clearly believed that salvation could only be found in exclusive and separatist measures? The amputation that the Society had practised on itself had found such a wide echo in predominantly continental anthroposophical circles that it had now become totally unrealistic even to think of reconstructing a new 'general' Society under such conditions. Thus, early in 1935, Dunlop was faced with three impossible prospects. On the one hand the original vessel which Rudolf Steiner had created for the *Vorstand* and the Society had been shattered; on the other hand nothing new could yet take root as the ground had not been sufficiently prepared; so for the time being, there remained only the third impossibility—that of directing a split-off movement, for this is what the Anthroposophical Society in Great Britain (apart from a minority of Dornach diehards grouping themselves around Harry Collison) had *de facto* become. What is more, Dunlop would have had to direct this movement in constant opposition to the so called 'real' Society. None of this could ever have been compatible with the aims of an individuality whose spiritual goals were as all-embracing as the 12 signs of the zodiac.

Given these circumstances, therefore, a moment had arrived in the course of this individuality's destiny where any further activity on the physical level must have appeared to him as 'spiritually uneconomical'. Were there not *other* possibilities for realizing truly universal anthroposophical impulses in another incarnation in the near future—in the spirit of the Michael Prophecy? So this individuality, counselled by the spiritual being of Rudolf Steiner to act straight out of the future, *brought about the death of that person we have come to know by the name of D.N. Dunlop*. Such, it would appear, is indeed the nature and 'reign' of the 'individuality' evoked by Ita Wegman—one which transcended all the interests and aspirations of the personality.

*

Immediately upon Dunlop's death, something of the individuality that had 'reigned' here came to expression in the features of his countenance. Several people bore witness to a surprising metamorphosis of this countenance after death. Many friends had the impression that they were perceiving something entirely different and new, and yet it was something familiar which they had sensed before, but was hitherto concealed and only active in the background of his being. Now it had suddenly unveiled itself, fashioning the facial features of the deceased man so that they depicted clearly the real 'contours' of his being. Amongst those who were impressed by this amazing phenomenon was also Wegman.

In her memorial address she describes how

> . . . the most remarkable metamorphosis took place in the face of Mr Dunlop after his passing away. This face took the traces of his individual Being, it show the imprint of the spirit so as it was true without the influence of nationality and education or the mark of daily struggle life. This face was like an Offenbarung [revelation]. And I must tell you that it was as if it sounded from out his head the sound TAO, and a picture came as if this face belonged to a man who has listened to the Offenbarungen [revelations] of the great spirit. A man standing in listening with effort the rushing of wind, making the impression to be one with all what is behind nature.[259] And then I remembered the words of Dr Steiner who said to me after a talk about Mr Dunlop that he is the right man to lead the Anthroposophical Society in Great Britain and that he has to teach about cosmic things, he has old western knowledge. And these words of Dr Steiner became forming that picture, my dear friends, if you stood before that transformed face, now open as a great mystery, nobody can say that he has known Dunlop as he was really; it was always only one side of his being he shows; the other sides were hidden . . . (WD)

*

With respect to our biography, Wegman's memorial address leaves us with two important tasks: the first is directed towards the past, the second towards the future. In the short final part of this book we shall attempt to elucidate these two aspects in relation to everything that has been developed in the preceding chapters. As regards the first task, whilst as it were 'reaping the harvest' of everything we have considered up to this point, we shall attempt to throw some light on a few of those 'hidden sides' of Dunlop's past. As for the other, we shall attempt to sketch out, in broad outlines, a picture of what might possibly be the *future* aspirations of this individuality. This will be undertaken primarily against the background of his deep connection with Rudolf Steiner and numerous other anthroposophical souls and friends—that is to say, against the background of what has been frequently touched upon as the 'Michael Prophecy'.

*

However, we must first draw the reader's attention to another series of driving forces and occurrences connected with the life and works of those men whom destiny had woven into a closely-knit circle around D.N. Dunlop during his Dublin years—W.B. Yeats, George William Russell and Charles Weekes. The two first-named in particular might appear to be very far-removed from Dunlop's later life and sphere of influence, although Weekes on the other hand acted as a kind of 'go-between' right up to the moment of Dunlop's death. That this appearance, however, is only superficial is clearly shown by certain events concerning the first two persons which took place during the last two years of Dunlop's life and immediately after his death.

AE, Yeats, Charles Weekes—A Circle of Destiny Closes

'. . . And for myself I would depart without repining, even with some gaiety,' continued AE with reference to 'Dan' in that letter to Charles Weekes from May 1935.

Let us recall how George William Russell, who was becoming more and more famous in the literary world under the pseudonym AE, had lost his wife in 1932, the same year as Dunlop lost his life's companion Eleanor.

In the meantime AE had not only become increasingly renowned as a theosophically inspired author and poet, he had also come to play a leading role, initially in Ireland, in the reorientation and reorganization of agricultural practices. Once again we may note a curious parallel to one of the fundamental impulses that had determined the life and work of the friend of his youth 'Dan'.

This activity of AE's as an altogether original and ingenious organizer was in a field that was apparently quite foreign to the literary sphere: commissioned by Horace Plunkett, the vice-president of the Irish Agricultural Department, he contributed decisively to the construction throughout the whole of Ireland of a network of Raiffaisen Banks with a view to providing economic support for small co-operatives of farmers all over the country. In 1905 he became editor of the *Irish Homestead*, a co-operative and agricultural magazine 'which attained world fame as a farming journal with a literary flair'.[260] In 1912 AE published a small book with the title *Co-operation and Nationality—A Guide for Rural Reformers from this to the next Generation.*

This aspect of AE's work and writing clearly illustrates how, for him too, the intensive study of theosophical ideas and ideals was a constant inspiration for activity on a practical level so that these ideals could be realized in the economic and social field. And indeed, 'co-operation as AE expounded it, grew into a cause associated with the redemption of mankind in a new social order',[261] as one commentator observed. For all AE's efforts were undertaken in the spirit of the statutes of the Theosophical Society: 'To form the nucleus of a Universal Brotherhood of Humanity, without distinction of race, creed, sex, caste or colour.' Like 'Dan', the friend of his youth, it was equally true of AE that 'mystic though he remained he could impress the hard-headed businessmen among whom he moved in his later years,' as George Adams[118] once put it, in an attempt to characterize D.N. Dunlop's extraordinary evolution. In these later years, after numerous lecture-tours in America, AE was even elected Honorary Advisor to the American Department of Agriculture.

In 1933, one year after the death of his wife, Russell planned to move to London for good. Charles Weekes offered to find him an appartment in Chelsea. If a suitable appartment had been found he would have come into the immediate vicinity of what was to be 'Dan's' last residence. 'The Chelsea district sounds attractive,' AE writes to Weekes on 8 July. A little further on in the same letter he remarks: 'I only know James Stephens well, of all my London friends, except you and Dan. All the others are acquaintances.'[262] This passage well illustrates how the inner bond to 'Dan' had remained deeply rooted in AE's being despite external distances and the long periods of time which might elapse between their meetings. Such a bond may appear in another light if, in connection with Rudolf Steiner's remark that Dunlop possessed 'old Western knowledge', we consider the following passage, from another letter. In writing to 'Willie', as W.B. Yeats was known in the Dublin circle of friends, AE, commenting on the 'Celtic traditional feeling', observed: 'A certain spirit of it I have but I am not Celt inside, not for many lives. *I remember vividly old America and Chaldea.*'[263] This letter is dated 3 April 1897. A few days before Russell had reported that 'the editor of our magazine', Dunlop, 'has just gone to America for a month'. We have shown that at an earlier stage AE had been deeply involved in Dunlop's inner experiences and later had himself been strongly drawn towards America at the very juncture when instead he found his destiny in Ireland. It seems indeed as though on this occasion too he wanted to accompany his friend, perhaps in order to clarify in his own consciousness the existence of certain ancient karmic roots which he may even have sensed on more than one occasion to be buried in far-distant times.

Now, in December 1934, AE did in fact undertake a journey to America for several months which was to be the last great voyage of his life—in order to lecture throughout the United States on 'rural policies'.

In March he was back in London, having had to break off his stay in America on account of illness. There is no evidence of his presence at Dunlop's cremation on 3 June, but Weekes will certainly have informed him of the most important details concerning the last days of his long-standing friend.

At the beginning of July, Russell had to undergo an abdominal operation in a clinic in Bournemouth. Suddenly old friends of his reappeared on all sides. Yeats, who had not written for a few years, sent him a very warm and cordial letter (AE had remained in touch with him all his life and, amongst other things, had even joined the 'Irish National Theatre Society' which Yeats himself had founded). Surrounded by numerous friends, Charles Weekes also amongst them, AE died on 17 July 1935 in Bournemouth. On the following day *The Times* published an obituary which ends with this statement: 'It was the unremitting energy of his transcendental faith which above all distinguished him, and that his faith was illusory, or that a soul so illuminated by intuitive wisdom should be finally extinguished, is not to be thought of.'

*

Let us take a last look at the relationship between AE and Yeats. In spite of the fact that there often was considerable tension between the two of them, the roots of their extraordinary friendship seem to go just as deep as those linking AE to 'Dan'. Furthermore, this relationship, and the reflection it found in cultural circles both then and since, appears extremely illuminating in itself as well as symptomatic of certain general cultural tendencies. Undoubtedly Yeats was from a technical angle more artistically talented and aesthetically refined as a poet than AE. It was no accident that in 1923, whilst Dunlop was preparing the Summer School in Penmaenmawr, Yeats rather than AE was put forward for the Nobel Prize and subsequently awarded it. However, it was AE, a man devoid of any literary ambition, who was the real poet *seer*. Everything he wrote or painted flowed directly from the wellsprings of his own real spiritual experience. For this reason his writings could be of the greatest interest to those who cherish and nurture a science of the spirit.

Let us call to mind for a moment the large proportion of educated people to whom Yeats is a well-known name and compare this to what must be the similarly large proportion of cultured individuals who have never even heard of AE! Such a comparison allows us to make a striking assessment of the prevailing criteria of our century in regard to artistic or literary achievement. Naturally this may change in the future, and perhaps a time will come when, precisely on account of his spiritual realism, AE's name will become an enduring concept within the consciousness of mankind while many of our present-day celebrities fade into the background against the horizons and interests of future generations.

Shortly after Russell's death, in a letter to a friend, Yeats summarized in clear and bold terms the whole relationship that had existed between AE and himself:

> AE was my oldest friend—we began our work together. I constantly quarrelled with him but he never bore malice and in his last letter, a

> month before his death, he said that generally when he differed from me it was that he feared to be absorbed by my personality. He had no passions, but as a young man had to struggle against his senses. He gave up writing poetry for a time because it stirred his senses. He wanted always to be free . . . My wife said the other night: 'AE was the nearest to a saint you or I will ever meet. You are a better poet but no saint. I suppose one has to choose' . . .[264]

One aspect of this 'saintliness' is testified in a refreshing and open-hearted manner in a letter to Charles Weekes. The latter seemed to be afraid that AE, as agricultural organizer and editor of an agricultural weekly, was in the process of neglecting or even squandering his great literary talent. Weekes feared the 'real' AE might be lost to the world. Even in his opening words and in the way he addresses his friend, AE just sweeps these fears away as though they were nothing more than a swarm of gnats:

> My dear boy, a man's success or failure is always with his own soul. You would like to see me well known, writing wise and beautiful books, hailed by the applause of the best critics. I might be all this and a failure in my own eyes, and wretched and unhappy. I am working for causes I feel to be good. I don't care in the least for recognition. In fact I loathe my personal publicity. I can't say that I have lived up to my highest possibilities. Nobody does, but I have not sunk to my worst, and many people do. I will go back to the stars without any flourish of trumpets, but I won't weep as I go back or whine about circumstance. Don't expect anything from me. I am not going anywhere I can be seen.[265]

This letter dates from 1913, the same year in which AE published his *Collected Poems* dedicated 'to D.N.D.—in memory of the household'. And in fact, as far as the essential core of AE's answer is concerned, it could just as well have flowed from D.N. Dunlop's hand—except that *he* would not have given it this tone of somewhat 'rugged' kindliness. However, there are still more profound qualities of being and aspirations that link these two friends to one another.

*

In a letter Dunlop addressed to E.C. Merry ('written in illness', probably in the 1930s), we find the following lines:

> Sorrow, thou art the child of a God's experience. The beauty of thy changing face gives ecstasy to Beauty herself . . . A God became Man and tasted Sorrow and was acquainted with grief. Sorrow! Long didst thou dwell in the Tree of Life together with Joy thy companion. When a God tasted Sorrow thy time was fulfilled, and *Man* knew thee for the first time. Every human sorrow since then tends to efflorescence in archetypal lineaments of World-Sorrow. Christ's sorrow is the Earth's Sorrow. To taste Sorrow is to experience Joy.

In the March 1893 number of *The Irish Theosophist*[266] Dunlop published a very short and simple poem by AE which can be brought into an inner relationship with this letter. If one bears in mind the common karma of these two friends and all the remarkable affinities and parallels between their lives, then we may arrive at what is, perhaps, the most beautiful element which they had in common—the ability to undergo suffering as part of a universal and divine experience.

PAIN

Men have made them gods of love,
Sun-gods, givers of the rain,
Deities of hill and grove;
I have made a god of Pain.

Of my god I know this much,
And in singing I repeat,
Though there's anguish in his touch,
Yet his soul within is sweet.

An Epilogue

Similarly, the following (undated) notes, which have been passed on by E.C. Merry, also no doubt stem from the last years of Dunlop's life; and if it is true to say that certain lines Dunlop had written *in memoriam* after Rudolf Steiner's death had constituted a kind of 'prologue' to the last ten years of his own life, then it is equally true that the following thoughts form a kind of 'epilogue' to it. We may even feel how the very *substance* of such thoughts, inspiring future activity with their impulses, can be carried over the threshold into the spiritual world; for this is a world to which not only the individuality himself who grasps them in his thought belongs, but one which is also the true 'home' of *these ideas themselves*.

> I dwell in my tent among the heavenly stars. There, there is cool shade and bright sun to meet every mood. There you will find refreshment for jaded hours lived in the world where the weary ones spend their time, knowing not how near are the immortal hills and the tall trees. How royal I feel! . . . May we not look together upon the wonderful battle going on where our 'shadows' are—the cosmic battle between Ahriman and Michael. I can see Michael's majesty as He waits for our help to give Him back His power. And He does not wait in vain! . . .

7

PERSPECTIVES

Desire has many voices, the loudest usually prevails.
The individuality has a single voice, which can be heard
in the quietness and stillness of the heart, stilling all disputes,
all strife. D.N.D.

'Connected with all the Ancient Mysteries'

At this point let us pause and look back over D.N. Dunlop's life in its entirety; not to establish the sum total of the most radical and significant events that figure in it, but rather with something quite different in mind. We want to cast into sharp relief a certain fundamental trait which permeates his whole life, by considering all those events, experiences and leitmotifs which seem to link this individuality to the great *Mystery Streams of mankind.* For many an impulse connected with these Mysteries is directly revealed, mentioned or touched upon by Dunlop or someone in his immediate entourage, whilst other links to the Mysteries are more concealed and can only be apprehended indirectly.

Of course no systematic exhaustive 'history of the Mysteries' can here be presented. We wish only to take up the various themes we have encountered in the course of Dunlop's life and consider them, both in their mutual relationships and as a *whole*, in the light of the Mysteries inherent in them. The following expositions therefore are necessarily of a very aphoristic and fragmentary nature.

*

Before briefly considering in chronological order the most striking elements linking Dunlop to the Mysteries, we might wish to ask: where did these Mysteries come from anyway and what was their task and function?

All the ancient Mystery Centres go back to the seven great Atlantean 'oracles' or, as Rudolf Steiner defined this expression in his book *Occult Science,*[267] to 'places where the intentions of spiritual beings were perceived'.

After the catastrophe that caused the destruction of Atlantis, the impulses that had lived in the Atlantean oracles subsequently flowed eastwards in two streams—one via Ireland, England, the north of France, Scandinavia and Russia into central Asia; the other, the 'Southern Stream', across southern Spain, North Africa, Egypt, Arabia, and likewise into Asia. In addition, there was another stream flowing directly into the American continent which we will return to presently. All along the paths taken by these two streams across Europe, Africa and Asia, numerous Mystery Centres were founded in post-Atlantean times. These were, as Rudolf Steiner once put it, 'something between a church and a school'.[268] It was from them that the predominating religious, scientific, artistic and social impulses—the 'culture' of antiquity—emanated. In accordance with the twofold stream proceeding from Atlantis, we are dealing here with two kinds of Mystery (or Initiation) Centres where a far deeper insight into the spiritual background of the universe and human life than was accessible to ordinary consciousness was imparted to certain carefully selected persons. Whilst in the northern Mystery Centres revelation was made of the great world or 'macrocosm', the initiate of the southern, 'microcosmic' Mysteries attained first and foremost to spiritual knowledge of *human* nature. This characterization, however, should be interpreted more as an emphasis rather than as a rigid definition of polar opposites, for indeed, there were numerous Mystery Centres where northern and southern impulses interpenetrated one another.

In *both* kinds of Mysteries the number 12 played a very decisive role. As the ego-consciousness even of those who had been chosen for initiation was not yet evolved enough to penetrate into the spiritual world in a fully conscious and spiritually independent manner it had to be reduced or 'dimmed' so that initiation could take place. To this end the initiator surrounded himself with *12* assistants, whose forces were there to protect the neophyte from certain dangers which threatened him—the danger of a 'cosmic dazzling' on the macrocosmic path to the 'higher gods', and the danger of being chained down by his own lower instincts upon the path to the 'lower gods'.[269]

Furthermore, the number 12 played a central role in the northern, macrocosmic Mysteries in another respect as well. In these Mysteries special care was taken that the neophyte should not come to consider the world from only one point of view but that he should find his way into a vision of the world which was all-embracing. In order to develop such a vision 'in the face of everything the human being might encounter in life, twelve points of view are enough; in the language of the Mystery Schools they were symbolized by the twelve constellations of the Zodiac.'[269]

In this light let us now review the course of Dunlop's life. The first obvious link to the Mysteries can be seen in the leitmotif of the '12' which, as more than once was emphasized, already appeared in a significant manner in the circle of friends that gathered on Sundays around the young boy on the Isle of Arran. In the same scene we also encountered another centrally important element of the Mysteries connected to this—the '*Logos*'. On the one hand this points to the Mysteries at Ephesus where the pupil learnt to know and experience the ruling power of the Universal Word as the creative force within the macrocosmic process of the world's becoming, as well as in the microcosmic human reproduction of the Word;[270] on the other hand, the *Logos is* also intimately connected with the central Mystery of the whole evolution of the earth—the incarnation of the Universal Word in Jesus of Nazareth.

Another theme related to the Mysteries can be seen to emerge a little later from the Imaginative, retrospective experience that Dunlop underwent in his early youth following his grandfather's death. As he himself later observed, the temple scene that appeared in it was related to the *Orphic Mysteries*. According to Rudolf Steiner all the later Greek Mysteries originated in the Orphic Mysteries which were also connected with the Mystery Centre situated at Colchis on the Black Sea; one need only think of the Quest for the Golden Fleece where Orpheus is first-named amongst the participants.[271] 'It was Orpheus who inaugurated the Greek Mysteries' and it was he who 'prepared the ground . . . for what was later imparted to mankind through the Christ-event.'[272]

Orpheus is described as being the son of the Muse Calliope, the

Muse of ritual song, and a Thracian river-god. This in itself indicates that as the founder of the Greek Mysteries he had to reckon with the fact that human nature in general was no longer capable of manifesting purely supersensible impulses but rather had already become extremely dependent on earthly geographical and climatic conditions. These same conditions made it possible for him to lose the faculty of clairvoyance connected to the etheric body, as indicated by the destiny of Eurydice. The general consciousness of mankind had begun to lose Eurydice and to be 'cut into pieces' in the physical world. Consequently, from the very outset the Greek Mysteries had the impulse to try by means of the schooling given within them to recover and preserve the old faculty of clairvoyance which was already fading into darkness. From this point of view all the later Greek Mysteries can be viewed as Initiation Centres whose goal was to win back Eurydice.

The reality of being 'dismembered' in a spiritual sense is expressed in the myth of Dionysos Zagreus and was something that the pupil of the Orphic Mysteries had to undergo in his own individual experience. He 'had to develop the inner strength of soul which would enable him, re-established as a self-enclosed individuality, to triumph over the disintegration of his being in the external world', in which he learnt 'to feel as if he were actually within the animals, plants and minerals, in air and water, in springs and mountains, in stones and stars, in other human beings . . . And many pupils of the Orphic Mysteries had undergone such experiences, had lived through this disintegration in the world and, had therewith attained the highest experience within reach in pre-Christian times as a kind of preparation for Christianity.'[273] Out of this force of the Ego, triumphing over the dismemberment in the external world, the power to subdue nature—*the power of Orphic Song*—was born.

Against this background we are now able to distinguish a certain trait of Dunlop's being, a certain mode of expression which otherwise is bound to remain enigmatic and strangely undefined. This now appears as a clear echo of that ritual power of song in which the 'Orphic' might of the Ego is revealed. It was

Willem Zeylmans who perceived it most distinctly and expressed it in the clearest terms:

> Conversation with Dunlop was a fascinating experience. At first he would usually say little, but would listen most intently. However, at the end of the conversation he was fond of developing his own points of view, putting them forward on a wide basis and taking up again all that had previously been touched upon in the course of the conversation. At the end he often expressed very deep ideas, full of spiritual content, expressed in a rather singing, almost ritual tone.[232]

*

At about the age of 18 Dunlop met his life-long friend George William Russell and it was from him that he had heard about the idea of reincarnation for the first time. Dunlop's move to Dublin was shortly afterwards followed by that strange, inner crisis which Russell so intimately witnessed. If, on the one hand, it was conditioned by certain inner, and apparently unresolvable questions, on the other it is equally clear that the whole of Dunlop's external situation—the whole of his happiness and fortune in life—was also then at stake.

In earlier times Ireland was the home of the Hibernian Mysteries whose mighty initiation-rituals have been described in three key lectures by Rudolf Steiner.[274] First of all the neophyte had to undergo the most intense trial of patience imaginable with respect to all knowledge and cognition; indeed, he was tested even to the point of having to pass through a stage of almost total doubt and despair with regard to the value of all knowledge that could be attained by logical or dialectical means. On the other hand, the pupil was also confronted with the question of human joy and happiness and the necessary role they have to play in human existence, and this experience was intensified within his soul to the point of becoming a real drama. The neophyte was then led to two colossal statues, one male, the other female, and here he himself became all question—question with regard to knowledge, question with regard to happiness, and above all, question with regard to how these two might be harmoniously combined. Thus in the preparatory stages of the Hibernian Mysteries the pupil was tried, so to speak, 'on the scales of knowledge and happiness.'[275] And after he had withstood the trial he was shown an image of the Christ-Being with whose force he would be able to solve this riddle and henceforth bring these two elements into a harmonious relationship with one another.

As within the Ephesian Mysteries, so too the actual contents of the Hibernian initiation teachings embraced both macrocosmic and microcosmic aspects. They consisted of a grandiose vision extending over the whole of earth- and world-evolution from Saturn to Vulcan and including the entire microcosmic evolution of man. Once he had become endowed with spiritual vision a picture of the whole evolution of the world unfolded before the initiate's eye. Rudolf Steiner names the Hibernian Mysteries as 'the last great Mysteries in which the secrets of man and the cosmos were able to express themselves'.[276]

So too, in the spiritual atmosphere and against the background of these Hibernian Mysteries, Dunlop had undergone a decisive crisis—that experience in Dublin in which he had been tried 'on the scales of knowledge and happiness', and subsequently, in an entirely inward manner of course, led on towards the Christ. Surrounded by the air of those same Mysteries he had begun, together with AE and a few other friends, to study the cosmological truths of Blavatsky's *Secret Doctrine.*

*

During D.N. Dunlop's sojourn in America at the end of the nineties the leitmotif of 'the 12' once more moves into the foreground of his destiny—this time assuming a more specific and concrete form. Dunlop begins to decipher the signs of the zodiac as the plan not only of the entire evolution of mankind but of the esoteric development of the individual human being as well. In the section entitled 'The Occult Path and the Zodiac' we attempted to present the elementary basis of his considerations. We discovered 12 structural principles working on a cosmic scale, totally transcending time; it was particularly striking to see how Dunlop related these principles, especially where any kind of esoteric development was concerned, to certain occult-physiological organs or functions of the physical body. It is also clear from lectures he later published in England, as well as from the gist of his first conversation with E.C. Merry, that Dunlop went to considerable lengths to try to understand and represent phenomena of the physical, psychic and spiritual life against the background of these eternal principles.

Rudolf Steiner's reference to the 'old Western knowledge' that Dunlop possessed seems first and foremost, as we will show in the section after next, to be connected with the spiritual impulses and consequences of this sojourn in America.[277] As this 'old Western' connection is certainly the most important factor of his karma and related to his future tasks as well, we will return to it presently.

*

In one of the first issues (August 1910) of the Theosophical magazine *The Path* which Dunlop edited, we find a few brief indications concerning the nine days of ritual and initiation between 2 and 10 September which constituted the 'Greater Eleusinia' (see Chapter 3, page 118). In a lecture given in 1915, Dunlop describes the four degrees of initiation that existed in the Eleusinian Mysteries and expresses the well-founded belief that 'in the Eleusinian ritual the Zodiac symbols were employed'. This supposition is not, to the author's knowledge, anywhere directly confirmed by Rudolf Steiner—at least not in the lecture dealing with these Mysteries which he gave on 14 December 1923.[278] However, what Rudolf Steiner does disclose, in a very impressive manner, is the fact that at least a certain part of these Mysteries was connected to a knowledge of nature and, more especially, a knowledge of the metals from a cosmological or planetary point of view; and this is an aspect of the Eleusinian initiation which would no doubt have constituted the 'instruction' corresponding to the first degree of initiation.

As was the case in the Hibernian Mysteries so too the mystery-pupil at Eleusis was brought before two statues—one representing the father, the other the mother-element: 'They conjured up the two opposing forces in his soul: the forces of the cosmos and the forces of earthly being.'[278] And in a similar way to what we have seen take place at Hibernia the pupil at Eleusis too was subsequently granted a vision of the coming Christ. In fact the focal-point of these Eleusinian Mysteries consisted of this vision of the future God of the Universe, as represented by the God Lakchos in a child-like form. He exemplified the ultimate goal of earth-evolution. This also comes to expression in the term employed to describe the neophyte—'Telest' (from the Greek 'telos', 'goal'), or, as Rudolf Steiner put it: one 'who had the task of looking to the goal of earth-evolution'. It is certainly not without reason that this term is also the root-concept behind the so-called 'Entelechy'. Considered from the point of view of the 'Telest', the 'Entelechy' may be defined as that principle within the man *which has the ultimate goal of earth-evolution in view* as it realizes and accomplishes its own being.

*

'A soul rising to a vision of Isis'—that is how E.C. Merry perceived and described an intimate aspect of Dunlop's striving when she first met him in his later years. The fact that it was *this* particular chord in Dunlop's soul which she discerned at the very beginning of their friendship presents us with an important clue in two respects. Not only does it point significantly to Dunlop's connection with those Egyptian paths of initiation leading to the 'lower gods', but we can also sense that it represents an important element of the mutual past and the interrelated destiny of these two friends—*similia per similibus*, as this faculty of recognition is explained by ancient philosophy.

In the section entitled 'Old Paths Meet', we tried to show how, in Dunlop's soul, the Isis-theme converged with what Rudolf Steiner demanded as a renewal of the Isis principle in our day and age. This convergence seems to have taken place in a particularly concentrated form against the background of Dunlop's 'old

Western knowledge', in other words against the background of a cosmologically orientated, spiritual vision of the world and of the human being. This Egyptian factor is also something to which we will return presently in connection with that 'old Western knowledge'.

Having thus cast a glance over Dunlop's life from this point of view, it remains now to focus on one or two of the Mysteries which Rudolf Steiner mentioned as being of special significance with regard to this individuality.

A New Templar Impulse in this Day and Age

Rudolf Steiner had not only drawn E.C. Merry's attention to Dunlop's connection with 'all the ancient Mysteries' but he also mentioned one specific incarnation to her as having taken place during medieval times—'that of a member of a secret society among the Templars', to quote Mrs Merry's exact words. (MD)

Rudolf Steiner alluded to the Templars in various different contexts, but it is probably in the lecture he gave at Dornach on 25 September 1916 that he described the nature and destiny of this order in most detail.[279]

Originally founded in 1119 by Hugo de Payns to protect the Holy Grave at Jerusalem, it was Bernhard de Clairvaux who endowed this order with its rules of conduct. Strict observance was required of its members, not only of all the 'usual' monastic vows of poverty, chastity and obedience, but also of certain 'unwritten regulations' which were particularly characteristic of the esoteric, Christian impulse of the order. In the above-mentioned lecture Rudolf Steiner describes how

> . . . they were to think of nothing except how they could completely fill themselves in heart and soul with the sacred Mystery of Golgotha, and how with every drop of their blood they could help bring the holy places within the sphere of influence of European authority. In each moment of their lives they were to think and feel dedicated with all their strength to this task alone, shunning nothing in order to

> realize it. Their blood was no longer to be their own but was to be devoted solely to the task we have indicated. Were they to meet a power three times as great as themselves, it was commanded that they were not to flee but were to stand firm . . . Whatever wealth they might acquire belonged to no one individual but to the order alone . . . A great and mighty task was set, not so much to thought as to deep feeling, which aimed at strengthening the individual and personal soul life with the intention that it might be entirely absorbed in the progressive stream of Christian evolution . . . Something quite remarkable and powerful had thus entered into the circle of the Templar Order without their having known the rules of Christian initiation other than through sacrificial service. At first in the Crusades, then in the spiritual work in Europe, their souls were so inspired by intensive devotion to the Christian impulse and the Mystery of Golgotha that consequently many Knights experienced a Christian initiation. We have before us the following event of world history: on the world-historical basis of the experience of a number of men, the Christian initiation, which is to say the vision of those spiritual worlds which are accessible to men through Christian initiation, arises from the fundamental depths of human development.

In an early lecture given in Berlin on 22 May 1905,[280] Steiner characterizes the spiritual background and motivating forces of the Knights Templar in connection with the architectural symbolism of Solomon's Temple. He indicates that, apart from a 'lesser' Mass for the uninitiated, the Templars also held a 'High' Mass in which the impulse of Christianity came to expression in a magnificent vista of the entire evolution of the world and of humanity. Special allusion was made in the High Mass to various levels of understanding which will arise with regard to Christianity in future times:

> Then [in the future], in the time of the sixth epoch, the time will arrive when man will have become so inwardly purified that he himself becomes a temple for the divine. At that time the sun will enter the sign of the Water Carrier. Thus the sun, which is really only the expression of our spiritual life, progresses in heavenly space . . . Thus proceeded the High Mass, from which all the uninitiated were excluded.

So in the heart of the Templar Order there lived an impulse based on an all-embracing vision of world-history, one which was able to acknowledge the special position of the Deed of Golgotha and also to grasp the various aspects of its future significance. One element that is particularly illuminating in the present context is the fact that in certain intimate circles of the Templar Order the historical evolution of humanity and the world was apprehended against the background of the precession of the equinoxes through the various signs of the zodiac. This means that the spiritual and cosmological impulse so characteristic of Dunlop's whole being also held sway in the Templar Order.

During the twelfth and thirteenth centuries this order, which developed into a powerful movement permeating the whole of the western world, innovated something like a primary form of international banking organization. Substantial sums of money could be made available to kings and princes, usually in the form of loans. In the course of the twelfth century some 80 cathedrals sprang up in Europe, largely financed by monies provided by the Templars.

In this regard the question has been raised in various quarters: how were the Templars able to obtain the monies necessary for the extensive construction of so many costly cathedrals? Furthermore, it has been established that the Templars made their payments primarily in silver (it is interesting to note that the French word 'argent' actually identifies silver with money), although they had considerable reserves in gold. In various settlements established by the order silver coins were even minted. But where then did the necessary raw silver come from? In a book published a few years ago under the title *Les Templiers en Amérique*,[281] the anthropologist and sociologist Jacques de Mahieu advances the theory that the greater part of the silver necessary for the construction of the cathedrals was shipped over from South America about two hundred years before the so called 'discovery of America'. The starting-point of Mahieu's thesis is a remarkable discovery in the French National Archives: a seal that is circumscribed 'Secretum Templi' ('the secret of the temple'), with a portrait of a South American Indian in the middle of it.

Mahieu further tries to prove that the Templars operated a secret harbour at La Rochelle from which proceeded shipping traffic to the as yet 'undiscovered' continent.

The only reason we have gone into this question here is because it may be linked to Rudolf Steiner's allusion to the existence of a 'secret society' in the Templar Order. In a lecture in St Gallen in 1917,[282] Steiner asserted that sea voyages had been undertaken from the north of Europe (especially from Norway) long before the 'discovery' of America, and also explained the reason for them. Now why should awareness of this fact not have existed (several hundred years after the Church had for very definite reasons put an end to the shipping traffic) within the initiated circles of those Templars who celebrated the 'High Mass'?

We would not in any way wish to affirm that D.N. Dunlop, during his Templar incarnation, was the *only* one to possess knowledge of such things. However, at the end of this biography, are we not to some extent entitled not only to pose the question, what impulses did this individuality receive from his existence as a Templar, but also another one as well: what impulses did he *introduce* into the Templar Order? For even if we are not in a position to practise spiritual research in concrete terms it appears to us highly probable that the individuality of D.N. Dunlop must have worked in the Templar Order, to a greater or lesser degree, *as a mediator of that cosmological knowledge which Rudolf Steiner mentioned.*

*

It was with a series of well-prepared arrests throughout the land that Philip IV, eager to lay hands on the Templars' gold, began his murderous onslaught against the order one day in October 1307. All the assets of the order were confiscated and the order itself dissolved by papal decree in 1312. Under the most brutal forms of torture, numerous Templars were forced into making 'confessions' as to the 'anti-Christian' nature of the order. In 1310, 55 knights who later disavowed these confessions were burnt at the stake. During a fake trial in 1314, Jacques de Molay, the Grand

Master of the Order, who until then had not been sentenced, declared that he 'was guilty of having lied under the pains of torture, however, now, before God and eternity, he bore witness to the purity and innocence of the Order.'[283] On that same day, 18 March 1314, he was burnt at the stake on Philip's orders on the little island in the middle of the Seine which at the time was named 'Isle aux Juifs' but subsequently became known as 'Ile aux Templiers'. Molay asked for his hands to be freed so that he might pray, 'and afterwards death took him', an eye-witness recalled, 'with such gentleness that the people marvelled at it'.[283]

*

To the best of the author's knowledge, Dunlop himself never made any direct mention of this significant medieval order. Nevertheless, given the remark that Rudolf Steiner made to Mrs Merry, we are bound to ask: how did the impulses which this individuality received and, perhaps more importantly, *introduced into* the Templar stream, evolve and take effect in his next incarnation?

*

If we once more look back over Dunlop's activity as a writer during the period of his theosophical activities, one of the monuments that still towers up before our gaze is that essay which we reprinted unabridged under the title 'Ceremonial Magic in Meditational Form'. This 'Meditation', with its will-enhancing attitude of sacrifice, universally transcending all personal considerations, may now in retrospect appear to us as the *key* to understanding Dunlop's Templar connection. It is a renewal and continuation of 'that great and mighty task . . . aimed at strengthening the individual and personal soul life with the intention that it might be entirely absorbed in the progressive stream of Christian evolution.'[279]

This 'Meditation' was published shortly before the outbreak of the First World War. At that time Dunlop had already been working as director of the BEAMA for three years. It is in relation to this activity of his in the technological and economical field (which soon afterwards led to the founding of the World Power Conference) that we can discover a second aspect of his connection to the Templars. But it appears less as a *result* of (past) Templar banking and organizational activities than as a *continuation* of the original Templar impulse in a form adapted to modern times.

During the last years of his life Dunlop lived at the upper end of a little road in Chelsea. Not far from his last residence there is a church dedicated to the memory of Thomas More. As Henry VIII's chancellor More had refused to recognize him as the supreme head of the Church of England and had suffered a destiny somewhat similar to that inflicted upon the Knights Templars by Philip IV more than two hundred years before. He was executed in 1535. One week after the above-quoted September lecture of 1916 on the Templars, Rudolf Steiner spoke of the great influence that More's soul was able to exercise *post mortem* upon the subsequent evolution of his age. In a manner which may surprise us to begin with, he explains how after death More's soul permeated and united itself with the whole spiritual atmosphere created by the destinies of the Templars—which likewise exercised a considerable inspiring influence on the further development of the age.[238] He describes the ingenious author of *Utopia* as 'a soul that has grown powerful because, in the physical body, it has experienced the supersensible and allows it to radiate out over succeeding evolution. It streamed into the other spiritual atmosphere I described about eight days ago [Lecture VI]. The spiritual atmosphere of the 14th, 15th, 16th, 17th, 18th centuries is, as we know, also permeated by the impulses that have arisen through the persecution and death of the Templars.' The external proximity of D.N. Dunlop's last residence to the Thomas More Memorial Church can almost be felt on a local level as a gentle hint to the biographer: it recalls the significant spiritual proximity in regard to their common source of inspiration as presented to Rudolf Steiner's spiritual eye. But of course, if Mrs Merry had not carefully noted Rudolf Steiner's remark, which served as our point of departure, then that small church dedicated to Thomas More would have continued to appear as just another of those many smaller or larger churches scattered over London.

Future Tasks and 'Old Western Knowledge'

While in 1930 D.N. Dunlop was recovering from that critical illness which brought him to the very gate of death, a spiritual impulse for a new kind of community rose up into the sphere of his waking consciousness. He spoke to Mrs Merry of the need to found certain 'new Mysteries of King Arthur', 'a new Order . . . of Twelve'. But a few days later he realized that the time was not yet ripe for it.

However, we cannot ignore the fact that this Mystery-motif of the 'Twelve', which is closely linked to the whole question of how spiritual communities can be formed, was something that was deeply anchored in Dunlop's soul, all the more so since a few years before his death and many years after his meeting with Anthroposophy it had again risen up before his inner eye with such tremendous urgency. So perhaps we should not content ourselves with seeking its origins in those *past* Mysteries which, even as we trace them back, become lost in the mists of time—Mysteries which, whether they concern humanity as a whole or the individual alone, have in a certain sense already been completed. It is just as likely that in this motif of the 'Twelve' there resides an element of the *future* also, a force that has yet to be discovered. In other words: if there really is something of the future in this element of the Mysteries, then we shall need to look for its 'roots' primarily in a kind of Mystery Culture which, with regard to humanity, *has not yet fulfilled its task*. This would also have to be a Mystery Stream capable both of taking the Event of Golgotha in its entirety into account, and of contributing something towards a future understanding of the Christ. For only a Mystery Stream that has been fructified by the Christ-Event can be said to be truly capable of growth and evolution in present and future times.

The first traces of such a Mystery Stream can be found in the allusion Rudolf Steiner once made to 'old Western knowledge'. It is substantiated in the first place by the fundamental impression made upon Ita Wegman when she saw the countenance of the deceased man: 'This face was like an "Offenbarung" [revelation]. And I must tell you that it was as if it sounded from out of his head the sound TAO, and a picture came as if this face belonged to a man who has listened to . . . the rushing of wind, making the impression to be one with all what is behind nature.' According to Mrs Merry's notes, Ita Wegman also added the following words as she contemplated this countenance: 'It reveals the Great Mysteries of the ancient West—the Mysteries of the *Father.*'

Now let us turn to a question which unavoidably arises at this point: what exactly is the Tao? It may be stated at the outset that the word is pronounced in exactly the same way as the modern German word 'Tau' which according to Rudolf Steiner is 'no other than that ancient . . . sound.'[285] (N.B. the English word 'dew' also derives its etymological origin and meaning from this word 'tau'.) Moreover, the Tao-cross (T) is the original form of the cross and this memory still lives on in the Latin word 'ros-crux', (for 'ros' means 'dew' or 'dewdrops') and in the corresponding word 'Rosicrucian'.

As regards the *spiritual* content of this sound which has existed for thousands of years, Rudolf Steiner gave the following description in a lecture in 1905:

> The Tao expresses, and for a large part of mankind already expressed thousands of years ago, the highest that man could look up to; it was thought of as the future goal of the world and of all mankind. It is the highest principle, which the human being bears in himself in a seed-like form, and which will one day ripen and blossom forth out of his innermost nature. The Tao signifies both the hidden depths—the grounds from which the soul has sprung—and a sublime. Those who understood the nature of the Tao spoke and even thought of it only with the greatest modesty and reverence. The Tao Religion is based on the principle of development and it says: 'what surrounds me today is one stage which will soon be superseded by another one. I must be aware of the fact that this evolution in which I participate has a particular goal and that I will continue to develop until I reach the

> sublime goal, Tao. There is a force within me that spurs me on to reach that goal; and when I feel this great force from within, guiding me together with all beings towards that goal, I know that it is the self-same guiding force that blows towards me out of the wind; sounds forth from the rock, streaks out of the lightning, rolls out of the thunder and sends its light to me from the sun. It is what appears as growth in plants; it is what appears as sensation and perception in animals; it is that power which continues to bring forth new forms, one after another, until it reaches that sublime goal whereby I know myself to be one with the whole of Nature. It streams in and out of me with every breath I take. It is the symbol of the greatest Spirit that is developing out of itself and which I feel as—life! This is the force of Tao that I feel. At the beginning . . . there was no talk of a God existing 'on the other side', no talk of anything *outside* the world, but only of a strengthening force that could assist the advancement of mankind.

After this characterization of the Tao and the feeling it evoked, Rudolf Steiner describes how it was fully experienced 'at a time when the human being was still closely linked to the divine origin of his being—as was especially the case with the peoples of *Atlantis*.' Thus it is here in old Atlantis that we must look if we wish to find the soil which nurtured the great Tao Religion, the sublime feeling of the Tao.

But what has all this to do with the ancient West? That is the next question we must ask. As already indicated, in his *Occult Science* Rudolf Steiner describes how, following the destruction of Atlantis, three migratory movements[286] provided the cultural impulses for humanity. Two of them crossed to Europe and Asia, thereby creating what was described as the Northern and Southern Mystery Streams. Both these migratory movements towards the east are, according to Rudolf Steiner, 'especially . . . important . . . for our present time'.[286] The third made its way to the American continent which, along with Europe, Asia and Africa, was gradually assuming the forms and contours it has today. If it is true to say that the major migratory movement which proceeded to America is not 'especially important' for us today, this can mean either that its importance is something of the past, or that it belongs to future times. Admittedly in a somewhat veiled form, we can ascertain from the final lecture Rudolf Steiner gave in the cycle entitled *The East in the Light of the West*[287] that the latter is in fact the case. For in that lecture (given on 31 August 1909) he explains the future significance of an ancient *Western* Mystery Stream which, in contrast to the two other *Eastward* moving Streams, had the task of preserving the old Atlantean clairvoyance for a more extensive understanding of the Christ in future times:

> Christ had to come into the world just at a time when the means of understanding were most contracted. The way had to be opened for the revival of the ancient wisdom during the ages to come and for placing it gradually in the service of the understanding of Christ. This could only be accomplished in the following way. Those men[288] who came over from old Atlantis into Europe and beyond brought with them great wisdom. In old Atlantis the majority of the people were instinctively clairvoyant; they could see into spiritual realms. This clairvoyance could not develop further; *it had to withdraw into separate personalities of the West.*[279] *It was guided there by a Being who once lived in deepest concealment*, withdrawn behind those who had already forsaken the world and who were pupils of a great initiate. *This Being had remained behind in order to preserve for later ages what was brought over from old Atlantis.*

The impulse to preserve the old Atlantean clairvoyance, which was guided by this hidden initiate, also included the very best and purest elements of the Atlantean Tao wisdom; this point is by no means undermined by the objection that in September 1916 Rudolf Steiner depicted predominantly Ahrimanic-Luciferic caricatures of the Atlantean Tao-Spirit—both in Asia and America.[289] For nobody could possibly suggest that the form of Tao-spirituality which subsequently degenerated into the 'Taotl-wisdom' of the American continent should be reckoned among those sources of wisdom that can be 'gradually placed in the service of an understanding of the Christ'. Therefore, from an overall view of the relevant passages in these lectures, we may simply conclude that there existed on the American continent, parallel to the Atlantean wisdom that had fallen into decadence, another pure extract of that same wisdom which was preserved by that particular initiate living and working in concealment. Rudolf Steiner says[287] of this guardian:

> . . . among the great initiates who had founded mystery places in the West for the preservation of the old Atlantean wisdom, a wisdom that entered deeply into all the secrets of the physical body, was Skythianos, as he was called in the early Middle Ages. And anyone who knows the nature of the European mysteries is aware that he is looking up to one of the highest initiates of the earth when is pronounced the name of Skythianos.[290]

The wisdom of Skythianos, then, includes the 'secrets of the physical body', which we could also call 'the secrets of the temple and its architecture'. Indirectly associated with this wisdom is the succinct description of the number 12 which Rudolf Steiner gives in the same lecture. To begin with he defines this number as the 'guideline for everything that exists side by side in space' and distinguishes it from the number seven which predominates 'wherever there are changes . . . that is to say time is involved' (for instance in the process of human development from childhood to old age).

Slightly further on Rudolf Steiner characterizes a certain 'inner relationship which exists with regard to time and space' and speaks of the 12 'fundamental points of the Zodiac'; they were already known to an ancient form of spiritual cosmology as the 12 signs from Aries to Pisces. What Rudolf Steiner then goes on to develop throws the first rays of light on the future mission of Skythianos; what is more, thanks to the distinction made with regard to the number seven, it now becomes clear to us that everything that was once associated with those '12 fundamental points' is of a nature totally transcending all that comes into existence and disappears again *with time*. It belongs to the 'realm of duration', as Rudolf Steiner expresses it in his *Occult Science*, or to what could also be termed, in the sense in which it perfectly transcends all time as such, the realm of *eternity*:

> These twelve points of the Zodiac were the actual, real world symbols for the very oldest divine spiritual beings, and in a certain

> sense they were thought to correspond with reality. Even when the earth was embodied as old Saturn, the forces issuing from these twelve directions were at work upon that old Saturn; so they were later the old Sun period, the old Moon period, and they will continue to be in the future. Therefore they have as it were the nature of permanence, they are far more sublime than that which arises and passes away within our earth existence. What is symbolized by the twelve signs of the Zodiac is far above what is transformed in the evolutionary course of our planet from old Saturn to old Sun, from old Sun to old Moon and so on. What goes on there is a process of arising and passing away, but the Zodiac outlasts planetary existence. What is symbolized by the points of the Zodiac is far above what plays its part upon earth as the opposition between good and evil . . . We have within the twelve points of permanence in the surroundings what is above good and evil. We have to seek out in space for the symbols of those divine-spiritual beings which, considered in themselves and without reference to their effects upon our earthly sphere, are beyond the differences between good and evil.[287]

In the same lecture Rudolf Steiner describes how, in the fourth century AD, one of the 'greatest councils was held that has ever taken place in the spiritual world belonging to the earth'; Manes, an even greater initiate than Skythianos, had gathered 'three significant personalities' about him 'in order to consult with them how all the wisdom which had once lived in Atlantis at the turn of time could gradually be reborn in future times . . . and the plan concerning the future evolution of culture on the earth which was then decided upon was preserved and was subsequently taken over into those European mysteries, the Mysteries of the Rose Cross.' The 'three personalities' in question consisted of the Buddha, who only reappeared in a 'physical reflection', Zarathustra, who was reincarnated at that time, and Skythianos who was likewise incarnated during that period.

It is clear from this lecture that these highly developed individualities are, in fact, Bodhisattvas. This is the name that is used in the East to describe those individualities who in Rudolf Steiner's sense have already passed through all the stages of evolution which can be completed by means of earthly incarnation. He also frequently describes these Bodhisattvas as the 'Masters of Wisdom and Harmony of Feeling',[291] and it is not by chance that the 'college' they form is made up of a total of 12 such individuals. What is the most distinctive task of these Bodhisattvas? In a word, it is to enable an ever deeper understanding of the Christ-Being and Christ-Deed gradually to arise. For 'the most worthy object of all understanding' is the 'Christ, who is a totally different Being from the Bodhisattvas'—a Being that can only be understood when *all* the forms of wisdom appertaining to the various Bodhisattvas are brought together. During the council summoned by Manes, 'a plan was made by means of which all the wisdom of the Bodhisattvas belonging to the post-Atlantean period would be able to flow more and more powerfully into the future life of mankind'.

While Manes, in accordance with this plan, has assumed a special mission connected with the development of the human ego, the individuality of the Buddha can be seen as the inspirer of all that is linked to the purification of the astral body. Zarathustra is intimately connected with the protection of the human ethereal body and Skythianos with a special form of wisdom which 'even penetrated into the depths of all the secrets of the physical body'. The clearly differentiated influence and collaboration of these four individualities has come to expression in a very fine essay by George Adams.[292] He was apparently stimulated by the lecture in Munich but also included and assembled other illuminating points of view from various other lectures and works by Rudolf Steiner.

If Skythianos, 'the great and honoured Bodhisattva of the West',[293] is particularly linked to the 'secrets of the physical body', we could also say that he is linked to secrets of the *Father or Saturn*. For, according to *Occult Science*, it was during the period of old Saturn that the first seed was laid of what was subsequently to become the human physical body of today. Moreover, the mysteries which are bound up with Saturn are connected in quite a unique way with the West. This is clear, for example, from the fact that Rudolf Steiner describes the Indian Root-Race inhabiting the North American continent, and preserving the original Atlantean Tao-spirituality, as the 'Saturn Race'.[294]

*

The conclusion may be drawn that Rudolf Steiner's allusion to D.N. Dunlop's possessing 'old Western knowledge' indicates that he was closely connected with the *Mysteries of the Father*, that is to say, with the Atlantean, Tao- or Saturn-wisdom preserved in the West by the initiate Skythianos. Indeed, the deep inner bond which links Dunlop to a certain form of wisdom concerned with the zodiac and, more specifically, with the 'secrets of the physical body' (as illustrated in the section 'The Occult Path and the Zodiac'), seems to point in the same direction.

In a lecture Rudolf Steiner gave during Advent of 1906,[295] the following enlightening allusion to the Atlantean Tao is to be found: 'This Tao later came to expression in the letter "T". Resting on the "T" there is a circle . . . which symbolizes the *all-embracing nature of the Father as Godhead.*' In the spirit of this illuminating exposition one might perceive the circle above the T as symbolizing the wisdom of the Zodiac.

Although in the Munich lecture Steiner does not immediately and directly link Skythianos to the lofty zodiac-conception, one may certainly conclude from his characterization of this Bodhisattva-individuality and his future mission on earth that this link does in fact exist. 'Today mankind is hardly able to bring to these great teachers of the Rose Cross *two* minimum elements of understanding—and even these two only represent the beginning of what will, in the future, be a truly vast and powerful understanding of Christianity.' The deeper comprehension of Christianity which is to be made accessible to the world by spiritual science is primarily concerned with integrating the Buddha-element, and subsequently the spiritual quality of Skythianos, into our understanding. 'We have to begin by integrating the most elementary principles which we have learnt from them into our culture. Christianity can learn about reincarnation and karma from the Buddha.' Then Steiner goes on to speak of the mission of Skythianos: 'Thus, an understanding of Skythianos will also gradually arise. It is his task not only to teach the reincarnation of man, but also to *instruct humanity in regard to what holds sway from eternity to eternity.*' That can only mean *in the whole context of this lecture*: a 'teaching' which is concerned with those 'ancient spiritual and divine beings' whose forces already began to converge at the beginning of Saturn evolution, working inwards from the 12 points of the periphery. These beings constitute an 'enduring element' *totally transcending all evolution within time* and they are seated in 'real and veritable world symbols'—in the 12 points of the zodiac.

Perhaps the following excerpt illustrates the point even more clearly:

> So as time passes the Being who is at the centre of our earthly world, that is to say the Christ-Being, will be more and more understood. For the teachings of the initiates are flowing ever more abundantly into the life of mankind. The spiritual scientist who today actively considers these things can only prepare the ground for two elements which will necessarily have a much more important role to play in the future spiritual development of mankind: the first is something which 'sinks' into the human soul as the Life of Christ.

This is directly related to the Buddha Impulse flowing through the whole of humanity.

> The second element which will contribute to an understanding of the Christ, will be an all-embracing *spiritual cosmology*.

The task of such a 'spiritual cosmology' will be to impart what holds sway from 'eternity to eternity' and we must look on the individuality of Skythianos as being the inspirer of this impulse.

*

What conclusions can be drawn from the last two sections with regard to Rudolf Steiner's allusion to D.N. Dunlop's past connection with the Mysteries?

In two respects we have been able to discover a more definite meaning behind his indication that Dunlop had been 'connected with all the ancient Mysteries'. *Firstly*, we have ascertained that Dunlop was connected not only with both Mystery Streams which developed parallel to the two great migratory movements proceeding *eastwards* after the destruction of Atlantis; he was also connected with the *westward* moving Mystery Stream which migrated to the ancient American continent. So he is related to *all three* of the main Mystery Streams of mankind—the new Mysteries which arose from the movement towards the East, and the surviving ones which moved westwards from Atlantis.

Secondly, we have been able to discover—and find confirmation in some details—certain factors linking Dunlop to specific Mystery Centres of antiquity (belonging both to the Northern and Southern Streams, and also to some cultivating impulses from both Mystery Streams together). As far as the Northern Mysteries are concerned, we need only think of Dunlop's connection to the 'Arthurian Mysteries' which, as Rudolf Steiner once pointed out, stemmed from the Mysteries of Hibernia. With regard to the Southern Mystery Stream, we need only remind ourselves of Dunlop's link to the Egyptian Isis-Mysteries.

Thus Dunlop's connection with 'all' the ancient Mysteries means that he was linked, in the first place, to the three principal Mystery Streams of mankind, and in the second, to a number of important Northern and Southern Streams which were representative of the Mysteries of antiquity. However, there is also a *third* aspect, the overriding importance of which has become increasingly evident in the course of our research: it is the profound significance of Dunlop's connection with the ancient Mysteries of the *West*. Rudolf Steiner seems to put great emphasis on this aspect too, when he speaks of Dunlop's tasks precisely in the context of 'old Western knowledge'. We may therefore regard Dunlop's association with the ancient Western Stream, which reaches right back to old Atlantis, as representing the most ancient 'roots' of his being, but also as providing the most fertile soil and the real foundation for all his activity and work into the far distant future.

At various moments in her life, E.C. Merry registered a number of quite distinctly different impressions about her great friend. Apart from the Templar incarnation which Rudolf Steiner had explicitly mentioned to her, she also felt D.N. Dunlop to be deeply connected with Rosicrucianism. However, the strongest karmic impression she had of him clearly emerges from the old Western background referred to here. In her 'reminiscences' of Dunlop she gives the following account of this impression:

> It was at about this time that Dr Steiner appointed D.N.D. to look after the interests of the medical work in England, and the Weleda Co. He devoted himself with great warmth of heart to this work, and I was astonished to find how much he seemed to know about medicines and healing generally. One day I had a remarkably clear vision which I believed at that time to be a vision of him in an old American incarnation. I saw an Indian seated on the ground. He was 'clothed' in his splendid aura which radiated from his head and down his spine exactly as the present day Red Indian wears his many-coloured feathers. In front of him burned a flame which the wind blew into the shape of a sickle; and at his feet was a serpent. He was in deep meditation, and his meditation formed for him the vision of a moon-coloured pillar of light which was surmounted by the half of a female form—a moon goddess. Orion was blazing in the sky, and the moon was setting on the horizon. In his meditation he was investigating the nature of healing plants. I painted a picture of this, and when I showed it to D.N.D. he told me that 'A.E.' the Irish poet, had seen the same picture of him.
>
> I mention this only because it illustrates the side of his nature with which I had then become acquainted. (MD)

This old Western incarnation seems to 'accompany' the later ones. It appears as something of a 'silver thread' which is carried over into all the later experiences which this individuality undergoes in the Northern and Southern Mysteries, acting as a kind of permanent catalyst with regard to all the impulses received from the various Mysteries. Thus, the 'Isis-motif', for instance, is subordinated to an all-embracing *cosmology* (as we pointed out in the section 'Old Paths Meet'). And the working of this individuality inside the Templar Order seems also to have been closely linked to the esoteric cosmology which formed part of the instruction of the 'High Mass'.

*

This varied wealth of experience which D.N. Dunlop had assimilated from the Mysteries, given a particular accent by his connection with the ancient West, must have brought him into a special kind of relationship with what Rudolf Steiner in 1924 often described and characterized as the 'Michael School'—that 'school' which, in the supersensible world, imparted a magnificent and momentous form of instruction over a period of several centuries. On 14 September 1924, Steiner gives the following characterization of this 'instruction':[296] 'Deeply significant was the teaching of that School. On the one hand it pointed again and again to the connections with the ancient Mysteries, to all that must come forth once again in a new form from the content of the ancient Mysteries so as to permeate modern civilization with spirituality. On the other hand it pointed to the impulses which souls devoted to spiritual life must have for their work into the future.'

In the incarnation following this cosmic instruction in the supersensible world, it must have been above all the search for such impulses, which are absolutely necessary for the future development of mankind, which led D.N. Dunlop to discover Anthroposophy and its founder.

From all this it follows that in D.N. Dunlop's case it is predominantly the impulse of the ancient Western Mysteries which has to 'come forth once again in a new form'. And when Rudolf Steiner specified, according to Ita Wegman, that Dunlop 'has to teach about cosmic things' then the preceding investigations should have made clear what this means in practical terms. It means that the future work and activity of this individuality in the service of the Michael Impulse and Anthroposophy will be accomplished under the cosmic influence or 'sign' of Skythianos, i.e. in accordance with the future mission of this individuality in the name of what 'holds sway from eternity to eternity' and embraces the 'secrets of the physical body'. It would of course be quite erroneous to *identify* D.N. Dunlop with Skythianos; all we want to do here is to draw attention to an intimate link which exists between these two particular individualities. For D.N.

Dunlop has not only revealed himself to us a servant and champion of the Michaelic cause but also as an individuality particularly well versed in the secrets of the 'Skythianos Mysteries'.*

At the Threshold of a Millennium

It was never our intention to compile a purely documentary account of Dunlop's life within the pages of this book. To have done so would have been to limit ourselves to a domain which, in Dunlop's terms, could only be described as that of the 'personality'. A historical vision of things which concentrates exclusively on the past, on documents or other *traces* of the living, will never be able to grasp the 'Entelechy' of the human being which belongs to the eternal region of the stars and only manifests itself, to a greater or lesser degree, in the life of the personality. In a historical portrait of that kind even D.N. Dunlop would at best appear as an interesting and remarkable figure—one in whom people might, for 'purely historical' reasons, begin to take an interest perhaps—but one whose life has, after all, come to an end and belongs to the past.

The present biography has been composed according to other criteria and from an entirely different point of view. It only remains here, at the end of the book, to summarize the two main factors which brought it to birth.

Time and time again, especially during the years of the First World War which claimed such an endless multitude of human lives, Rudolf Steiner spoke of the life after death and of the continued existence of the so-called 'dead'. He emphasized the importance of consciously taking up the impulses which had once lived in individualities no longer incarnated on the earth in order to ensure a cultural continuity within the evolution of mankind. This is especially important today because from now on and to an

* **Editor's note:** Dunlop's association with these mysteries is developed further in the author's book *Clairvoyance and Consciousness* (Temple Lodge Press, London 1991).

ever greater degree it will be the responsibility of the human being to create this continuity *consciously* and by himself. By taking up the spiritual impulses of no longer incarnated souls, men will in future times bring a completely new and necessary element into their own cultural evolution.

Whoever attempts to 'reckon' in a realistic and practical way with the continued existence, activity and evolution of the so-called 'dead' must first of all develop a kind of active 'inspiration' and receptiveness with respect to the impulses they are constantly trying to bring into the world of the so-called 'living'. The development of this inspirational attitude or faculty is not dependent on whether or not one is, in the widest *sense of the term*, 'clairvoyant'. The decisive point is whether or not one is in a position to take the *thoughts* one has assimilated from Anthroposophy, and worked over in one's mind, so seriously that they actually begin to create new organs of perception; and long before they are able to actually function, this might be experienced as the birth of not only new thoughts but of new inner attitudes of feeling towards the world and its phenomena. Of course this will only be the case if we are able to treat such 'pure' thoughts—and in the present context this primarily concerns the purely universal thoughts of life after death, life before birth, and the destiny of man—as linked to practical realities, so that the moment such thoughts have been understood according to the inherent inner structure of their elements one no longer afterwards doubts them. The faculty to *understand*, to grasp pure, abstract thoughts is anyway, as Rudolf Steiner made perfectly clear in his fundamental philosophical works, already an act of clairvoyance—one which is, of course, often overlooked by the human being today who does not recognize the inestimable value of these 'pearls of clairvoyance'[297] within real energetic thinking.

In other words, once certain thoughts have been *clairvoyantly grasped* and experienced in their self-evidence, one does not need to wait passively for any additional 'demonstration' or 'real proof' of that which has already been perceived in thought. It makes no difference at all whether we are tempted impatiently to seek such 'real proof' in the sense-world or in the supersensible world of perceptions outside the world of thought. It is precisely the inner patience required in understanding *without yet 'seeing'* which contributes to creating the supersensible organs of perception. For it is a well-known fact that, when one has thoroughly understood certain spiritual-scientific thoughts with regard to some spiritual reality or other, one often has to wait, sometimes a considerable period of time, before the concrete perceptions corresponding to these thoughts also present themselves. Consequently, an attitude which while understanding does not yet take this understanding seriously enough, but keeps on waiting for something else (an attitude of *naive realism*, in terms of *The Philosophy of Spiritual Activity*) will generally only result in the thought not finding its way to the heart, and there will be no possibility whatsoever of developing the inspirational attitude hinted at above.

It is this naive inclination to seek 'real' demonstrations or 'proof' of concepts corresponding to supersensible realities which is probably one of the greatest hindrances to taking such thoughts really seriously—especially as this tendency does not simply disappear the moment we begin to assimilate spiritual thoughts. Consequently, in order to understand this whole problem special attention must be paid to a particular aspect of the 'spiritualization of thinking', a process which Rudolf Steiner often described as being one of the most important tasks of Anthroposophy. It is the following: once the results of spiritual scientific research have been communicated in the form of pure concepts and thoroughly *understood* (by healthy common sense), everything depends on whether one develops the faculty to apprehend and feel that they do, indeed, correspond to quite definite realities, even though, as one *thinks* them, one does not yet have the corresponding perceptions.

The moment this is achieved, one is bound to take the continued existence, evolution and activity of the so-called 'dead', especially with respect to their influence within the sphere of the so-called 'living', *just as seriously as the existence and activity of the living themselves*. However, in order to practise this inspirational attitude with regard to quite specific and real individualities, something else is necessary too. It is an ability from time to time, and in full consciousness, to 'make room' in one's own soul for another influence; so that another individuality and its activity may not merely be experienced and 'appreciated' from outside, but also allowed to 'take place' as it were in one's own soul life. This means developing a certain faculty of selflessness, or rather, intensifying and reinforcing this faculty which is already used in everyday intercourse with human beings—for it is present in every *true act of listening with inner understanding*. If this faculty is not consciously cultivated and reinforced it will become increasingly difficult to ensure spiritual continuity in the future evolution of mankind. 'But it would have a momentous effect,' Rudolf Steiner declared on 3 December 1916,[298] 'if this form of selflessness were to become somewhat wider spread in the world, if those living at a later moment in time were to take up the impulses of the dead in a really conscious attempt to ensure a certain continuity of evolution. Now this might be due to pure congeniality or again to some relationship of a karmic nature—but in both cases it is an act of tremendous significance if it is cultivated in full consciousness—if we are able to work consciously in the same spirit as those who are trying to transmit the rays of their activity to us from the spiritual world.'

So this is where we stand. We are left with the possibility, or rather judging by these words, the necessity, of taking up these impulses and making a conscious connection with the past—an act which is of vital importance with regard to the Anthroposophical Movement since the death of Rudolf Steiner and of those individualities who were part of his immediate entourage. For it is obvious enough that what has been stated with regard to the continuity of evolution in general is especially relevant with regard to the continuity of the Anthroposophical Movement in particular.

*

The *second factor* determining the point of view adopted in this biography is connected with what has been mentioned on several occasions as the 'Michael Prophecy'.[299] This prophecy not only involves the free decisions of those anthroposophists who belong more to the Aristotelian spiritual stream of humanity and who already incarnated at the beginning of this century; it also embraces those Platonic spirits who were above all responsible for directing the School of Chartres in the twelfth century as well as the vast circle of pupils connected with that school.[300] Rudolf Steiner repeatedly referred to this state of affairs in the karma lectures of 1924. Whether or not these two groups of souls succeed in working together on the earth at the end of the century is something Rudolf Steiner explicitly presents to us as being a *possibility,* 'for today everything depends on the freedom of the will'. He points out that the factual realization of this project could be thwarted by human beings of the twentieth century if the opportunity 'is not taken seriously but lost in joking' and, in the same lecture, makes it clear that the successful collaboration of these two parties united with each other will depend in a certain sense upon 'whether or not the Anthroposophical Society understands how to devote itself in the right way to the cultivation of Anthroposophy'.[301]

Anybody looking back over the history of this Society, with its various crises and expulsions, but also with its uplifting elements as for instance the educational movement, will not find it easy to judge whether or not there has indeed been the right 'devotion' towards the 'cultivation of Anthroposophy', i.e. whether the conditions making it possible for Platonists and Aristotelians to join forces and work together on the earth have been adequately fulfilled in the sense of Rudolf Steiner's words. At all events, as 'today everything depends on the freedom of the will' we should not draw the over-hasty conclusion that the opportunity for collaboration has already been 'lost in joking'. Above all, we cannot exclude the possibility that, in accordance with the Michael Prophecy, there may be a number of anthroposophical souls who, having been incarnated at the beginning of the century, are now seeking or, indeed, may already have embarked upon a new earth-existence and activity. For this particular use of free will, which will become increasingly prevalent in the future, must, of course, also be granted to those souls who, during their last anthroposophical incarnation, permeated themselves with the content of the Michael Prophecy to the point where they felt themselves to be truly bound up with it.

Despite the possibility that this opportunity may have already been 'lost in joking', there are no reasons for assuming that the realization of the Michael Prophecy, *in its most far-reaching consequences*, is entirely dependent upon whether or not (or to what degree) Anthroposophy has been, or will be in future, 'cultivated in the right way'. Nor do these far-reaching *consequences* depend entirely upon the extent to which the Michael Prophecy itself (which is of such vital importance to the Anthroposophical Movement, being primarily concerned with the tasks for the world and for mankind of those involved in it) is really taken seriously by anthroposophists in general. However, one thing that really *does* depend upon this serious attitude is the factor of *continuity*—both within the Anthroposophical Movement and Society as such. The task of consciously taking up and realizing the impulses of returning anthroposophical souls will be considerably facilitated if a number of people have already acquainted themselves with the biographies of these individualities—of course, in such a way as to enable us not merely to arrive at a certain 'historical knowledge of the personality', but to begin actually to develop an organ for the Entelechy itself, embracing as it does both the past and future of the souls concerned.

But what if the opportunity offered to mankind by the Michael Prophecy has, indeed, been 'lost in joking'? In this case the inspirational attitude, the attempt to take up and continue the impulses of 'those who are trying to transmit the rays of their activity to us from the spiritual world', would appear to be all the more urgent and relevant. This is so regardless of whether one is seeking to 'take up' these impulses on a physical or spiritual level. In an age which is characterized by consciousness and freedom of will, what is needed in both cases is a real practical knowledge of the Entelechy.

Many of Rudolf Steiner's pupils really did take up the Michael Prophecy and inwardly integrate it into their lives in a very real sense. Thus, for example, Count Polzer-Hoditz wrote an essay shortly after Rudolf Steiner's death in which we find the following allusion to it: 'Rudolf Steiner will reunite us all once more in the sun-spheres of Michael's realm, and together we will return to the earth soon afterwards, in order to accomplish what he promised in his last lecture: we will be able to intervene in the very decisive crisis which mankind will be undergoing in order to bring a remedy.'[302]

In a similar way to Count Polzer-Hoditz, Ita Wegman refers in the original draft of her speech after Dunlop's death to the way in which 'Rudolf Steiner is gathering all those who have finished their task'. This is an allusion to that 'gathering' to which Rudolf Steiner referred in his 'Last Address' when speaking directly to those who were present in Dornach at the time: 'You will find all those with whom you are to prepare the work that should be accomplished at the end of this century, and that should lead mankind past the great crisis in which it is involved.'[303] These words point to a supersensible 'preparatory council' concerning the work to be accomplished at the end of this century and one in which both groups of souls will in the meantime have participated: those who incarnated with Rudolf Steiner at the beginning of the century, as well as those souls belonging to the Platonic stream. This 'heavenly council' can be apprehended as a 'higher octave' of a preceding 'council' which had been held in the thirteenth century and in the course of which the decision had been taken to bring about a future collaboration between Platonists and Aristotelians.

Not only the life and development of the human being but also that of humanity as a whole passes, in the space of the three times 33⅓ years that make up a century, through the three stages of soul-life: thinking, feeling and willing. During the first third of the century Anthroposophy was presented as a *teaching* for a modern-day humanity which had the potential to make full and free use of its capacity to think. During the second third what mattered most was that this teaching should find its way into the human *heart*. (Viewed in the context of the Anthroposophical Movement as a whole, this was a phase of intense inward-looking activity—one provoked, in the widest sense, by the terrible events of the War.)

The *end* of the century, W.J. Stein once wrote to anthroposophical friends in an Easter letter of 1933, will be 'the deed . . . the trial of will'.

Stein too was aware, in the deepest sense, of his own connection with the Michael Prophecy, as the following lines from the same letter testify. Referring to the crisis within the Society at that time, he observes that it will no longer be the prerogative of earthly kinds of 'Vorstand'—which take upon themselves to expel certain persons from the Society—to decide whether or not someone is a representative of the 'right method' or not. In future this task will fall to 'sacred powers of a very different kind' (an allusion to the highest hierarchies). Moreover, when these individualities, whose destinies are interwoven with the Michael Prophecy, reappear, Anthroposophy will live in them not only as a teaching, and as a form of intense, inwardly individualized feeling, but above all as *new faculties*—'organs' as Stein puts it.

> Some people believe it necessary to create special institutions in order to 'keep the teaching pure', but for those who will incarnate later, this teaching is not only written in books, it is inscribed in our organs, and in the great Book of Life whose pages are turned by sacred powers very different from those of any 'Vorstand'. This teaching is written in our blood and pulsates within our veins. And to the extent that it has become an organ, to the extent it has become an integral part of ourselves through love, to that extent it will at the point of culmination realize itself in our willing, in our destiny and in our return. That is the miraculous work which is to be accomplished—*per spiritum sanctum reviviscimus.*

D.N. Dunlop was not given to expressing, in a direct or immediate way, the kind of spiritual decision which, in a Michaelic age of freedom, can only be weighed and actively taken in the innermost sanctuaries of the human ego. However, in the pages of this book we have presented a number of elements which lead us to suppose that, together with Polzer-Hoditz, Stein and of course many others who have left no specific literary statements, Dunlop too both felt and knew himself deeply connected with the Michael Prophecy. Indeed, from this point of view we may wish to glance back at the words he had already published in 1910 with regard to the end of the century. They speak of the 'great treasure' of individual freedom. As the foundation-stone of a future spiritual society it must be protected in its entirety and carried through all the tempests and struggles of the century. Its custodians will be those 'who are strong in sympathy and tolerance for a growing mankind . . . and who are determined not to give up that freedom . . . Only these will ultimately stand the shocks brought to bear upon the Society by the opposers of human development, both within and without our ranks' and form 'a nucleus of the universal brotherhood of mankind'.

Given the predicament in which our civilization finds itself today—the countless fundamental problems of unemployment, Third World debts, population growth, problems of nutrition and energy supplies, as well as a series of environmental catastrophes, just to mention what immediately comes to mind—it is likely that the individuality of D.N. Dunlop, united with Rudolf Steiner and many other friendly anthroposophical souls, will have a significant task to fulfil in the near future. At least we may presume that this individuality, with his particularly valuable 'old Western knowledge', is already inspirationally at work in an effort to help solve the great world problems of today. Have his unfulfilled intentions not remained seeds of future development, the realization of which was temporarily interrupted in 1935?

*

The following words, which Rudolf Steiner addressed to members of the Anthroposophical Society during a lecture in Arnheim on 19 and 20 July 1924,[304] represent a special kind of legacy. They can orientate us with regard to the whole impulse of the Anthroposophical Movement (which naturally also includes those anthroposophical souls no longer or not yet incarnated on the earth), and the important task it must accomplish in the world:

> Men must work together with the Gods, with Michael—Michael inspires men in order that there may appear on the Earth a spirituality

> consonant with the personal Intelligence of men, in order that one can be a thinker—and at the same time be a truly spiritual man. For this is primarily what Michael's dominion means. This is what must be wrestled for within the Anthroposophical Movement. And then those who are working today for the Anthroposophical Movement will appear again on Earth at the end of the twentieth century and will be united with those who were the great teachers of Chartres. For that is the agreement reached in that heavenly conference at the beginning of the thirteenth century, that the Aristotelians and the Platonists are to appear together, working for the ever-growing prosperity of the Anthroposophical Movement in the twentieth century, in order that at the end of this century, with Platonists and Aristotelians in unison, Anthroposophy may reach a certain culmination in earthly civilization. If it is possible to work in this way, in the way predestined by Michael, then Europe and modern civilization will emerge from decline. But verily in no other way than this! The leading of civilization out of decline is bound up with an understanding of Michael.

However, there is another aspect which must be taken into consideration as well: this 'leading of civilization out of decline' is also bound up with a great battle—one in the sphere of knowledge, which has to be waged against 'all kinds of demonic-Ahrimanic powers'. For today mankind is not only placed into a realm which is touched by the rays of Michael and the impulses of the Michaelic School in the supersensible world, it has also come into the sphere of influence of an 'opposing Ahrimanic School' which was founded parallel to the Michael School. This is a point Rudolf Steiner put forward with particular urgency during the lecture the following day:

> While Michael above was teaching his hosts, there was founded immediately below the surface of the Earth a kind of sub-earthly, Ahrimanic school. So one can say that the Michael School was in the super-earthly world; in the region directly beneath our feet—for the spiritual is also actively at work in the sub-earthly region—the opposing Ahrimanic school was founded. And in that particular period, when no impulses were streaming down from Michael bringing heavenly inspiration to the Intelligence, when the Intelligence on the Earth was, for the time being, left to itself, the

> Ahrimanic hosts strove all the harder to send their impulses up from below into the development of the Intelligence in mankind. It is a truly overwhelming picture that can stand before one's eyes. Let one imagine the Earth's surface—Michael above, teaching his hosts, revealing to them in mighty, cosmic language the ancient Initiate-Wisdom, and below, the Ahrimanic school in the sub-strata of the Earth. Upon the Earth, the Intelligence that has fallen from the Heavens is unfolding. Michael holding his school in heavenly isolation from the earthly world—no impulses stream down from above—and the Ahrimanic powers sending up their impulses with all the greater strength.

A point which may strike us as particularly illuminating in this description is the tremendous difference between the modes of action of these two spiritual powers. The free spirit of Michael is only accessible to the human being if he approaches it by himself, actually grasping and spiritualizing his earthly intelligence in total freedom of will—'no impulses stream down from above'. The Ahrimanic powers on the other hand try forcefully to prevent man from unfolding the spiritual activity of his free being. They know no restraints and intervene directly in that sphere which can potentially give birth to free and conscious activity, or has already given birth to it. They would like to see him deny the spirit and, in desperation, give himself over to the earth and all its powers—there to remain forever. But what are the principal means used by these Ahrimanic beings to achieve their ends? Firstly, they exploit the stream of fixed, mechanical spirituality which flows through the world today by means of the printed word. This very effective form of spirituality increasingly betrays the presence of two polar-opposite, contrasting elements. On the one hand it unleashes all those instinctive aspects of human nature which tend to deaden human consciousness; on the other, it trains the human being to adopt a coldly lucid, spiritually hostile form of intellectuality. However, even if it is true that in the future the most important things will be passed on 'by word of mouth', it is equally certain that no one who truly represents Anthroposophy can or indeed should try to avoid this mechanical art. Any attempt to do so would only mean 'delivering up the art of printing to the most powerful enemies of Michael wisdom; we should be making it impossible for our anthroposophical work to thrive, as thrive it must, until the end of the century is reached. What we must do is to ennoble the art of printing through our reverence for what lives there in the Michael wisdom. For what is it that Ahriman is intent upon achieving in opposition to Michael through the art of printing? Ahriman is intent upon conquest of the Intelligence. There is evidence of it everywhere today. Conquest of the Intelligence, which asserts itself wherever conditions are favourable.' And where in fact are these conditions most favourable? Wherever human beings do not form their thoughts, or feel, or act out of a self-possessed, clear-thinking state of consciousness but rather as a result of certain states of being in which, for some reason or other, ordinary waking consciousness has been dampened or 'lowered'. It is then that the most effective Ahrimanic attacks take place: 'We find that at the times when a diminution or lowering of the consciousness takes place in human beings, these Ahrimanic spirits then entrench themselves within human consciousness, they make men so to speak "possessed".'

Rudolf Steiner also makes clear what the effects of such diminished states of consciousness can be on the social level when doors are left open to negative forces: 'In the year 1914, many individuals in a lowered state of consciousness became entangled in the outbreak of the terrible World War. And within the lowered consciousness of such men the hosts of Ahriman promoted the World War—promoted it through human beings. The real causes of that War will not ever be brought to light by external documents contained in archives.'

Numerous events and phenomena connected with the origins of the Second World War, as well as many contemporary developments and occurrences, are inexplicable without this kind of spiritual-scientific analysis, as no unprejudiced spectator of twentieth-century history will be likely to deny.

The efforts undertaken by the anti-Michaelic demonic beings hitherto have been mighty indeed. However, the following words (which immediately follow Rudolf Steiner's allusion to 'the leading of civilization out of decline' and the necessity of 'understanding Michael') make it perfectly clear that the efforts of these beings in the near future will, in a certain sense, become even greater:

> I have now led you towards an understanding of the Michael Mystery which at present reigns over the thinking and the spiritual strivings of mankind. This means that . . . through Anthroposophy something must be introduced into the spiritual evolution of the Earth, for all kinds of demonic-Ahrimanic powers are taking possession of men. The Ahrimanic powers in many a human body were exultant in their confidence that it would no longer be possible for Michael to take over his rulership of the Cosmic Intelligence which had fallen down to the Earth. And this exultation was particularly strong in the middle of the nineteenth century, when Ahriman already believed that Michael will not again recover his former Cosmic Intelligence which had found its way from the heavens to the Earth . . . It is a great matter, it is a tremendous matter!

*

Let us also recall at this point some words which Dunlop addressed to E.C. Merry shortly before his death. Viewed from a historical distance, the supra-personal import of these words may now appear as a kind of encouraging 'plea' to all those who have actively placed themselves within the stream of the Anthroposophical Movement:

> May we not look together upon the wonderful battle going on where our 'shadows' are—the cosmic battle between Ahriman and Michael. I can see Michael's majesty as He waits for our help to give Him back His power. And He does not wait in vain . . . He does not wait in vain!

Are not these the words of one who understands and *fights* for the Michaelic Cause? One who is aware of the cosmic battle raging behind the scenes, behind the various civilizational conflicts of our times? And one whose will and determination to sway the tide of battle in favour of Michael has become as strong and steadfast as a rock of granite? At all events, not long after the *beginning* of this century, in early 1912,[305] D.N. Dunlop wrote the following lines, and we, who now find ourselves at a short distance from the *end* of the century, may well reflect on his words as we approach the threshold of a millennium:

> The most wonderful relationships that occur are between those who are following the path of spiritual unfoldment. They began in the beginning and have been going on through all the ages ever since. That relationship, where one is the teacher in one incarnation and the pupil in the next, is characterized by an immortal sympathy which nothing can obliterate. Through all the mixture of blood, races, families, tribes, these kindred spirits find each other, and their relationships are not determined so much by degrees of knowledge, as by the spirit of the work in which they are engaged.

APPENDIX

That is something which every anthroposophist should have written before his soul: the fact that initiative forms an integral part of his karma, and that much of what he encounters will depend on the extent to which he is actively *able to bring these initiatives to consciousness.* *Rudolf Steiner, 4 August 1924*

Chronological Table of Events

1841 The battle of the Spirits of Darkness begins.

1861 27 February: Rudolf Steiner is born in Kraljevec.

1865 13 June: William Butler Yeats is born.

1867 10 April: George William Russell (AE) is born.
28 July: Alexander Dunlop marries Catherine Nicol at Kildonan (Isle of Arran)

1868 28 December: Birth of D.N. Dunlop at 3 Clark Street, Kilmarnock.

1873 (?) Death of Catherine, the mother. D.N.D. is put in the care of his grandfather on the Isle of Arran.

1875 17 November: H.P. Blavatsky and Colonel Olcott found the Theosophical Society.

1876 17 December: Eleanor Charlotte Kynaston is born in Eton.—D.N.D. attends school in Kildonan.

1876 (?) D.N.D. proclaims the Logos from the prologue of St John's Gospel, to a circle of 12 friends.

1879 November: the Fall of the Spirits of Darkness; the beginning of Michael's rulership.

1882 30 June: the grandfather Daniel Nicol dies at the age of 78 in Kildonan (Arran). D.N.D.'s Imaginative experience. He moves to Ardrossan where his father is working as an architect and attends the Ardrossan Academy, South Beach.

1885 (?) Apprenticeship period in an office of the Howe Machine Company in Ardrossan. D.N.D. discovers a 'World History'. Following a dispute with his father he leaves Ardrossan.

1886–7 Glasgow period. D.N.D. works as an employee in a bicycle shop; he reads historical, philosophical and occult works.

1887 D.N.D. meets AE during a visit to Ireland about the time of his first lunar node (in July).

1888–9 First journey to America; meetings with the American (Swedenborgian and mystic) Thomas Lake Harris, whom he may have known from Ireland. D.N.D. moves to Dublin; as proprietor of a vegetarian restaurant he works to begin with as wine and tea merchant, then as a clerk in an insurance company.

1891 He moves into the Theosophical Lodge at No. 3, Upper Ely Place, which is run by the engineer Frederick J. Dick. Study group on H.P. Blavatsky's *Secret Doctrine*.

8 May: H.P. Blavatsky dies in London. Probably between May and August: Dunlop's nocturnal visionary experience, as described by AE in *The Secret of Power*.

July: first meeting with AE's friend Yeats, an occasional visitor.

12 August: D.N. Dunlop marries Eleanor Fitzpatrick.

30 September: D.N.D.'s first lecture—'Buddha and Christ'.

Autumn (?): D.N.D. moves out of Ely Place and takes up lodgings with his wife at Drumcondra Road.

1892 January: birth of D.N.D.'s first child, Edith (later Young).

October: the first issue of the magazine *The Irish Theosophist* appears.

1893 Together with AE and Yeats, D.N.D. attends the Convention of the European Section of the TS in London.

1894 June: birth of Ronald, D.N.D.'s only son (later a painter).

1895 (?) D.N.D becomes general secretary of the Cooney Manufacturing Company.

1896 21 March: William Quin Judge dies.

26–27 April: D.N.D. attends the Theosophical Convention in New York; he meets Catherine Tingley, Judge's successor in America, for the first time. He also visits Canada.

July: Tingley's 'crusaders' arrive in Ireland.

1897 D.N.D. attends Theosophical Conventions in New York (April), Philadelphia (May), and Stockholm (August).

September: last issue of *The Irish Theosophist*. D.N.D. moves with family to New York; he works in the Pierce and Miller Engineering Company and also in his spare time as private secretary for Tingley, writing numerous articles in *The Crusader* and *The New Century*. First meeting with his (later) friend H.W. Percival (?)

1898 19 February: D.N.D. present at the first constitutional congress of the Universal Brotherhood founded by Tingley in 1896. He becomes one of 12 members of the 'cabinet'.

1899 Autumn: D.N.D. moves to London and works for the Westinghouse firm—from 1902 onwards as sole manager of the European publishing department.

1900 June: birth of second daughter, Aileen (later eurythmist). The family lives at Wandsworth.

1901 D.N.D. becomes President of the newly founded Battersea Lodge.

1902 D.N.D. begins to contribute numerous articles ('From a Student's Easy Chair') to *The Theosophical Review*.

1903 Yeats introduces James Joyce to D.N.D. in London.

1904 June: D.N.D. attends European Federation Congress of the TS in Amsterdam.

1905 July: D.N.D. attends the European Federation Congress of the TS in London.

1906 June: D.N.D. attends the European Federation Congress of the TS in Paris. He lectures on William Morris. First meeting with Rudolf Steiner (?)

1907 17 February: H.S. Olcott, co-founder of the TS, dies at Adyar.

1909 D.N.D. launches the idea of theosophical summer schools in *The Vahan*.

1910 D.N.D. opens the Blavatsky Institute in Hale, Cheshire. It is visited by Annie Besant amongst others and exists until the outbreak of the First World War. D.N.D. gives regular lecture courses on Theosophy. Some of this material is published in *The Path* (1909–14) which he co-edits with Charles Lazenby. (1910–13) D.N.D. organizes five theosophical summer schools. Significant articles from this period: 'The Function of Mind', 'The Christ-Drama', 'Some Symbols of Magic', 'Friendship'.

1911 Founding of the 'Star in the East': attempts are made to proclaim Krishnamurti as World-Teacher.
D.N.D. founds the British Electrical and Allied Manufacturer's Association.

1912 October: D.N.D. begins to reprint a series of articles on the zodiac by H.W. Percival, editor of *The Word*.

1913 AE publishes his *Collected Poems*, dedicating them to D.N.D.

1915 The monthly magazine *BEAMA* comes out. From 1923 onwards it appears under the title *World Power*.

1916 D.N.D. publishes his books *British Destiny* and *The Path of Attainment*.
Foundation of the Federation of British Industries.

1918 *The Science of Immortality* comes out. D.N.D. directs the anthroposophical Human Freedom Group which meets every week.

1919 D.N.D. opens the second Annual Conference of the Braille and Servers of the Blind League with a lecture entitled *Duty*.
(Probably towards the end of the year): *The Path of Knowledge* comes out. It contains the first reference to Rudolf Steiner's *Occult Science*. Foundation of the Electrical Research Association.

1920 At the Annual Convention: D.N.D. gives a lecture on *Nature-Spirits and the Spirits of the Elements*.
14 December: D.N.D. applies for membership of the Anthroposophical Society.
Foundation of the Electrical Research Association.

1922 January: Within the Human Freedom Group: first meeting between D.N.D. and E.C. Merry.
April: Josef van Leer introduces D.N.D. to Rudolf Steiner in London—probably between 14 and 16 April.
8 May: D.N.D. withdraws from the TS.
August: E.C. Merry meets Rudolf Steiner for the first time in Oxford.
November: Rudolf Steiner visits the bedridden Dunlop at his home in Wimbledon. Birth of the idea of summer courses and a series of 'World Conferences'. On 19 November D.N.D. asks Rudolf Steiner to take over the presidency of the Anthroposophical Society in Great Britain.

1923 18–31 August: Within the framework of a First International Summer School in Penmaenmawr Rudolf Steiner gives the cycle of lectures *The Evolution of Consciousness*.
2 September: foundation of the Anthroposophical Society in Great Britain. Harry Collison is elected General Secretary.
24 December–1 January 1924: Christmas Conference: foundation of the General Anthroposophical Society.

1924 30 June: H.R.H. The Prince of Wales opens the first World Power Conference in London. The conference ends on 12 July.
11–22 August: Rudolf Steiner gives the cycle of lectures *True and False Paths in Spiritual Investigation* at the second International Summer School in Torquay. He asks D.N.D. to see to it that the book he had compiled with Ita Wegman's collabora-

tion, *Fundamentals of Therapy*, is published in English. Before the year is out, Dunlop founds the British Weleda Company.
17 August: Rudolf Steiner visits Tintagel with a group of friends (including D.N.D. and E.C.M.).
End of August: leave-taking in London.
September: third lunar node in D.N.D.'s life.

1925 30 March: Rudolf Steiner dies in Dornach.

1926 30 August–8 September: First Sectional Meeting of the World Power Conference in Basel.

1927 24 July–5 August: Third International Summer School at Gareloch, Scotland. The theme is 'Health and Disease'.

1928 20 July: inauguration of the first Anthroposophical World Conference in London. The conference ends on 1 August. Michaelmas: opening ceremonies of the Second Goethenum in Dornach.

1929 The comprehensive survey *Power Resources of the World* is published with a Foreword by D.N.D.
Towards the end of the year Harry Collison and his supporters withdraw from the Anthroposophical Society in Great Britain.

1930 January: D.N.D. is re-elected General Secretary of the Anthroposophical Society in Great Britain.
First half of the year: D.N.D. falls seriously ill.
June: Second Plenary Meeting of the World Power Conference in Berlin.
August: Kamp Stakenberg in Holland.

1932 21 January: death of D.N.D.'s wife Eleanor.
3 February: death of AE's wife Violet.
March: W.J. Stein undertakes a one-month lecturing-tour in England. D.N.D. founds a World Economic Association in Birmingham. June: in view of an attack made by Boos he considers founding an International Association for the Advancement of Spiritual Science.
July: Anthroposophical Youth Conference in Glastonbury.

1933 6 June: D.N.D. invites W.J. Stein to come to England. Anthroposophical Summer School in Bangor (Wales).

1934 27–28 March: General Meeting of the Anthroposophical Society in Dornach. In reply to a motion to change the Statutes a number of members present a 'Declaration of Will'. The meeting ends with the resolution of the membership to accept the decisions made by Albert Steffen, Marie Steiner and

Guenther Wachsmuth as binding decisions of the whole *Vorstand*.

July: founding of the 'United Free Anthroposophical Groups' in Stuttgart.

21–31 August: Anthroposophical Summer School in Westonbirt. D.N.D. is interviewed by W.J. Stein.

1935 April: first number of the magazine *World Survey*.

At the General Meeting of the Anthroposophical Society in Dornach, Ita Wegman and Elizabeth Vreede are expelled from the *Vorstand* and a number of leading anthroposophists from the Society, including D.N.D. The Anthroposophical Society in Great Britain is also severed *in toto* from the General Anthroposophical Society.

30 May: Daniel Nicol Dunlop dies in London.

17 July: AE dies in Bournemouth.

12–23 August: Harrogate Summer School.

1939 28 January: death of W.B. Yeats.

29 November: death of Eugen Kolisko in London.

1943 4 March: death of Ita Wegman.

31 August: death of Elizabeth Vreede.

1948 At the General Meeting of the Anthroposophical Society in Dornach the expulsion decisions of 1935 are unanimously rescinded.

27 December: death of Marie Steiner.

1956 16 June: death of E.C. Merry.

1957 7 July: W.J. Stein dies in London.

1963 The Anthroposophical Society in Great Britain rejoins the General Anthroposophical Society.

1968 The World Power Conference is renamed World Energy Conference.

1980 Eleventh Congress of the World Energy Conference in Munich with Peter von Siemens as acting President.

1986 Thirteenth Congress of the World Energy Conference in Cannes.

1989 Fourteenth Congress of the World Energy Conference in Montreal.

1990 The World Energy Conference is renamed World Energy Council.

D.N. Dunlop: Interview with W.B. Yeats

A few evenings ago I called on my friend, Mr. W.B. Yeats, and found him alone, seated in his arm-chair, smoking his cigarette, with a volume of Homer before him. The whole room indicated the style and taste peculiar to its presiding genius. Upon the walls hung various designs by Blake and other less well-known symbolic artists; everywhere books and papers, in apparently endless profusion.

In his usual genial way he invited me to have a cup of tea with him. During this pleasant ceremony little was said, but sufficient to impress me more than ever with the fact that my host was supremely an artist, much in love with his art. With a passion deep and entrancing he adores his art: 'his bread is from her lips; his exhilaration from the taste of her.' The Muse finds in him a tongue to respond to her most subtle beauties. In song was handed down the great Solar Religion that advanced the people of antiquity; in song those of a later day received that which caused them to emerge from their cold isolation and kiss 'the warm lips of Helios'; and in these days, too, we look to the poets for that inspiration which will

'Overflow mankind with true desires,
And guide new Ages on by flights of living Lyres.'

Tea over, I disclosed the object of my visit. 'Mr. Yeats,' I said, 'I understand that you saw a great deal of Madame Blavatsky in the earlier days of the Theosophical movement in England, and so I thought you might have something to say regarding her, which would interest the readers of the *Irish Theosophist.*'

'Yes,' replied Mr. Yeats, 'I had the privilege of seeing Madame Blavatsky frequently at that time, and so many interesting little incidents crowd in upon me, that I find some difficulty in selecting what might be most interesting to your readers.'

'Well,' I replied, 'suppose you begin by giving your personal impressions.'

'Madame Blavatsky,' said Mr. Yeats, 'struck me as being a very strong character. In her ordinary moods, rather combative, and inclined to rub people's prejudices the other way. When depressed, she dropped her combativeness, and, thrown back on herself, as it were, became most interesting, and talked about her own life. A clever American, who was not a Theosophist, said to me once: "Madame Blavatsky has become the most famous woman in the whole world, by sitting in her arm-chair, and getting people to talk to her." '

'I have heard it stated,' said I, 'in connection with the Coloumb incidents,[305] that Madame Blavatsky showed great lack of insight into character.'

'For so powerful a personality,' replied Mr. Yeats, 'she did seem to lack something in that respect. I remember, for instance, on one occasion she introduced me to a French occultist, whom she spoke of very highly, and even urged me to read his books. Within a short time he was expelled from the Society for what appeared excellent reasons. "I have had to expel him," said Madame Blavatsky to me; "he sold a love elixir for two francs; had it been forty francs I might have overlooked the fact." On another occasion she told me, quite seriously, that I would have a severe illness within six months, and I am waiting for that illness still. Attempts are made by people very often,' continued Mr. Yeats, 'to wash humanity out of their leaders. Madame Blavatsky made mistakes; she was human, and to me that fact makes her, if possible, the more interesting. Another peculiarity was her evident lack of proportion. An attack on the Theosophical movement (she did not seem to mind personal attacks) in some obscure little paper, was to her of as much importance as if it appeared in the *Times*.' In reply to another question, Mr. Yeats remarked that she had met De Musset a few times, and Balzac once. She had worked a little at occultism with George Sand, but, to use her own words, both were "mere dabblers" at the time.

'What did you think of Madame Blavatsky as a talker?' I asked.

'It has been said of Dr. Johnson,' replied Mr. Yeats, 'that the effeminate reader is repelled by him; and the same might be said of Madame Blavatsky as a talker. She had that kind of faculty which repelled the weak, and attracted those of a stronger temperament. She hated paradox, and yet she gave utterance to the most magnificent paradox I ever heard.'

'As you heard her talk a good deal, perhaps you will kindly relate to me any interesting sayings that occur to you,' said I.

'With pleasure,' replied Mr. Yeats, lighting another cigarette. 'I called on Madame Blavatsky one day, with a friend—a T.C.D. man. She was trying to explain to us the nature of the Akas,[307] and was entering into an exceedingly subtle metaphysical analysis of the difference between foreknowledge and predestination—a problem which has interested theologians of ancient, as well as modern times—showing the way in which the whole question was mixed up with the question of the Akas, when suddenly she broke off—my friend not following, and said, turning round, and pointing to one of her followers who was present: "You with your spectacles and your impudence, you will be sitting there in the Akas to all eternity—no not to all eternity, for a day will come when even the Akas will pass away, and then there shall be nothing but God—Chaos—that which every man is seeking in his heart."

'At another time, when I called, she seemed rather depressed. "Ah!" she said, "there is no solidarity among the good; there is only solidarity among the evil. There was a time when I used to blame and pity the people who sold their souls to the devil, now I only pity them; I know why they do it; they do it to have somebody on their side. As for me I write, write, write, as the Wandering Jew walks, walks, walks."

'On one occasion, too,' said Mr. Yeats, continuing, 'she referred to the Greek Church as the church of her childhood, saying: "The Greek Church, like all true religions, was a triangle, but it spread out and became a bramble bush, and that is the Church of Rome; then they came and lopped off the branches, and turned it into a broomstick, and that is Protestantism."

In reply to a question, Mr. Yeats said, quoting her own words, with reference to Col. Olcott:[308] 'Ah! *he* is an honest man; I am an old Russian savage'; and, referring to Mr. Old, she said, with a hearty enthusiasm that, in certain respects, he was above all those about her at that time.

'Can you remember anything in the nature of a prophecy, Mr. Yeats, made by Madame Blavatsky, that might be of interest to record, notwithstanding the fact that you are yet awaiting your prophesied illness?' I asked.

'The only thing of that nature,' replied Mr. Yeats, 'was a reference to England. "The Master told me," said she, "that the power of England would not outlive the century, and the Master never deceived me."

'I am very much obliged to you, Mr. Yeats,' said I, 'for the kind manner in which you have responded to my enquiries regarding Madame Blavatsky; perhaps you will pardon me if I ask you one or two questions about your own work now. Do you intend, at any time, publishing a book on "Mysticism"?'

'Yes; at no very distant date I hope to publish a work dealing with mystics I have seen, and stories I have heard, but it will be as an artist, not as a controversialist.'

'And what about your present work?' I asked.

'*Celtic Twilight*,[309] a work dealing with ghosts, goblins, and faeries, will be out shortly; also a small selection of *Blake's Poems*,' he replied. 'Then, I am getting ready for publication, next spring, a book of poems, which I intend calling, *The Wind among the Reeds*;[310] and, as soon afterwards as possible, a collection of essays, and lectures dealing with Irish nationality and literature, which will probably appear under the title of "The Watch Fire".'[311]

After due apologies for my intrusion, I bade my host good evening, and withdrew feeling more than satisfied with the result of my interview.

Mr. Yeats has often been spoken of as a dreamer, and many strange stories are afloat which go a long way to bear out such a statement. But, in my opinion, he combines the man of thought with the man of action; he is 'whole of heart and sound of head', and Ireland may, indeed, be proud of one who promises to rank among her most worthy sons.

H.R.H. The Prince of Wales: Opening Speech at the Inauguration of the World Power Conference on 30 June 1924

It is with great pleasure that, as President of the British Empire Exhibition, I now welcome the delegates who are assembled in session to discuss the many vital problems connected with the first World Power Conference. I feel this to be an occasion of great importance, for it may prove the beginning of a series of conferences, whereby the combined knowledge and judgment of the world may be devoted to the solution of the many difficulties confronting, not only science and research, but also economic progress throughout the world. We have become accustomed to the idea of an international clearing-house for many things, and in the League of Nations, with its Labour Office and International Court of Justice, have seen international co-operation at work in political and labour questions and in law; but the deeper questions connected with industrial progress and equipment, with natural resources, with the conservation of energy and of fuel, with standardization in design and manufacture, have hitherto, I believe, been examined by each country in isolation, with results that are apparent to everyone. In this effort to create for industry, and especially power, what the League of Nations intends for politics, lies, I think, the true significance of the World Power Conference, and, in the belief that something more fundamental than merely technical discussions will result, I extend a cordial welcome to the distinguished representatives here to-day.

The study of power, if we consider only the technical aspect, is still in a comparatively elementary stage; no effort has hitherto been made to find out on what foundations our present industrial structure is built, and what part power plays in this structure. It is difficult to conceive any modern industry where power in some shape or form does not play a part. Power, whether in the form of steam, gas, oil, water, or electricity, is the one great instrument in the possession of man by which he is capable of extracting from nature everything of value that nature can offer, and of converting this natural wealth into something of immediate use. As one expert says: 'The social structure itself is in a sense bound up with the effective use of power for industrial purposes, and there are many reasons to support the view that the weakness of the social structure in an industrial State is due to inefficient or inadequate utilization of power.'

You are all familiar with the main objects of the World Power Conference, and have each in your own degree contributed to our knowledge of certain aspects, so that it is unnecessary for me to discuss the matter in detail; but there is one consideration which has specially appealed to me. You each represent the views of the main countries of the world on certain questions relating to power. Though your individual views may not necessarily coincide, the mere fact of discussion, in an atmosphere of cordial appreciation, must do much to tighten those personal contacts which form the inspiring motive of progress in every great activity connected with the modern industrial State, in finance as well as in science and in research. All three, finance, science, and research, are universal, but the utilization of the results derived from those three activities is not universal, and in this disparity lies one of the greatest obstacles to progress. We should find inspiration in the vision of over thirty countries here contributing, each in its highest capacity, to the discussion of one subject of more than merely temporary importance. You are at grips with fundamentals and from your deliberations will result the first enunciation of a policy applied internationally, which may contribute very largely to the harmony and economic progress of the world.

You have before you, in the reports submitted to the World Power Conference, the raw material for a survey of the power resources of the world; you can now explore many countries which have hitherto been veiled in mystery, and assess at their true value the possibilities of an immense industrial development in many of them; you may from this material erect the structure which will go beyond the confines of one country, or group of countries, and include all those parts of the world where man can hope to prosper. International co-operation may emerge from the realm of the ideal, into the realm of practical utilization, as the result of your deliberations, and I sincerely trust that full success will attend them.

Collison–Dunlop–Marie Steiner: Correspondence

For the Information of Members of the Anthroposophical Society in Great Britain*

Notice from the Executive Council

It is necessary to explain to Members of the Anthroposophical Society in Great Britain the position as regards the 'Anthroposophic News Sheet' now being published at the Goetheanum, and its effect upon our own News Sheet, which has been published for ten years, and upon our Quarterly magazine, published for eight years. We are of opinion that the best and fairest way of conveying the necessary information is to publish in full the communications that have passed on this matter in order that the circumstances may be completely understood.

The first official indication of the decision taken to publish a News Sheet for English-speaking members from the Headquarters of the General Anthroposophical Society was the following letter:

* Published in *Anthroposophical Movement*, Vol. X, No. 22, November 1933.

2nd September, 1933

D.N. Dunlop, Esq.,
35 Park Road,
London, N.W.1.

Dear Mr. Dunlop,

In order to give English-speaking members all over the world the opportunity of a closer contact with the centre of the anthroposophic movement, the Goetheanum at Dornach, and at the express desire of English-speaking members in various countries, it has been decided to bring out every week an English edition of the News Sheet for members founded by Rudolf Steiner ten years ago under the German title: 'Was in der anthroposophischen Bewegung vorgeht: Nachrichten für deren Mitglieder,' and published at Headquarters. The English edition will also be published at Headquarters by the General Anthroposophical Society under the title of 'Anthroposophic News Sheet,' and it is hoped that English-speaking members will look upon it as their central organ and give it their support. No doubt you will be able to appreciate the importance of the initiative which has been taken.

A communication to this effect is being sent to all English-speaking members whose addresses are available at Dornach. The first number of the 'Anthroposophic News Sheet' will appear at Michaelmas.

Yours sincerely,

(Signed) ALBERT STEFFEN.
MARIE STEINER.
DR. GUENTHER WACHSMUTH.

The printed circular announcing the new publication is as follows:

GOETHEANUM.
SCHOOL FOR SPIRITUAL ACTIVITY IN SCIENCE AND ART.
Dornach, near Basle, Switzerland.

To the English-speaking members of the General Anthroposophical Society.

September, 1933.

At the express desire of English-speaking members in various countries, the initiative has been taken of bringing out a weekly anthroposophic news sheet for English-speaking members throughout the world, published at Headquarters by the General Anthroposophical Society, Dornach, Switzerland, under the title of 'Anthroposophic News Sheet'.

It will consist of translations of all articles contained in the Dornach news sheet (German title: 'Was in der anthroposophischen Gesellschaft vorgeht: Nachrichten für deren Mitglieder') founded by Rudolf Steiner ten years ago, and, in part, of English extracts from the weekly paper 'Das Goetheanum,' also founded by Rudolf Steiner and published at Headquarters.

Six or more *Supplements* will appear annually. By kind permission of Frau Marie Steiner, each supplement will *contain a complete lecture by Rudolf Steiner*, in addition to Rudolf Steiner's lectures appearing in the weekly News Sheets.

Subscribing members will therefore enjoy the advantage of obtaining at regular intervals lectures by Rudolf Steiner and news of the events taking place within the Society. English translations of Rudolf Steiner's lectures will in future be confined to this Anthroposophic News Sheet published at Headquarters as a central organ for English-speaking members throughout the world.

The Anthroposophic News Sheet may also be used by English-speaking members in various countries for the publication of communications and notices of special interest.

The annual subscription without the Supplements will amount to 15 Swiss Francs, with the Supplements to 17 Swiss Francs.

All communications regarding subscriptions, notices to be included, etc., should be addressed to the office of the Anthroposophic News Sheet, Goetheanum, Dornach, Switzerland, c/o Miss Dora Baker.

Accompanying words. By Albert Steffen.

Before and after the Christmas Foundation Assembly, Rudolf Steiner has always referred to the Goetheanum as the centre of the anthroposophical movement. He created the first 'Bau' (Building) as a work of peace in the midst of the great war, in collaboration with people belonging to all the nations that were fighting against each other on the battlefields. When the old Goetheanum was consumed by the enemy's fire-flames on New Year's Eve of 1922–23, he formed the model of the second Building; with united strength we will complete it, as his legacy.

Again, after the new foundation of the General Anthroposophical Society, he said that the centre of spiritual life had to be looked for in the Goetheanum at Dornach.

'Anthroposophy is a way of knowledge, seeking to lead the spiritual in man to the spiritual in the universe'—thus begins the first guiding sentence to members. The essential being of anthroposophy is of a universally human kind, and its methods appeal to the single human being, no matter where he may stand in life according to his destiny, no matter within which profession or nation he may have to fulfil his duties. No two human beings are alike, but this very difference should unite anthroposophists, for it completes, enriches and widens them, whereas in the case of non-anthroposophists it generally divides them. Why is this? Because it is given to us to realize that just as the Sun is the one source of light for the whole earth, so can Anthroposophy, the Wisdom of Man, be found only in the *one* truth. May this spirit be the fertile soil on which the News Sheet for English-speaking members will shoot up and grow. Whether it will thrive—this will depend on the hearts of those who love the Goetheanum.

Miss Dora Baker ensures its good success, through the activity she has carried out thus far, through her connections with English-speaking collaborators and the perfect knowledge of the languages in question.

We consider it a good omen that the first number can already appear at Michaelmas.'

*

This circular was sent from the Goetheanum direct to Leaders of Groups outside London without any covering letter and a certain number of copies were sent to Mr. Dunlop at Rudolf Steiner House for the London Groups.

At a special meeting held at the Rudolf Steiner House on October 1st, the above circular and matters arising therefrom were discussed with Leaders of Groups. Careful consideration has since been given by the Executive Council to a matter which so directly affects our own publications.

On October 16th, the following letter was received from Mr. Collison, withdrawing permission for the publication of English translations of lectures by Dr. Steiner in our periodicals—'Anthroposophical Movement' (our fortnightly News Sheet) and 'Anthroposophy' (Quarterly):—

25 Hereford Square, S.W.7,
14th October, 1933.

Dear Mr. Dunlop,

I regret to have to call your attention to what seems to have been overlooked, namely, my consent to the publication of the translation of an article of Dr. Steiner's appearing in No. 6 Supplement to the 'Anthroposophical Movement,' Vol. X, No. 18. I do not remember having been asked, and I generally make a note. No doubt you will be able to give me the explanation.

I have also to inform you that the initiative has been taken to bring out a weekly Anthroposophic News Sheet for English-speaking members, published at Headquarters by the General Anthroposophic Society, Dornach, and the first number appeared at Michaelmas.

To avoid unnecessary overlapping and duplication the English translations of Rudolf Steiner's lectures in periodicals will in future be confined to this publication emanating from the central authority.

Yours sincerely,

(*Signed*) H. COLLISON.

To this letter from Mr. Collison the following reply was sent:

Rudolf Steiner House,
35 Park Road,
London, N.W.1,

October 18th, 1933.

Dear Mr. Collison,

Miss Osmond has handed me your letter of October 14th. You must be aware that the procedure with regard to the publication of Dr. Steiner's lecture in the News Sheet Supplement (No. 6) is exactly the same as that followed for many years. We have never been in the habit of asking your permission for each individual lecture published in the News Sheet Supplements, as you gave this permission many years ago, and until now, although these lectures have been coming out quite regularly, you have never once taken exception to this procedure, neither have you objected to their publication. Indeed, you will remember that early in the year 1932 you raised the question with me of paying a royalty to Frau Dr. Steiner for these News Sheet Supplement lectures in addition to the royalty for lectures published in the Quarterly. I wrote to Frau Dr. Steiner on the subject but received no reply. I hope you will find this explanation satisfactory.

With regard to the second and third paragraphs of your letter, it was, of course, clearly indicated in the May number of the Anthroposophic News Sheet published by you that some arrangement of this kind was already then in contemplation. Later on I received a letter dated 2nd September, signed by Herr Steffen, Frau Dr. Steiner and Dr. Wachsmuth, telling me a little more fully what you now state in your letter, but in this letter from the three Members of the Vorstand no reference was made to the fact that, as stated in your letter, 'to avoid unnecessary overlapping and duplication, the English translation of Rudolf Steiner's Lectures in periodicals will in future be confined to this publication emanating from the central authority.' This matter was only referred to in the printed circular sent to Group Leaders in this country.

It was naturally a surprise to us that a step which so seriously affects a Group of the General Anthroposophical Society—the Anthroposophical Society in Great Britain—should have been taken in this way.

In answer to the third paragraph of your letter, while it is possible that lectures published in our News Sheet might overlap with those it has now been decided to publish from Dornach, this does not in any way apply to the Quarterly. This latter periodical is sold to the public, whereas the new Anthroposophic News Sheet is being confined to Members of the General Anthroposophical Society. The reason you give, therefore, and which in your letter to Miss Osmond of the same date is applied to the Quarterly as well, namely, 'the avoidance of unnecessary overlapping and duplication,' can hardly be said to hold good. Will you tell me whether you think there is any possibility of the decision being reconsidered in the case of anthroposophical periodicals which are sold to the public?

I am sending copies of this correspondence to the Members of the Vorstand at the Goetheanum.

Yours sincerely,

(*Signed*) D.N. DUNLOP,
General Secretary.

Mr. Collison's reply to the above letter is as follows:

25 Hereford Square, S.W.7,
23rd October, 1933.

Dear Mr. Dunlop,

I have to thank you for your letter of 18th October and for reminding me of the arrangements for lectures in your News Sheet. It is quite correct.

Since you have sent the correspondence to Dornach it is as well to await their reply. Meantime I must abide by the ruling on Dr. Steiner's lectures and cancel any previous permission.

Yours sincerely,

(*Signed*) H. COLLISON.

Copies of Mr. Collison's letter dated October 14th and of Mr. Dunlop's reply dated October 18th were sent to all Members of the Vorstand, the following individual letter being sent to Frau Dr. Steiner:—

Rudolf Steiner House,
35 Park Road,
London, N.W.1,
October 18th, 1933.

Dear Frau Dr. Steiner,

With reference to the changes consequent upon the decision to publish the 'Anthroposophic News Sheet' from the Goetheanum, I enclose for your information copies of letters from Mr. Collison dated October 14th, one addressed to Miss Osmond and one to myself, and also a copy of my reply.

If Mr. Collison's action is in line with your wishes, then I can only say that I regret very deeply that we should thus suddenly be deprived of the inestimable benefit of publishing for Members of the Society and also for the public, English translations of Dr. Steiner's lectures. I do hope that you will consider continuing the permission hitherto given in connection at least with anthroposophical periodicals sold to the public, such as our Quarterly magazine.

Yours sincerely,

(*Signed*) D.N. DUNLOP.

At the time of going to press no reply has been received to the above letter.

A letter has been sent to the three Members of the Vorstand who signed the letter dated September 2nd (see above), and to Mr. Collison, advising them of the decision taken by the Executive Council to publish the correspondence, for the reason given in the first paragraph of this notice.

The Executive Council have also decided to continue the publication of our own News Sheet, 'Anthroposophical Movement', and of our Quarterly, 'Anthroposophy.'

For the Executive Council:

D. N. DUNLOP,
General Secretary.

W.J. Stein: A Letter to F. Zur Nedden[312]

36 Kingsway, London W.C.2.

4 June 1935

Dear Sir,

Most respectful thanks for having written and for the assurance that you are ready to intercede in favour of retaining the headquarters of the World Power Conference in London. It is certainly a point of great importance. For not only does London have all the necessary scientific aids such as libraries, it also provides essential connections to industries and organizations. Moreover, from a psychological point of view, England is better suited under present world-conditions than most other countries for this purpose. Lastly, continuity is an important factor. Mr. Dunlop expressed no last wishes and I had the impression that for him the best guarantee of continuity was to be found in human beings rather than in anything that could be written down in fixed terms. He believed in humanity and for him the living human being was the *real* continuous factor. It will certainly not be easy to preserve all that Dunlop achieved during his life and still more difficult to gradually realize what was only planned. Mr. Dunlop was silent; he liked to weigh his plans in stillness, to wait a long time and then, in the objectively and psychologically right moment, to transform into deeds as much as seemed possible to him. I had the good fortune to be so to speak 'educated' by him. And he instructed more by his exemplary attitude to things than by the words he spoke; more by goodness than by forceful urgency, more by a simple ability to wait than by any haste in action.

He was full of plans, and every now and then he would give those near to him a glimmering of what it was he was planning. I will try to relate something of what I assimilated from our conversations which might, perhaps, be of importance for the future. He was convinced that the right kind of organization demanded that one bide one's time, that one wait for the moment when what had to be done was so to speak 'in the air'. 'Now anyone could really see it', he would say. When things had reached this stage one could act. And one was acting in accordance with an evolutionary necessity. Not out of egoistic or other petty motives. Such knowledge gave him the power to wait. As a much younger man this was something that really astounded me. He waited, waited and then suddenly everything was there—others were actually *doing* what he had been planning for so long, for it was indeed time that it happened.

When one did anything with Mr. Dunlop one felt freer than if one did it quite alone. For there was something about his interest and his love that encouraged you to unfold your real self. At the crematorium there were so many flowers that it was impossible to bring them all into the chapel. More than half of them lay outside in front of the door and people passing by paused to ask who had died and what manner of man it was. They had been sent by individual persons and corporations alike and people of all ages and classes were amongst the mourners. Two memorial addresses were given by two friends. Dr. Zeylmans van Emmichoven, a Dutchman, spoke for those on the Continent and Mr. Wheeler, an Englishman for Dunlop's English friends.[313]

Nearly all his employees were there and countless friends. Many had come from the Continent. In these speeches again this point was touched on—that he made people so free. That is why he had everybody's confidence as an organizer. One knew that if *he* did it, it would be done in such a way that everything of relevance and importance would be treated and there would be no room for personal considerations. Mr. Dunlop was a great admirer of German culture. He had a deep, inner belief in the kinship between Germans and Anglo-Saxons. He often spoke of an Anglo-Saxon-Germanic culture. For him it was an absurdity to consider England and Germany as not belonging together. In his actions he was extremely well-disposed towards Germany, but if ever one asked him whether he was a 'Germanophile' he would reply: 'I'm only being fair. If you deprive one country of its full possibilities then you deprive everyone of them.' Such ideas as this won him many friends in Germany. And to all of them he had personal, human relationships.

When I asked him whether there had been a moment in his life where he had really 'awakened' he gave me the following account. He said: 'I was nine years old.[314] My father was working on the mainland and I was alone with my grandfather on a small, Scottish island. We had a house there. I don't remember my mother. I only know of a rocky corner where you could watch the sea surging up. I was told that she had often sat at this very place. And so with time I imagined that mother evoked in me this vision of the sea.' He lived alone with his grandfather. One evening when it was really stormy he sat at the window and looked into the huge waves. Then he went to bed. But the wind was howling and it was so eerie that he went to his grandfather and crept into bed beside him. He fell asleep in the arms of the old man. That night his grandfather died. The boy awoke and found himself in the arms of a dead man. 'At that moment I was awakened,' he said, 'I had a kind of vision of the future, and all my ideas go back to it.'

Mr. Dunlop's idea was that the World Power Conference would gradually permit another organization to come into existence, one of a purely economic nature. He took the view that the different states as such could not come to a real understanding with respect to economic problems because they always took their own interest too seriously and did not adequately grasp the fact that the interest of others is just as important. It was via this approach that Dunlop came to love Germany. To him Germany seemed to be *the* country whose real vital interests the other countries had forgotten. Thus for him the German problem became a world-problem. Dunlop wrote a book during the war—*British Destiny* (1916). In it one finds such thoughts as this: 'History does not preserve the memory of any statesman, philosopher or thinker who is not really great; their fame does not survive the centuries unless they have enunciated and endeavoured to carry into practice those immortal Principles which inhere in Man and characterize the race. If they identify themselves with what is eternally true, they become part of the tradition of their country, and even that of all countries, when their insight has been especially profound. These eternal Principles are the causes of existence, the source of all life; they are everywhere in operation . . . The nation that interprets them most clearly leads evolution.'[77]

Dunlop's idea was to use *World Survey* as a start, in an attempt to go beyond the limitations of a purely technical world organization. Little by little the economic life was to be drawn into, and included in the orbit of the World Power Conference. His sense of reality would not allow him to regard the achievement of this aim as *certain*. He never forced people or circumstances. He just waited. For this reason he attached *World Survey* to the World Power Conference with a certain degree of independence. For him it was a matter of some importance that it should not be the paper of the World Power Conference as such but only under its auspices and there to serve this organization. He certainly wanted to create the world-wide economic organization. He knew that it was just as necessary as the technical one. However, whether or not the technical organization was ready to extend its objectives to this point was something it would have to decide for itself. Dunlop respected the independence of the organization he had created. He was ready to pursue a modified version of his own idea if the inner life of his organization was ready to take a different path than that he had originally foreseen. This respect for people he worked with and their will, made him into an immortal organizer.

Dunlop saw perfectly well that there are many forces within the World Power Conference that are against the extension of technical considerations into the economic field. So he took precautions. But he did want to achieve his goal. Hence *World Survey*. This *World Survey is* the seed of a world organization founded on totally unpolitical, purely economic grounds. Whether or not anyone understands this or wants it, that is something that must now become evident. But Dunlop knew that nothing can be forced upon mankind. He wanted to achieve his goal step by step according to a grandiose ability to wait. There is no country on earth that could have a greater interest in the creation of this world-wide economic organization than Germany. He planned it for Germany. Not because he was 'pro-German' but because he knew that things will not arrange themselves in the world without Germany finding its proper place. He said once: 'As the "I" within the soul, so the German Being stands in the world.'

Other nationalities would not understand such words so he merely *acted* in accordance with them and wrote no more books after 1918. He said: 'I forbade myself to speak or write because I found that it was my task to put people into the right places.' Dunlop is really a very great man.

These are the things which he has placed in my heart. I want to work for them. And if they are well received by those to whom they were addressed then something great will come. If not, mankind will have to wait.

I am alarmed to see how long this letter has become. But perhaps you will forgive me when you consider the greatness of everything at stake. We have not only to preserve, but also to continue his work.

Yours respectfully,

W.J. STEIN[315]

Rudolf Steiner and the Fulfilment of a Quest*

Any attempt to describe a meeting we regard as the most significant turning-point of life must, in the nature of things, include some account of earlier experiences, for they are its background and forerunners. Apologies for personal references are therefore out of place in such a narrative and the very variety of experiences described in this volume as a whole will constitute much of its value. The stories told by the younger and older generations will become vivid by their inevitable contrast and unite the tellers and the readers more closely.

It is probable that more than one contributor met Rudolf Steiner in

* [Editor's note from original publication in *Anthroposophical Movement*, Vol. XII, No. 7, July 1935.] This article was sent by Mr. Dunlop in response to a request that he should contribute a chapter to a book which was in contemplation last autumn. The volume proposed to set on record experiences which had come to the several writers on meeting Rudolf Steiner for the first time. The request was for descriptions of 'where one stood before the meeting', the meeting itself, and 'what came of the meeting.' The member who had initiated the idea of such a book has kindly allowed us to publish Mr. Dunlop's contribution here.

comparatively early years. Others, like the present writer, were already at grips with industrial and economic life in the last decades of the nineteenth century—a time when those whose thoughts turned at all to things beyond the world of sense were confronted in many circles and societies with manifestations of a supersensible world shining too often as will-o'-the-wisps and not as the stars of heaven. It was a time when, in religion, sects were multiplying everywhere, and dogma, narrowness of vision, rigidity were rife; in the world of science, materialism had reached its prime.

Two memories have remained clearly with me and may be recounted here as symptomatic of the course which my spiritual life was afterwards to take. One is of childhood, when on Scotch hills outside the cottage where for some years I was brought up, I would collect other children around me and read to them the Gospel of St. John, dimly aware that here was something magical, infinitely more real than all the lessons at the village school. The other memory is of the excitement aroused by volumes of a 'World History' shown me when at the age of about seventeen I was working in a dingy office for wages of a few shillings a week. This book seemed to open a door to universality, to a wide Earth of which I knew so little, but which I instinctively loved. I know now, as I look back over my life, that, in some form, a feeling of the reality of the spiritual world was always there. It was a matter of finding the Teacher, for a deliberate seeking after spiritual knowledge began, in my case, with the very first stirrings of independent thought.

I mention these things only in order to explain how Rudolf Steiner afterwards became for me the interpreter of a certain realm of experience, as well as teacher in the realm of spiritual knowledge. Having in very early youth to cope with the stubborn problem of earning daily bread, I had no opportunity for classical or scientific education of any kind. But before very long, after long hours of work, my evenings were spent in reading mystical and occult literature picked up, for the most part, on second-hand bookstalls in back streets of Glasgow. It is for others to tell how Rudolf Steiner became their master too in the domain of the highest University scholarship. So far as I was concerned, the sunlight of his teachings and his personality rose upon a different background.

At the end of the nineteenth century, the works of H.P. Blavatsky were making a greater stir in the West than is often realized. Her writings attracted around that strange, enigmatical personality, minds of calibre and students of mystical and occult philosophy all over the world. The Stanzas of Dzyan seemed to be a voice of thunder from a bygone age, carrying their own conviction of spiritual reality, but remote and imperfectly understood. For years I was engrossed, in company with the Irish poet 'A.E.' and others whose names have since become well known, in the study of H.P. Blavatsky's works, and an overwhelming wish was born in me: to meet an Initiate in the physical body, to be able to recognize, here on Earth, a *knower* of spiritual truth, and then to take my share in spreading this truth for the 'well-being of humanity.' But the time of fulfilment was not yet. Many disillusionments were still in store through the years of activity in more than one branch of the Theosophical Society which followed the reading of H.P. Blavatsky's works.

To some extent, therefore, experience which helps mightily to sift the true from the false in the realm of occultism was already behind me when, for the first time, I found Rudolf Steiner's teachings. I had seen him about the year 1906 in a crowded Convention of the Theosophical Society and his face and bearing made an unforgettable impression. But his books and lectures were at that time unavailable in English and it was my lot to see many strange and wayward developments in Theosophy before finding him as the teacher for whom all my life I had been looking. I stood aloof from these developments in the Theosophical Society, incurring the disapproval and often the firm opposition of orthodox followers of Annie Besant and C.W. Leadbeater, but opportunity for direct contact with Rudolf Steiner's teachings came only later.

The manifest absurdities and trivialities filling Theosophical literature, above all from the year 1907 onwards, gave rise to a natural caution when Rudolf Steiner's works first came into my hands. They were utterly different in tone and content, but I felt they must be approached with reserve and balance.

I had always longed to hear of the *Cosmic* mysteries connected with Christ and His incarnation, and here, in Anthroposophy, was the first indication that rang true. But I confess quite frankly that, at the beginning, earlier prejudices arose in strong reaction to these new teachings. Was Anthroposophy, after all, based merely on the assertions of psychic faculties as yet unproven? Would room be left in Rudolf Steiner's teachings for the exercise of that 'healthy human reason' which now seemed to have deserted so many thousands of Theosophists? Was this new spiritual teaching capable not only of theoretical but of *practical* application to human life and activity, to art, to science in all its branches, to therapy, education, religion, economics, industrial and social life? Would it speak as a reminder and revealer of knowledge already hidden in the soul and not as another body of doctrine to which there was no inner assent?—And Rudolf Steiner himself—that was the greatest question of all!

Many such problems were alive in me before the opportunity came for meeting him face to face. I knew that really deep acceptance of a new form of knowledge must always be an act of *will*—not only of mind and feeling. I realized how easily human beings may be carried away by the glamour of a great personality, and in mature age conviction has to wrestle with a stubborn background of experience. I was studying Rudolf Steiner's works continually, but I knew that no final decision was possible for me until in his actual presence I could perceive whether the undoubted greatness indicated by his seership expressed itself too through him as a human being, as a man among men. In the West we want to 'see for ourselves!'

But the first meeting brought instant recognition: here is the knower, the Initiate, the bearer of the Spirit to his age. The human relationship was established immediately: a clasp of the hand which lasted for many minutes; a conversation which while it took its course in ordinary language seemed to lie in a realm of understanding infinitely deeper, and was filled with an undescribable sweetness and warmth. I felt as though the meeting had been—as indeed Rudolf Steiner himself once hinted—of the nature of a re-union after years, maybe lives, of wandering and seeking. I came away from that first meeting, and from others, with my heart on fire with thankfulness that a quest had found fulfilment.

In personal contact Rudolf Steiner seems to give his whole being in understanding of the other. He saw possibilities, not failings, and just because of this, the highest in human beings was drawn out and cherished. He was conscious of his spiritual mission and he needed others to work for this mission in the world. Human beings weighed down by fear of mistakes or their own shortcomings are incapable of vital thought or action in the age of the Consciousness Soul, and Rudolf Steiner's treatment of individuals was the very truest way to make *men* of those who recognized him. He treasured and stimulated the good within them, knowing that the power of the Spirit was mighty enough to transmute failings, once that Spirit was allowed access to mind, heart and will. Towering as he did above everyone around him, it would have been more than easy to have bent everyone to his slightest will. But his whole attitude belied servility. In all my life I have never experienced such an absence of any attempt to force opinions or intentions. He made one feel: here, in the service of *his* mission, there is, in very truth, 'perfect freedom'. The soul began to breathe in his presence, and to have wings—to have feet as well, planted on free and independent soil for action.

Such was my first impression of him, and it grew in strength and conviction on every subsequent occasion. It is only natural that he should have been surrounded with a great deal of awe, in spite of the fact that utmost simplicity was one of his most marked characteristics. He expressed infinite gratitude for any small service rendered to the cause of Anthroposophy, or for the slightest care for his personal comfort, to which he himself paid no heed. There was sparkling humour and lightness of heart, and a more courteous gentleness than I have ever met in another human being. Unequalled sanity of judgment in things of the world went hand in hand with clearest vision of the Supersensible and the power to make it a reality in the souls of those who listened to him. My impression of him many times at Penmaenmawr in the year 1923, and near the site of King Arthur's Castle at Tintagel in 1924, was that his consciousness was fully awake in the spiritual and physical worlds at the same time. A glance at his eyes was enough to indicate that mysteries beyond our ken were revealing themselves to him, while all the time his waking consciousness was far more alert than ours.

His loving appreciation of initiative was more than apparent in every contact I had with him personally, and there was instant readiness to accede to requests, if they were sincerely made. In several discussions he had with me as to the development of the work of the Anthroposophical Society in England, I was often conscious of diffidence at making my own suggestions, even when this was at his own request. But here again, they were met with the response and understanding of an intimate friend.

Only a few weeks before his last illness, I spoke to him during the Summer School at Torquay of my fears for his physical health. Firmly, but with infinite gentleness he drew me aside and conveyed to me that ordinary conceptions of illness should not be applied to his condition. Those few words of explanation revealed to me far more than their ordinary meaning. I felt then, and afterwards, that the veils of mysteries connected with the transmutation of the physical organism itself may sometimes be lifted, and a spiritual alchemy made manifest.

There could only be one outcome of such a meeting: through weal and woe to work for the spreading and application of the wisdom of which he was the bearer. Was not every sphere of human activity crying out for this new, creative impulse? I was grateful beyond words when Rudolf Steiner asked me to undertake a task in connection with the medical work he was developing in collaboration with Dr. Ita Wegman, and to bring out the book then in course of writing.

Understanding of the world as it actually is, ability to bring spiritual knowledge right down into the practical life of men, into the stubborn spheres of technical industry and economics, as well as into the thinking, the moral life and the actions of men—that is one side of Rudolf Steiner's challenge. The other is the development of the inner life of soul which generates love for human beings and the wisdom to promote their spiritual and social well-being. Rudolf Steiner once said: 'To cultivate Spiritual Science is no abstract pursuit. To cultivate Spiritual Science means to open the doors to those influences from beyond the Earth, which have been seeking to come down to the Earth since the last third of the nineteenth century.'

Those who knew him in the physical world, those who have known of him since his death or will yet come to know him—with them lies the destiny of the future, for they can open or help to keep closed, as they will, these 'doors' by which the spiritual influences, revealed in all their power by Rudolf Steiner, can pour down and perform alchemy upon the Earth. The Inspirer of the twentieth century has lived among us, and lives among us still. Is it not for us to work as labourers unto harvest?

Ludwig Count Polzer-Hoditz: Two Addresses Harrogate Summer School 1935

Opening Address of 12 August 1935*

Before coming to this Summer School in the North of England out of the Midst of Europe, there often has stood before my soul the picture of our dear friend Mr. Dunlop. Only lately through Mr. Kaufmann and through what Dr. Walter Johannes Stein wrote in memoriam of Mr. Dunlop in the 'Mitteilungen'† I learnt something more about his active

* *Translated into English by George Adams-Kaufmann.*

† *Mitteilungen für die Mitglieder der Anthroposophischen Arbeitsgemeinschaften in Deutschland*, ed. Jürgen v. Grone, No. 1, July 1935.

and successful life. This combined with my own remembrance of personal meetings and gave me the impression of a most lovable and beautiful human soul.

As I have been told, I owe my being here to a large extent to Mr. Dunlop's wish that I should partake at this Summer School, and I think that Rudolf Steiner has guided the threads of fate so that we can find each other to tie nearer relations between Anthroposophs here and Anthroposophs living in the Eastern part of the heart of Europe.

Anglo-Saxon souls led by Rudolf Steiner, living in full light and activity of nowadays life, and over there, in the East of Central Europe, souls of Slavs, bearing germs to prepare mankind for further evolution: they try to meet one another.

And so I feel ready to work with you in acceptance of the will of ever wakeful destiny, in pursuit of human-spiritual understanding which is not subject either to space or to time. This is to be understood as a most warmhearted greeting.

*

Closing Address of 22 August 1935

When one has been active in the anthroposophical movement for nearly 30 years and at the end of this time has to go through the painful experiences which have resulted from recent events in Dornach and when one is called upon to play an active part therein, then one is deeply thankful for the days which we have been able to spend together here at this anthroposophical Summer School.

I have found again the friendly atmosphere that there was in former times, when Rudolf Steiner was still among us. I have found so many old friends of mine who worked together with Rudolf Steiner. All this has been a great help to me for what we have to do in the future. So I should like to thank all those who have struggled with the difficulties of the time and have brought about the possibility of this anthroposophical Summer School in such a wonderful way. Above all I will give my thanks to our dear friend Mr. Dunlop whose spiritual presence is certainly with us.—Next our chairman Mr. Wheeler, Mr. Kaufmann and all the speakers and those who have helped in the organization here.

I must take what I have experienced back again to the East. There I will tell again how important it seems to me for the position of the anthroposophical movement and for the world that the English

Anthroposophical Society is becoming strong, that from here strength may stream out to the threshold of Europe where German and Slavs meet together.

I should like to close with these words which Rudolf Steiner often spoke to us at the end of a gathering: 'Auf Wiedersehen'—we shall be still together though separated by space.

George Adams-Kaufmann: A Speech in Memory of D.N. Dunlop—Our Community[316]

D.N. Dunlop was our friend. He was known as such to many who saw him at anthroposophical gatherings, lectures, group meetings, summer schools, committees, manifold activities. He was a friend to many others who perhaps never saw him, or through difference of language could not converse with him; who benefited none the less by his initiative and good will, and partook in the warm life he imparted. Some of us also were privileged to know him as a friend more intimately.

A strong and good friend has gone from us across the Threshold. We may do well to be mindful together, at such a moment, of our life's source and of its goal; and of the true resolves of the spirit, whereby we are here together.

To earthly consciousness, our life's beginning is enveloped in darkness. It is a darkness no less complete than that which hides from us the other end of life, the afterdeath. As we look back, we see in memory the familiar scenes of youth and childhood, a few first memories, dim or outstanding, mostly isolated—then, nothing more. As we look forward, we know that Death stands at the end of the way, and here again is utter darkness for our earthly consciousness.

Spiritual Knowledge, joined to the moral intuition of our soul, made vivid by our interest in the great stream of human history, tells us with inner certainty that we came down to Earth from the Spirit-world, and thither shall return. Now our community with other human beings is enlarged and deepened. These others too, who are beside us now on Earth, came down from the same Spirit-land, they were with us there, and will be with us again in spiritual worlds in the future. Our being-together on the Earth, in its beginnings and endings, in its bereavements, in the apparently blind inevitability of the fates that rule it—dark as it is to earthly consciousness—receives 'light into the darkness' when we know this. While it tells universally of the facts of human life in any age or incarnation, this knowledge has an especial significance when applied to the incarnation in which we are living now—the close of the 19th and the first half of the 20th century. Rudolf Steiner has told us of the conditions that prevailed in spiritual worlds, and of the *why*, and *how*, and who were those who resolved to incarnate, to take part in the spiritual movement of this time on Earth. Our friend and we, each and all of us, had this destiny in common: to come down to Earth at this juncture and work together in preparing the first beginnings of a new Age of Light.

Thinking of this, let us look back for a moment on the period of his life. D.N. Dunlop was born in the Western Highlands in 1868, about seven years after Rudolf Steiner's birth. Great spiritual transformations were now about to take place, deeply affecting the spiritual life of mankind on earth and in spiritual worlds. In 1879, we remember, came the beginning of the new period of Michael. Seven Archangels, belonging to the seven planetary spheres, succeed one another in the main leadership of earthly history, in periods of three to four hundred years. The last rulership was that of Gabriel, the Archangel of the Moon, from about the 16th century till the last third of the 19th. From 1879 onward, Michael the Sun-Archangel took his place, heralding a profound change in the tendencies of human spiritual life. But this was not the only transformation. Another of the great cosmic rhythms or cycles of time—this of far longer duration—came to an end with the close of the 19th century. Kali Yuga, the five thousand years' Age of Darkness prophesied in ancient Eastern wisdom, came to an end in 1899; the new Age of Light began.

This was our time: at once the beginning of a new Michael period (the period of the Sun, and therefore spiritually most important within the sevenfold cycle), and of the new great Age of Light—the emergence of mankind from materialism, the ascent from merely physical and intellectual into the first beginnings of a new clairvoyant consciousness: 'Imagination,' as Rudolf Steiner calls it. 'For, in the Michael epoch . . . gradually into the prevalent intellectual consciousness of mankind the power of Imagination will enter.'

It is a new beginning, of overwhelming significance and also of great difficulty for mankind. As to the life of mankind as a whole, it is a crossing of the Threshold, of the abyss of existence where the dread Guardian stands.[317] Old standards crumble and old values fade. Souls lose their inner certainty, even in matters hitherto felt to be fundamental and secure. The economic, social and inter-racial life of the world is shaken. The balance of the soul and the true fount of life have to be sought anew, in all domains.

Souls must resolve to incarnate at this moment, to experience this first beginning of a new age, and in experiencing help prepare the way for a future which can but gradually blossom forth out of the midst of trial and difficulty. Many such souls there were. Far more, perhaps, than we imagine, made this resolve with consciousness in the last life between death and new birth. In his lectures on the history and conditions of the Anthroposophical Movement and Society (June 1923[318]), Dr Steiner tells of these souls, who upon Earth found their way into diverse spiritual, mystical and kindred movements of the late 19th century, and in our time into the Anthroposophical Society.

'During the time between death and new birth, the moment comes when the human being begins to look once more in the direction of the Earth. For a long time before birth, the soul seeks connection with the line of generations, at the end of which are the two parents who will give him birth. Not only to the great-great-grandfather, but away back into much earlier generations, man is already looking down, uniting himself with the stream that flows through the generations of his forebears.

'For the majority of souls now living, it is true to say that in the time when they are thus preparing to come down again to Earth they already have a burning interest in that which is going on on Earth. They as it were look down from the spiritual world to the Earth and are interested keenly in what is going on among their fathers' fathers . . .

'On the other hand, notably in the present time there are a number of souls who, even in the time when the pre-earthly life thus inclines once more towards the earthly, are not so greatly interested in what is going on on Earth; whose main interest is directed rather towards other questions. "How do we grow to maturity in the spiritual world?" Until the very last moment when they find their way to Earth again, it is as though they were still interested paramountly in the spiritual world. While other souls have a deep craving for the earthly life, these souls until the very last have a vivid interest in that which is taking place in spiritual worlds. And when at last they find themselves embodied on the Earth, they arrive here with a consciousness that springs more from the spiritual side, inclining not so much towards the motives which impel those who content themselves with the broad highway of life. They grow beyond the prevailing impulses of their environment; with their spiritual aspirations, above all, they grow out of this environment. They are thereby predestined to find ways of their own . . . It is to this latter kind that the souls who then find their way into the Anthroposophical Movement, belong.'

More profoundly, in the lectures given a year later (July and August, 1924) upon the Karma of this Movement, we are told of the deep resolves that were formed and the decisive experiences undergone by those who were gathered in the schools of Michael in spiritual worlds, in the decades and centuries before the beginning of the new Michael epoch on the Earth. To find our way aright to-day, in view of our late bereavements and impending tasks and tests, we need to look again into these great perspectives.

D.N. Dunlop was undoubtedly one of the best and strongest—and, withal, one of the most characteristic of the souls whose earthly life, spanning the closing third of the 19th and the beginning third of the 20th century, centred upon the spiritual tasks here mentioned. Wheresoever he lived and moved: in groups of the Theosophical Society in earlier years, in the Anthroposophical Society until his death, and in a whole variety of modern movements, social or cultural, intellectual or mystical—with which he came into contact from time to time, his virile influence was felt. Obituaries which have appeared in the technical and industrial press speak of him not only as the prominent leader that he was, but as a quiet, self-effacing worker behind the scenes; one who did not often appear in the limelight, but to whose initiative many important developments were primarily due. So too he worked in the cultural and spiritual movement of our time. Deep in his being was the quality of *initiative*, of which Dr Steiner speaks in the aforesaid Karma lectures of 1924. The Universal Spirit, says Dr Steiner,[319] has impressed this archetypal picture more strongly upon the destiny of anthroposophists than is the case with other men. The anthroposophist must say to himself:—'Somewhere or other, more or less deeply in my soul, there will emerge the necessity for me to discover the inmost initiative of my life—initiative which will enable me to undertake something or to make some judgment or decision out of my own inmost being.' Verily, this is written in the Karma of every single anthroposophist: Be a man of initiative, and beware lest through hindrances of your own body, or hindrances that otherwise come in your way, you do not find the centre of your being, where is the source of your initiative. Observe that in your life all joy and sorrow, happiness and pain will depend on the finding or not finding of your own individual initiative. This should stand written as though in golden letters, ever before the soul of the anthroposophist. Initiative lies in his Karma; what he encounters in this life will much depend on the extent to which he becomes conscious of it in his Will.

In Dunlop's being, this fundamental, Michaelite quality of human will was awakened. This was what drew men to him. Sometimes, when he spoke in meetings devoted to the spiritual life, there was in his speech a warmth and outpouring of expression, somewhat unusual among the rather terse and astringent conventions of the present phase in the epoch of the 'consciousness soul' (or Spiritual Soul). The Spiritual Soul, as Dr Steiner tells us in the last Christmas letter which he wrote, begins its evolution in a cold element of light. It will be fired-through with love as we awaken in the spirit to the great facts of cosmic and all-human evolution. But we cannot go back to the more instinctive warmth of cosmic feeling which preceded the soul's temporary isolation in consciousness. Instinctive knowledge of this truth renders the intellectual people of our time not unjustly sensitive to any warmth of feeling which may seem too easy. Yet the same intellectual mind often fails to recognize out of what depth the feeling issues, or what experience of life there is behind it, to give it substance. 'In its true essence,' says Dr Steiner, 'the spiritual soul is not cold. It only seems so in the initial stage of its evolution, for it is then only able to reveal the quality of Light which it contains, not yet the Warmth of Worlds, from which in truth it springs.'

Some people loved, some were repelled by Mr Dunlop's warmth of expression. Yet, very soon, if one had any will to work together, one encountered in him the real essence which lay beneath it, and this ultimately drew men to him, no matter what their first impression of his personality might be. We may perhaps describe this essence of the man as straightforward Will, combined with deep Patience. This Will, and this Patience, were alike grounded in the fundamental Good of his being, which lived through all his changing days and ways in an unfaltering knowledge of the eternal stream of spiritual life and of the love of the Gods, the 'spiritual guidance of Man and of Mankind.' In a peculiar way, Dunlop lived forth this certainty, this faith. It fired with resolve his will, which at some critical moments would become absolute, unbreakable. Yet at the same time it endowed him with gentle patience, humour to bide his time, power to suffer with equanimity the great rebuffs, and the far harder-to-bear, the everlasting petty ones. So did we come to know his unbelievable gentleness, and his will, which was at times like lightning and like the rock into which it strikes. There were eternal truths of the Way of Initiation which had become the fibre of his being. He had attained what is called, in *Knowledge of the Higher Worlds*, the 'spiritual balance.' 'On one of the scales there lies an "open heart" for the needs of the outer world, and on the other scale, "inner fortitude and unfaltering endurance".'[320]

These qualities in our friend brought him near to Rudolf Steiner. Dunlop was one of those in whose company Dr Steiner seemed to feel ease and happiness. He came to him without reserve or repression, with a spark of the absolute fire, so that Dr Steiner was able to unfold to him many things. He came to him in purest thankfulness and asked to receive in full measure, as only the courageous and the strong can ask.

It was for this reason also that things flourished under Dunlop's hand or in his presence. Men do not come, in the long run, only to hear *about* the spiritual in a theoretic way, however wise the thoughts. Dunlop as chairman of a Group, or of a Summer School, had that about him which lay neither in his warmth of words, nor in his rather saturnine silences, but deeper down. In the whole tenor of his being was the witness to the eternal Spiritual Guidance, which will act, when the moment comes, with an all-welding fire, and which can also wait, knowing well 'the love that warms the centuries of Time'—love, which is ultimate substance of all human souls, and in the rhythms of wise Time will at long last awaken to receive, in every one, the Will of Christ.

He, then, was one of those with whom we have been together in times gone by, and shall be again. What is it, to be friends in the way he and we were friends? Fair are the friendships and brotherhoods that arise on the ground of common human destinies, the bonds of blood, the ties of partnership and calling. Yet there is something different about those which are founded on the united seeking for the spiritual life. Forces are there called into play which relate not only to the community of mother-tongue, or memories of childhood spent or earthly tasks resolved upon together, but to experiences and tasks which souls have had and will have together in the spiritual worlds, among the Gods. Therefore the Threshold of the Spiritual World, with its stern laws, is always near at hand when communities are formed on Earth for the sake of the eternal, spiritual life. (That is the reason too, why in such societies—when one forgets the laws—the professed brotherhood will turn so subtly and, alas! so easily into its opposite: misunderstanding, bitterness and strife.)

The community in spiritual striving, which we have had and still have with him, relates us to the life in spiritual worlds in the past, and in the future also. What we receive in Occult Science, through the clairvoyant researches of the Initiates whose consciousness is raised to higher worlds, is a downpouring from the Divine-spiritual to the Earth. It comes, in a manner of speaking, by the same path by which we ourselves come, when we descend from spiritual worlds upon the way of birth. It is born of the Divine: *Ex Deo Nascimur.* The Divine-spiritual Beings who brought forth humanity on Earth, have from time immemorial bestowed upon the world the sacred Wisdom. It was Divinely given Wisdom: Theosophia, in pre-Christian time; it has become, through the Christ-Impulse and the Holy Spirit upon Earth, Anthroposophia. All we receive through Anthroposophy is like a gift of communion with the Divine world whence we come. It renews for our imagination the knowledge of those things we learnt in spiritual schools before our descent to Earth. Thus the clairvoyant research of the true Initiate bestows upon the earthly life the gifts from Heaven. And the receiving of it *can* and indeed *should* be for the anthroposophist something akin in strength and power to what the members of a religious community receive through word and ceremony of the sacred cult, the religious worship in which they join. Of the latter, Dr Steiner said that it has the effect of recalling, for souls on Earth, the community of spiritual life which was theirs during the life before birth.

But Anthroposophy is not only the receiving of the spiritual knowledge communicated by Initiation. What is essential above all is the understanding of it by dint of human thought, and the resultant working of it out in earthly life. Something new is added to the spiritual cosmos when human beings experience the Spiritual in the form of thoughts, when they lift their thought to the understanding of the spiritual worlds. For this reason, says Dr Steiner, the Gods have brought Man into being: that They might plant the seed of Wisdom in mankind on Earth and receive it back again, transmuted, in the new form of human thought—and all that springs from human thought. During the after-death existence, following upon the earthly life in which we devoted ourselves to spiritual science, we find abundantly that this is so. Our thoughts devoted to the Spirit become the seeds which blossom forth and bear fruit in yonder realm. 'We receive what is imparted to us from higher worlds, not as an idle gift to make it more convenient for us when we have left the physical plane, but to the end that we may change it into the currency of Earth. Only so much of it as we have thus transmuted, will help us onward in the afterdeath existence.'* It is the new thing in the age of the Spiritual Soul, that communities of human beings can thus be formed in the pursuit of conscious spiritual knowledge. Everyone who has felt the blessing of an anthroposophical group-meeting or gathering of any kind for spiritual study, has had experience of this. It is a community-creating force based not merely nor even paramountly—as in religious congregations—on the renewing of a past community of life in spiritual worlds, but above all, on that which man upon Earth is preparing for the spiritual future of the world. Religious communities are *given*, inasmuch as the Gods bestow that which finds expression in the settled forms of cult and public worship. Anthroposophical community has to be *created* far more actively and as it were *ab initio* by ourselves, for it is rather rooted in that spiritual stream which flows, returning, from a free mankind on Earth into the realm of Gods. In Dr Steiner's words:—'Just as man brings the spiritual world down to the earthly when he establishes a sacred form of religious cult or ritual, so can he take what he has seen, what he has learned to know and understand on Earth, and, as he raises it to the Ideal, lift it into the supersensible and spiritual. We bring down the Heavenly to Earth, into a realm of pictures full of living power, in celebrating a religious cult. We lift ourselves with our soul's life into the supersensible when we experience spiritually, idealistically, what we here have within the physical world . . . We can then say to ourselves: "What you have seen and perceived in this world of the senses—raise it to the Ideal, and it will suddenly become alive. It will become alive when you rightly permeate it with will and feeling, when you let your whole inner life be rayed-through with will and give true enthusiasm to it . . ." We should call forth the feeling that this is so in every single one who takes part with us in the receiving of anthroposophical life. This must become not only abstract conviction but living inner experience, so that in a room where we are doing Anthroposophy together we are not only sitting there as so many individuals who receive what they hear or read and make it into their several thoughts, but more than this. For by the very receiving of anthroposophical ideas, by the whole process that takes place as we do so, a real Spirit-being becomes present in the room where we are studying Anthroposophy. As in the forms of cult and ritual the Divine forces are made present in the sense-world, so must we learn with heart

* 'Spiritual Science, its Tasks and Aims'. Lecture at Stuttgart, 13 November 1909.[321]

and soul, through the whole tenor of our soul to allow the presence of a Spirit-being in the room wherein the word of Anthroposophy resounds. We must be able to make spiritual our speaking, our thinking and our impulses of will—not abstractly spiritual, but with the feeling as though a Being were there, looking down upon us, hearing us, hovering over us, present in the spirit . . .

'Only then do we really comprehend the Spiritual, when we not only possess the idea of it in the abstract and can reproduce it theoretically whether for ourselves or others, but are able to believe—with a belief that carries proof—*that in our spiritual comprehending, Spirits are having spiritual communion with us.* Anthroposophical community cannot be realized by any outward arrangements; it must be summoned from the deepest source of human consciousness itself.'* D.N. Dunlop had in him the true idealism and enthusiasm of which Dr Steiner speaks. He was in this regard an anthroposophist in the fullest sense. His religion was of the future, namely, of the way which leads from free creative Humanity on Earth to the spiritual Cosmos, where all the Gods are expectant. Fire was kindled in him when this note was touched. His outer work in life, and the peculiar way he had of confirming the good, the creative, the truly human—it can be said without exaggeration—in many thousands whom he encountered in all walks of modern life, bore witness to the genuineness of this inner fire. Those who imagined Dunlop not to be a thinker as a true Michaelite must be, took a too narrow view of thinking and of the forms of life and word which give it voice. Alas for the too narrow view and its poor consequences!

He is now in spiritual worlds. We all of us shall be there again, some sooner and some later. What do we look to find there? How do we realize the working of those our friends, who with him and with our great Teacher are there already? We think of Michael, and of the Holy Spirit. It is a deep secret; souls must have courage to take hold of this. Michael among the Archangels is, above all, the one who attends, to receive what human beings upon Earth—in their science, in their industry, in their culture, in all social life—think and do out of true spiritual courage. He is attentive to receive it and pass it on into the realm of the Gods, into the realm of the Holy Spirit where as fertile seed it will blossom forth into new creative power. The other Archangels are more concerned in passing down to Earth-humanity what the Gods bestow upon us. Michael on the other hand looks to humanity; His task

* Lectures to the Delegates' Congress at Stuttgart, February 1923.[322]

is to encourage, to awaken, to beckon on what is truly free in man, so as to give to the Gods from an awakened Manhood what They are waiting to receive; without which the further progress of the Cosmos and of ourselves, is no longer possible.[323]

In the life after death we shall find ourselves in the realm of the Holy Spirit where these things are made true. So much of the spiritual gift as we changed into true currency of Earth, so much will help us there. There it will grow abundantly. And we shall find ourselves chosen for brave future tasks. What blossoms forth in Spirit-land out of the seeds which were sown by anthroposophical study and activity on Earth, becomes an *excess* of creative power, to endow us for a future life of service. But the experience of this excess, of this abounding grace in the Holy Spirit, will not merely be for each of us alone; we shall know it also in community with one another. We shall look back to this Earth-life which we had together in the first difficult beginnings of the new Age of Light, with overwhelming thankfulness to the Gods. We shall look forward, and be confirmed in Brotherhood.

We, who remain on Earth, continue. We have stood once again before the awful suddenness of Death. Yet the Death we witness in such moments of bereavement is but the consummation of a myriad instances of Death which are there through all our life. In every opening of the senses to the outer world, this differential Death is present, which at the end is integrated. Wherever human beings meet and look one another in the eyes, Death is there. And whatsoever they institute and arrange, is, from the moment of the doing, given to the world where Death prevails. Even the teachings of the Initiate enter the world of Death as soon as the book is printed. Human beings speak to one another, write for one another, confer, and in their deeds, commit themselves to one another within the world of Death. In the very realizing of their good conceptions—whether School, Society or Building—they entrust the Spirit to the world of Death. Such was our living with our friend, and all we did together. Such are the things we still shall do with one another in good faith and courage. Mindful of this, we know that all our life only has comfort and meaning when we can say with inner truth: Death becomes Life in Christ, *In Christo Morimur*, words we repeated in the solemn moment when we gave the body of our friend to the elements. And when we think of what has here been said, of the awakening in the Holy Spirit which is made possible for man by the Christ-Impulse and His Archangel Michael, we can unite in spirit with our friend and with all friends who have gone on before us, saying: In the Holy Spirit we shall come to life again. *Per Spiritum Sanctum Reviviscimus.*

Obituary on D.N. Dunlop from the *BEAMA News Sheet*

Mr. Dunlop was perhaps most widely known as Director of the B.E.A.M.A. The original conception of that organization was his; and, after it was firmly established, he was inevitably carried by its success into all the ramifications of the electrical world, and he seized every opportunity, afforded by the rising tide of electrical science and industry, of advancing the common cause. Many of his most brilliant conceptions are perhaps not now generally recognized as such and many possibly forgotten. The B.E.A.M.A. itself was the most successful of them, but the early days of the Electrical Research Association, when co-operative effort was almost unknown, saw him in the van of progress; and he should be given (for he never took it) full credit for the creation of the Electrical Development Association, a branch of activity which was particularly attractive to him as a trained publicist. He had the Scot's *nous* to perceive that 'business' always comes first, but that those valuable instruments of electrical progress, education, research, standardization, etc. should be put into motion concurrently; and they received their impulse from him. The committees on which he found himself, either as Chairman (always a willing one) or member, were as the sands of the sea in number, some of them, perhaps (as is not unusual) rather shifting sand. Much has been said in disparagement of the committee method of arriving at action: but in his case, there were some fundamental principles behind. He *believed* in the committee meetings as a means of settling rivalries. A case in point is the Fair Trading Council, an attempt to reconcile very many conflicting views within the home industry. Several such enterprises, originated by him, will occur to everyone. Talk, conciliation, reconcilement: those were his methods, and in many cases, they brought everyone into final agreement. His patience was endless, his suavity acknowledged by all: he might not ineptly be called 'the great conciliator'.

And how, after all the talk, were the original conceptions brought down to bedrock fact in action and work? The answer seems to be that he had the priceless gift of choosing the right men and winning their loyalty. His time was always at their disposal at any hour of the day or night, without notice. He was rarely known to reprimand anyone for haste or error resulting from over-enthusiasm; and nothing that he said left a sting behind. He would have heartily agreed that, as with Nature, there are no punishments but only consequences. A vivid personality, almost baffling description, he has been described as a Scotch metaphysician; and, undoubtedly, his private philosophic studies engendered in him a detachment of mind enabling him to face delays and opposition with patience and equanimity in the sure belief that he was endeavouring to create something that would meet with approval in the future even if the present did not receive his proposals with enthusiasm.

Selected Bibliography

A. Books
B. Articles in periodical publications edited or co-edited by D.N. Dunlop
C. Articles in other periodical publications.
D. Obituaries

A. Books

In the Light of Theosophy, 'by a Fellow of the Theosophical Society', Hale 1911, published by the Blavatsky Institute.
Protean Man, London 1912, first published in 1893 by *The Irish Theosophist*, reprinted in *The Path*.
The Basis of Friendship, Hale 1912 (?), reprinted from *The Path*.
Symbols of Magic, London 1915, reprinted from *The Path*.
Studies in the Philosophy of Lorenz Oken, reprinted from *The Vahan*, London 1916.
British Destiny—The Principles of Progress, London 1916.
The Path of Attainment, London 1916. The book consists of three revised lectures which Dunlop had given to members of the Blavatsky Lodge in London in autumn 1915.
The Science of Immortality, London 1918. This book contains revised lectures from *The Path* Vol. II but also some new essays.
Duty, London 1919. A lecture given in London at the second Annual Conference of the Braille League.
The Path of Knowledge, London 1919 (?)
Nature-Spirits and the Spirits of the Elements, 'The Blavatsky Lecture', London 1920. Given at the Convention of the TS in England and Wales.

B. Articles in periodical publications edited or co-edited by D.N. Dunlop

Titles accompanied by an asterisk indicate revised versions of lectures.

1. *The Irish Theosophist*—a monthly magazine devoted to universal brotherhood, the study of Eastern literature and occult science (Dublin, Vol. I, 1/October 1892; Vol. V, 12/September 1897; editor D.N. Dunlop).

'Interview with Mr. W.B. Yeats', Vol II, No. 2, November 1893.
'Notes by the Way, The Sex Problem', Vol. III, No. 7, April 1894.
'By-Paths in Occult Progress', Vol. V, No. 6, March 1897.

In addition to this *The Irish Theosophist* also contains a wealth of leading articles and commentaries by D.N. Dunlop on current theosophical activities and other events. For the history of the Theosophical Movement during those years this magazine represents an important and largely unexploited source. Fortunately, the five volumes have been reprinted by the Edmonton Theosophical Society, Canada 1989/90.

2. *The Lamp* Vol. I–IV (March 1896–August 1900) edited by Albert E. Smythe and co-edited by D.N. Dunlop in 1900. This monthly theosophical magazine was published in Toronto.

'Some Little Observations', Vol. III, No. 8, November 1899.
'Our English Letter', Vol. III, No. 10, December 1899 and No. 11, January 1900. (In these letters D.N.D. gives the reasons why he left the cause of the 'Universal Brotherhood'.)
'The Greater Mood', Vol. IV, No. 2, April 1900.
'The Only Reality', Vol. IV, No. 3, May 1900.

3. *The Path*—A Monthly Magazine (Hale/London), Vol. I, 1/July 1910–Vol. IV, 12/June 1914) edited by D.N. Dunlop and Charles Lazenby from July 1910 to February 1912, D.N. Dunlop alone from March 1912 to June 1913, and D.N. Dunlop and W.W. Leisering jointly until June 1914.

'Editorial' (the question of expulsions/end of the century), Vol. I, No. 2, August 1910.
'The "Spiritual Will"', Vol. I, No. 4, October 1910.
'Through Sex', Vol. I, No. 12, June 1911.
'Birth and Death',* Vol. II, No. 1, July 1911. 'Friendship',* Vol. II, No. 2/3, August September 1911.
'Individuality and Personality',* Vol. II, No. 4, October 1911.
'The Soul',* Vol. II, No. 3, September 1911.
'Breath',* Vol. II, No. 6, December 1911.
'Will',* Vol.II, No. 7, January 1912.
'The Masonic Examination', Vol. II, No. 10, April 1912. 'The Function of Mind',* Vol. II, No. 12, June 1912.

'Some Symbols of Magic', Vol. IV, No. 10, April 1914. 'The Christ Drama according to St. John',* Vol. IV, No. 12, June 1914.

4. *BEAMA News Sheet*, a quarterly bearing the same name as the industrial corporation of which D.N.D. was the director from 1917 onwards (Vol. I, 1/January 1915–Vol. VIII, 12/December 1922), edited by D.N. Dunlop.

'The Philosophy of Co-operation', Vol. I, No. 1, 1915.
From January 1923 onwards the magazine *BEAMA* came out under the continued editorship of D.N. Dunlop but under the new title of *World Power*.
'The Significance of the World Power Conference', Vol. II, No. 8, July 1924.

5. *Anthroposophy, A Quarterly Review of Spiritual Science*, London 1926–1933; edited from Easter 1928 onwards by D.N. Dunlop.

'The World Conference on Spiritual Science', Vol. III, No. 3, Michaelmas 1928.

6. *Anthroposophical Movement, News for English-speaking Members of the Anthroposophical Society*, London 1924–1975. Dunlop was its unsigned editor from January 1931 to 1935.

'Rudolf Steiner and the Fulfilment of a Quest', in: *Anthroposophical Movement*, issue in memory of D.N. Dunlop, Vol. XII, No. 7, July 1935.

7. In April 1935 the first number of the last magazine to be published by D.N.D. came out—*World Survey*, a monthly magazine published under the auspices of the World Power Conference, Vol. 1, No. 1/April 1935; No. 5/August 1935.

'World Unity and World Problems', No. 1, 1935.
'Power Mankind Economics', ibid.

C. Articles in other periodical publications

1. *The Theosophical News, A Weekly Report of Activities*, Boston 1896.

'An Irishman in Philadelphia', Vol. I, No. 48, May 1897. 'European Convention Successfully held at Stockholm', Vol. II, No. 11, August 1897.

2. *The Crusader, Devoted to the Cause of Universal Brotherhood*, ed. Basil Crump, London 1897.

'Notes by the Way', Vol. II, No. 7, September 1898.

3. *The New Century*, weekly publication, ed. Katherine Tingley, 1897.

'Theosophy and Practice', Vol. I, No. 11, December 1897.
'Address at First Brotherhood Congress, Chicago, 20 February 1898', Vol. 1, No 21, March 1898.

4. *The International Theosophist*, ed. Alice L. Cleather and F. J. Dick 1898.

'Report of American Convention', Vol. 1, No. 1, April 1898.

5. *The Theosophical Review*, monthly magazine, ed. Annie Besant and G.R.S. Mead.

'A Deep Sense of Portals Opening', Vol. 31, No. 183, November 1902.
'From A Student's Easy Chair', Vol. 34, No. 204, August 1904.

6. *The Vahan*

'Proposed Theosophical Summer School', Vol. 18, No. 11, June 1909.
'The Path to Power', Vol. 25, No. 3, October 1915.
'The Way of the Soul', Vol. 25, No. 8, March 1916.
'A New Year's Prayer' (original version of the meditation reproduced on page 267, Vol. 26, No. 5, Christmas Supplement, December 1916.

7. *The Theosophist*, ed. Annie Besant.

'The Mystic Path' (lecture-notes), Vol. 35, No. 12, September 1914.

8. *Theosophy, a monthly magazine devoted to the interest of Brotherhood, Religion and Occultism*, 1921–

'The Mystery of Matter', Vol. I, No. 1, January 1921.

'The Ego and the Senses', Vol. I, No. 3, March 1921.

9. *Anthroposophy*, monthly magazine 1920–26.

'In Memoriam Rudolf Steiner', Vol. IV, No. 8, June 1925.

10. *The Occult Review*, ed. Ralph Shirley.

'Rudolf Steiner, a Study', Vol. 41, No. 5, May 1925.

D. Obituaries

1. *Anthroposophical Movement*, Vol. XII, No. 7, July/August 1935 (Owen Barfield, George Adams's memorial address [see page 404], Montague Wheeler, W.J. Stein, Rudolf Hauschka).
2. *BEAMA News Sheet*, Vol. III, 5 June 1935 (see Appendix page 414).
3. *British Industries*, July 1935.
4. *The Canadian Theosophist*, Vol. XVI, July 1935 (Albert E.S. Smythe).
5. *The Electrical Contractor and Retailer*, July 1935.
6. *Electrical Industries*, Vol. XXXV, 5 June 1935.
7. *The Electrical Review*, Vol. CXVI, 7 June 1935 (M.J. Railing).
8. *The Electrical Times*, Vol. LXXXVII, 13 June 1935 (Hugh Quigley).
9. *The Electrician*, Vol. CXIV, 7 June 1935.
10. *The Engineer*, Vol. CLIX, 7 June 1935.
11. *Engineering*, Vol. CXXXIX, 7 June 1935.
12. *The Metropolitan-Vickers Gazette*, Vol. XV, July 1935.
13. *Mitteilungen dür die Mitglieder der Anthroposophischen Arbeitsgemeinschaften in Deutschland*, No. 1, July 1935 (W.J. Stein).
14. *New Thought*, Vol VIII, July 1935 (Alice M. Callow).
15. *The Present Age*, Vol. I, No. 1, December 1935 (W.J. Stein).
16. *The Times*, 5 June 1935.
17. *World Power*, June 1935.
18. *World Survey*, Nos 3, 4 and 5, June–August 1935 (international representatives of the World Power Conference).

Three other appreciations from much later years are:

Willem Zeylmans van Emmichoven, 'D.N. Dunlop', in *Mededelingen van de Anthroposofische Vereeniging in Nederland*, November 1949.

Gerlind Zaiser, 'In Memoriam Daniel Nicol Dunlop', in *Was in der anthroposophischen Gesellschaft vorgeht*, Vol. 45, No. 51/52, 1968.

David Clement, 'Some Personal Reminiscences of D.N. Dunlop', in *Anthroposophical Quarterly*, Vol. 18, No. 3, 1973.

Notes and References

All indications given with regard to Rudolf Steiner's works or lectures refer to the Rudolf Steiner Bibliography (abbr. Bibl.), unless otherwise stated.

Introduction

1 The 'Strader-machine', Hans Kühn, see 'Vom Strader-Apparat', in *Mitteilungen aus der anthroposophischen Arbeit in Deutschland,* No. 98, 1971; also H. Knobel, 'Zur Stradermaschine', ibid., No. 100, 1972.
2 In London on 27 August 1924. See *Karmic Relationships*, Vol. VIII, Bibl. No. 240; Rudolf Steiner Press, London 1975.
3 *Anthroposophical Movement*, Vol. XII, No. 7, London 1935, p.103f.
4 London 1935, p.5–16.
5 See page 393 for the whole of this letter.
6 See bibliography of obituaries in the Appendix (page 420).
7 An unpublished manuscript compiled on the basis of an interview with C.H. Gray in the Summer of 1986, Central Office Archives of the World Energy Conference, London.

Chapter 1

8 David Booth, David Perrott, *The Shell Book of the Islands of Britain*, p.110. See also Robert Mclellan: *The Isle of Arran*, 3rd ed. 1985.
9 The grandfather, a fisherman, was called Daniel Nicol; thus the *whole* of his name re-emerges in that of his grandchild.
10 Presumably the 'Black Cave' at Bennan Head, from which the coast of Ireland is just visible on the distant horizon.
11 According to the death-certificate Daniel Nicol died on 30 June at Kildonan at the age of 78.
12 The 'Telest' (from the Greek 'telos', 'goal') refers, according to Rudolf Steiner, to one 'who had the task of looking to the goal of earth-evolution'. This is also the root-concept behind the so-called 'Entelechy' which might be defined as: that principle of the Ego inhering in the human being *which has the ultimate goal of earth-evolution in view* as it realizes itself and accomplishes its own Self-being.

13 See Rudolf Steiner, *The Fall of the Spirits of Darkness*, Rudolf Steiner Press, 1992.
The spiritualization of thinking is a leitmotif which runs, like a silver thread, through the whole of Rudolf Steiner's works. It consists of and indeed combines two essential impulses (or rather demands) for modern evolution:
(i) The possibility that the human being has within himself to break through into sense-free thinking and discover the true being of his Self (or 'I'), free from the body, within this same activity.
(ii) The fact that this sense-free (pure) thinking should no longer be used exclusively to serve the comprehension of the sense-world and the technology which sets out to master it. It must increasingly and equally be used to comprehend *supersensible* facts and *spiritual* truths. From the very first philosophically-orientated works of his early life right up to the karma lectures of 1924, we find this 'string' touched upon again and again, even if the terminology varies at times. In the year 1924 it emerges as clearly and intimately linked to the impulse of the time spirit Michael.

14 Alan Denson (ed.), *Letters from AE*, London 1961, p.249. Denson has added a series of short biographical sketches to this collection of letters including one on D.N. Dunlop. These sketches have proved extremely useful especially for Chapter 2 of this book.

Chapter 2

15 London 1916, p.215.

16 And yet right from the start their spiritual paths, although closely entwined with each other, also exhibited fundamental differences. One striking symptom of this was that Russell was much less impressed by Sinnett's *Esoteric Budhism* than he was by Mabel Collins's *Light on the Path*.
See: Henry Summerfield, *That Myriad-Minded Man*, Gerrards Cross 1975, pp22ff., and Peter Kuch, *Yeats and AE*, Gerrards Cross 1986, *passim*.

17 AE (George William Russell), *The Candle of Vision—The Autobiography of a Mystic*, Wheaton 1974, p.4f; also contained in the collection *The Descent of the Gods*, Gerrards Cross 1988, pp.84ff.

18 Rudolf Steiner, *Knowledge of the Higher Worlds—How is it achieved?* Bibl. No. 10, 6th ed. 1969, p.93.
19 AE, 'Song and its Fountains', in *The Descent of the Gods*, p.394.
20 *The Candle of Vision*, p.15.
21 Lecture of 16 April 1920.
22 A detailed account of Harris is given in *The Markham Review*, 4 (February 1969). The founders of the Brotherhood (in 1861) consisted of himself, his family, and 'certain other chosen and invited persons who numbered at first about twelve in all'.
23 K.H.R. Frick, *Die Erleuchteten*, Bd. II, Graz 1978, p.380.
24 Dunlop told Stein in 1934: 'Harris once met Laurence Oliphant in Piccadilly. Harris touched him on the shoulder and said: "I want to change your life. Try to become the correspondent of *The Times* in Paris. Go to Paris, but one day a stone will be thrown through your window. Understand this as a sign that you must go immediately to California." All this happened. Oliphant found an excellent successor for his work for *The Times* and left Paris.' (St) See also: Margaret W. Oliphant, *Memoir of the Life of Laurence Oliphant*, Vol. II, London 1891, p.80.

As it happened Dunlop did not, at this particular moment in time, have a very high opinion of Oliphant. This can be clearly deduced from an article on Harris which he published a few years later in *The Irish Theosophist*. In it he discusses Harris's 'Brotherhood of the New Life' (to which both men and women belonged), as well as Harris's controversial ideas on sexuality. As regards Oliphant directly, Dunlop wrote: 'With his writings it is unnecessary to deal, as there can be no doubt he was indebted to Mr. Harris for most of what was really of any value.' On the other hand we can perceive clearly in this article how Dunlop, looking at this from the theosophical standpoint he had now assumed, was also considering Harris's views from a certain distance: 'To the Theosophist neither Mr. Harris's nor Mr. Oliphant's symbolism seems to rise above the "psychical states", where the distinctions of sex still exist. To those who recognize that "in the True there is no sex" their philosophy is inadequate . . . On no subject is it so desirable to have a sound philosophy.' These were the words with which Dunlop opened his article on 'The Sex Problem'. That this was and remained his view later on is borne out by the fact that he gave several lectures in England during the pre-war years that dealt with sexuality from a theosophical point of view. See 'The Sex Problem', in *The Irish Theosophist*, Vol. II, No. 7, Dublin 1894.

About Harris, Laurence Oliphant's niece and first biographer wrote: 'The great novelty in him was that he required no adhesion to any doctrine, and did not demand of his converts that they should agree with him upon anything but the necessity of living a Christ-like life.' Ibid., p.5f.

25 W.B. Yeats, *Autobiographies*, London 1955, pp.236ff.

26 In the appendix to *Autobiographies* Yeats gives a brief account of his former adherence to this controversial order; it ends with these words: 'My connection with "The Hermetic Students" ended amid quarrels caused by men, otherwise worthy, who claimed a Rosicrucian sanction for their own fantasies, and I add, to prevent needless correspondence, that I am not now a member of a Cabbalistic society.'

For Yeats's connection with the 'Golden Dawn' see also Ellis Howe, *The Magicians of the Golden Dawn*, London 1972.

27 Edith Young, *Inside Out*, London 1971, p.7. See also Yeats, *Autobiographies*, p.249f. and Austin Clarke, *A Penny in the Clouds*, London 1968, p.56.

28 John Eglinton (pseudonym for William Magee), *A Memoir of AE*, London 1937, p.17f.

29 On 30 September of that same year Dunlop also delivered what seems to have been his first lecture at the Dublin Lodge. It was on 'Buddha and Christ'—a subject which was to have a dramatic significance for the whole future of the Theosophical Movement!

30 Eglinton, op. cit., p.16f.

31 D.N. Dunlop, *The Path of Attainment*, London 1916, p.80.

32 'The Candle of Vision', in *The Descent of the Gods*, p.105.

33 *Song and its Fountains*, ibid. p.394.

34 E.A. Boyd, *Ireland's Literary Renaissance*, 1923, p.220.

35 It appeared in *The Irish Theosophist* (see section 'Horizons New'); reprinted in *The Path*, March 1911.

36 A significant choice of pseudonym. It is used from the very beginning to symbolize the positive character and outcome of these experiences. In Latin Felix means 'the happy one'.

37 *Knowledge of the Higher Worlds*, see note 18, p.207f.

38 ibid., p.22.

39 'The Candle of Vision', in *The Descent of the Gods*, p.115. On the concept of the 'Aeon', see also Rudolf Steiner, *Christ and the Spiritual*

World—The Search for the Holy Grail, Rudolf Steiner Press, London 1963. Lecture given 28 December 1913.
40 Edith Young died in 1987.
41 One more daughter, Aileen, was born to them; she later became a eurythmist.
42 Printed in *The Theosophical Society in America*, New York, 1896, p.6.
43 K.R.H. Frick, op. cit., p.268.
44 It appeared in *The Irish Theosophist*, Vol. V, No. 6, March 1897, pp.109ff.
45 Lecture given on 10 June 1923. See *The Anthroposophic Movement*, London 1933.
46 ibid. Lecture 11 June 1923.
47 *Spiritual Hierarchies*, Anthroposophic Press, New York 1931. Lecture given 12 April 1909.
48 *The Course of My Life*, Bibl. No. 28, Chapter VII. Anthroposophic Press, New York 1986.
49 James Joyce, *Ulysses*, London 1960, p.202.
50 ibid. p.178.
51 ibid. p.210.
52 ibid. p.237.
53 Edith Young, op. cit., p.8f.

Chapter 3

54 *The Irish Theosophist*, Vol. V, No. 12, Dublin 1897.
55 ibid. Vol. V, No. 3, Dublin 1896.
56 *The Path*, Vol. III, No. 9, March 1913.
57 Edith Young, op. cit. p.27.
58 A total of six articles were printed on the 'Zodiac'; the sixth one is a specific contribution to the interpretation of the 'Stanzas of Dzyan' in *The Secret Doctrine. The Path*, Vol. III, No. 4, No. 5, No. 6, No. 7, No. 10; Vol. IV, No. 11 (October 1912–May 1914).
59 Vol. III, No. 6, p.201f.
60 Vol. III, No. 5, p.161ff. On the gland of Luschka see also Hubert Luschka, *Der Hirnanhang und die Steißdrüse des Menschen*, Berlin 1860.
61 It should be noted that according to Percival the principle of the Balance ('Libra') only indicates 'the division of the trunk of the body, to distinguish between the feminine and masculine bodies'. It is only with Virgo and Scorpio that the actual female and male sex-organs are respectively symbolized. Therefore the principle of

Libra is relevant to a condition of man before the separation of the sexes in the Lemurian epoch, when he was still androgynous. Hence, it was only at a later period that the Virgo and Scorpio principles *appeared on a physical level.* This also accords with another fact: 'the history of astronomy reveals that the signs of the Zodiac, and the gods corresponding to them, were conceived as being tenfold.' See Günther Schubert, 'Die Kategorien des Aristoteles', in *Beiträge zur Rudolf Steiner Gesamtausgabe*, Nr. 29, 1970.

62 ibid. No. 7, p.245.
63 ibid. No. 6, p.205.
64 Alan Denson (ed.), *Letters from AE*, p.99.
65 *Twenty-one Years—A Preview of the Progress and Achievements of the BEAMA*, London 1933, p.viif.
66 Published on 7 June 1935.
67 *The Path*, Vol. I, No. 6, Dec. 1910, p.123.
68 Dunlop was ably and courageously assisted in these activities by his comrade Charles Lazenby (on whom see *The Canadian Theosophist*, Vol. 69 No. 5, 1988).
69 *The Path*, Vol. I, No. 1, July 1910, p.1.
70 *The Open Door* (Supplement to *The Path*, No. 3, December 1911).
71 *The Path*, Vol. I, No. 2, August 1910, p.30.
72 ibid. appendix to the August number.
73 ibid. (June 1912), p.353ff.
74 The following was published under the unassuming title: 'Editorial Notes—Some Symbols of Magic' in *The Path*, Vol. IV, No. 10 (April 1914), p.363ff.
75 Published as 'Editorial Notes' under the title 'The Christ Drama According to St. John', in *The Path*, Vol. IV, No. 12 (June 1914), p.431ff. It is composed from notes of a lecture.
76 *British Destiny*, London 1916, p.47f.
77 ibid. p.48.
78 ibid. p.2f.
79 ibid. p.3f.
80 ibid. p.77f.
81 R. Steiner, *The Philosophy of Spiritual Activity*, Rudolf Steiner Press, London 1966, p.8.
82 Op cit. p.82f. The final chapter of *British Destiny* is entitled 'A National Industrial Federation'. In this chapter Dunlop states that because 'the difficulties of industrial administration are increasing every day . . . a wise anticipation should inspire the preparation of

a policy to reconcile the antagonisms between different interests . . . The obvious thing is a conference of a few men with the co-operative spirit . . . This Federation . . . could lay the lines for much co-operative work, and could consummate many plans for the consolidation and mutual understanding of all departments of Industry.'

It was the industrial magnate Dudley Docker, himself a vice-president of BEAMA, who translated such notions into action by founding the Federation of British Industries in July 1916, shortly after the publication of Dunlop's book. The FBI proved an immediately successful foundation and expanded greatly in subsequent years. Eventually in 1965 it amalgamated with the British Employers Confederation and the National Association of British Manufacturers to form the present Confederation of British Industries (CBI), a body of major importance on the British industrial-political scene.

See R.P.T. Davenport-Hines: Dudley Docker, Cambridge 1984, pp.105ff.

83 *I Planted Trees*, p.34f.

84 *The Daily Telegraph*, 11 June 1982.

85 David Clement, 'Some Personal Reminiscences of D.N. Dunlop', see *Anthroposophical Quarterly*, Vol. 18, No. 3, London 1973.

86 London 1916.

87 This does not mean that there were not also genuine 'Master Letters'; however, in the history of the Theosophical Society there can be no doubt as to the disastrous effects of those that were *not*. Concerning this problem see R. Steiner, *Zur Geschichte und aus den Inhalten der ersten Abteilung der esoterischen Schule*, GA 264, 1984, preliminary remarks to Part II by H. Wiesberger, p.263f.

As far as fraudulent 'Master Letters' are concerned, we can consider the 'Coulomb Affair' as being symptomatic. This whole affair, which concerned the elections after Colonel Olcott's death in 1907, illustrates the dubious 'influence' of 'Masters' on the physical plane. See also Rudolf Steiner, *The Anthroposophic Movement*, op.cit., lecture given on 12 June 1923; also R. Steiner, 'Zur bevorstehenden Präsidentenwahl der Theosophischen Gesellschaft', in *Luzifer-Gnosis—Gesammelte Aufsätze*, 1960, p.615f.

In his autobiographical sketch Dunlop refers to these occurrences after Olcott's death when he mentions the 'manifest absurdities . . . filling Theosophical literature, above all from the year 1907 onwards'.

On the general history of the Theosophical Society see also Josephine Ranson, *A Short History of the Theosophical Society*, Adyar 1938. On the 'Coulomb Affair' see Charles Ryan, *H.P. Blavatsky and the Theosophical Movement*, San Diego 1975, p.177f.

88 *The Path of Attainment*, 1916, p.25f.
89 An illuminating assessment of the phenomenon of 'psychic shells' or 'shadows', which easily become a source of illusion for those with mediumistic tendencies, can be found in R. Steiner's lecture in Berlin, 18 October 1905, included in *The Foundations of Esotericism*, Rudolf Steiner Press, London 1983.
90 *The Path of Attainment*, p.50ff.
91 ibid. p.57.
92 ibid. p.67f.
93 ibid, p.77.
94 ibid. p.79.
95 ibid. p.71.
96 ibid. p.82.
97 ibid. p.80.
98 ibid. p.85f.
99 ibid. p.98f.
100 References to the 'light of kundalini' and to the spiritual functions of the pineal gland and pituitary body are to be found, for instance, in *Foundations of Esotericism*, see note 89.
101 *The Path of Attainment*, p.94f.
102 ibid. p.105.
103 ibid. p.105f.
104 *The Path of Knowledge, s.a.*, p.56f.
105 ibid. p.39f.
106 ibid. p.65.
107 *The Path of Attainment*, p.72f.

Chapter 4

108 *The Science of Immortality* p.27. In 1919 a French translation of this book appeared.
109 For in addition to the work which he already had as director of BEAMA he became actively involved in other new enterprises during the immediate post-war years. We have already noted that

it was thanks to him that the Electrical Development Association was founded in 1919, and he was also among the founders of what in 1920 became the Electrical Research Association. (See obituary in Appendix, page 414).

The EDA had the prime function of arousing interest in electricity by lectures, demonstrations and printed matter. With the reprivatization of British electricity in 1989 it continues its activities today, still based in London, as the development department of the present Electricity Association.

The Electrical Research Association (ERA) proved enormously successful. In 1973 it transformend itself into an independent company, ERA Technology. It provides industries and government agencies with research and development in electronics and electrical engineering and has a growing influence in major European collaborative projects in these fields. See H.G. Taylor, *An Experiment in Co-operative Research* (1970).

110 *Duty—Report of an Address* by D.N. Dunlop, London 1919, p.15.

111 *Nature-Spirits and the Spirits of the Elements*, London 1920, p.3.

112 ibid. p.9.

113 ibid. p.17.

114 ibid. p.24.

115 ibid. p.26.

116 *Spiritual Hierarchies*, Anthroposophic Press, New York 1983, Bibl. 110, lecture given 12 April 1909.

117 ibid. Chapter 'Practical Aspects'.

118 W.J. Stein mentions the scene in his obituary of Dunlop in the first issue of *The Present Age*, see note 4; E.C. Merry records it in her unpublished notes on D.N. Dunlop; George Adams describes it in a contribution he made, 'Rudolf Steiner—Recollections by some of his Pupils', to *The Golden Blade*, London 1955.

119 See *Spiritual Relations in the Human Organism*, Mercury Press, New York 1984, Bibl. No. 218.

120 See *Rudolf Steiner und die Zivilisationsaufgaben der Anthroposophie*, edited by Marie Steiner, Philosophisch-Anthroposophischer Verlag, Dornach 1943, p.149.

121 Bibl. No. 227, *The Evolution of Consciousness*, Rudolf Steiner Press, 1979.

122 See note 120; p.106f.

123 See Rudolf Steiner's report in *Das Goetheanum*, No. 6, 1923.

124 Bibl. No. 227, lecture given 24 August 1923. See Rudolf Steiner, *The Evolution of Consciousness*, Rudolf Steiner Press, London 1979.

125 See R. Steiner, *Awakening to Community*, Anthroposophic Press, New York 1974, Bibl. 257, lecture given 23 January 1923.

126 See note 120, p.150.

127 Guenther Wachsmuth, *The Life and Work of Rudolf Steiner*, New York 1955, p.508.

128 See Rudolf Steiner, *Ein malerischer Schulungsweg—Pastellskizzen und Aquarelle*, Rudolf Steiner Nachlaßverwaltung, Dornach 1986, Textbeilage p.38ff. This contains the important notes concerning 'the Sketch of the Druid Stone (*Zur Druidenstein-Skizze*) made by the painter William R. Nedella after his conversations with Rudolf Steiner. Concerning the geographical location of the 'original' landscape appearing in the sketch, Nedella affirms that 'this place actually exists on the English coast and was visited by Rudolf Steiner'. This can only refer to Penmaenmawr and its surroundings. In connection with this drawing it must, however, be said that during his journey to England in 1923 Steiner had already been stimulated by his earlier stay in Ilkley; for there is a 'Swastika-stone' near Ilkley which he expressly sought out and whose spiritual function he described in Dornach on his return from England on 9 September (see *Rudolf Steiner und die Zivilisationsaufgaben der Anthroposophie*, p.169f.; see also note 120). On 14 September Rudolf Steiner again referred to the powerful presence of the Druid culture in the atmosphere around Penmaenmawr (see Bibl. No. 228).

Concerning the sketch of the Druidic Stone, see Frank Teichmann, 'Druid Stone Sketch and St John's Tide Imagination' in *Anthroposophy Today*, No. 7 (1989); also John Wood, 'A New Look at Old Stones', ibid. No. 1 (1986).

129 *Ita Wegmans Erdenwirken aus heutiger Sicht*, Arlesheim 1976, see contribution made by M.P. van Deventer, p.8.

130 J.E. Zeylmans van Emmichoven: *Wer war Ita Wegman*, Vol. 1 (1990), p.146.

131 *Rudolf Steiner und die Zivilisationsaufgaben der Anthroposophie*, see note 120, p.150.

132 From as yet unpublished notes compiled by E.C. Merry immediately after Dunlop's death; these notes (consisting of 25 pages) will be indicated hereafter as (MD).

133 This forms the final part of Rudolf Steiner's closing speech on 31 August 1923; omitted from the volume *Rudolf Steiner und die*

Zivilisationsaufgaben der Anthroposophie, it stems from a copy in the Dornach archives.

134 *Rudolf Steiner und die Zivilisationsaufgaben der Anthroposophie*, see note 120, p.150f. Rudolf Steiner goes on to say how 'the choice of this particular locality has proved to be a very fortunate "sleight of hand", for what once lived in middle and northern Europe before the Mystery of Golgotha traversed the earth has been able to arise up spiritually within this place: it was something that was awaiting the Mystery of Golgotha, something, however, that at first found no continuation, as I described this morning, with Christianity coming up from the South. It is something that in a certain sense is still waiting now.'

135 *Das Schicksalsjahr 1923 in der Geschichte der Anthroposophischen Gesellschaft* (GA 159), p.610.

136 ibid. p.603ff.

137 From as yet unpublished notes drafted by Ita Wegman for a memorial address following Dunlop's death on 30 May 1935. The author is indebted to E. Zeylmans, Reutlingen, for making them available.

138 Collison's adherence to Freemasonry, which Rudolf Steiner does not *directly* touch upon in his address, is confirmed by George Adams in his contribution to the collaborative work *Rudolf Steiner—Recollections by some of his Pupils* (see note 118).

139 *Das Schicksalsjahr 1923*, op. cit., p.608.

140 ibid.

141 ibid.

142 This is reported by David Clement in *Some Personal Reminiscences of D.N. Dunlop*, see note 85.

143 30 December 1923; see *Die Weihnachtstagung* (GA 260).

144 See *Our Summer Course in Torquay*, in *Anthroposophical Movement*, Vol. 1, 24 August 1924.

145 *My Meeting with Rudolf Steiner—A Testimony to the Spiritual Guidance of Destiny* (a manuscript from her literary remains that has not been published as a whole).

146 *Life Story—An Autobiographical Experience of Destiny*, Mercury Art Publications, 1987.

147 *Ancient Myths*, Anthroposophic Press, New York, 1978, Bibl. No. 180.

148 See *The Search for the New Isis the Divine Sophia*, Mercury Press,

Spring Valley, New York 1983, Bibl. No. 202, lecture 24 December 1920.

149 Bibl. No. 243, *True and False Paths in Spiritual Investigation*, Rudolf Steiner Press, London 1985.

150 Rudolf Steiner, *Karmic Relationships—Esoteric Studies*, Vol. VIII, Bibl. No. 240, Rudolf Steiner Press, London 1975, lecture in Torquay 12 August 1924.

151 ibid. lecture 14 August 1924.

152 'A Day at Tintagel in August', 1924, with an introduction by Mabel Cotterell, *Anthroposophical Quarterly*, Autumn 1956, p.4f.

153 Guenther Wachsmuth, op. cit., p.564.

154 According to E.C. Merry's report on this visit in *Life Story* (see note 146), Rudolf Steiner also spoke on the spot about the painter Böcklin.

155 Bibl. No. 240; lecture given on 21 August 1924 (see note 150).

156 In the same lecture Rudolf Steiner characterizes the 'Grail-stream' which is the polar opposite to the 'Arthur stream' though its direct complement. This Grail-stream already reckoned with the gradual individualization of the Michaelic intelligence: 'And so in olden times . . . we find the intense striving to ensure Michael's dominion over Intelligence through the Arthurian principle, and in the Grail stream proceeding from Spain, the striving to take account of the fact that Intelligence must in future be found on earth, that it no longer flows down from the heavens. The import of what I have just described to you is the very breath and life of the whole legend of the Grail.' Finally, Rudolf Steiner sets out how the great School of Chartres was orientated right between the northern Arthurian stream and the southern Grail-stream. 'And like shadows cast by the castle of King Arthur and the castle of the Grail, supersensible, invisible impulses made their way, not so much into the actual content of the teachings, as into the whole attitude and mood-of-soul of the pupils who gathered with glowing enthusiasm in the lecture halls—as we should say nowadays—of Chartres.'

157 An observation made by Mrs Merry, see note 152. Indirectly this can be concluded from Rudolf Steiner's lecture in London of 27 August 1924 (see *Karmic Relationships* Vol. VIII, op.cit.), where on the one hand he speaks of knights 'who were gathered around King Arthur in the first centuries after the Mystery of Golgotha', and on the other of 'the Arthurian Knights of the Round Table standing high up on the rocky crags before the Mystery of Golgotha.' So the

activities of 'Arthur' and his Round Table evidently spanned a period of several hundred years.

158 Colin Wilson, *Rudolf Steiner, the Man and his Vision*, Aquarian Press, Wellingborough 1985, p.115.

159 Op cit., p.116.

160 In Bibl. No. 238, *Karmic Relationships* Vol. IV, Rudolf Steiner Press, London 1983.

161 Wilson op. cit., p.117.

162 'One day Rudolf Steiner told me how mercilessly the anti-Michael demons were setting to work to prevent the rise of the work of Michael and indeed destroy it . . . These anti-Michael demons, to whom also Klingsor and his hosts belong, were hard at work, and threatened derisively to come into their own if the Michael-impulses that had begun so strongly should not be able to break through.' This is related by Ita Wegman in a letter 'To All Members,' 4 October 1925, see *Anthroposophical Movement*, Vol. 11, No. 40.

163 In Torquay (see note 150), on 12 August, 1924, Rudolf Steiner spoke of the objective, spiritual difficulties involved in actually *speaking* about the concrete results of karmic research. He described how these forces of resistance had been paralysed by the Christmas Foundation Meeting: 'even after having lived with these questions for decades, every time one wanted to utter them, it was as though the opponents of Michael always gathered round and sealed one's lips—for about certain matters silence was to be maintained . . . since the Christmas Foundation Meeting through the way and opportunity vouchsafed to me for occult work, the demons who hitherto prevented these things from being voiced have been compelled to remain silent.'

164 Lecture given on 21 August 1924, in Bibl. 243, see note 149.

165 In Bibl. No. 254, *Occult Movements in the Nineteenth Century*, Rudolf Steiner Press, London 1973, especially lectures given on 11, 17, and 18 October 1915.

166 Emil Bock, *Studien zu seinem Lebensgang und Lebenswerk*, Stuttgart, 2. Aufl. 1967, p.260.

167 See *Karmic Relations—Esoteric Studies*, Vol. VI, Rudolf Steiner, Press, London 1971.

168 'There is no feeling and no enthusiasm to be compared with the sentiments of warmth, beauty and exaltation that are kindled through the pure, crystal-clear thoughts that relate to higher

worlds. The highest feelings are, as a matter of fact, not those that come of themselves, but those that are achieved by energetic and persevering work in the realm of thought.' (Rudolf Steiner, *Theosophy*, Chapter 1, 'Body, Soul and Spirit', Rudolf Steiner Press, London 1970.) If this is true in general with regard to the integration of thoughts into the whole human being, it is particularly true of thoughts pertaining to the mysteries of reincarnation and karma.

169 Ita Wegman, 'To all Members', *Anthroposophical Movement*, Vol. II, No. 40, see also note 162.

170 Rudolf Steiner & Ita Wegman, *Fundamentals of Therapy*, Bibl. No. 17, Rudolf Steiner Press, London 1983.

171 See note 148.

172 This is a reference to the two lectures he gave on 24 August and the one on 27 August 1924, included in Bibl. No. 240, *Karmic Relationships* Vol. VIII, Rudolf Steiner Press, London 1975.

173 At the founding of the German Section of the Theosophical Society in 1902, Rudolf Steiner had announced the title of a lecture he was to give as 'Practical Exercises in Karma'. He describes in a lecture he gave on 24 August 1924: 'However, the people who were present at the founding of this Section were terribly shocked when they heard what the title was to be. Indeed, to this very day I could give a perfectly detailed account of the waves of astrality, the quaking and trembling of these persons—especially of the more elderly gentlemen who emanated from the Theosophical Movement of that period—when they heard that I was going to speak about practical karma.' (This passage is missing from the English translation of this lecture referred to above.)

174 See Ann Taylor, *Laurence Oliphant*, Oxford 1982. See also note 23.

175 See Richard Seddon, *The Mystery of Arthur at Tintagel*, Rudolf Steiner Press 1990. See also note 157.

176 See note 156.

177 See George Adams's contribution to 'Rudolf Steiner—Recollections by Some of his Pupils', in *The Golden Blade*, London 1955, p.20.

Chapter 5

178 From a release to the press; Central Office Archives in London.

179 Fifteenth Sectional Meeting of the World Power Conference, Tokyo 16–20 October 1966, *Transactions*, Vol. VII., p.3545.

180 The three faculties Rudolf Steiner describes in the second part of his

Philosophy of Spiritual Activity (see note 81) as being necessary for the accomplishment of any free act.

181 *Speeches by H.R.H. The Prince of Wales*, London n.d., p.279f. For the whole of this speech see also pages 384–86 of this book.

182 *A King's Story—The Memoirs of the Duke of Windsor*, New York 1947, p.216.

183 *The Times*, 2 July 1924.

184 See Rudolf Steiner's lecture 12 September 1919, in *The Inner Aspect of the Social Question*, Bibl. No. 193, Rudolf Steiner Press, London 1974. In connection with the possibility the individual human being has to pass the threshold *consciously*, see *Knowledge of Higher Worlds—How is it achieved?* Bibl. No. 10, Rudolf Steiner Press, London 1969.

185 See W.J. Stein, *The Earth as Basis of World Economy*, a special number of *The Present Age*, Vol. II, No. 7, in which Marshall's work *Economics for Industry*, is cited. In this work Marshall makes the demand that the expression 'national economy be replaced by the expression "economy".'

186 Printed in *Transactions of the World Power Conference, Basle Sectional Meeting 1926*, Birkhäuser Verlag, Basel 1926, Vol. I, p.1198f.

187 From an obituary which appeared in the magazine *World Survey*, Vol. I No. 3, June 1935.

188 In the Basel *National-Zeitung*, 6th of September 1926.

189 *Transactions of the World Power Conference* (see note 186), Vol. II, p.1535f.

190 On 9 September 1926.

191 Printed under the title *Die Weltkraftkonferenz—Rückblick und Ausblick*, an undated extract from the newspaper, Economic Archives, Basel.

192 *Power Resources of the World (Potential and Developed)*, London 1929, with a forword by D.N. Dunlop.

193 *The Global 2000 Report to the President*, Washington, US Government Printing Office, 1980.

194 Basel *National-Zeitung*, 24 June 1930.

195 This description appeared in the *Neuer Zürcher Zeitung*, 18 June 1930.

196 On 1 August 1930.

197 The source here is an eight-page letter to a certain Mr Whiston which includes a kind of curriculum vitae.

198 We do not know the exact name Dunlop himself used for this organization. W.J. Stein describes it as a 'Weltwirtschaftsbund'.

199 Stein's 'interview' might already have taken place in July 1932 at Glastonbury, where he was lecturing and Dunlop was also present.
200 *World Survey*, April 1935, p.1f.
201 ibid. p.5f.
202 ibid. No. 3, June 1935, p.67.
203 W.J. Stein, *The Earth as Basis of World Economy* (see note 185), p.8.
204 ibid. p.5.
205 ibid. p.8ff.
206 Compare the fundamental principles of Rudolf Steiner's expositions on this subject in *The Mission of the Folk-Souls*, Bibl. 121, Rudolf Steiner Press, 1970.
207 This part of Stein's account was later expanded by him into his (posthumously published) work *The British: their Psychology and Destiny*, 1958 (new edition London 1990).
208 *Deutsche Zeitung und Wirtschaftszeitung*, No. 54, 7 July 1956.
209 Printed in *Fifth World Power Conference*, Vienna 1956, Vol. I, p.275.
210 It is worth noting that this change took place approximately 33 years after Dunlop's death.
211 In this respect the recent foundation in Switzerland of the Anthro-Tech Association may augur well for the future.

Chapter 6

212 D.N. Dunlop, 'In Memoriam', in *Anthroposophy, Memorial Number*, August 1925, p.86f.
213 *Rudolf Steiner—'Erkenne dich im Strome der Welt'*, published in the series *Texte zum Nachdenken*, presented by Gerhard Wehr, Herder Verlag, Freiburg/Basel/Wien 1986.
214 The action and influence of these beings, as well as that of the Luciferic powers diametrically opposed to them, are described by Rudolf Steiner from a number of different points of view in his works, e.g. *Occult Science—An Outline*, Bibl. No. 13, Rudolf Steiner Press, London 1963; *The Threshold of the Spiritual World*, Bibl. No. 17, Rudolf Steiner Press, London, and in numerous lectures. What he writes on this subject in *Anthroposophical Leading Thoughts* (Bibl. No. 26, Rudolf Steiner Press 1985) is in a sense a kind of legacy.
215 *Willem Zeylmans van Emmichoven—Ein Pionier der Anthroposophie* by Emanuel Zeylmans, Arlesheim 1979, p.153f.
216 Rudolf Hauschka, *Wetterleuchten einer Zeitenwende*, Frankfurt 1966, p.88.

217 Extract from a letter addressed to the author by Sidney Hunt, Scotland, 30 July 1986.
218 'To All Friends', see also *Anthroposophical Movement*, 26 June 1927.
219 'Ossian and Fingal's Cave', a short address after a performance of Mendelssohn's *Hebrides Overture* on 3 March 1909; Bibl. No. 127.
220 'To All Members', *Anthroposophical Movement*, Vol. IV. No. 36, 4 September 1927.
221 See 'A World Conference', *Anthroposophical Movement*, Vol. IV, No. 43, 23 October 1927.
222 Erich Weismann from Reutlingen in Germany; this detail is reported by E. Zeylmans. See also *Eugen Kolisko—Ein Lebensbild* (1961), p.189.
223 See *Anthroposophical Movement*, Vol. V, No. 34, 26 August 1928.
224 Under the title 'The World Conference on Spiritual Science', Vol. III, No. 3, 1933, p.383.
225 The post of President of the Anthroposophical Society was never as such revived. It seems not to have been until after Dunlop's lifetime that the post of General Secretary was officially upgraded to that of 'Chairman'.
226 'To All Members', printed in *Anthroposophical Movement* from 17 May to 9 August 1925 (from 23 August onwards, the title of Ita Wegman's contributions was changed from 'Leitsätze' to 'Leitgedanken').
227 One particular statement made by Dunlop during an Extraordinary Meeting of the General Secretaries of the Anthroposophical Society in the autumn of that year is symptomatic of his attitude towards the schismatic tendencies within the *Vorstand* at that time. The statement is recorded (see *Memorandum*, note 253) in the form of a reference to the relationship between the President and the rest of that body, 'comparing the Vorstand to a human hand which has five members; the first of which however, should not be more prominent than the others'. If Rudolf Steiner had designated a successor before his death, someone to take over the *esoteric* functions which he himself as President had been able to fulfill, then the whole situation after his death would have been very different. However, no such successor had been named by him; and who could, in all seriousness, claim that he was spiritually competent to exercise these esoteric functions—in the sense indicated by Rudolf Steiner? Steffen's reply to this objection was 'that the President *did* have a special role to play, otherwise there was no need to have a

President'. In so far as Steffen meant something over and above the 'special role' the President might have to play in organizational matters and the like within the framework of the whole Society, to this extent he was indeed attributing a greater degree of 'esoteric' spirituality to the President—in this case, to himself—than to the other members of the Vorstand.

See Bodo von Plato, *Zur Entwicklung der Anthroposophischen Gesellschaft*, Stuttgart 1986; Lili Kolisko, *Eugen Kolisko—Ein Lebensbild*, published privately 1961; Fred Poeppig, *Rückblick*, Basel 1964; for the 'quarrel over the urn' see *Marie Steiner—Briefe und Dokumente*, Dornach 1981, p.89f. Further sources will be indicated in the relevant contexts.

228 See Emanuel Zeylmans, *Willem Zeylmans van Emmichoven* (see note 215), p.167f.

229 Towards the end of the 'Last Address' at Dornach, Michaelmas Eve, 1924, Rudolf Steiner pronounced the following words: 'If in the near future, in four times twelve human beings, the Michael-Thought becomes fully alive . . . if in four times twelve such human beings, leaders arise having the mood that belongs to the Michael festival, then we can look up to the light that through the Michael stream and the Michael activity will be shed abroad in the future among mankind.' Rudolf Steiner Press, London 1967.

230 In the lecture he gave on 4 April 1912, in *The Spiritual Beings in the Heavenly Bodies and in the Kingdoms of Nature*, Bibl. No. 136, Anthroposophic Press 1981.

231 'Meine holländische und englische Reise', *Das Goetheanum*, Jg. I, No. 39, 7 May 1922. Translation J.B. and C.V.

232 Willem Zeylmans van Emmichoven, op. cit. p.154.

233 Extract from a short obituary by W.J. Stein in *Anthroposophical Movement*, Vol. XII, No. 7, July/August 1935, p.122f.

234 Op cit. p.113: from a letter received from Dr Rudolf Hauschka, addressed to members of the Anthroposophical Society in Great Britain.

235 George Adams, *Physical and Ethereal Spaces*, reprinted in revised version, Rudolf Steiner Press, 1965.

236 See for instance his lecture of 27 January 1910 in *The Reappearance of Christ in the Etheric*, Bibl. No. 118, Anthroposophic Press, New York 1983.

237 'Christmas and the Mystery of the Logos', *Anthroposophical Move-*

ment, Vol. I, 1924, p.225. (However, we have quoted G. Adams's translation of this passage, see note 238.)

238 George Adams (Kaufmann) in his memorial address *Our Community*, reprinted in *Anthroposophical Movement*, Vol. XII, No. 7, July/August 1935, p.106ff. and as an appendix to this book.

239 'If I managed to break-through', see Stein's reminiscences in *The Death of Merlin*, Edinburgh 1989, p.65f., also J. Tautz's contribution: *Der Lehrerumkreis um Rudolf Steiner*, Stuttgart, 2. Ed. p.59f.

240 Printed in the collection of documents entitled *Marie Steiner—Briefe und Dokumente*, on the occasion of the thirty-third anniversary of her death, by the Nachlaßverwaltung in Dornach. An original draft also exists. Stein did *not* send off the letter; doubtless he feared to open up old wounds and thereby do more harm than good. See also the announcement made by Marie Steiner at the same time at the General Meeting, 28 March 1948 included in the same volume p.144, see note 227.

241 The various proceedings and votes at this General Meeting can be studied in some detail in Lili Kolisko, *Eugen Kolisko—ein Lebensbild* (see note. 220), p.305f. See also: *Bericht über die Vorgänge bei der Generalversammlung in Dornach am 27., 28. März 1934* (printed manuscript), by Jürgen von Grone; see also the abbreviated version of the minutes in *Anthroposophical Movement*, Vol. XI, No. 16.

242 Thus Boos describes the Basle Sectional Meeting of the *World Power Conference* as the *first* World Power Conference; Dunlop is described as 'industrial magnate' which inevitably leads to a very one-sided association of ideas.

243 See 'Declaration of Will' published before the General Meeting 1934 by a group of leading members in protest against the proposal to change the Statutes of the Society. Included in Lili Kolisko, op. cit. p.333ff., as well as in *Anthroposophical Movement*, Vol. II, No. 16.

244 See 'Extraordinary General Meeting' in *Anthroposophical Movement*, Vol. XI, No. 11, 14 June 1934. At this meeting the following resolution was carried by an overwhelming majority: 'With a view to continuing, to the best of our ability, the world-wide tasks of the Anthroposophical Movement under the new conditions, we ask the Executive Council to enter into consultation with the representatives of independent Groups in other countries, so as to find the most suitable forms for our united work in the future.'

245 Lili Kolisko, ibid. p.362.

246 Founded during a conference in Stuttgart on 30 June–1 July, in the

presence of Elizabeth Vreede, it was an alliance between the Anthroposophical Societies in Great Britain and Holland as well as other free anthroposophical groups already existing in Germany. See Lili Kolisko, op. cit., p.264f., also Bodo von Plato, op. cit. p.86f.

247 George Adams-Kaufmann, *The Present Situation in our Society*, in *Anthroposophical Movement*, Vol. XI, No. 13, July 1934, p.101f.

248 See L. Kolisko, op. cit. p.360; also, Elisabeth Vreede, *Zur Geschichte der Anthroposophischen Gesellschaft seit der Weihnachtstagung 1923*, privately printed for members, Arlesheim, February 1935.

249 'Summer School at Westonbirt', *Anthroposophical Movement*, Vol. XI, No. 16, 13 September 1934.

250 Reprinted in *Anthroposophical Movement*, Vol. I, No. 33, 24 August 1924.

251 Circulated to members of the Anthroposophical Society.

252 This formulation was also used by Albert Steffen in his opening speech in order to characterize the 'United Free Anthroposophical Groups' founded on 30 June 1934.

253 This 'Memorandum' came out in March only three weeks before the General Meeting, under the title: *Denkschrift über Angelegenheiten der Anthroposophischen Gesellschaft in den Jahren 1925 bis 1935*, Manuskriptdruck für Mitglieder, Dornach 1935. The English translation, entitled *Memorandum*, inspired Owen Barfield to publish a perceptive assessment by way of rejoinder: 'The Anthroposophical Society', in *Anthroposophical Movement*, Vol. XII, No. 5 (may 1935).

254 This speech was first published in its entirety in the magazine *Erde und Kosmos*, Vol. XII, No. 1, 1986. After it was made, Count Polzer-Hoditz sent a copy to Ita Wegman, which was then translated into English by George Adams in a copy made specifically for Dunlop's benefit. The expulsions of 1935 were unanimously rescinded at the General Meeting in 1948.

255 Constance Winney, London.

256 See the lecture he gave on 6 September 1915, *Chance, Providence and Necessity*, AP 1988, Bibl. No. 163.

257 The author wishes to thank Emanuel Zeylmans for the kind permission of using the draft of this address.

258 The illness in question lasted from February 1934 right into the autumn of that year.

259 These words may remind us of those spoken by the Red Indian which Rudolf Steiner freely evoked in a lecture he gave in Oslo on

12 June 1910; see: *The Mission of the Folk-Souls*, Bibl. No. 121, Rudolf Steiner Press, London 1970.

260 From the preface to AE's work *Co-operation and Nationality*, new edition Dublin 1982.

261 John Eglinton, op. cit. p.78.

262 Alan Denson (ed.), op. cit. p.204.

263 op, cit. p.16f.

264 From a letter dated 26 July 1935 addressed to Dorothy Wellesley, in *The Letters of W.B. Yeats*, edited by Allan Wade, London 1954, p.838.

265 John Eglinton, op. cit. p.61.

266 *The Irish Theosophist*, Vol. I, No. 6, p.56. Also *Homeward—Songs by the Way*, p.22.

Chapter 7

267 Bibl. No. 13, *Occult Science*, Rudolf Steiner Press, London 1963, p.194.

268 Freely translated from a lecture he gave on 29 June 1909. But see *The Gospel of St. John in its Relation to the Other Three Gospels, Particularly to the Gospel of St. Luke*, Bibl. No. 112, Anthroposophic Press, New York 1982.

269 From a lecture given on 7 September 1910, *The Gospel of St Matthew*, Bibl. No. 123, Rudolf Steiner Press, London 1965.

270 See Rudolf Steiner's indications on this subject on 2 December 1923 in *Mystery Knowledge and Mystery Centres*, Bibl. No. 232, Rudolf Steiner Press, London 1973.

271 In the epic work *Argonautica* (*c.* 240 BC), by Apollonius of Rhodes.

272 Freely translated from a lecture given on 16 January 1911. But see *Background to the Gospel of St. Mark*, Bibl. No. 124, Rudolf Steiner Press, London 1968.

273 Rudolf Steiner, 27 December 1910, in *Occult History*, Bibl. No. 126, Rudolf Steiner Press, London 1982.

274 On 7, 8, 9 December 1923. See *Mystery Knowledge and Mystery Centres*, op. cit. Rudolf Steiner also spoke of the Hibernian Mysteries from another point of view in *World History*, Rudolf Steiner Press, London 1977.

275 Freely translated from a lecture given on 2 December 1923; but see note 274.

276 9 December 1923; see note 274.

277 Of course it is also possible to see a connection to the Hibernian Mysteries here and to the Arthurian Mysteries emanating from them. However, Ita Wegman's impression of the 'Tao' points to the Saturn Mysteries which, following the destruction of Atlantis, primarily lived on in the Saturn-race inhabiting the North American continent. As a fairly substantial 'shipping traffic' between north-western Europe and the American continent was maintained right into the first centuries AD, 'old Western' might be associated equally with the European or the American West. However, on pages 347–59 we will demonstrate how the *main accent* lies on the link to the old American West.

278 See *Mystery Knowledge and Mystery Centres*, op.cit. See also note 274.

279 Printed in *Inner Impulses of Human Evolution*, Bibl. No. 171, Rudolf Steiner Press, London 1984.

280 Quoted from *The Temple Legend*, Bibl. No. 93, Rudolf Steiner Press, London 1985.

281 Jacques de Mahieu, *Les Templiers en Amérique*, Editions Robert Laffont 1981. See also Louis Charpentier, *Les Mystères Templiers*, Paris 1967.

282 In the lecture he gave on 16 November 1917, in *Individuelle Geistwesen und ihr Wirken in der Seele des Menschen*, Bibl. No. 178. (*Geographic Medicine and the Mystery of the Double*, Mercury Press, New York 1986) As Rudolf Steiner specifies in this lecture 'in former centuries Norwegian ships sailed over to America and *studies were made of certain illnesses there.*' One particular being was deeply implicated in all the illnesses that were studied in the West in this way—the being Rudolf Steiner describes in the same lecture as the human 'Doppelgänger' (or spiritual 'double'). This 'double' is particularly related to the sub-earthly forces of electricity and magnetism. It was known that such magnetic forces could be found especially in America—forces which, exuding from the earth, bring the human being into a special kind of relationship to this 'double'. People 'set out from Europe in order to study illnesses in America which were, so to speak, brought about by the forces of magnetism; *and it is there that we must look if we want to find the mysterious origin of old European medicine.* There it was possible to observe the whole course of an illness whereas in Europe, where people were more susceptible to the influence of the double, this was not possible.' Thus 'visits' were made to the West in order to 'study the very significant role that the "double" played within the

Indian Race with its quite different constitution.' The importance of this knowledge concerning the human 'double', which was once sought after in the West and in future times will have to be re-acquired, can be gauged from the following remark made by Rudolf Steiner: 'This "double" is nothing more and nothing less than the "originating author" of all physical illnesses that emerge spontaneously from inside the human being. And really to know him is itself organic medicine.'

283 M.J. Krück von Poturzyn, *Im Brennpunkt der Geschichte, Historische Miniaturen*, Stuttgart 1983, p.52f. See also: M.J. Krück von Poturzyn, *Der Prozeß gegen die Templer*, Stuttgart, 2. Aufl. 1982.

284 From a lecture given on 1 October 1916, in Bibl. No. 171; see note 279.

285 See Bibl. No. 264 op. cit., p.326f., a public lecture given on 16 November 1904.

286 *Occult Science*, op. cit. Chapter IV. See also Guenther *Wachsmuth, Werdegang der Menschheit*, Dornach 1973, p.111f.; Wachsmuth uses a graphic illustration to show the migratory movement of the Atlantic Saturn Mysteries to North and South America.

287 *The East in the Light of the West*, Bibl. No. 113, Anthroposophic Press, New York 1940. Lecture given on 31 August 1909. It is worth noting that before it went into print Rudolf Steiner read through this cycle of lectures and made the annotations to it himself, something he very rarely did.

288 The 'men who came over from old Atlantis into Europe and beyond' constituted what is described in *Occult Science*, as well as in the fifth lecture (27 August) of this cycle (above), as the northern and southern streams which both moved eastwards. Consequently, the conservation of the old Atlantean clairvoyance, which 'withdrew perforce into separate personalities in the West', is connected with the *third* stream which went over from Atlantis to America.

289 See the lectures given on 17 and 18 September 1916, in Bibl. No. 171; see note 279.

290 Rudolf Steiner made relatively few allusions to Skythianos (later referred to in this lecture as 'the great and honoured Bodhisattva of the West'); perhaps the clearest exposition is in this Munich cycle of lectures (see note 287).

Two other illuminating references can be found in the same year in the lectures given on 31 May (*The Principle of Spiritual Economy*, Anthroposophic Press, New York 1986, Bibl. No. 109) and 14

November 1909 (*Deeper Secrets of Human History*, Rudolf Steiner Press, 1985, Bibl. No. 117). On 31 May 1909 Rudolf Steiner described Skythianos as 'a highly developed personality of ancient origins who, in a later incarnation in Central Asia, directed the Occult Schools and later became the teacher of the 'inner Schools of Europe'. On the second occasion he explains how Skythianos, 'who had also lived in ancient times, surrounded during a certain period by the people of Skythia', had the task of impregnating the Slavonic peoples 'with a particular form of the Mystery of Golgotha'. This he accomplished by introducing 'Greek-Byzantine culture' into the Slavonic world, his influence proceeding from Constantinople as his 'Initiation Centre'.

Skythianos is also mentioned in connection with Manes and Buddha in some notes that Elisabeth Vreede took at a lecture given by Rudolf Steiner entitled: 'Über Meisterpersönlichkeiten im Zusammenhang mit den Auferweckungen in den Evangelien' Bibl. No. 264, 1984 (not yet translated into English).

From an overall view of these passages extracted from various lectures we may conclude in broad outlines that Skythianos was connected to an Eastern, a European and a Western mission; furthermore, the spheres of influence which correspond to his Eastern and European missions appear, in a certain sense, to interpenetrate one another. For on 14 November 1914 Rudolf Steiner specified in connection with the forces which had inspired the first forms of European culture that this initiate's sphere of influence 'reached right into Siberia'. On the other hand, Constantinople, the centre of his Eastern Slavonic mission is situated at a comparable kind of distance to Middle Europe. Whilst his European and Eastern missions were fulfilled (or rather embarked upon) in the past, his *Western* mission, particularly emphasized by Rudolf Steiner in the Munich cycle of lectures, has still to be accomplished in the future.

An illuminating, concrete confirmation of this mode of Skythianos' influence and action (embracing East, West and Centre), can be found in a remark that Friedrich Rittelmeyer passed on to Stein. On 9 July 1924, the latter noted it as follows: 'Rittelmeyer said: on a certain occasion when he had been required to write a short account of Rudolf Steiner's life, Dr Steiner had told him, in the presence of Frau Dr Steiner, that he had had two "Initiators"—Christian Rosenkreutz and Master Jesus (Zarathustra). The latter had drawn his attention to Fichte. The former had worked through Felix Balde' (Stein means Felix Koguzki, on whom Rudolf Steiner *modelled* the character of Felix Balde in his Mystery Plays. Schuré points to Master Jesus (strong of will) in his biography: '*Skythianos moves between six other Masters. He maintains the link.* Two in the East, two in the West, Master Jesus and Christian Rosenkreutz in the Centre.' See also Bibl. No. 264, p.246, where further reference to this remark is made.

291 See H. Wiesberger, 'Die Meister der Weisheit und des Zusammenklanges der Empfindungen im Werk Rudolf Steiners', in Bibl. No. 264, p.241ff. See also note 87. This is only the earthly aspect of a Bodhisattva; there is also a supersensible, 'avataric' side of such beings. See E. Vreede, T.H. Meyer, *Die Bodhisattvafrage*, Basel 1989.

292 George Adams, *The Mysteries of the Rose-Cross*, London 1989.

293 Rudolf Steiner spoke of two Masters in the East, two Masters in the West, two in the Centre, and one who maintained the link (see end of note 290). Sometimes he used the word 'West' to designate the whole area of the Mediterranean Sea forming part of the Western world. He named Christian Rosenkreutz and Master Jesus as the guiding Master-individualities corresponding to this part of the globe, speaking of both of them as 'Masters of the West'. We may conclude from this that it is in the *far West* that must be sought the main sphere of influence of Skythianos, as *the Bodhisattva of the West.*

294 See *The Mission of the Folk-Souls*, Bibl. No. 121 Rudolf Steiner Press, London 1929. Morning lecture of 12 June 1910. It is clear from this lecture that the Great Spirit of old Atlantis, which survived in the Red Indian Saturn race, was deeply linked to an element that had held sway in humanity before the differentiation between one race and another had begun to emerge. Rudolf Steiner asks what it was that 'the Red Indian valued most highly', and observes that 'it was that he was still able dimly to sense something of the former greatness and majesty of a period which existed in the old Atlantean epoch when the separation of the races had hardly begun to take effect.'

295 Lecture of 17 December 1906, in *Ursprungsimpulse der Geisteswissenschaft*, Bibl. No. 96, 1974 (*Signs and Symbols of the Christmas Festival*, New York 1969).

296 In *Karmic Relationships—Esoteric Studies* Vol. IV, Bibl. No. 238, Rudolf Steiner Press, London 1983.

297 See Rudolf Steiner, *The Occult Significance of the Bhagavad Gita*, Bibl.

No. 146, Anthroposophic Press, New York 1984. 'No one could think abstractly, could have thoughts and ideas, if he were not clairvoyant. In our ordinary thinking the pearl of clairvoyance is contained from the start. Ideas arise in the soul through exactly the same process as what gives rise to its highest powers. It is immensely important to learn to understand that clairvoyance begins in something common and everyday. One only has to recognize the supersensible nature of concepts and ideas . . . In the 18th century what was considered a great dictum was uttered by a pioneer of thinking: "O, Man, make bold to use thy power of reason!" Today a greater word must resound in men's souls: "O, Man, make bold to claim concepts and ideas as the beginning of thy clairvoyance."'

298 In *Die Verbindung zwischen Lebenden und Toten*, Bibl. No. 168 (not yet translated into English).

299 See also Hans Peter van Manen, *Christussucher und Michaeldiener*, Dornach 1980; Wilhelm Rath, *Von dem Zusammenwirken der Platoniker und Aristoteliker im Hinblick auf das Ende des zwanzigsten Jahrhunderts, in: Mitteilungen aus der anthroposophischen Arbeit in Deutschland*, Johanni 1964; further: Emil Bock, *Rudolf Steiner*, op. cit.

300 We cannot here discuss in detail everything that Rudolf Steiner brought forward in the 1924 karma lectures in order to depict these two streams both of which played a central part in the spiritual history of mankind. However, we may characterize these two polar-opposite and yet complementary movements from an *elementary* point of view by considering them in the light of the Northern and Southern Mystery Streams earlier mentioned. The spiritual movement that goes back to Plato seeks the spiritual and supersensible more by opening up the inner 'windows' of the soul which command a certain view over the world of creative archetypal images or ideas; the souls belonging to the Aristotelian stream, on the other hand, seek the reality of the Spirit particularly in its activity behind the veil of all natural phenomena and even in these phenomena themselves. From this point of view it is easy to understand why it was particularly the most important representatives of this second stream, above all in the Dominican Order, who prepared the ground for the modern scientific frame of mind. With regard to the preparations made to ensure the collaboration between Platonists and Aristotelians, see for instance Rudolf Steiner's lecture on 13 July 1924, in Bibl. No. 237, *Karmic Relationships—Esoteric Studies*, Rudolf Steiner Press, London 1977.

301 Lecture in Arnheim; 18 July 1924, in Bibl. No. 240, *Karmic Relationships—Esoteric Studies*, Vol. VI, Rudolf Steiner Press, London 1971 p.141.
302 Ludwig Polzer-Hoditz, *Erinnerungen an Rudolf Steiner*, Dornach 1985, p.232.
303 From 'The Last Address' given by Rudolf Steiner on 28 September 1924, see note 229.
304 Bibl. No. 240, *Karmic Relationships—Esoteric Studies*, Vol. VI, Rudolf Steiner Press, London 1971.
305 D.N. Dunlop, *The Masonic Examination*, in *The Path*, Vol. II, No. 10, April 1912.

Appendix

306 In 1884 or thereabouts Mr and Mrs Coulomb launched a libellous campaign against H.P. Blavatsky in Adyar. Efforts were being undertaken from certain quarters to render her 'harmless'. The stir caused by this campaign also made itself felt in the press and did considerable damage to the Theosophical Movement. (See Charles J. Ryan, *H.P. Blavatsky and the Theosophical Movement*, San Diego 1975; also Rudolf Steiner's lecture of 12 June 1923, where he explains which occult circles were behind the affair and why they used the Coulombs in an attempt to discredit H.P. Blavatsky in the eyes of the public, and how they exploited her naivety; see also note 87. As a result of the Coulomb affair a very one-sided investigation was made by the Society for Psychical Research: see Leslie Price, *Madame Blavatsky Unveiled? A new discussion of the most famous investigation of the Society for Psychical Research*, Theosophical History Centre, London 1986.)
307 A reference to the etheric substance which forms the basis of the Akashic Record.
308 Henry Steel Olcott (1832–1907), co-founder of the Theosophical Society and Founder President until his death.
309 *Celtic Twilight* was Yeats's first work in prose. It came out in 1893.
310 Published in 1899.
311 Presumably Yeats is referring to his collection of essays published under the title *Ideas of Good and Evil*.
312 The certified engineer F. Zur Nedden acted as general reporter at

the second World Power Conference in Berlin 1930. Stein wrote this letter about two weeks *before* his dismissal from the editorial staff of *World Survey*.

313 See bibliography of obituaries (page 420).

314 Presumably Stein made a mistake here with regard to Dunlop's age. At this point in time Dunlop was 13½ years old (see also Chapter 1 of this book).

315 This document is a transcript of an unsigned letter found in Stein's literary remains.

316 This came out under the title 'Our Community', in *Anthroposophical Movement*, Vol. XII, No. 6, London, June 1935.

317 See, for instance, Rudolf Steiner's lecture of 11 April 1919, in Bibl. No. 190, 3. Aufl. 1980 (not yet translated).

318 Bibl. No. 258; lecture of 10 June 1923, *The Anthroposophic Movement*, Rudolf Steiner Press, 1992.

319 Bibl. No. 237; lecture of 4 August 1924. *Karmic Relationships*, Vol III, Rudolf Steiner Press, 1977.

320 Bibl. No. 10; *Knowledge of the Higher Worlds*, (op.cit.) 'The Conditions of Esoteric Training'.

321 Bibl. No. 117, *Deeper Secrets of Human History*, op.cit.

322 Bibl. No. 257; lecture of 27 February 1923, *Awakening to Community*, op.cit.

323 Bibl. No. 233a; lecture of 13 January 1924, *Rosicrucianism and Modern Initiation*, Rudolf Steiner Press, London 1965.

Sources of Quotations

Sources of quotations introducing the seven chapters of this book:

Introduction	From: 'Birth and Death'; address given by Dunlop on 7 May 1911, reprinted in *The Path*, Vol. II, No. 1, London 1911.
Chapter 1:	From: 'A Morning Prayer', see page 267
Chapter 2:	From: 'Friendship', address given by Dunlop on 18 June 1911, reprinted in *The Path*, Vol. II, No. 2, 1911.
Chapter 3:	From an undated letter to E.C. Merry.
Chapter 4:	From: 'Rudolf Steiner and the Fulfilment of a Quest'; see complete text in Appendix.
Chapter 5:	From an undated letter to E.C. Merry.
Chapter 6:	From: 'Rudolf Steiner and the Fulfilment of a Quest'.
Chapter 7:	From 'Individuality and Personality', reprinted in *The Science of Immortality*, London 1918, p.40.

AFTERWORD

First a few half-buried reminiscences. I believe the first time I saw D.N. Dunlop was at the General Meeting in 1929 when he was on the platform together with Mr Collison. It was the meeting that resulted in his taking over the leadership of the Anthroposophical Society in Great Britain. There was much dissension. I was still a relatively junior and uninstructed anthroposophist and had a rather vague idea of what was going on, and why. What sticks in my memory is that at one point the political issue threatened to rear its head. Mr Collison was a true blue conservative. One or more of the speakers had shown leftward leanings and in response to them Collison in his speech insisted that the existence of the Society had been made possible by capital. Dunlop, when his turn came, poured oil on potentially troubled waters. Politics were not our concern; there was room in the Society for opinions of every colour including apparently—and here he picked up a rose from a flower vase on the table—red!

In the following year I was elected or co-opted a member of the Executive Council and attended a whole series of meetings under his chairmanship. This was really the closest association I had with him. The external man became a familiar figure to me, and perhaps I should mention here the two marks of the external man that *anyone* to whom he became a familiar figure is unlikely to omit from his mental picture. Namely the Yeatsian broad black ribbon descending from his pince-nez and the white spats that are so evident in the group photograph from 1924 (see plate 18). Untutored and perhaps unreliable memory tells me that he always kept these on, though they must have been very uncomfortable in warm weather. It also tells me that—off the stage—I have never seen them on anyone else!

Less trivially, there are things in one's experience of a person that one does not 'notice' at the time but of which one was in fact so conscious that, when attention is drawn to them, perhaps years later, they rank as reminiscences. This happened to me when I came to Edith Young's reference on page 37 to that 'engaging twinkle in his eye', which is most nearly apparent in the 1925 photograph (see plate 23). Perhaps in the author's terminology it is the Individuality trying to shine through the personality, as to which more later. Whatever it is, it was much evident in those Council Meetings. In the years leading up to 1935 they were difficult and often protracted ones. The dissensions in Dornach extended down to its members, some of whom resigned when matters came to a head in that year. Often there was correspondence with the *Vorstand* to be dealt with, and here one of the difficulties was that our letters not infrequently remained unanswered. Through it all Dunlop's quiet geniality was a valuable healing influence. I recall in particular how he was wont to lay stress on the practical activities, in education, medicine, etc., which were steadily growing while the Society appeared to be falling apart.

Sometime before the fateful General Meeting in 1935, at which Dunlop himself among others was expelled from the General Society, leading up to it there was another meeting in Dornach which I have not often seen referred to. It was a meeting of elected representatives of the various national societies, with Albert Steffen in the chair, and it continued through two successive days into the small hours of the morning. D.N. Dunlop, Cecil Harwood and I myself attended it on behalf of the Anthroposophical Society in Great Britain. It was a violently contentious meeting and there is much that I could tell about it. But I mention it only because it is connected with another reminiscence of Dunlop, though he did not speak at the meeting. The three of us were not travelling together, because Dunlop went 1st Class. But I have a very vivid memory indeed of Basel railway station on the return journey, and of Dunlop smiling and waving to us from a seat on the platform as we walked past him to our end of the train.

I have dwelt on these all too slight and scattered personal

recollections, not because I imagine they could be as important to others as to myself, but because I was particularly requested to do so. All this time I knew very little indeed of the real Dunlop. I had heard a few references to his predominant role in BEAMA, but they meant very little to me—even after an uncle of mine, who was employed on the marketing side by one of the electrical companies, told me that Dunlop had spoken to him after a meeting and had asked if I were any relation. Of his pre-anthroposophical life, his links with such well-known figures as W.B. Yeats, AE., Richard St Barbe Baker, his own published writings, his growing international significance as the founder and indeed leader of the World Power Conference, of all this I knew nothing until after his death and then only what I heard or read in scraps. No wonder that, when I read, on its first appearance in German, Thomas Meyer's biography with its wide range and almost quixotic wealth of detail, I was a good deal surprised by a revelation for which I am also deeply grateful. To discover buried treasure anywhere is a joy, but to discover it in one's own little back garden is a special kind of joy; and my limited personal acquaintance with the later Dunlop is the back garden I have in mind.

Here it is worth remarking that in the matter of range and detail, this Englished version goes beyond its original. It comprises for instance a fuller account of Dunlop's theosophical activities and of his experiences in America, where he was shown the 'Keely engine', and there are some additional letters in the Appendix. Even without these I can imagine some less well-disposed reader complaining that the range is *too* wide. Here is what purports to be a biography of one individual and we keep finding ourselves in miniature, but still quite detailed, biographies of others such as W.J. Stein and E.C. Merry. I can understand, he might say, that a good deal of attention had to be paid to the inner histories of the Theosophical Movement and the Anthroposophical Society, but elsewhere surely our author has wandered too far afield.

To a certain extent Thomas Meyer rebuts this putative objection himself, when he observes (page 359): 'It was never our intention to compile a purely documentary account of Dunlop's life within the pages of this book. To have done so would only have been to limit ourselves to a domain which, in Dunlop's terms, could only be described as that of the "personality". A historical vision of things which concentrates exclusively on the past, on documents or other *traces* of the living, will never be able to grasp the *Entelechy* of the human being . . .' This distinction between the personality and the Individuality, also referred to as the Entelechy, because it denotes the totality of a biographical process extending over many lives, which is stressed throughout the book, has positively determined its character and, with that, its structure. One could even say that the book is both a biography and a treatise on biography as a *genre*. A narrative of the life, character and significance of a personality is one thing, and up to now it is all that biographers have attempted. An account of the life, character and significance of an Individuality is, or rather will be, another. In dealing with the subject's relations with another human being for example it must have to do with elements in that relation that extended beyond the bounds of birth and death. And that entails concern with their future as well as with their past both on earth and in the realm they inhabit between death and a new birth. A friendship or other relation between two personalities can indeed be delineated with sympathy and penetration, but it has significance for them alone. A similar relation between two Individualities on the other hand has a bearing on the well-being or otherwise of the entire human community. Not only is it likely to have arisen from the bosom of that community in a remote past—when human consciousness was altogether different in character from what it is now—but it is equally likely to have some bearings on the future development of that community, its welfare and its destiny. It is, or it is going to be, correspondingly difficult to achieve. But it is for that reason that the author's narrative is laced with frequent digressions into something like a survey of the world surrounding it.

I am free to make such cool assertions as the above without embroidery, regardless of the fact that most of my contemporaries would dismiss them out of hand. Not so the author. He too had, as far as space would permit, to justify them in the act of using them, hence the interventions in his text of what some would again regard as digressions into argument. A pioneer cannot simply pitch his tent on any hitherto uninhabited spot he chooses and start living in it. He has first to screen it from rain and snow and clear the ground of any irregularities and injurious matter that spoils it for his purpose. Today not only are there far too many biographies of no particular value pouring almost monthly from the press, but there is also a mental climate that renders virtually unthinkable the future he foresees for the art. If Meyer has indeed produced, as I have suggested, a pioneering treatise on the *genre* of biography and its future development, it is precisely because he has done that, not as his primary objective but as incidental to one actual biography impressively researched and lovingly handled, that it is to my mind so convincing.

Had such a treatise been his *primary* object, it may be questioned whether his choice of subject to try it on would have been a wise one. D.N. Dunlop stood for some years somewhere near the centre of the Anthroposophical Movement, and the Anthroposophical Movement, together with the Michael impulse, stands somewhere near the centre of the whole evolution of human consciousness. This must, I think, have intensified the difficulty, inherent in the *genre* as he sees it, of reconciling the extremes of centre and periphery. If the technique he has evolved for interweaving cosmic and terrestrial, individual and personal, goings on is not beyond criticism, that is hardly surprising. But criticism on those lines might well be deferred until someone else has evolved a better one.

Shall I attempt a value judgement? Galloping inflation has deprived the common currency of all significance. We live in an age when literary 'prizes' are awarded five or six times a year and 'best sellers', judging by the *Radio Times*, are three a penny. By contrast the circulation this book can expect is a dispiritingly small one. But so is the first and most visible of the expanding rings made by a small pebble dropped into a large pool. In this matter of literary values I have for a long time now been in the habit of applying my own private gold standard. Does a book's content make its own positive contribution, however slight, to the total evolution of human consciousness? And I find *A Man of Our Time* passing that test with first class honours.

Owen Barfield
Forest Row, Sussex
November 1989

INDEX

C

D

E

T

U

V

W

Y

Z

JOHANNES TAUTZ

W.J. Stein, A Biography

In this definitive biography the author has produced a comprehensive account of the life of one of Rudolf Steiner's most important co-workers. W.J. Stein was indeed one of the pioneers of Anthroposophy and a true student of the spirit. In 1928 he wrote the esoteric classic *The Ninth Century and the Holy Grail*, a book which has received much attention over the years. Stein, aside from being a writer was—amongst other things—a Waldorf school teacher, lecturer and traveller.

Tautz catalogues Stein's intricate path of destiny with meticulous care and great warmth, and explores his association with many famous and influential individuals—amongst them Kemal Pasha, Winston Churchill, King Leopold of Belgium and D.N. Dunlop.

298pp; illus; 210 × 135 mm; sewn softback; £12.95;
ISBN 0 904693 23 6

TEMPLE LODGE